MAGAZINE OF BOTANY.

PAXTON'S

MAGAZINE OF BOTANY,

AND

REGISTER OF FLOWERING PLANTS.

"Flowers of all hue."

VOLUME THE SIXTH.

LONDON:
PUBLISHED BY W. S. ORR & CO., PATERNOSTER ROW.

MDCCCXXXIX.

LONDON:
BRADBURY AND EVANS, PRINTERS TO THE QUEEN,
WHITEFRIARS.

TO HER ROYAL HIGHNESS

THE

DUCHESS OF CAMBRIDGE,

WHO,

WITH THE NUMEROUS VIRTUES AND EXCELLENCES WHICH ADORN, AND EVEN ENNOBLE
SUCH ILLUSTRIOUS RANK, COMBINES AN ENLIGHTENED ADMIRATION OF NATURAL
BEAUTIES, AND AN UNOBTRUSIVE BUT BENIGNANT AND PRINCELY
PATRONAGE OF BOTANICAL INTERESTS,

This Sixth Volume

OF

THE MAGAZINE OF BOTANY

IS,

THROUGH HER ROYAL HIGHNESS'S GRACIOUS PLEASURE,

MOST SUBMISSIVELY DEDICATED,

BY

HER ROYAL HIGHNESS'S VERY OBEDIENT HUMBLE SERVANT,

JOSEPH PAXTON.

ADVERTISEMENT.

Considering the already elevated and rapidly rising condition of botanical and floricultural science, it is peculiarly encouraging to the editor of the Magazine of Botany to find that, with so many other and more talented individuals exerting their powers in the same service, his humble efforts to aid in spreading a higher intellectual appreciation of these interesting subjects, meet with such stedfast and munificent support.

The completion of another volume furnishes an appropriate occasion for surveying attentively the paths we have traversed during the past year. Such a review, while engendering some degree of self-satisfaction, begets also a feeling of genuine humility. We candidly opine that, to the critical discernment of the professed botanist, some trifling inaccuracies will be apparent; at the same time, we may securely venture to affirm that these are neither numerous nor important. It is to the gardener, and the cultivator of every rank—whether engaging manually in the necessary operations, or only experiencing delight in their supervision—that we have especially endeavoured to adapt the present volume; and for the latter class we have striven so to blend the *utile et dulce*, that nothing distasteful or unedifying might be presented to their inspection.

In the world of floricultural fashion—for, as in all other pleasing pursuits, the *élite* of its votaries have recognized and fluctuating favourites—epiphytal Orchidaceæ still maintain an almost undivided sway. Of these, the noble collection at Chatsworth, and frequent visits to the best nursery establishments, have enabled us to publish figures of many novel and splendid species; and from the same sources, we have continued to collect and embody a fund of useful information respecting their culture, such as few persons possess similar opportunities of obtaining. The like distinguished facilities, with yet greater disposition to improve them, will be perpetuated throughout the ensuing season.

We have not omitted to note the attention which the more rare and grotesque kinds of Cactaceous plants are just beginning to attract. The recent large importations of these curious objects, and the excellent practice —but lately adopted—of increasing them by seeds, have, in conjunction with their exceedingly singular forms, obtained for them an augmented share of popular regard; and in our lowly office of caterers to the prevalent floral taste, we shall speedily devote to their illustration, or to directions concerning their management, such a space in our Magazine as their importance or interest appear to merit.

Perhaps on no portion of our work can we now look with greater complacency than on its coloured representations of plants. Either in the choice of subjects, or the accuracy, beauty, and effect of the execution, we are perfectly willing, indeed desirous, to invite comparison with any other similar periodical. Our recorded intention of figuring none but ornamental and beautiful plants has been most scrupulously fulfilled; and is the only restriction by which we acknowledge ourselves bound.

To those of our correspondents or friends who have kindly favoured us with drawings or other assistance, we beg to record our grateful sense of obligation; and we would reiterate the assurance to our subscribers, that no practicable means of rendering this publication additionally and enduringly attractive shall remain unheeded or untried.

CHATSWORTH,
December 20, 1839.

LATIN INDEX

TO

THE COLOURED FIGURES OF PLANTS.

Æschynànthus ramosìssimus, 195
Amphicome argùta, 79
Aristolòchia hyperbòrea, 53

Balsamìna Mastersiàna, 75
Brássia maculàta, 5

Chorizèma vàrium, 175
Cœlógyne Gardneriàna, 73
— Wàllichiàna, 25
Convólvulus pentánthus, 219

Dendròbium aggregàtum, 145
— Cambridgeànum, 265
— formòsum, 49
— Paxtòni, 169
Díplacus puníceus, 221

Epácris coccíneus, 123
Érica trícolor, var. supérba, 3
Erýsimum Perowskiànum, 245

Gardìquia multiflòra, 223
Gesnèria Douglàsii, var. verticillàta, 29
— oblongàta, 103
Gladìolus ramòsus, 99
Gompholòbium polymorphum, 151
Grammatophýllum multiflòrum, 217

Hòvea púngens, 101

Ipomœ'a Leàri, 267

Læ'lia autumnàlis, 121
Lílium aurantiacum, 127
Lisiánthus Russelliànus, 31
Lobelia heterophýlla, 197
— ígnea, 247

Málva Creeàna, 55
Miltònia cándida, 241

Nuttállia papàver, 173

Pentastèmon argùtus, 271
— speciòsa, 171
Phàius Wállichii, 193
Philibértia grandiflòra, 7
Potentílla Hopwoodiàna, 149

Roélla élegans, 27
Rudbéckia Drummóndii, 51

Saccolàbium calceolàre, 97
Sálvia pàtens, 1
Sphenógyne speciòsa, 77

Tecoma jasminoìdes, 199
Thunbérgia aurantiàca, 269
— Hawtayneàna, 147
Thysanotus intricatus, 243
Tweédia cœrùlea, 125

VOL. VI.   c

ENGLISH INDEX

TO

THE COLOURED FIGURES OF PLANTS.

ÆSCHYNANTHUS, most branching, 195
Amphicome, finely cut-leaved, 79

Balsam, Mr. Masters', 75
Bindweed, five-flowered, 219
Birthwort, northern, 53
Brassia, spotted-flowered, 5

Chorizema, various-leaved, 175
Cinquefoil, Mr. Hopwood's, 149
Cœlogyne, Mr. Gardner's, 73
— Dr. Wallich's, 25
Corn-flag, branching, 99

Dendrobium, beautiful, 49
— cluster-flowered, 145
— Duchess of Cambridge's, 265
— Mr. Paxton's, 169
Diplacus, scarlet-leaved, 221

Epacris, scarlet-flowered, 123

Gardoquia, many-flowered, 223
Gesneria, Mr. Douglas's whorled-leaved, 29
— oblong-flowered, 103
Gompholobium, multiform-leaved, 151
Grammatophyllum, many-flowered, 217

Heath, superb three-coloured, 3
Hedge Mustard, orange-flowered, 245
Hovea, pointed-leaved, 101

Ipomœa, Mr. Lear's, 267

Lælia, autumnal-flowering, 121
Lily, orange-flowered, 127
Lisianthus, Duke of Bedford's, 31
Lobelia, flame-coloured, 247
— various-leaved, 197

Mallow, showy red-flowered, 55
Miltonia, white-lipped, 241

Nuttallia, poppy-flowered, 173

Pentstemon, cut-leaved, 271
— showy, 171
Phaius, Dr. Wallich's, 193
Philibertia, large-flowered, 7

Roella, elegant, 27
Rudbeckia, Mr. Drummond's, 51

Saccolabium, slipper-shaped, 97
Sage, spreading, 1
Sphenogyne, showy, 77

Tecoma, jasmine-like, 199
Thunbergia, Hawtayne's, 147
— orange-flowered, 269
Thysanotus, intricate-stemmed, 243
Tweedia, light-blue-flowered, 125

WOODCUT ILLUSTRATIONS.

VOLUME THE SIXTH.

Aristolochia hyperborea, 54
Brassia maculata, 6
Cœlogyne Gardneriana, 74
Grammatophyllum multiflorum, 218

Lælia autumnalis, 122
Miltonia candida, 242
Pentstemon speciosus, 172
Phaius Wallichii, 194

Salvia patens.

VEGETABLE PHYSIOLOGY.

It may appear superfluous to notice a subject which has called forth the powers of investigation of many of the ablest philosophers of Europe; but when we consider, that no two writers have agreed, that various and opposing functions have been ascribed to the same vessels, and that, to this hour, no one has been able to determine with accuracy, and beyond doubt, the channels through which the sap ascends, we may be permitted to collect and embody a few hints, which we hope may excite inquiry among those who have time and inclination to undertake investigations of a nature so delicate and obscure.

The name of that great and good man lately deceased, who during so long a period honourably filled the president's chair of the London Horticultural Society, must command attention. He it was who, perhaps, approached most nearly to the truth; and we are enabled, through the communications of a friend who was favoured with a very extensive correspondence with Mr. Knight, to present to our readers some extracts copied verbatim from original letters, whence that gentleman's views on many important particulars may be pretty clearly ascertained.

The *Sap Vessels*—those which conduct the ascending current—have generally been thought to be *hollow tubes:* some puncturated, some spiral; arranged in bundles, or more or less detached. Mr. Knight, in the earlier part of his life, entertained the same opinion; and it is somewhat remarkable that the late Sir James Edward Smith mistook Mr. Knight's "*central*" vessels for those termed "*spirals,*" for he thus expresses himself:—" The same idea has been adopted, confirmed by experiments, and carried to a much greater perfection by Mr. Knight, whose papers in the Philosophical Transactions for 1801, 1804, and 1805, throw the most brilliant light upon it, and I think establish no less than an entirely new theory of vegetation, by which the real use and functions of the principal organs of plants are now, for the first time, satisfactorily explained. In a young branch of a tree or shrub, or in the stem of an herbaceous plant, are found, *ranged round the centre* or pith, a number of longitudinal tubes, or vessels, of a much more firm texture than the adjacent parts, and when examined minutely, these vessels often appear to be constructed with a spiral coat."

Now, Sir J. E. Smith believed the spiral vessels to be here alluded to, though Mr. Knight had distinctly written that, "to these" (his *central*) "vessels, the spiral tubes *are everywhere appendages;*" and again, "the spiral tubes will neither carry coloured infusions, nor in the smallest degree retard the withering of the leaf, when the central vessels are divided."

In a letter dated September 22, 1830, Mr. Knight thus expresses his then opinion, and it will be pleasing to observe the honourable testimony he therein bore to his esteemed friend M. Dutrochet.

"I had proved that the specific gravity of the sap of trees, *in the spring,* increases in proportion to its distance from the ground, and that a good deal of saccharine matter is formed in the alburnum of trees in the spring, which contained none in the winter: but M. Dutrochet was not acquainted with these circumstances, nor with others published in the Philosophical Transactions, by which I conceive myself to have proved that *it is through the cellular substance of the alburnum, and not through its tubes, as I once thought, that the sap ascends.*"

M. Dutrochet corresponded with Mr. Knight on this his new view, but as slow progress only could be made by letters when the distance between the parties was nearly five hundred miles, he resolved to pay Mr. Knight a visit, an act which that gentleman considered as very honourable to his zeal, particularly as he did not speak, though he read, English. " He spent nearly three weeks with me, and our opinions before we parted became perfectly in unison. We both agree that the water and nutriment absorbed from the soil ascend through the cellular substance of the alburnum, and pass through vessels, *cellular in structure*, which surround the bundles of spiral tubes. That the nutriment absorbed becomes the true sap, or living blood of the plant, by *exposure to light* in the leaf; that it descends by the *bark* (wherever plants have bark), by which the matter that forms the layer of alburnum is deposited, and that, whatever portion of the true sap is not thus expended, *sinks into the alburnum* through the misnamed *medullary processes*, and joins the ascending current. As autumn, however, approaches, the expenditure of sap diminishes; and it then *accumulates in the alburnum*, to be employed in forming the young shoots and leaves of the ensuing spring. I am in possession of a thousand facts to support this hypothesis, but not of one in opposition to it. Sir E. Smith had mistaken my meaning respecting the central vessels, though I must admit that I did not express myself with sufficient clearness. I am quite certain that *neither* the *spiral* tubes, nor the threads which compose them, carry any aqueous fluid."

With these high testimonials before us, we conceive that we have commenced a series of articles of great consequence, under favourable auspices, and hope, ere long, to add a few remarks in elucidation of terms which at present may be rather abstruse to the young student.

INFLUENCE OF SOLAR LIGHT ON VEGETATION.

THE interesting papers in the late numbers of your Magazine of Botany on the " Influence of Light on Vegetation," induce me to offer a few remarks which may assist in any researches into the subject.

The effects of light on the vegetable world, whether upon the fruit, leaves, or blossoms of its members, present, indeed, a beautiful subject. A blossom seems to feed on light, expanding in the morning to imbibe it, and closing at night, as if to sleep, sated with light. Many even closed during the eclipse of May 15th, 1836, near Belfast, where the obscuration was considerable; proving thereby, that the closing of flowers and the convolution of leaves is to be attributed to the absence of light, and not to the effects of dews; and I regret having mislaid a memorandum of the particular flowers which I witnessed partly closed on that occasion. I have caused the wild anemone (*A. nemorosa*) to erect its stem, and expand its flowers at night, by placing it between two candles, though the heat of warm water had no effect on it; and a plant of *Hibiscus Africanus*, that had not expanded a flower for several days during the late gloomy summer, though in a high moist temperature, gradually opened a blossom when placed near candle-light. But my present observations regard principally the effects of light, modified by transmission through the glass of hot-houses, and the difference between such light and direct solar light.

The first remark I would make is, that we must maintain a distinction between rays of light and rays of heat, for the sun emits rays of these two kinds; and though they both proceed from their source, as it were intimately interwoven with each other, yet the effect of transparent substances is to separate them; for one substance may transmit almost every ray of light, and yet exclude nearly every ray of heat, and *vice versâ*.

It is convenient to consider all transparent bodies,—e. g. glass, air, water, and ice,—as sieves of infinite fineness, by which the sun's beams are, as it were, sifted; some rays passing through, some being arrested, or absorbed, and others reflected back. The atmosphere is an instance of this, as it retains almost all the blue rays, letting the others pass through.

Now, the usual glass of our hot-houses transmits more rays of light than any *coloured* glass would; but does it also transmit more rays of heat than dark coloured glass would? This deserves consideration; for, if a plant has been subjected to rays of heat of one particular quality, when exposed to the direct light, it will be acted upon by rays of a different quality; and this may cause the destruction of its leaves, unless it be gradually inured to the change by shading.

If any one wishes to prove the difference between the transmission of light and heat, let him place a piece of stained black (not superficially blackened) glass between the sun and the bulb of a thermometer, and the quicksilver will immediately indicate the difference between heat thus transmitted, and heat transmitted through a piece of common glass. Much more heat, though much less light, will be transmitted through the black than through the common glass.

Again, there are rays issuing from the sun distinct from the rays of heat and light:—rays of chemical and magnetic influence; and who can tell to what extent glass may not intercept and transmute these rays? Hence may arise that inelastic state of the air confined in hot-houses; for no doubt can exist respecting the chemical and magnetic rays of the sun possessing a great influence in regulating the component gases of the atmosphere.

This is not unprofitable theorising. It is a subject lately opened to the scientific world by the experiments of Messrs. Melloni, De la Roche, and Berard, and is of great importance to the horticulturist, who at the present day requires facts instead of empiricism, and prefers scientific accuracy to blind practice. He must therefore consider whether he require, for the particular object in view, more light, or more heat; and, in accordance, use a glass of due colour and quality. In the cultivation of Orchidaceæ, for instance, where heat, not light, is usually most required, a greyish, or a purplish thick glass, might obviate the necessity of shading, or a sheltered situation, and give the plants the sober-toned light which they enjoy in their native shades, where they dwell "hidden from day's garish eye." The first collections sent to Paris perished through exposure to unmitigated light.

Most of the plants cultivated in our stoves seem to be sufficiently furnished with light, even where the roof is only imperfectly glazed. In their natural situations they generally grow thickly together, their summits only receiving much light; and the vapours that are constantly diffused (perceptibly or not) through a tropical atmosphere, with the immense dilatation of the air by heat, greatly modify the light of even a tropical sun; without considering the rains that accompany and modify it when vertical. Thus, the banana, the fan-palm, and numerous other plants, really thrive without injury from the effects of glass.

There is, however, another class, which, from growing on dry rocks, and beneath a hot, clear, and *raw* sky, require all possible heat and light, as the Cactus tribe. But, in the greenhouse tribes of plants, the Azalea, Erica, Camellia, Olive, &c., we have to deal with plants natives of climates remarkable for the intense purity of their air and consequent brightness of sky and light, though without very great heat; as the cloudless climes of Attica and Provence, and the fresh and crisp air of the middle regions of tropical mountain ranges. Such plants require more light than glass will transmit, and yet more heat than our open sky affords; and they are consequently the most difficult of culture, either losing their leaves or casting their flower-buds. They require a glass that transmits all possible light, even to the partial exclusion of heat, for heat can be artificially produced:—not so light.

A classification founded on the natural circumstances of every plant, seems the safest method of considering their wants, whether as regards light, heat, air, moisture, or soil; of these light is the most difficult to provide for them, in the proportion in which many require it; and it is a nice point to decide how much is best for them, in the different stages of their hybernation, active growth, periodical sleep, flowering and fruiting states. Nothing but an unwearied course of experiments can teach this hitherto little known branch of horticulture. The colouring of the fruit, the expansion and closing of the blossoms, the different surfaces of the leaf, the motions of the leaf, the twining of tendrils, and the shedding of petals, are some of the objects of such experiments. I will conclude with one remark on air and moisture, having made so many upon light.

Unless the water with which plants are supplied is abundantly mixed (in fact diluted) with air, it is a fluid too thick to nourish them duly. Hence the great superiority of showers over irrigation; for every drop of rain descends through the atmosphere, absorbing air, as a sponge descends through water, filling as it sinks.

But if water be artificially heated, in order to elevate it to a proper degree of temperature, the air it contains is expelled by the heat. In supplying such water to plants, it it advisable to restore the air it has lost, to render it fit for imbibition by the delicate pores of plants. This can easily be done by distributing it to them through a syringe or engine; by which means it will be mixed with a quantity of air. This is a remark of some moment, and by no means a superfluous refinement, if we consider how dainty a delicate plant is with respect to moisture and air.

ON TRAINING ROSES, AND OTHER CLIMBING PLANTS, TO POLES.

Of the many diversified forms and modes of growth which plants exhibit, the climbing or twining habit would seem to be the most graceful and interesting. As man is accustomed to regard more tenderly and fervently such objects as depend upon, or, as it were, cling to, him for protection and support; so, in the vegetable world, those plants appear to excite the greatest interest which require the assistance of their more robust neighbours to maintain them in their needful position, and uphold them from grovelling prostration. We will not say that the mere presentation to the mind of any object in dependent circumstances necessarily awakens sympathy and attachment, but that it is a powerful incentive to those feelings, and especially when associated with delicacy and beauty, every one will be prepared to admit: and whether from this peculiarity in human nature, or from pure admiration of their delightful wreathing and fantastic contortion, we have always observed that climbing plants are acknowledged favourites with persons of refined taste and sensitive minds.

Their sprightly and elegant disposition, the enchanting irregularity and negligence with which their branches are arranged and entangled, and the beautiful manner in which the extremities of these protrude and depend so as best to exhibit their varied blossoms, each contribute to heighten their attractions and invest them with increased powers of captivation. We allude chiefly to their appearance in a natural state, for when subjected to artificial cultivation, the operations of training and pruning deprive them of much of that pleasing simplicity which intrinsically characterizes them, and which is the principal cause of our attachment.

It is much to be regretted that the unnatural method of training these plants to walls or trellises should be so generally substituted for that which nature teaches us is the most graceful and ornamental, and by far the best adapted to the purpose of displaying their peculiar habits and beauties—supporting them by poles or the stems of trees. We are far from wishing the former of these modes discontinued or abated, as it constitutes an agreeable variety, and frequently secures an ornament to what would otherwise be an unsightly surface; we would only urge the adoption of the latter as the preferable, because the more facile and suitable, method. Having before avowed ourselves the advocates of that system of cultivating all kinds of plants which assimilates most closely to the usual procedure of nature, we are happy to be afforded an opportunity of illustrating and enforcing our theory by showing the propriety and advantage of its application to the tribe now under consideration.

The natural habitats of climbing plants are too well known to require description. Most of our readers, we presume, have witnessed the common honeysuckle twining closely around the stems of trees in neglected forests, and interweaving its slender branches with those of the tree to which it clings for support. Those plants which have not the advantage of the vicinage of trees, attach themselves to the nearest shrub, and exhibit their beautiful flowers at every aperture in the branches; or, failing also in this particular, trail along the surface of the ground. So far as general mode of growth is concerned, this may be considered a fair type of most climbing plants: all are incapable of supporting themselves in an erect position, and, consequently, are not frequently met with, except where trees or shrubs exist or abound.

These circumstances very naturally suggest the idea of encouraging them to ascend poles, or the stems of trees, in a state of cultivation; but, strange to say, there are few gardens in which this system is practised, much less is it adopted to any extent. They might also lead to the supposition that these plants require a shaded situation; but this is not the case, at least with those from temperate climates, and to which these remarks are confined. Although found growing naturally beneath the shade of trees and shrubs, they are invariably seen struggling to obtain an exposure, and either protrude their shoots through the opening branches, or tower above the summits of their supporters, and fall carelessly upon the mass of verdure they have surmounted.

Climbing plants of the description just alluded to, are best adapted for planting at the base of small trees in a conspicuous plantation or shrubbery, and to these they may be allowed to attach themselves; or, if necessary, proximity can be secured by a band of matting or string, till they have embraced them sufficiently to render further attention needless. It is particularly advisable to permit them to commence twining themselves; as many of them grow in a peculiar direction, which, if altered, would considerably retard their progress and detract from their beauty. No just conception can be formed of the great additional charms they would impart to our ornamental plantations; for when they had become firmly established, and had grown to their natural size, the trees or shrubs would be seen covered with an extensive variety of showy flowers, and present an appearance at once striking and picturesque. The usual sheltered situation of shrubberies, or the protection which the shrubs themselves would afford, render it probable that many half-hardy climbers might be grown within their boundary, provided the mode of growth were congenial to their habits; and even with no other variety than our hardy species of *Clematis, Caprifolium*, &c. presents, these departments, which look pleasing enough at a distance, but become unsightly when approached, might be converted into decided and lasting attractions.

There is another description of climbing plants, however, which from their natural disposition to branch, or in which such a tendency may be readily induced by pruning, possess peculiar adaptations for training to detached poles; and it is to these species, and this mode of supporting them, that we solicit especial attention. None but those who have once seen this system successfully practised, can possibly have any idea of the effect which a pillar of roses or other suitable plants produces in villa scenery, when all their branches are bending to the earth, as it were, beneath the weight of the multitudes of flowers with which they are laden. Their appearance, whether in the flower-bed or in the lawn, whether arranged opposite to each other on either side of a portico, an entrance, or a walk, or disposed solitarily and irregularly over any part of the pleasure-ground, is truly enchanting. In short, roses thus treated have all the concentrated beauty of the head of a standard elongated into a pillar, without any of the formality of its summit, the lack of congruity in its parts, or the bareness and inelegance of its stem.

In growing climbing roses to poles, it is necessary that a situation be chosen for planting them where they will be slightly sheltered from cold and bleak winds; but this shelter should always be at such a distance as not to screen them from the full influences of the sun, otherwise their shoots will suffer from cold during the winter, on account of their not being thoroughly matured; or, should they escape this, their flowers would not subsequently be so abundantly developed. A clayey soil is undoubtedly the most suitable for them. In the nursery of Mr. Rivers of Sawbridgeworth, we saw a number of these plants growing in a sub-soil which had been taken out from a depth of five or six feet, for the purpose of forming a pond. It was stiff and adhesive, and the roses were flourishing in the greatest luxuriance. Similar instances have likewise fallen beneath our observation, and are corroborative of the above opinion with regard to soil. Richness by no means appears an essential quality, since it is the constant moisture of the soil above noticed, and likewise the absence of all deleterious vegetable matter, that constitute its congeniality.

Poles of the requisite size and strength may be easily procured from the thinnings of larch plantations, and they will stand for several years without renewing. If the bark be removed, (which is a very injudicious practice,) they should be carefully painted previously to being used; but, both for durability and appearance, it is far preferable to allow it to remain. Care should be taken to apportion the length and strength of the poles to the estimated height of the plant, for they will look exceedingly clumsy and unsightly if too large or too long. When contiguous to any erection, their height must also be regulated by its dimensions, as, if they were permitted to soar much above it, a want of conformity, which would greatly disparage their appearance, would be consequent. Pruning, when necessary, must be performed with the greatest judgment. Many kinds of climbing roses will not brook much pruning, while others may be subjected to it to almost any extent. In general, those with weak and flexible shoots may be left to hang down naturally, after they have attained the desired height, thinning them only when they are too numerous; but such as are stronger and more luxuriant occasionally need shortening, to prevent them from growing too diffuse. Where other climbing plants besides roses are trained in this manner, they must be pruned according to their nature. *Wistaria consequana*, which makes a splendid display when attached to a pole, should be very vigorously pruned, as it is by close pruning alone that it can be induced to flower freely. Several species of *Rubus* create a pleasing variation if thus treated, but none are so ornamental, and at the same time so admirably suited to the purpose, as roses.

In small villa gardens, and those attached to the numerous suburban residences of gentlemen engaged in the metropolis, as also in the humble plot of the cottager, or the extensive demesne of the nobleman, a few poles of climbing roses might be introduced with great advantage; and we hope shortly to witness this commendable practice most extensively adopted. Should these remarks have the slightest tendency to encourage the attempt, the design for which they were written will be abundantly realized. However this may be, we are confident that the sight of a flowering specimen in full perfection, would be a sufficient incentive to any lover of nature to append this most ornamental feature to their collection.

FLORICULTURAL NOTICES.

NEW AND RARE PLANTS, FIGURED IN THE LEADING BOTANICAL PERIODICALS FOR DECEMBER AND JANUARY.

CLASS I.—PLANTS WITH TWO COTYLEDONS (DICOTYLEDONEÆ).

THE MALLOW TRIBE (*Malvaceæ*).

MÁLVA CREEANA. Showy red-flowered Mallow. A neat and interesting species of Mallow, of the history of which nothing is known beyond its having been received at the Edinburgh Botanic Garden from Messrs. Lucombe and Pince, nurserymen of Exeter, in the year 1837. Being a profuse flowering plant, it is highly deserving of cultivation in the greenhouse. We have seen it thriving most luxuriantly in the open border throughout the summer months, forming an exceedingly attractive ornament when thus treated. Its flowering season is said to be the months of June and July, but although the flowers may attain their greatest perfection at that period, it continues blooming until the approach of winter. *Bot. Mag.* 3698.

THE EVENING PRIMROSE TRIBE (*Onagràceæ*).

FUCHSIA CYLINDRIACEA. Cylindrical-flowered Fuchsia. By no means a handsome species, though certainly worthy of attention, on account of the brilliant red colour of its flowers, and their somewhat remarkable character. Unisexual flowers, and short stamens, constitute this plant quite a novelty in the genus *Fuchsia;* at least, to British gardens. The former character, however, is the most singular, and has suggested the propriety of founding a new genus for the species of this description which are found in Mexico. To this Dr. Lindley objects; but observes that such characters will serve to "form an excellent sectional distinction." It is recommended as being well adapted for hybridization with those species whose flowers are larger, but of less brilliant hue. The flowers are small, being little larger than those of *F. microphylla;* they are produced on long peduncles, which are rendered half-pendent by their weight, and are extremely graceful. Male plants are stated to bear flowers of nearly twice the size of the females, and much more handsome. This should influence the cultivator in purchasing the species. It is of Mexican origin, and was raised in the gardens of the Horticultural Society, from seeds presented by G. Barker, Esq., of Birmingham. *Bot. Reg.* 66.

THE PURSLANE TRIBE (*Portulacàceæ*).

CALANDRINA DISCOLOR. Discoloured-flowered Calandrina. This very showy species is even far superior to the handsome *C. grandiflora*, both in the size and beauty of its flowers, and in their remaining expanded throughout the whole day. It is a half-hardy, suffruticose plant, received by the Horticultural Society from the Berlin Botanic Garden, in 1835. Although a perennial species, it is found to succeed admirably under the treatment generally bestowed on annuals, and is a most delightful feature in the flower-garden. Flowers develop themselves in constant succession from the end of June till the occurrence of frost, when the seeds may be collected, and the plants left to perish. The seeds may be sown, and the plants managed, precisely as half-hardy annuals; planting them in the beds of the flower-garden after the cessation of spring frosts. *Bot. Reg.* vol. ii. p. 4.

THE COMPOSITE-FLOWERED TRIBE (*Compósitæ*).

MARSHALLIA CÆSPITOSA. Tufted Marshallia. A very elegant plant, with an interesting admixture of pink and white rays in its beautiful involucre. It has been discovered "by Mr. Nuttall, in the Red River territory, by Berlendier at Villa de Austin in Texas, and by Drummond in Galvester Bay of the same country." Seeds sent to this country by the latter gentleman have germinated successfully, and this species has flowered in the Glasgow Botanic Garden. Its stems grow in tufts for a foot or more in height, from which character it derives its name. The leaves are long, linear-lanceolate, and are produced only from the lower part of the stems. The plant is well calculated for growing in beds, but has been kept in a cold frame. The flowers appear in July and August. *Bot. Mag.* 3704.

THE HONEYSUCKLE TRIBE (*Caprifoliàceæ*).

LEYCESTERIA FORMOSA. Figures of this ornamental shrub have appeared simultaneously in the January Numbers of the *Botanical Register* and *Botanical Magazine*. In the latter the leaves, and in the former the flowers, are best represented. The character of the plant, as developed in an artificial climate, is far from being so good as the accounts of Indian botanists had led us to anticipate. The foliage is large and handsome, and the flowers appear to be produced numerously in terminal pendent racemes; but the most showy feature is the large bracteæ at the base of the flowers, which are beautifully veined and tipped with crimson. Dr. Lindley suggests that this latter character may be more prominently exhibited as the plant becomes older, and more inured to our system of cultivation. It is a native of the Himalaya mountains, and is figured and described by Dr. Wallich in his admirable work on the Asiatic Flora. Plants have been raised in the Garden of the Horticultural Society, from seeds transmitted by Dr. Royle from India. It is found to be a hardy evergreen, requiring a considerable degree of moisture, and a situation slightly sheltered and shaded, though the colour of its bracts would most probably be heightened by exposure to solar light. Propagation is effected by cuttings or layers.

THE FIGWORT TRIBE (*Schrophulariàceæ*).

COLLÍNSIA HETEROPHÝLLA. Variable-leaved Collinsia. A charming annual, closely resembling *C. bicolor* in general appearance, and in the colours of its flowers. Indeed, so striking is the similarity, that Sir W. J. Hooker himself almost questioned the propriety of considering it a distinct species. The principal points of difference are, that the present plant has its lower leaves divided into segments, its calyx covered with coarser hairs, the divisions of the corolla more rounded, the lobe of the middle lip nearly acute, and the border to the upper side of the throat almost entire. The flowers are also larger and more showy. This species was discovered by Mr. Nuttall in the vicinity of the Columbia river, North America, and seeds were forwarded from Mr. Buist of Philadelphia, to the Experimental Garden, Edinburgh, whence plants were obtained which flowered during the summer of 1838. It is justly considered to be the handsomest species of the genus. *Bot. Mag.* 3695.

THE MINT TRIBE (*Lamiàceæ*).

LEONÓTIS NEPETÆFOLIA. Catmint-leaved Leonotis. The beautiful clusters of bright scarlet flowers which are formed in such dense profusion around each articulation of the stem, impart to this plant a most ornamental character. Otherwise it has little to recommend it to general notice, the foliage being rather coarse and straggling, and the plant frequently growing too vigorously if kept in the stove. We have seen it cultivated, however, with much greater success in the greenhouse, and in this situation it has formed an interesting object. It inhabits various places on the continent of India, and the adjacent islands, but is also found in Brazil, Trinidad, and Demerara. Flowers are produced freely in the summer months, if the plant is afforded a due degree of light. *Bot. Mag.* 3700.

CLASS II.—PLANTS WITH ONE COTYLEDON (MONOCOTYLEDONEÆ).

THE BLOOD-ROOT TRIBE (*Hæmodoràceæ*).

ANIGOZANTHUS FLAVIDUS ; *var.* BICOLOR. Two-coloured yellow-haired Anigozanthus. In this fine variety there is almost sufficient distinction to constitute a new species; but, besides the colours of its flowers, and the branching nature of its stem, Dr. Lindley states that he has "sought in vain for any other peculiarity." The striking combination of green and scarlet in its flowers, (from which circumstance it has received its name,) has a peculiarly pleasing appearance; while its vigorous mode of growth further enhances its value. Its native country is the Swan River Colony; from whence, we believe, it was introduced to England by Captain James Mangles, R.N. A place in the greenhouse has hitherto been assigned to it, but it is said to succeed very well when planted in a cold pit, and duly protected in the winter. An increase may be obtained by seeds or offsets, and the plant requires to be kept in a light and airy position, watering it liberally while in the growing stage. *Bot. Reg.* 64.

THE ORCHIS TRIBE (*Orchidàceæ*).

COMPARETTIA COCCINEA. Scarlet Comparettia. One of the prettiest and most elegant little orchidaceous plants we ever witnessed. With the graceful habit of the neatest *Oncidium*, it has flowers of a very brilliant scarlet colour. Messrs. Loddiges, who flowered this delightful plant in August 1838, suppose it to be a native of Brazil, but Dr. Lindley presumes some mistake has arisen on this subject, as he possesses dried specimens from Xalapa. The character of the flowers of this species is very singular. Within the external spur, which forms a part of the sepals, is another spur, which cannot be discerned till the plant is dissected. This structure is extremely uncommon in Orchidaceæ. The foliage of this plant is also very interesting, being of a beautiful purple colour beneath, and the liveliest green on the upper surface. We imagine that a block of wood would be the most suitable material for growing it upon, as it would appear to require some care in the administration of water, on account of its small and slender nature. *Bot. Reg.* 68.

DENDROBIUM SULCATUM. Furrowed Dendrobium. A very handsome species of this charming genus. The stem is deeply furrowed, and articulated, and the flowers appear from the joints of the old shoots. Orange is the predominant colour in the flowers, but the labellum is of a somewhat deeper hue, and has two slight blotches of brownish red at its base; when magnified, this latter is an extremely beautiful object, and exhibits a hairy surface, with a delicately fringed margin. It is one of the numerous features of Dendrobieæ brought from India to Chatsworth by Mr. J. Gibson, and flowered at Chatsworth in April, 1838. It is stated to be nearly allied to *D. Griffithianum*, differing from it in the form of the labellum, and the mode of producing its flowers, which appear in clusters of three on each peduncle. *Bot. Reg.* 65.

CATTLEYA GUTTATA ; *var.* RUSSELLIANA. Spotted Cattleya ; Lord Edward Russell's variety. Few superior collections of Orchidaceæ are without the splendid species of which this plant forms a variety. The present plant is very distinct in its characters from the original. Besides growing larger and stronger, the flowers are of greater size, more expansive, and less spotted; the labellum is short, very obtuse, and deep pinkish-red towards the extremity. It was introduced to the collection at Woburn Abbey by Captain Lord Edward Russell, R.N., having been presented to that nobleman by the director of the Botanic Garden at Rio, where it had been previously received from the Organ Mountains. It flowered at Woburn in August, 1838. Although superior in all its characters to *C. guttata*, it wants the beautiful spots with which the flowers of that species are so profusely studded. The same treatment as is given to the rest of the genus will be found suitable. *Bot. Mag.* 3694.

BRASAVOLA MARTIANA. Dr. Von Martius's Brasavola. A rather interesting species of a pretty, but not showy, genus of plants. It has long terete leaves, from near the base of which springs a branching peduncle, bearing several pale-green flowers, which have a white and beautifully fringed labellum. The latter is the most pleasing feature, and, though it exists in two other species, these are altogether of a very different form. Dr. Von Martius first discovered this plant on the banks of the Rio Negro, in Brazil, and specimens of it were imported from Berbice by Messrs. Loddiges, in whose collection it has flowered. A loose stony soil appears to be the kind of earth which the species of Brasavola prefer, and very little moisture is required to their roots. They may be multiplied by dividing the stem, so as to leave one shoot to each division. *Bot. Reg.* vol. ii. p. 5.

STANHOPEA TIGRINA. Tiger-flowered Stanhopea. This is the magnificent species which we have previously noticed as flowering in the nursery of Messrs. Rollison, but which we certainly considered different from the *S. tigrina*, which is so admirably figured in the splendid work on Orchidaceæ, now publishing by J. Bateman, Esq. The flowers of this species are larger and more showy than those of any of its allies. It was first imported into this country from the vicinity of Xalapa, by Messrs. Low and Co., of Clapton, and has flowered in the superb collection of J. Bateman, Esq., of Knypersly, as also at the nursery of Messrs. Rollison, Tooting. The fragrance of the flowers of this species is delightfully aromatic, "resembling a mixture of melon and vanilla." Its cultivation may be conducted in a similar manner to that of the other species, observing to place it in a pot or basket in such a manner as to allow its flower-scape free egress from the soil. *Bot. Reg.* vol. i. p. 1.

NEW, RARE, OR INTERESTING PLANTS IN FLOWER IN THE PRINCIPAL SUBURBAN NURSERIES.

ANTENNARIA TRIPLINERVIS. A rare and very pretty little greenhouse plant, with flowers of the description termed everlasting. It grows to about six inches in height, and has leaves of a somewhat elliptical form, which are covered with a whitish pubescence, and exhibit three distinct ribs or nerves. The dense clusters of neat white blossoms first appear on the summits of the shoots about the month of October, and continue in unfading perfection till the present time. Though not a showy plant, it is a very interesting one, and quite a desirable ornament to the greenhouse at this season. Plants of it are now in a flowering state in the nursery of Messrs. Young, Epsom.

BEGONIA OCTAPETALA. One of the largest, but the least handsome, species of the genus. Attaining usually the altitude of eight or ten feet, with very fine foliage, it appears of a shrubby disposition, and has a rather majestic appearance in a collection of large stove-plants. But the flowers, which are terminal, are small, white, and comparatively insignificant, and it is scarcely worth growing, except for the beauty of its leaves, and the mass of verdure they compose. We believe it to be a rare species, and it is now blooming in the stove of the Epsom nursery.

CORRÆA CORDATA. An hybrid *Corræa*, of a very definite character, and at present extremely scarce. The most distinctive and ornamental features of this plant, are its very compact habit, and smooth, ovately-cordate foliage. In these respects, it is decidedly superior to any previously known. Its average height is from two to three feet, but even the latter standard will probably be exceeded when the species becomes more established, if judiciously cultivated. The flowers, which are now expanded in the greenhouse of Messrs. Low and Co., Clapton, are of a deep rose colour. They will, however, undoubtedly be larger, and of a richer hue, when produced at a more propitious season.

CORRÆA MILNERII. Another hybrid production, but by no means so distinct as the latter. In its rugose, hairy, oval leaves, it approximates very closely to *C. speciosa*, and the flowers are also of a reddish crimson hue; the growth of the plant is, however, less straggling, and the blossoms are larger, and moreover of one uniform colour. Both this and the preceding plant, and also another called *C. rosea*, which we have not yet seen, were raised by an individual of the name of Milner, and are in the possession of Messrs. Low and Co., in whose nursery a plant of *C. Milnerii*, which is not more than six inches high, is now producing its showy flowers.

DENDROBIUM LONGICORNU. This extremely rare and interesting species of one of the most beautiful genera of orchidaceous plants, perfected its blossoms in the collection of Messrs. Rollison, Tooting, about two months since, and these have not yet faded. It is not surpassed by any of its congeners, either in gracefulness of form or delicacy of the flowers, although the latter possess but little brilliancy of colour. Independently of the flowers, this species may be distinguished from all others by its slender stems being covered with small black hairs, which do not project horizontally, but lie close along the surface, and incline upwards. These, however, disappear entirely from the old stems soon after they have shed their foliage. The flowers seem to be produced in pairs, on pedicels an inch in length; when fully developed, they are of a tubular form, gradually expanding from a slender, almost pointed, spur, to a tube of three-fourths of an inch in diameter. The sepals are three in number, simple, white, linear, acute, and elongated into a spur at the base. The two petals are similar in form and colour, but much undulated at the margins. The labellum is large, expanding into a semi-circular shape, yellow, with beautiful orange-red longitudinal streaks; it is three-lobed, the central one of which is small, delicately fringed and undulated, and forming an acute, recurved point. The species is a native of Eastern India, and grows admirably on a block of wood.

EPIDENDRUM LENTIGINOSUM. With much of the usual character of the species of *Epidendrum*, which have stems in the form of pseudo-bulbs, this species has a neatness of appearance, and a degree of beauty in its flowers, of which many others are destitute. Its most peculiar characteristic, and that from which it derives its name, is the liberal manner in which the petals of its flowers are spotted with small circular stains of deep brown. The remainder of the flower is of a yellowish-green colour. Messrs. Loddiges, of Hackney, imported specimens directly from Demerara, and it is flowering very beautifully in their orchidaceous house.

LÆLIA ANCEPS. We notice this charming orchidaceous plant for the purpose of inviting attention to two splendid specimens which are now exhibiting their lovely blossoms in the rich collections of Messrs. Loddiges and Rollison. The exquisitely delicately texture and colour of the petals and sepals of its flowers, and the rich purple hue of the labellum, are almost beyond compare, even amongst orchidaceæ. The flowers would really appear transparent, if colourless, and, when viewed obliquely, display a number of minute, glistening crystallizations on their surface, which contribute much to enhance their beauty. The long, slender flower-stem, which becomes half pendent with the weight of its surmounting pairs of blossoms, imparts to it an air of gracefulness and gaiety which is quite in accordance with the appearance of the flowers. It is indispensable to every collection of the tribe, and should always be grown on a piece of wood, covering the roots with moss, and suspending the whole from the roof of the house.

LINUM TRIGYNUM. Several plants of this old but uncommon and exceedingly ornamental species, are blooming most profusely in the nursery of Mr. Knight, Chelsea. The dwarf habit, broadly ovate foliage, and large lively yellow-coloured flowers, the centre of which merges gradually into a rich saffron tint, constitute *Linum trigynum* a very valuable ornament to the stove. We have alluded to it for two reasons; first, on account of its striking beauty, and secondly, because it produces its handsome blossoms at this comparatively sterile period. It is usually treated as a stove plant, but appears to succeed well in a house, the temperature of which is kept intermediate between that of the stove and greenhouse, and it might possibly thrive in the greenhouse itself. To either of these structures it is a decided acquisition. Its native country is the East Indies, and it is remarkable for resembling in its structure an order of a Linnæan class to which the genus does not belong.

MAXILLARIA AUREO-FULVA. This is a singular and very pretty species, as also a rare one. The flowers (by which it is principally distinguished, and to which its specific name refers) are of a colour between golden and brown, and occasionally these shades are pleasingly blended. When expanded, the blossoms are about the size of those of *M. picta*, and the pseudo-bulbs and foliage are peculiarly neat. It is blossoming very freely at Messrs. Loddiges.

PIMELEA INCANA. A most interesting species, which has very recently been introduced to our collections. It is liberally clothed with a whitish down, (whence the name,) and the leaves are small, oval, and obtuse. Its pure white blossoms are produced in clusters at the extremities of the shoots, and their beauty is greatly heightened by the appearance of the two bright yellow anthers which are prominently protruded from each on short slender filaments, and recline on the surface of the corolla. Messrs. Rollison possess a plant of it now most pleasingly in flower, and it should be in the collection of every admirer of simple and pretty plants.

QUEKĒTTIA MICROSCŌPICA. Minute and almost imperceptible as are the flowers of this curious little orchidaceous plant, they are interesting, when examined closely, even by the naked eye; but, placed beneath a microscope of tolerable power, they are said to become extremely beautiful. It is without doubt the smallest orchidaceous plant yet discovered, and though it possesses no attractions for the vulgar eye, the lover of the tribe will discover in it much to admire, especially if aided by a powerful lens. It has small, cylindrical, stem-like leaves, which taper gradually towards the summit. The predominant colour of the flowers is yellow. A specimen of it is blooming with Messrs. Loddiges at this time.

OPERATIONS FOR FEBRUARY.

OUR monthly calendar of operations necessary to be performed in the various departments of floriculture having already been conducted through five successive annual volumes, it may easily be imagined that the subject is now nearly exhausted. To avoid any useless and tedious reiteration, in the last volume of this Magazine we deemed it advisable to generalise the instructions as much as possible, neither detailing every process, nor enumerating each individual plant to which any particular treatment was required. In accordance with this practice of submitting general principles rather than petty precepts, we propose commencing and continuing the present volume, and beg to refer the reader, who may be desirous of obtaining more particular information, to the directions contained in those previously issued.

During this and the succeeding months, the time of the gardener is usually occupied in attention to the preservation of all kinds of tender plants. In plant structures, besides the expulsion or exclusion of frost and damp, a state of profound torpor must be maintained. Although, by abating the supply of moisture, this object may be partially attained, the due regulation of temperature is of much greater moment. As the sun's beams are not now sufficiently intense to furnish heat commensurate with the excessive calorific radiation, the value of interposing any substances which may obstruct the latter will be fully recognised by the economical cultivator. A very trifling degree of artificial heat, accompanied by a close covering of garden mats over every part of the glazed surface, will be much more effectual in preserving plants from frost than the employment of active heat to twice the extent, without any covering to the glass.

OPERATIONS FOR FEBRUARY.

To the amateur, or gardener of limited means, a knowledge of this fact is of very great importance; as, by availing himself of the system here recommended, an immense saving of fuel may be effected. But the practice is even still more valuable in maintaining the plants in a healthy condition, and consequently should be adopted even where economy is not so much regarded. Its beneficial result to the plants is twofold, combining ample protection from cold, with the maintenance of that dormancy which we before stated to be so desirable, neither of which objects is ensured by any other method. Without a covering to the glass of some material which will diminish radiation, whatever quantity of heat may be at command, the upper and tender shoots of plants that are within a few feet from the glass, are almost inevitably injured when frosts are very intense. Their susceptibility of injury is also greatly increased by the excitation which must and does always accompany an elevation of temperature. Thus, when in frosty weather a high temperature is created and maintained, a stimulus is imparted to the roots and lower portions of plants, which, upon being communicated to their upper extremities, induces growth; and the shoots thus formed are exceedingly liable to be destroyed when any augmentation of frost occurs.

By the practice of the method above suggested, no danger of this kind will be incurred, and the plants will be kept in a uniformly dormant state. The partial refraction of light which it will occasion, cannot be productive of injury to any plant if its shoots are fully matured and completely torpid; and even this will be obviated during the day, except in extreme frost, since the covering may be safely removed while the sun is shining, or the temperature only moderately low. In fine weather, indeed, a greater degree of light will be afforded by this system than could else be obtained; as the cultivator will be enabled to place his plants much nearer the glass than he otherwise could with security.

These principles apply with equal force and propriety to the management of pits and frames, and also to tender plants in the open ground. If they are closely enveloped in some thick covering which will prevent or retard radiation, the natural heat of the ground, and also the latent heat of the plants themselves, will render them perfectly secure from external cold. The preservation of tuberous or other roots, which are taken from the ground during winter, may likewise be included in these remarks. If duly sheltered with dry straw, and all apertures or glazed surfaces in the apartment in which they are kept carefully covered, no artificial heat will be necessary, unless it be for dispelling injurious moisture.

When a complete thaw succeeds a severe frost, all herbaceous plants and bulbs that have been planted in the autumn should be examined, and those which have been so near the surface as to be left exposed by the contraction of the soil during congelation, must be carefully reinstated.

Bulbs or other plants intended for early flowering, should be immediately placed in a moist heat, and their growth attentively watched, for the purpose of removing all obstructions, and affording every desirable facility. Gentle syringing is, or should be, an essential feature in forcing, though a moist atmosphere will have precisely the same effect, and is much more congenial to plants.

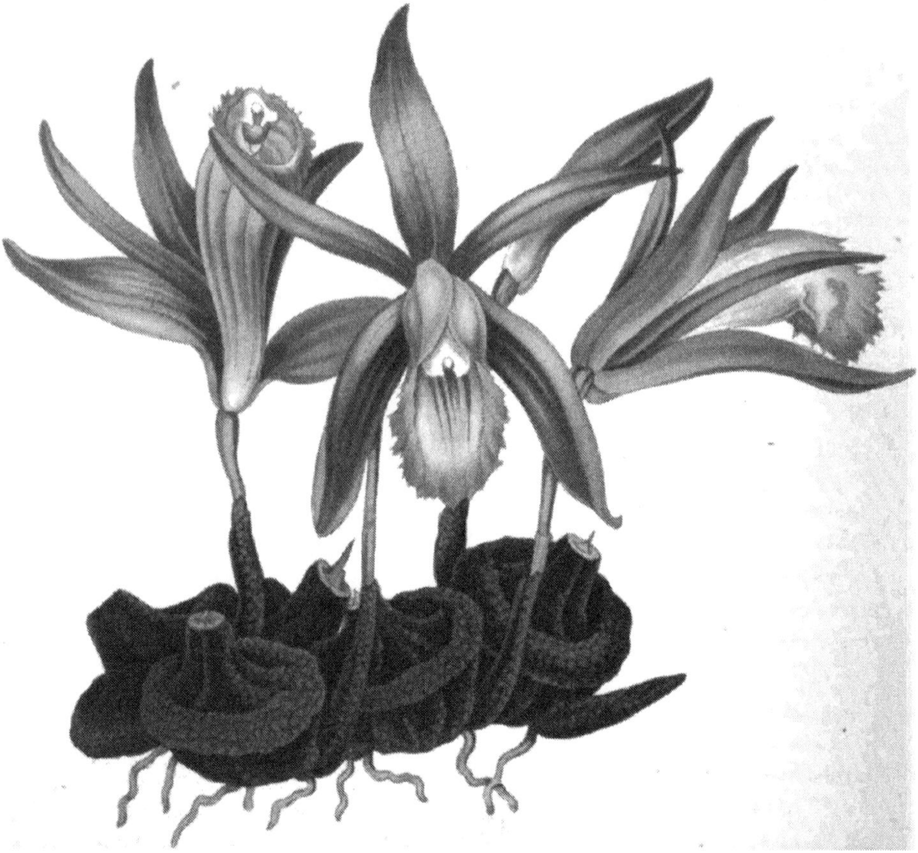

CŒLÓGYNE WALLICHIÀNA.

(DR. WALLICH'S CŒLOGYNE.)

CLASS.
GYNANDRIA.

ORDER.
MONANDRIA.

NATURAL ORDER.
ORCHIDACEÆ.

GENERIC CHARACTER.—*Sepals* connivent or spreading, free, equal, similar in colour to the petals. *Petals* occasionally resembling the sepals, but sometimes linear. *Labellum* cucullate, frequently three-lobed, with depressed streaks or crests on its surface, but sometimes quite entire, and without crests. *Column* erect, free, with a winged margin, expanding at the summit, or cucullate, with a two-lipped stigma. *Anthers* two-celled, covered, not divisible in the middle; inserted below the apex of the column. *Pollen-masses* four, free, inclining to one side; occasionally cohering.

SPECIFIC CHARACTER.—*Leaves* lanceolate, plaited. *Labellum* indistinctly three-lobed; middle one ovate, toothed, two-lobed at the extremity, entire, with a pointlet; lateral lobes imperceptible; surface crested, with five incomplete teeth; having a short spur at the base. *Column* divided at the summit, inferior lip of the stigma tapering gradually into three abrupt points.

RARELY is the signal beauty of this charming plant excelled, even amongst Orchidaceæ. The compactness and elegance of its habits, its singularly moulded and prettily mottled pseudo-bulbs, and the remarkable comparative size and showiness of its flowers, constitute it a perfect gem of its class, and ensure for it unexceptionable favour.

His Grace the Duke of Devonshire's collector, Mr. J. Gibson, found this species growing most abundantly on the Khoseea Hills, in Eastern India, and specimens were received at Chatsworth in the autumn of 1837. It inhabits almost every variety of locality on the summit of those hills, sometimes attaching itself to rocks, either on the arid knoll or washed by the mountain rivulets, but is more frequently met with on the branches of trees, in shady and moist woods. Occasionally it is seen in situations fully exposed to the influence of the sun, but it evidently thrives in greater perfection where partially shaded from its blaze.

The habits, and consequently the cultivation, of this plant are rather peculiar. Its pseudo-bulbs are of only annual duration, and shed all their foliage previous to the production of flowers. This will account for the absence of that feature in our figure. As with many other plants of the tribe, the flowering is the immediate precursor of the growing season. The former of these occurs about the commencement of cold weather, or usually in the month of November. At this period, the flower-shoots are seen to protrude themselves from the base of the pseudo-bulbs; and, after the blossoms have faded, the sheath which envelops their peduncle expands at the base, ultimately exhibiting a perfect new bulb. When these latter are matured, the old ones decay, and the plant, now in full leaf, remains in a state of torpidity till the following October; about which time it loses its foliage, and the flower-buds again begin to swell.

With one trifling exception,—viz. the period of potting,—our present subject may be treated in precisely the same manner as is recommended for *Phaius albus* p. 159 of the last volume of this Magazine. While a mixture of heath-soil, potsherds, and sphagnum will be found an excellent compost for planting it in, drainage is too important a point in the operation of potting to be left unnoticed here, as this species requires the greatest possible care in that respect. Shallow pots, where procurable, are decidedly to be preferred. From the period at which its growth ceases to that immediately succeeding the decay of its flowers, a cold house is the most appropriate situation in which it can be placed. On attaining this epoch, it should be repotted, and removed to a moist stove, retaining it there during the whole of the time in which any disposition to grow is apparent, and returning it to a cool house when its growth is concluded.

Propagation is easily effected by separating one of the pseudo-bulbs while in a dormant state, and treating it as the parent plant.

In its native districts, this lovely species grows in such astonishing profusion, that the surface of the rocks, in favourable situations, is literally strewn during the flowering season with its delightful blossoms; and as these are produced on such short peduncles, their appearance resembles a superb and richly decorated carpet. Such a picture would have even enhanced the beautiful description of the immortal Milton, when, alluding to the nuptial bower of our first parents in pristine innocence and bliss, he says,—

> "Under foot the violet,
> Crocus, and hyacinth, with rich inlay
> Broider'd the ground, more colour'd than with stone
> Of costliest emblem."

Happily the species can be cultivated with tolerable facility, and our hothouses afford us the means of emulating nature in developing and displaying this admirable little flower, though on ever so limited a scale.

According to Loudon, the generic designation is from *koilos*, hollow, and *gyne*, woman; which alludes to the structure of the stigma, or female organ of reproduction.

This species was named in compliment to Dr. Wallich, the distinguished explorer of East Indian vegetation, and able director of the Calcutta Botanic Garden. A drawing of it has been published by that gentleman in his *Raræ Floræ Asiaticæ*.

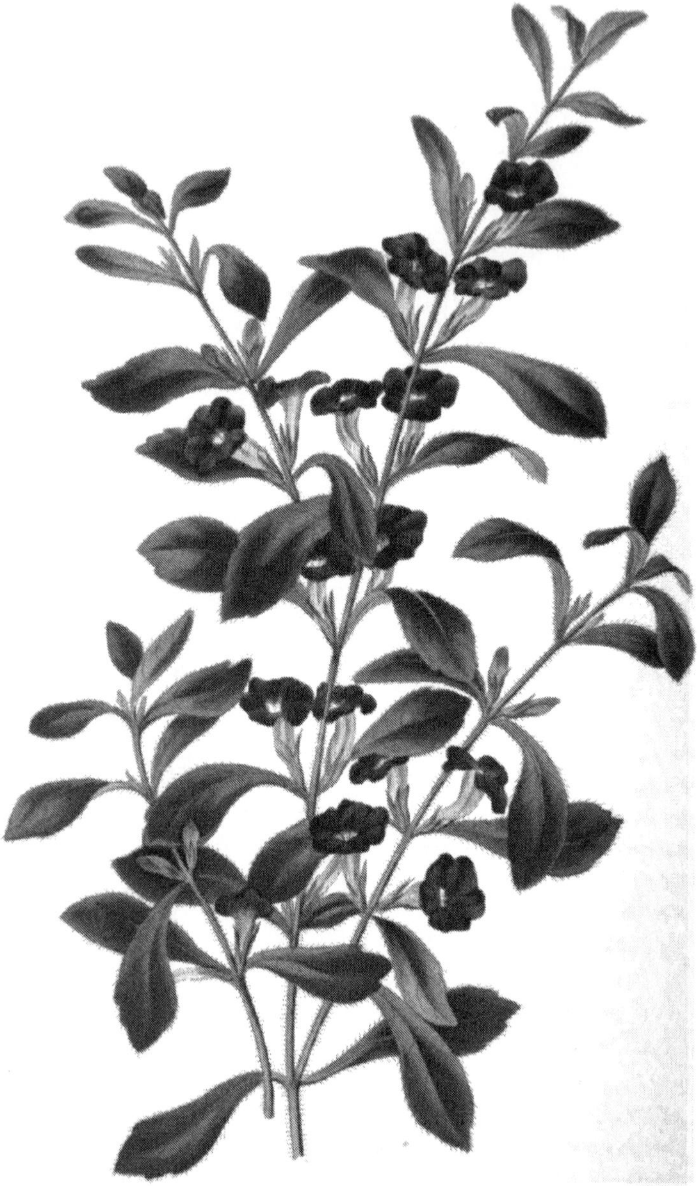

ROÉLLA ÉLEGANS.
(ELEGANT ROELLA.)

CLASS.
PENTANDRIA.

ORDER.
MONOGYNIA.

NATURAL ORDER.
CAMPANULACEÆ.

GENERIC CHARACTER.—*Corolla* funnel-shaped, with a stameniferous tube. *Stigma* bifid. *Capsule* two-celled, cylindrical, inferior.

SPECIFIC CHARACTER.—*Plant* an herbaceous perennial. *Stem* rounded, erect, much branched, hairy, as well as the leaves. *Leaves* partially spatulate, sessile, opposite, slightly crenate, acute. *Flowers* solitary, axillary. *Calyx* five-cleft, segments awl-shaped. *Corolla* with a five-parted limb, lobes rounded, with a slight indentation in the middle, recurved at the margin; bright blue, with a stain of purple in its throat.

In no subject that we have before had the satisfaction to figure, do we remember to have seen so much real elegance and simple beauty. Whether in the general contour of the plant, the precise and pleasing conformation of its parts, or the attractive colour of its pretty blossoms, it is a truly delightful object, and forms an exceedingly ornamental feature in the stove.

There are few of the characters of a plant which exercise so great an influence over the popular suffrage as the hue of the flowers. Almost every admirer of these, the most attractive of natural productions, evinces some partiality to a particular tint; but although this predilection may be as varied as the stains produced by nature's freakish limner, there is evidently a strong and prevailing attachment to flowers of a blue colour. Without enquiring into the source of this preference, which may, however, no doubt be traced to the associations with which we are wont to connect all colours, the brilliant and intense blue of the blossoms of this interesting plant cannot fail to inspire sensations of both pleasure and admiration in the beholder.

It must greatly increase the value of this species in the estimation of our readers, if, like us, they are fascinated with the richness of its flowers, when we state, that our attention was first attracted to it about two years since in the stove of Messrs. Young, Epsom; and notwithstanding our subsequent visits to that establishment have been monthly, we scarcely remember an occasion on which at least one or more specimens were not in flower.

Our figure represents only a single branch, but the plant seldom exceeds nine or ten inches in height, and forms a peculiarly neat and symmetrical object. Although its habit appears to be herbaceous, we have never observed it destitute of stems or leaves, so that these are evidently produced in constant succession. It is probable that the plant is suffruticose, but neither its superficial aspect nor a close examination warrant us in making such an assertion.

As its general mode of growth seems to be different from most other herbaceous stove plants, some variation from the usual course of treatment is necessary in its cultivation. With regard to soil, it prefers a sandy loam, with a very trifling addition of heath-mould. The smallest pot into which the roots can be inserted, without undue compression, will be the most suitable, as too much pot-room is decidedly prejudicial. As with other stove plants, a period of dormancy is beneficial; still it must be supplied with water during the entire season, and will not be injured by being continually subjected to a moderately high temperature. Indeed, if kept in a hothouse, it will flower during the whole of the winter months. Especial care should be taken to place it in a position alike free from the shade of other plants and the droppings from them or from the roof of the house, caused by the condensation of vapour, or admitted from the exterior surface. It should be kept on a dry stage or shelf, but a slightly-humid atmosphere will be rather propitious than otherwise.

Seeds are liberally matured, and germinate successfully if sown in very light soil in shallow pans, and these plunged in a moderate bottom heat. Cuttings also succeed very well under the ordinary treatment, with all due precaution in preserving them from superabundant moisture.

We regret that the native country of this plant has hitherto baffled our inquiries. It was received at the Epsom nursery from the Glasgow Botanic Garden, and our figure was prepared from a plant which flowered beautifully in the stove of Messrs. Young, in May, 1838.

The generic name was applied by Linnæus in commemoration of Mr. George Roelle, professor of anatomy at Amsterdam.

Gesneria Douglasii verticillata

GESNÈRIA DOUGLÀSII; *var.* VERTICILLÀTA.

(MR. DOUGLAS'S GESNERIA; WHORLED-LEAVED VARIETY.)

CLASS.	ORDER.
DIDYNAMIA.	ANGIOSPERMIA.

NATURAL ORDER.
GESNERIÀCEÆ.

GENERIC CHARACTER.—*Vide* vol. i. p. 224.

SPECIFIC CHARACTER.—*Plant* herbaceous. *Root* tuberous. *Leaves* produced in whorls around the middle of the stem, ovate, crenate. *Flowers* terminal, pedunculate, umbelled. *Corolla* with a nearly equal limb.

Var. VERTICILLATA.—*Peduncles* usually simple, very dense, whorled.

WERE a sectional division of the genus *Gesneria* desirable, it might with great facility and propriety be separated into two parts; *viz.* those species which possess corollas with a bilabiate limb, and such as have them expansive and nearly equally divided. With the latter section would be classed the fine variety here figured.

An interesting deviation from the usual scarlet colour of the corolla of the species, is exhibited in our present subject. It is also greatly superior to G. *Douglasii* in habit, in foliage, and in the size and beauty of its flowers. The hue of its blossoms is not brilliant, but it is delicate and of various shades, while the numerous spots or streaks render it still more attractive. The dense clusters or whorls in which they are produced, the long, slender, red peduncles on which they are supported, and the showy crimson petioles and veins of the leaves, all tend in some measure to heighten the appearance of the plant, and multiply its claims to attention.

Tubers of this variety were originally imported by J. Allcard, Esq., from Rio, and in the collection of that gentleman it first produced its flowers in April, 1836. From G. *Douglasii* it differs, as we before observed, in the greater size of all its parts; but the character which forms its principal distinction, and from which it has received the name by which it now appears, is the disposition of its inflorescence in whorls, whereas, in the original species, it is produced irregularly, and in a decided panicle.

The cultivation of the species of *Gesneria* is pretty generally known to be comprised in two particulars,—a season of excitement, and a period of renovation or rest. Both these are absolutely essential, and the circumstances necessary to occasion either of them must be continued throughout their entire duration, slightly modified, however, at the commencement or conclusion of these eras, according to the capabilities of the plant. Thus, when a specimen of any kind of *Gesneria* is beginning to grow, the supply of moisture must be very limited, and be increased as the growth advances; and, on the other hand, when it evinces signs of decay, a similarly gradual but retrogressive course should be pursued.

A dry and cold house is far preferable to a stove for preserving the dormant tubers of these plants, because, in such a situation, they are prevented from shrivelling, and require no water; two objects which cannot possibly be conjointly attained in a hothouse, and without which complete torpidity is not ensured. As profound dormancy is necessary during a certain period, so also is vigorous stimulation alike useful in the contrary state. Hence, a moist bottom heat, caused by fermentation, is more appropriate than increased temperature created by combustion, because accompanied by the requisite humidity; this being also furnished in a manner most congenial to the plant.

Gesnerias may be incited to grow at various periods, as their flowers may be desired; but it is better to allow them to take the natural course, and to repot and place them in a humid heat when they exhibit a tendency to shoot. The soil used should be a compound of light loam, heath-mould, and rotten manure, of which the first-named should constitute a moiety of the whole. There appears no reason why they should not be susceptible of hybridization, and it is probable that an hybrid between the present plant and *G. Cooperi*, or other similar species, would be both novel and interesting.

They may be propagated by cuttings, which succeed best when taken off at an early period of their growth from the base of the plant, with a small portion of the tuber attached. Where a number of plants is desired, the specimen should not be allowed to flower, and the young shoots must be kept cut down within half an inch of their base. They root rapidly in sandy loam, under judicious treatment.

Messrs. Rollison, of Tooting, obligingly furnished us with an opportunity of obtaining a drawing of this plant in May, 1838. Its usual time of flowering is the months of May and June.

The derivation of the generic name is given in vol. v. p. 54.

Lisianthus Russelianus.

LISIÁNTHUS RUSSELLIÀNUS.
(DUKE OF BEDFORD'S LISIANTHUS.)

CLASS.	ORDER.
PENTANDRIA.	MONOGYNIA.

NATURAL ORDER.
GENTIANACEÆ.

GENERIC CHARACTER.—*Anthers* inclining to one side, generally recurved. *Corolla* funnel-shaped, withering, five-lobed. *Stigma* two-plated. *Capsule* with an inflexed valve, divided into two parts of two or four cells each, or more frequently completely two-celled; placentæ in pairs on both sides of the division.

SPECIFIC CHARACTER.—*Plant* biennial. *Stem* one to two feet high, erect, rounded, slightly branched, smooth, and glaucous. *Leaves* ovate, very acute, three to five-nerved. *Flowers* paniculate. *Calyx* deeply divided into distant, awl-shaped lobes. *Corolla* deep blue, very showy, five-parted, campanulately funnel-shaped; lobes obovate, spreading.

MUCH as the merits of this species have been extolled in various publications, and by eminent individuals, there exists an impression among floriculturists, which has recently been greatly strengthened, that it is far from being so handsome as it is generally reputed. Our previous notices of it have, perhaps, been somewhat vague, because we have preferred leaving any remarks which we wished to make till an opportunity was afforded of illustrating and confirming them by a correct representation. Such we have at length the gratification to submit, and affirm that we are not acquainted with any plant which is more entitled to the epithet ornamental than the one now figured.

Concerning the beauty of this plant, but one opinion can be entertained by those who have witnessed its magnificent flowers. The erroneous notion which has obtained respecting it, and which we now hope to remove, has originated in the following circumstance. A species or variety of *Lisianthus* has been introduced, (by seed from Jamaica, as we are informed,) the general aspect of which might easily be mistaken for the present species, by those whose knowledge of its appearance is but imperfect. The plant in question has also flowered in several collections, and its blossoms are of a deep blue colour. Here, however, all resemblance ceases; for the flowers approach very nearly, in size and form, to those of some species of *Chironia*. It is needless to add, that this is *not Lisianthus Rus-*

sellianus, but a plant of a very inferior character; and, having been repeatedly (perhaps unintentionally) sold as such, the misapprehension above-mentioned has arisen.

Seeds of this species were collected in San Felipe de Austin, Texas, by the late Mr. Drummond, and sent to Britain in 1835. It flowered first at Bothwell Castle, Scotland, and in the Glasgow Botanic Garden, in 1837. Although it is said to possess naturally all the appearance of an annual, yet, from the length of time which precedes its flowering, and the additional circumstance of its not decaying after that period, there can now be little doubt as to its being at least a biennial, and most probably a perennial. In this respect, we may again remark the difference between this, the genuine species, and the one before noticed, as the latter dies almost immediately after producing its flowers.

So little has at present been ascertained respecting its cultivation, that we are unable to propose any routine with confidence. It is to be feared that it will never become so inured to our climate as to adorn the open border, since the apparent season for flowering is at too late a period of the year. Indeed, when kept in a greenhouse, it is almost necessary to remove it to the stove upon the appearance of its blossoms, as they will not otherwise be finely developed. A slight excitement in the spring, by artificial heat, is recommended as a means of hastening the expansion of the flowers; but this must be practised with extreme caution, and accompanied with an abundant supply of light. Great care is requisite in shifting the plant, as its roots are few and fragile. A rather rich loamy soil, slightly elevated in the centre of the pot, and perfect drainage, are essential; while water must be applied only in proportion to the necessities of the plant, and, in the winter months, with considerable prudence.

This plant may be increased by seeds or cuttings. The former, when produced, vegetate rapidly, but the plants do not flower, at the earliest, for two or three years; while the latter, which strike readily under the usual treatment and care, would probably flower much sooner.

We have much pleasure in directing those of our readers who may wish to procure plants of this handsome species, to the nursery of Messrs. Young, Epsom, from whence our drawing was taken in the month of November, 1838. Most other London nurserymen, we believe, also possess plants of it.

Lisianthus is derived from *lysis*, dissolution, and *anthos*, a flower. This refers to the medical qualities of the original species; for, by its cathartic nature, it is said to have the power of dissipating humours.

INFLUENCE OF CLIMATE ON PLANTS.
SOLAR HEAT.

In the last volume of this Magazine, some practical remarks were inserted on the agency of solar light. As we have reason to believe that they have been in some measure instrumental in promoting a rational inquiry into the influence exerted by that most vitally important agent, and the extent of modification required to suit the constitutions of different plants, we now request the attention of our readers while we attempt to fulfil our original design by submitting a few observations on the effects of a still more essential principle—heat.

It would scarcely accord with the character of this work, and the design of the present article, to discuss the question of the nature of heat. Whether it be indeed a substance, or merely a mode of existence,—a particular variety of form, or the vibration of rudimental atoms,—is far from being accurately determined. Believing that the majority of men of science incline to the opinion that it is an impalpable substance, and this hypothesis being likewise much more tangible and intelligible, we have adopted the mode of language which treats of it as such. Nor do we intend to institute any inquiry into latent heat, or the precise means of its development. We write on the subject for practical purposes, and solely with reference to botanical art and science. In this dissertation on solar heat, we shall therefore consider it as an active principle, noting the effects of its presence or absence upon vegetation, with applicatory deductions and illustrations; and the few remarks we may deem it necessary to make on its general laws, or the mode of its agency, will be as deferential and cursory as possible.

Heat—solar heat—is that great, undefined, and undefinable natural agent, which is the principal source of all the changes undergone by plants and vegetables, from the first germination of their seeds, to the period of their actual disorganization and decomposition. Being universally diffused, it pervades all their parts, and incites and invigorates their various functions when in health; but the moment disease and decay seize them, its apparent mode of operation is reversed, and it has a direct tendency to hasten their dissolution. In either health or decay, heat fulfils most important ends in vegetable economy; for, while in the one case it is the means of infusing life and vigour into what would necessarily be inert structures without its agency, in the other it prepares materials for the nourishment and support of succeeding generations, which are destined to flourish on the ruins of their progenitors and predecessors.

These diverse effects of heat, although apparently attributable to two distinct and discordant properties, result from precisely the same cause, and are realized by a similar process; since, in either instance, the substance of plants is dilated and rarefied. Heat expands all things; and when it appears to act contrariwise, such appearance is illusory. There may be only heat sufficient to evaporate the more soluble portions, and the residue may contract; but, in every case, there is an expansion and diffusion of invisible particles, this causing the visible ones to become more closely compressed; and if the heat were rendered more intense, the latter would probably be dissolved likewise. Heat evolves from the soil, rarefies, and then returns the fluid gaseous aliment of plants, which subsequently passes into, or is absorbed by, the minute orifices of the spongelets of their roots. Still influenced by caloric, this aliment is impelled and circulated throughout all their continuous and ramified arteries, depositing, in its passage through stem, leaf, or flower, its grosser elements, according to chemical affinity and assimilation, which deposite, by accumulation, is its actual growth or increase, while the rarer elements are constantly evaporated (by the continued influence of heat) through the innumerable pores.

There is thus, in a healthy plant, an unintermitting supply, appropriation, and expenditure; and as the supply exceeds the expenditure, so much is the appropriation, and so much the growth. If the supply be suspended, or the plant unable to absorb it, or the circulation in any manner interrupted, and the plant debarred from appropriation; in either case the influence of heat is continued upon the plant's substance, expanding and volatilizing into the atmosphere its more fluid matters, while the earthy portion subsides, and eventually mingles with the surrounding soil. Any derangement of the channels of circulation,—such as may be produced by a close ligature, by twisting the plant, by severing its stem, or a more inscrutable injury,—of course causes the gases which would have entered them to be dispersed abroad, and thus diverts the supply; while evaporation being unceasing, and its progress in fact facilitated as decomposition advances, the plant is speedily reduced to its component elements.

That the action of heat is alike indispensable to the growth and decay of plants, is further evinced by the fact, that, in a temperature below the freezing point, these processes are mutually arrested. Moisture, however, assists in promoting the decomposition of vegetable substances; but water is only a consequence of heat, at least in the form in which it is supplied to the earth. The progress of volatilization is accelerated or retarded, according to the degree of uniformity in which heat and moisture exist, either collaterally or independently, and the extent of alternation to which they are subjected. In a temperature uniformly high, with a commensurate supply of moisture, plants decay most rapidly; at a similar temperature, but in the absence of all humidity, the solid particles retain their texture for a great length of time; and in a lower one, under the same circumstances, still longer. In the latter case, alternations of moisture and drought will greatly facilitate the disorganization of a plant, but in the former they only impede its progress.

Of the popular opinion that exposure to the atmosphere is necessary to induce vegetable decomposition, we may observe that it is to a great extent erroneous. Air can have no effect whatever in either causing or hastening this process, except in so far as it is the medium through which solar heat and moisture are conveyed.

Neither is the submersion of any dead vegetable substance in water at all effectual in preventing its dissolution, unless, as is the case in all natural bodies of water, by this fluid being considerably colder than the atmosphere. The fallacy of either of the above notions is easily demonstrated by placing any part of a plant in a close vessel, filled with boiling water. If the water be kept boiling, and the supply replenished as it evaporates, the vegetable tissue will ultimately be destroyed, and its succulent portion, together with the water, be completely volatilized. This simple experiment proves incontestibly that heat and moisture—when the former is sufficiently intense, and the latter proportionately supplied—will speedily reduce all vegetable matters to a state of gaseous fluidity.

Heat performs an essential office in generating those tiny mosses which first appear on newly-formed islands, mountain ranges, and architectural ruins; and, by the action of the same principle, these are converted into soil, successive tribes are produced in superior gradation, which likewise decay in their turns, and thus the surface of these barren districts is eventually clothed with both soil and vegetation, and rendered competent to sustain both animal and human life. As already hinted, all the food of plants, which is supplied to them either naturally or artificially, in the form of decayed vegetable or animal substances, is rendered soluble and qualified for absorption through the agency of heat. Aqueous aliment, which is a much more important article of vegetable sustenance,—whether absorbed in a pure state by the leaves, or percolated through soil,—is also primarily produced entirely by solar heat. The rains and dews which distil upon plants, and on which they ever depend for support, have their origin in the watery vapours constantly exhaled by the heat of the sun, which, passing into a cooler atmosphere, are condensed into the various modifications of dew and rain, and being thus increased in density and weight, descend, by the law of gravitation, again on the earth.

The most remarkable properties of heat are those of a diffusive and imponderous character. By the latter of these it is enabled to pass unrestrainedly through the atmosphere, and permeate the densest substances. To the former we are indebted for that equability of temperature which is caused by what is termed the radiation of heat. This process is continually going on from all parts of the earth's surface, as well as from all substances, both solid and fluid, with which it is overspread. Hence, when, from the natural obliquity of the sun's rays, or from their total obscuration, the atmosphere is at a much lower temperature than the surface of the ground, heat is radiated from the latter, and from vegetation, to such an extent, that not only does the atmospheric vapour condense, but congeal upon them. Perhaps, also, the trifling evaporation caused by radiation from such bodies, may increase the quantity of hoar frost which is engendered upon humid ones during the spring and autumnal months, these being preceded in the one case, and succeeded in the other, by more intense and durable congelations. It is under similar circumstances, and entirely owing to the abstraction of heat by radiation, that ice is formed on the surface of water; while the incrustation thus produced, being a bad conductor of heat, is subsequently instrumental in preventing a like dispersion of heat from the lower strata.

Different kinds of substances possess very variable capacities for absorbing, conducting, and radiating heat; these depending chiefly on the nature of their surfaces and texture: radiation and absorption being the transmission of heat to and from the atmosphere, while conduction is the communication of it to and from any other materials. In general, those bodies which are of the loosest texture, are the best radiators and absorbents of heat, since they admit the air to all their parts most freely, while those are the more perfect conductors which possess a substance of a uniformly dense and compact nature. The extent to which any body acquires dew, when exposed to a clear and saturated nocturnal atmosphere, has been established as a criterion for determining its radiating powers. This ingenious theory is based upon the fact, that, when vapour is brought in contact with any substance, in proportion as the temperature of that substance diminishes, to the same degree will the vapour be condensed, and adhere to it in the form of dew. All metals, particularly those with smooth and polished surfaces, are thus proved to be imperfect radiators of heat; while glass, and those substances which are of a very porous nature, are speedily deprived of heat when placed in a cold atmosphere. Most vegetable bodies radiate heat profusely; subject, however, to great variations, according to the nature of the fluids therein involved. Semi-fluids, such as oils and resins, dissipate heat much less freely than aqueous fluids; hence the different capacities of plants containing either of them for enduring cold.

The power of conducting or absorbing heat from contact with other substances, is seldom co-existent and at the same time co-extensive with the radiating power; but generally resides in the same body in inverse proportion. Substances with a dense continuous tissue conduct heat most rapidly, there being more immediate and uninterrupted communication between their particles: whereas, those which are more porous admitting air, or being partially exposed to air throughout, radiate more liberally. The conduction of heat in porous substances is evidently obstructed by the irregularity of their tissue, and the interposition of minute vesicles of air, which, however, facilitate radiation; while from a denser substance radiation is far less extensive, but, by the contiguity and uniformity of its constituent particles, conduction is readily effected. Metals possess the latter property in a very remarkable degree, as is evinced by the rapidity with which they reduce the temperature of any warmer substance which is applied to them. Glass, on the other hand, is an extremely slow conductor of caloric, as are also wood and other vegetable matters. The capacity of any body for the absorption of radiant heat, varies materially from its capacity of absorption by conduction; the former being generally commensurate with its radiating power, since, in both instances, the heat is conveyed through the same medium.

An increase of temperature may be produced by a variety of means. Chemical combinations, friction, percussion, and electrical elicitation, are the most effective of them; but the sun is the principal and most cogent natural source of heat. All other celestial luminaries appear to be either incapable of generating it, or are too far removed from us to render any emission of it perceptible from the rays which reach our globe. Indeed, the moon may be supposed rather to possess the power of attracting and abstracting it, for we have repeatedly remarked that frosts are most severe (and frequently occur only) when the moon's disk is visible, and particularly when she is in the latter quarter of her revolution. During the period immediately succeeding the spring and autumnal equinoxes, when the moon rises unobscured, in a calm atmosphere, after twilight in the evening, it is almost invariably accompanied by a greater or less degree of frost: and when it is not seen above the horizon till near or after midnight, this is still more frequently the case. Hence it is that many tender plants have been injured in the morning at this period, because the atmosphere was not sufficiently cold at night to induce the cultivator to protect them, he being at the same time ignorant of the above facts.

Now we know that the absence of wind and clouds would alone facilitate radiation from the ground, and that the temperature of the earth's surface is always lower after midnight, on account of the prolonged absence of solar rays, and the protracted radiation; but the result of our observations is not confined to this period. On the contrary, we have noted the occurrence of the same phenomena when the moon was far advanced in the second quarter, and consequently when she rose before sunset. Frosty evenings at this period have very frequently been succeeded by rainy mornings, after the declension of the moon; while precisely the reverse has occurred in the later stages of the lunar revolution. This hypothesis receives additional strength from the circumstance of frosts invariably being much slighter in those situations which are by any means shaded from the lunar rays; and which, by their distance from the bodies which sheltered them, cannot be supposed to derive any heat from them, or to be at all assisted by them in retaining their temperature, otherwise than by their refracting the moon's beams. We do not, however, profess to assert this as an established principle, or one that is not liable occasionally to be departed from; but it certainly appears to us to be founded in reason, and supported by facts: it is therefore well deserving of the unbiassed attention of the inquiring gardener.

Cold—the direct converse of heat—is by many ignorantly considered a distinct principle, or entity. So far from this being the case, it is merely the state produced by the abstraction or absence of heat; in fact, a consequence, and not a cause; a condition, and not a constituent. When we say, therefore, that certain plants are injured by cold, although the mode of expression appears to imply that cold is an active agent, we must be understood to mean that the injury is occasioned by the excessive radiation of heat from their substance, on account of its distributive property. It will thus be perceived that the effects of cold are due to the withdrawal, and not the introduction, of an element; and that the temperature of those bodies which radiate heat most rapidly, is more speedily reduced to the medium of the surrounding atmosphere.

(*To be continued.*)

REMARKS ON BRITISH PLANTS.

The engrossing love of novelty which characterises the present age, is almost sufficient to deter us from allowing any observations upon the plants which flower beneath our feet, and adorn the living landscape around us, to obtrude upon the pages of our Magazine. Objects presented to our daily gaze; springing spontaneously from the soil; and flourishing in blended beauty and prodigal profusion, without requiring the slightest attention or assistance at the hand of man; are naturally enough regarded with that stoical indifference which imbues us when we hearken to a tale familiar to our ears from childhood, or scan a remark that has met our observation unnumbered times before. They occasionally obtain from us a passing glance, and that is all. A large proportion of those who traverse nature's domain, never stay to look at them, much less to examine and admire them. To pluck a wild or hedge-row flower, is absolutely considered puerile, and subjects the unsophisticated offender to derision. Thus the plants to which our father-land is indebted for all its loveliness, and on which we are in various ways more or less indirectly dependent for our very existence, are despised as unworthy of notice, and grow, blossom, and decay, unheeded and without regret.

It were easy to show that this stolid apathy to the works and beauties of creation in our own immediate vicinage, is not only irrational, but culpable; as the contemplation and investigation of such a subject is productive of instruction and delight, of the highest possible description. Nor can a situation be found in which natural productions are likely to be met with in such rich perfection as when luxuriating in a congenial and grateful clime, and in their native soil. We are happy, however, to find, that the above stigma attaches chiefly to the unenlightened portion of the community, over whose minds ignorance, indolence, or prejudice, usurp and maintain an undisputed sway.

The vegetation of the British isles is by no means so varied, so highly developed, or so striking, as that of countries lying nearer to the equatorial line. It nevertheless comprises many very delightful species; some of which are extremely valuable in ministering to the necessities of animal life. To the ornamental or attractive flowering species, the following remarks will principally refer; as we are anxious to render the study of British plants an agreeable and fascinating, as well as a beneficial recreation.

An able botanist has justly observed, that in no country has the native vegetation been so thoroughly explored and described as in Britain. Very few discoveries of undescribed plants have been made during many years past, and some of these have doubtless become accidentally naturalised from other, and in several instances remote, districts. Such, it is true, have now taken possession of the soil, and mature and reproduce themselves with all the vigour and certainty of indigenous tribes; but no doubt can be entertained respecting their foreign origin, and a variety of circumstances may have occurred or conspired to accomplish their acclimatization. It is very questionable whether any further unknown species will be hereafter discovered, although there is a great probability of new varieties arising from casual impregnation.

By the fact of a group of plants being elaborately described, we are presented with unequalled facilities for recognising and familiarising ourselves with them; but there is another particular of equal importance, which is, we believe, peculiar to the plants of this country. It is the circumstance of their distribution being so precisely ascertained, that there are few species to which a distinct locality has not been assigned. This is especially the case with the rarer kinds; and though some are found scattered over almost all parts of the islands, yet the districts which they inhabit more abundantly are, in general, accurately defined. The value of this can be duly appreciated by those only who are desirous of acquiring an acquaintance with our native plants. To such it supplies at once definite objects for research, and an infallible guide to the attainment of those objects. Indeed, the landscape may be said to be a text-book for the student of British botany, and a description of the structure and locality of plants the key by which he is enabled to refer to the proper department, and meet with the specimen desired.

British plants are, for many reasons, well worthy of enlightened and devoted study. Their intrinsic beauty;—the means which they afford for acquiring a knowledge of systematic, and also of physiological botany;—their properties and uses, whether as food for the animated tribes, for medicine, for mechanism, or in the arts;—the powerful incentives with which they furnish the invalid, the nervous, or the dyspeptic, to exercise and activity, those most invaluable auxiliaries in promoting convalescence and conserving health;—their touching poetical associations, and their happy influence in soothing the wounded spirit, or subduing the agitated soul:—severally and unitedly establish their claim to the attention of all classes of society. With each and all of these we would urge upon our readers the advantage of entering at once (if they have hitherto neglected to do so) upon this interesting pursuit; but, for the practical and lucid insight into the science of botany which it is calculated to afford, and the attachment to that study which it generally inspires, we would particularly suggest its importance to the young gardener and botanic pupil.

Those alone who have bestowed any attention on the plants of their native country, know the immense benefit which a person aspiring to the mastery of botany derives from such observation. We speak experimentally. Our earliest knowledge of the organs, the structure, the conformation, ay, and the functions of plants, was obtained while collecting and examining the charming productions of our domestic soil. The listlessness of our first efforts soon gave place to interest, and this was speedily succeeded by enthusiasm; a thirst for a more extensive

[illegible]

[illegible] in our very [illegible]

[illegible] and [illegible]

[illegible] easy to show that this [illegible] ... in our own immediate vicinage, is not ... the [illegible] [illegible]ulation and investigation of such a ... and [illegible] of the highest possible description. ... in which natural productions are likely to be met ... when [illegible]ating in a congenial and grateful clime, ... are [illegible], however, to find, that the above stigma ... [illegible] portion of the community, over whose ... prejudices usurp and maintain an undisputed sway.

The vegetation of the British isles is by no means ... [illegible] or so striking, as that of countries lying nearer ... nevertheless comprises many very delightful species; ... valuable in ministering to the necessities of animal life. ... attractive flowering species, the following remarks will ... anxious to render the study of British plants an agreeable ... as a beneficial recreation.

An able botanist has justly observed, that in no country ... [illegible] been so thoroughly explored and described as in B... discoveries of undescribed plants have been made during ... some of these have doubtless become accidentally naturalised ... several instances remote, districts. Such, it is true, have now ... the soil, and mature and reproduce themselves with all the ...

[illegible]

which [illegible]
value [illegible]
objects [illegible]
Indeed. [illegible]
botany. [illegible]
he is [illegible]
desired.

[illegible]
study. [illegible]
knowledg[illegible]
men, wi[illegible]
the [illegible]
in [illegible]
the [illegible]
all [illegible]
the [illegible]
this [illegible]
of botany [illegible]
is generally [illegible]
gardener and [illegible]

[illegible] has the [illegible]
[illegible] other plants [illegible]
[illegible] species in [illegible]
[illegible] pseudo-bulbs
[illegible] long, and
[illegible] large, and
[illegible] wood, or
[illegible] The
[illegible] win
[illegible] Mor.

acquaintance with botanical science was induced, and the gratification of this only served as a stimulus to higher and more critical attainments. We mention this, because well aware that novitiates frequently experience so many difficulties and discouragements in the outset, that they sometimes relinquish the pursuit, in despair of ever attaining any proficiency. We will venture to assure them, however, that the elementary initiation once surmounted, (which, by a little persevering application may very soon be effected,) progress will be easy—success certain; while, as the science becomes more familiar to them, their attachment to it will proportionately increase, and they will ultimately find it capable of imparting an untold amount of unsullied satisfaction and unvitiated pleasure.

For studying the flowers peculiar to this country, a manual of British botany, a glossary of botanical terms, and a small magnifying-glass, are essential. If the student also possess opportunities for forming an herbarium, this will likewise be a valuable acquisition. We will suppose the tyro equipped with the three requisites above-mentioned, and starting on a botanical excursion. We observe, by the way, that this is far preferable to collecting the specimens, and carrying them home for examination, for reasons which must be obvious to every one. He discovers a plant which is unknown to him, surveys it, ascertains its class and order in the Linnean system, and turns to that section of his "British Flora" to search for a generic character to which it will correspond. The habits of the plant, its leaves, its flowers, its capsules, and seeds, are all subjected to a scrutinizing investigation; and at length it is assigned with certainty to its proper genus.

This may be all decided with tolerable facility, but then its specific distinction has to be determined. If the species are numerous, and very varied, he must first inquire whether it is an annual or perennial herb, a shrub, or a tree. Having clearly affixed to it one of these characters, there may yet be several species of the genus to which it will apply. He will then ask if it is evergreen or deciduous; whether its mode of growth be erect or procumbent, compact or spreading; and after satisfying himself upon all these points, the form and colour of its members will next engage his attention. He succeeds at last in discovering a specific character most closely in accordance with its essential features, except that his specimen is perhaps only two inches high, while the plant is described as being twice that size; it is also remarkably hairy, whereas that circumstance is either unnoticed, or barely alluded to; and all its parts are more diminutive than he finds them reported. To add to his perplexity, the colours of the flowers are much darker; and he searches again and again for a more applicable description, but to no effect—it is nowhere to be found. More than once he resolves to abandon the attempt, and as often re-resolves to search again.

Now all this embarrassment proceeds from inattention to a very trifling matter; viz. the situation and soil in which the plant is growing. A moment's consideration of this subject would have solved the difficulty. The work he has consulted states that the plant grows usually in moist and shaded places, whereas, the specimen in question was procured from an open plain of dry, and sandy, or gravelly soil. Its hairiness, the diminutive size of its parts, and the deeper colour of its flowers, are thus at once accounted for; for it is the peculiar tendency of such a situation to impart these characters. In prosecuting this search after the name of an individual plant, a definition and illustration of many botanical terms will have been obtained; it is probable that the nature of some particular organ will also have been satisfactorily discovered; and its successful issue will encourage the individual to extend his observations, from each of which similarly gratifying results may be anticipated.

In thus minutely examining the organs of plants, not only will their names be impressed upon the memory, but all their hidden beauties descried; and as peculiarities of structure or variations of character in the same species present themselves, an inquiry will be awakened concerning the nature and operation of their functions, which will inevitably lead to a full investigation, and consequent elucidation, of that extensive, but intensely-interesting subject—vegetable physiology. Before concluding this article, we would remind the young botanist, that it is always advisable to procure a number of specimens of a species, if possible, before comparing it with any established characters'; as the appearance and habit of plants are so much influenced by local circumstances, that the attempt to attach a specific distinction to a plant of which only one specimen is possessed, very frequently proves abortive,'solely from this cause.

FLORICULTURAL NOTICES.

NEW AND RARE PLANTS, FIGURED IN THE LEADING BOTANICAL PERIODICALS FOR FEBRUARY.

CLASS I.—PLANTS WITH TWO COTYLEDONS (DICOTYLEDONEÆ).

THE GERANIUM TRIBE (*Geraniàceæ*).

GERÀNIUM TUBERÒSUM; *var*. RAMÒSUM. Tuberous Geranium, branched variety. A small, but pretty, and most profuse-flowering hardy perennial variety. It differs from the original species in its stems being much branched, and very leafy. The flowers are usually axillary, of a pinkish-red colour, and are produced in pairs. The Hon. W. F. Strangways collected specimens of this plant near Potenza, and its numerous blossoms impart to it a rather ornamental appearance in the flower border, although, in this respect, it is inferior to many of our British species. The tubers of the roots are described as being as large as walnuts, and the plant may be easily multiplied by detaching them. *Bot. Reg.* 10.

THE COMPOSITE-FLOWERED TRIBE (*Compósitæ*).

SENÈCIO CRUÉNTUS. Blood-red Senecio. This species is said to be one of the parents of all the beautiful hybrid plants, usually called Cinerarias, which now decorate our greenhouses so profusely in the spring months. The flowers are smaller and less beautiful than those of many of its progeny, and from the repeated impregnations between this plant and *S. maderensis*, it is now rarely met with in its natural character. From a most valuable account of the climate of the Canary Islands (of which the above plant is a native) by Messrs. Webb and Berthollet, in which are included ample particulars respecting the locality it usually inhabits, Dr. Lindley deduces that the plants we are accustomed to call hybrid Cinerarias decidedly belong to the greenhouse, and should be kept in a moderate temperature, with a greater proportion than usual of atmospheric humidity. They would also appear to require but a partial exposure to light. *Bot. Reg.* 7.

THE CORNFLAG TRIBE (*Iridáceæ*).

PHALOCÁLLIS PLÚMBEA. Lead-coloured Phalocallis. In the general appearance of the flowers of this beautiful plant, a striking resemblance to the species of *Marica* is perceptible. It has been named by the Hon. and Rev. W. Herbert, in whose collection at Spofforth it flowered in the autumn of 1838. Unfortunately it is found to display but one blossom on the summit of its stem, and this expands before sunrise, and fades before noon. The flowers are principally of a pale lead colour, but their internal structure is both curious and very pleasingly marked with yellow and brown. The gentleman above-mentioned presumes that it will be found to succeed in an open border with a southern aspect. *Bot. Mag.* 3710.

THE ORCHIS TRIBE (*Orchidàceæ*).

MAXILLÀRIA TENUIFÒLIA. Slender-leaved Maxillaria. Two distinct modes of growth are observable in the plants constituting the genus Maxillaria; the one with prostrate and the other with ascending rhizomata or stems. To the latter section belongs the present species, which produces its pseudo-bulbs in a successional series, one above the other. It is less interesting in its habit than many other species, but the flowers are peculiarly beautiful; for, though small, they are most liberally blotched with scarlet on a greenish-yellow ground. In its cultivation or propagation, not the slightest difficulty is experienced, as it will thrive either in a pot filled with the usual materials, or on a block of wood, and may be increased to any extent by separating a single bulb from its rhizoma. Mr. Thomas Hartweg, who has been sent on a botanical mission to Mexico by the Horticultural Society, discovered the species here noticed in the vicinity of Vera Cruz, Mexico, and it has flowered in the gardens of the Horticultural Society at Chiswick. *Bot. Reg.* 8.

SOPHRONÌTIS GRANDIFLÒRA. Large-flowered Sophronitis. With the combined habit, appearance, and beauty of a *Cattleya*, this charming plant has the dwarfness and compactness of the elegant little *Sophronitis cernua*. To the latter plant it is now connected, and while its flowers infinitely exceed those of that species in size, they are even superior to them in richness and intensity of hue. The pseudo-bulbs resemble those of the genus *Cattleya*, but are not more than three inches long, and have only one leaf at their summit. The flowers are terminal, solitary, large, and of a brilliant scarlet colour. It would doubtless flourish on a log of wood, or might be kept in a pot, with proper attention to drainage and watering. " The credit of introducing this plant alive to this country is due to Mr. Gardner, who found it in the Organ Mountains of Brazil, and sent it home in 1837." *Bot. Mag.* 3709.

ONCÍDIUM FÓRBESII. Mr. Forbes' Oncidium. One of the most splendid, and decidedly the rarest, species of Oncidium at present known in this country. Mr. Gardner originally discovered it in the Organ Mountains, and transmitted it to Woburn Abbey, the seat of His Grace the Duke of Bedford. It is stated that only one specimen rewarded Mr. Gardner's researches, and this has flowered under the care of Mr. Forbes, gardener to the distinguished nobleman above-mentioned, after whom it has been named. The flowers are large, and their petals and labellum are almost completely obscurated by a rich scarlet colour, the margins only, and the centre of the flower, being yellowish white. It approaches nearest to *O. crispum*, but is altogether stronger, and has much more showy and handsome flowers; in this respect being inferior to none of its allies. *Bot. Mag.* 3705.

NEW, RARE, OR INTERESTING PLANTS IN FLOWER IN THE PRINCIPAL SUBURBAN NURSERIES.

CACTÆ. In an extensive collection of this singular tribe, recently imported by Messrs. Low and Co., from the Spanish Main, South America, are several new and remarkable species. One of these, which evidently belongs to the genus *Cereus*, and bears a slight resemblance to *C. senilis*, is peculiarly interesting. Instead of the thickly-set, rigid, and coarse hairs which characterise the species just mentioned, the present plant is only partially covered with a white, woolly substance, of an extremely delicate texture. The plant grows erect, about a foot in height, and is of nearly the same dimensions (an inch and a half in diameter) throughout its entire length. The ribs or angles are more distant, prominent, and perceptible, than those of *C. senilis*, and the spines grow in tufts. Several striking species, of a larger size, and with a most formidable array of aculei, some of which are full three inches in length, and are arranged along the edges of the ribs precisely after the manner of a chevaux-de-frise, are among the collection. Many orchidaceous plants likewise accompany them, and all are in an admirable state of preservation.

COMESPÉRMA GRÁCILIS. An excellent specimen of this charming plant is now expanding its pretty blossoms in the nursery of Messrs. Young, Epsom. It is trained on a perpendicular, flat, wire trellis, of a circular form, and rather more than a foot in diameter. The profusion of flowers, especially towards the summit, is truly astonishing. For the abundance, the bright blue colour, and the general beauty of its blossoms, as well as the circumstance of their being developed at the present season, it merits especial attention. Its diminutive size, and slow growth, are fully compensated by the qualities above noticed. The mode of training is mentioned to state that the practice adopted at Epsom is preferable to allowing it to grow erect, as the young branches and flowers are thus induced to cover the old and unsightly stems, thereby effectually concealing them.

DENDRÒBIUM NÒBILE. All admirers of orchidaceæ would doubtless experience considerable gratification, and receive a powerful stimulus to their ardour in the cultivation of the tribe, by witnessing a magnificent specimen of this noble plant, which is now flowering in the collection of Messrs. Loddiges. It is difficult to say whether the superior management with which the plant has evidently been favoured, or the exquisite beauty of the flowers with which the skilful culture is repaid, is entitled to the most distinguished notice. Both are certainly of the highest order; and it may suffice to say that we have seldom seen or known either surpassed. It is a rapid-growing species, with light blush-coloured flowers; the labellum being of a most superb purple hue, and somewhat recurved, but obtuse, at the extremity.

EPIDÉNDRUM MACROCHÌLUM. The extensive genus *Epidendrum* contains a few species which are really interesting and beautiful, and amongst these the present plant may indisputably be included. With large, smooth, roundish, pseudo-bulbs, and neat foliage, it has also flowers of a very attractive character. The sepals and petals are of a purplish-brown colour, while the labellum is pure white. The latter is large, (hence the specific name,) and has a rich purple stain near its base, which, together with the bright yellow summit of the column immediately above it, present a most pleasing appearance. Messrs. Loddiges have several specimens now in flower.

GREVÍLLEA ——(?) A new species of *Grevillea* has, during the last year, been cultivated in the London nurseries, which has excited some attention on account of the unusual character of the leaves. These are somewhat wedge-shaped with deep longitudinal lobes. The flowers are now exhibited in the Epsom nursery, and in this respect it proves to be one of the least valuable species of this not very ornamental genus. They are produced in terminal clusters, and are white, with yellow anthers. It is scarcely worthy of a place in the greenhouse, except for the singularity of its foliage. We are not aware that it has yet received a specific appellation.

GRIFFÍNIA HYACINTHÌNA. This is an old but very scarce bulbous stove plant, yet we know of none more deserving of attention. Its large, deep green, glossy leaves, (of which there are seldom more than two on each plant,) the shortness of the flower-spike, and the showy clusters of beautiful blue blossoms by which it is surmounted, impart to it a compactness of appearance almost unknown among bulbs, and an ample degree of the beauty for which some of them are so deservedly famed. Nor are the flowers of that fugitive character so common to plants of this description, but continue to expand in succession for a considerable time. As it blossoms during the winter months, no collection of stove plants should be without it. We observed it flowering most beautifully last month in the nursery of Messrs. Rollison, Tooting.

ONCÍDIUM LUNÀTUM. The curious crescent-like form of the labellum of the flowers of this plant, has suggested its specific name. It is a small species, of dwarf habits, and slightly resembling *O. triquetrum*. The flowers are very numerous, and exceedingly pretty, being of a dull white ground, and liberally streaked with brownish purple. It is an excellent species for growing on pieces of wood, suspended from the roof of the house; as, in such a position, it could receive the necessary care with regard to the administration of water, and its blossoms would be more favourably exhibited. Specimens of it are flowering in the orchidaceous house of Messrs. Loddiges at the present time.

ONCÍDIUM CAVENDÍSHII. A noble species, imported from Mexico, and inferior to *O. Lanceanum* in the colours and fragrance of its flowers alone. It has short, thick, fleshy leaves, which are quite destitute of spots, and large yellow flowers mottled with brown. These latter are produced in strong, dwarf spikes, after the manner of the species above mentioned, from which it differs in general appearance by the shortness and rigidness of its foliage, and the absence from it of any other colour than green. In the nursery of Messrs. Loddiges it is now blooming profusely.

PECULIARITIES IN THE CULTURE OF RARE OR ORNAMENTAL PLANTS.

FÙCHSIA FÚLGENS.—As in the literary world, so also in the scientific, and consequently in the floricultural, each season records one or more particular novelties, which may or may not contain real excellence, but which the patrons of the pursuit are always anxious to bring within their personal knowledge, to possess, and, if possible, to improve. Judging from the eagerness with which *Fuchsia fulgens* has been cultivated, the numerous prizes which have been awarded for it at horticultural exhibitions, and the distinguished and engrossing attention it has received in gardening works, we presume we are correct in asserting, that this fine species has held no mean rank among such floral *lions* or attractions of 1838.

Much as we contemn the practice of involving any subject in mysterious uncertainty, particularly when in itself extremely simple, it will be admitted that something has yet to be learned respecting the cultivation of this plant. It may be, indeed is, perfectly true, that nothing can be more easy than its summer treatment; but, what are the best methods of preserving it through the winter, and of inducing it to grow, or accelerating its growth, or rendering it strong and healthy in the spring, is far from being satisfactorily determined. The following hints, which are the result of close observation of the habits of the present species, will, perhaps, prove useful, and certainly cannot be considered irrelevant.

The rapidity and luxuriance with which the stems of this plant grow during the summer and autumn, and their consequent succulence and immaturity at the commencement of winter, render them not only exceedingly liable to decay, but preclude, if they survive, the possibility of their producing vigorous lateral shoots or fine flowers in the succeeding year. Indeed, were it possible to induce them to ripen their wood sufficiently, it is very questionable whether the old stems would flower so beautifully as those young ones which might easily be obtained immediately from the roots.

Under these circumstances, and with a full consideration of the nature of the plant, we are disposed to believe, that if its treatment were assimilated to that of the dahlia, it might be rendered available as an ornament to the flower-garden, and cultivated to the highest perfection with the least possible trouble. We do not intend that every particular in the management of the dahlia should be unhesitatingly adopted in the culture of this plant, but only the most prominent and essential articles, and these with a slight degree of modification. The propriety of this will be seen by comparing the character of the two plants. The *Fuchsia* now under discussion has tuberous roots, is dormant during the winter, commences growing in the spring, by throwing up a number of young shoots from its roots, (provided its stems of the previous year's growth have been removed,) and would not be injured, but rather benefited, by having its stem or stems cut down in the latter part of the autumn. These are well known to be precisely the habits of the dahlia.

To elucidate our suggestion, and define the extent to which we would practise it, a brief outline of the treatment we propose to bestow on this species will be necessary. Commencing with the vernal season, we would remove the plants (which had been taken from the earth in the previous autumn) from their winter repository about the month of March, and place them in pots or beds of soil in a greenhouse or frame. They should be fully exposed to light, and even to the open air in fine weather, and duly protected with mats when frost occurs, but not subjected to artificial heat. In this situation, with occasional gentle waterings, they will soon emit a number of stems from the roots, some of which may be taken off for propagation, and one or more left to grow, as may be desired.

With the ordinary attention afforded to growing plants, they will be ready for transferring to the open border at the usual period; and, whether planted singly or collectively, there can be no doubt they would make a most brilliant display in the flower-garden. Premising, from the luxuriant character of the plant, that a perfect freedom for the roots is the most favourable to its superior development, and considering that it would thus obtain this desirable privilege, accompanied likewise by the beneficial influence of an unconfined and pure atmosphere and unmitigated solar agency, it appears impossible to arrive at just conclusions relative to the extent of improvement which the adoption of the system here propounded is calculated to effect on this favourite plant.

In the autumn, prior to the usual period for the occurrence of frost, a small quantity of some loose and dry material may be placed around the base of the stem of each plant for protection, and as soon as the leaves and shoots are injured by frost, the stems may be cut down to within two or three inches of the base, and the roots taken from the ground. They should be removed with a portion of soil attached, and immediately placed in a dry shed, loft, or other apartment, plunging them in light and rather dry earth. If the apartment be a close one, and the roots copiously covered with dry straw, they will not require any attention during the winter, except an occasional examination, to ascertain that they are secure from frost, and to counteract any tendency to either an excess of moisture or drought. Care should be taken to remove them from this situation either before or immediately after their growth has commenced, when they may be tended as previously suggested.

These hints are not given at a venture; for, although we have not had an opportunity of testing their propriety, they are based upon an almost unerring foundation—the habits of the plant. The method herein proposed is divested of every difficulty which could create an objection, and appears to us the best adapted to ensure an augmentation of the splendour and attractions of this most magnificent species. As such, we leave it with our readers, to adopt or improve, according as it may harmonize with their own opinions or experience.

OPERATIONS FOR MARCH.

MARCH is, almost to a proverb, the month for seed-sowing; and it may likewise be considered the season for the general excitation of all kinds of plants. Contrary to the usual practice of diminishing the temperature of the plant-stove as the spring advances, we would recommend a gradual but decided augmentation. All tropical plants are naturally subjected, during their growing stage, to an intense and continuous degree of heat, and to cultivate them successfully this treatment must be imitated. If, as we have before suggested, the winter be allowed them for repose, the system now advocated is not only practicable, but precisely that which will prove the most suitable.

The advantages of this method are great and manifest. Both economy and superior beauty will be the result. First, the plants will be thus vigorously incited during the period in which alone their growth can be of a healthy nature. Secondly, a high temperature, accompanied by a corresponding degree of light, and supplied only for a definite time, will cause them to perfect and mature their shoots, and thus render their flowering or fruitful organs more prolific, besides placing them farther beyond the reach of injury from subsequent cold.

Lastly, a considerable quantity of fuel will thus be saved, as that which by this system is consumed in the spring and summer months, will be very trifling compared with the usual expenditure required for maintaining an incessantly high temperature throughout the winter.

In effectuating this principle, the elevation or diminution of temperature must be gradual, and closely in accordance with the duration or extent of solar influence. In proportion as these particulars are kept in view and acted upon, will be the success of the operation. At the present season artificial heat may be constantly, but moderately applied, and as the sun's rays become more vigorous and durable, the temperature may be increased. Ridiculous as this may appear to some, a little investigation will prove it to be the only rational mode of proceeding; for, to subject plants to a great heat without a due supply of light, is contrary to nature, and highly prejudicial. Whereas, the influence of the sun not being so prolonged in our climate as it is in tropical regions, we should take advantage of the period in which it is afforded, to endeavour, by seasonable co-operation, to bring to maturity those objects which will not flourish without its aid.

The maintenance of an equable degree of temperature during day and night indiscriminately, must be understood as being quite irrelevant to the principle above propounded, and perfectly incompatible with our views. While, however, we would by no means attempt to preserve this equability, we would not suffer the temperature to be too greatly deranged, and certainly not to a greater extent than 20 degrees Fahrenheit. Moisture, whether atmospheric, or in the form of water, whether applied to the roots, or sprinkled over the entire surface of the plant, must always be administered in quantities commensurate with the degree of heat, and this rule should in no instance be departed from, except in particular cases during the decline of the season.

Greenhouse plants, and those in pits, frames, or such as are kept in pots in any other situation, will in some degree fall under the preceding remarks. Although, in their case, no artificial heat is required, water performs the part of a stimulant; and the same principle of apportioning its supply to the extent of solar agency, holds good in reference to them likewise. In preparing any of these for the flower-garden or borders, the action upon them of any other than solar heat should be avoided as much as possible, since it induces a weak, sickly state, which is inimical to their future development and beauty.

Seeds of annual plants of every description, if sown at this period, ought not to be rapidly excited by a too powerful heat. Where any stimulation of this kind is employed, it should be of a very gentle nature; and, except with extremely tender species, the more it is dispensed with, the greater will be the luxuriance, beauty, and hardiness, of the plants.

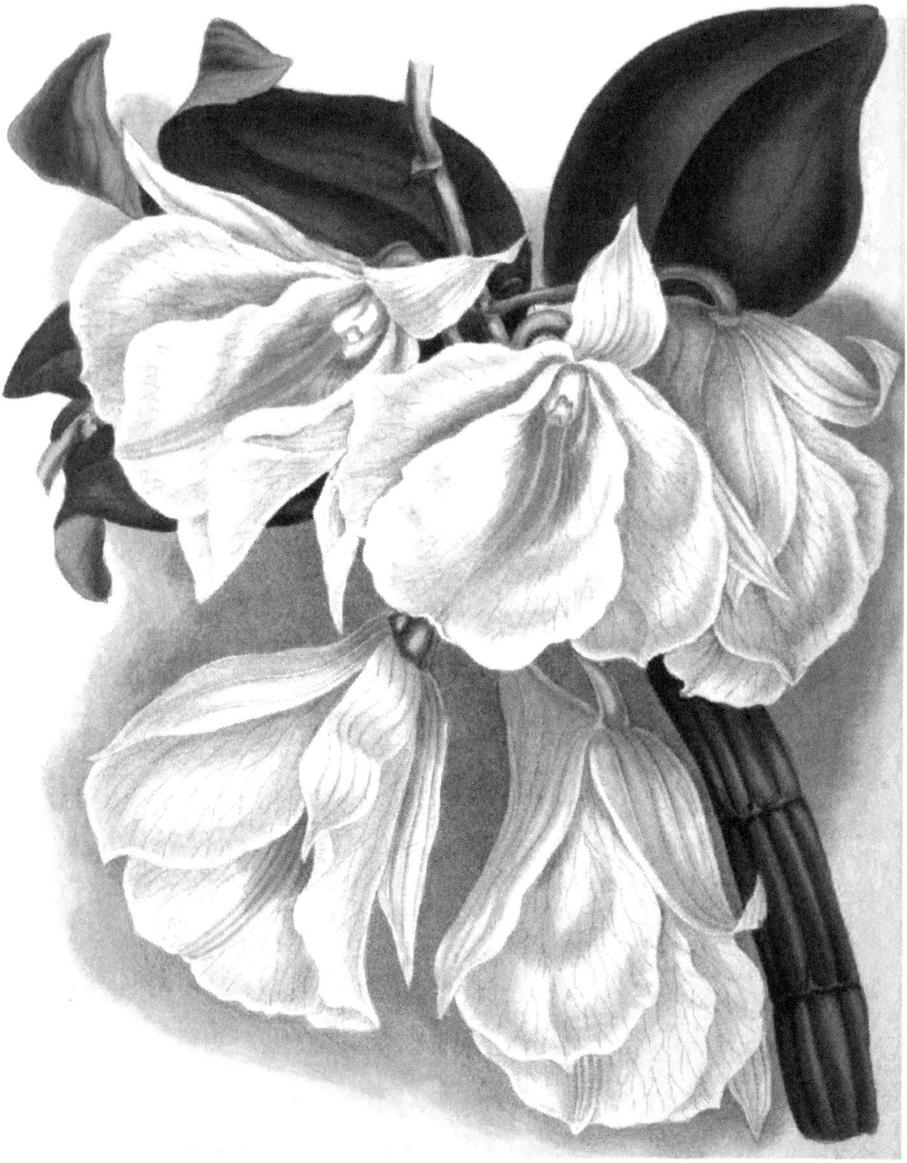

DENDRÒBIUM FORMÒSUM.
(BEAUTIFUL DENDROBIUM.)

CLASS.
GYNANDRIA.

ORDER.
MONANDRIA.

NATURAL ORDER.
ORCHIDACEÆ.

GENERIC CHARACTER.—*Vide* vol. iii. p. 77.

SPECIFIC CHARACTER.—*Stems* terete, pendulous, slightly hairy. *Leaves* opposite, ovate, obliquely emarginate at the summit, obtuse. *Racemes* short, terminal, four or five flowered. *Bracts* small, ovate. *Flowers* large, white. *Sepals* oblong, acute; lateral ones elongated into an obtuse spur at their base. *Petals* two, broader than the sepals, partially covered by the labellum, acute. *Labellum* ovate, extended beyond the petals, retuse, comnate with the base of the column.

It must be highly gratifying to the admirers of orchidaceæ to witness the annual accession to our collections of so many noble species, of which little or nothing is previously known. The number of these delightful plants that has been imported within the last few years, is wholly without a precedent in the annals of floriculture. Yet, notwithstanding this immense influx, the reserve is still ample; indeed, new and unexplored districts are continually presenting themselves, the beauty of whose vegetable offspring seems to invite their removal to countries where they can be admired and enjoyed by those nobler beings for whose gratification more especially they unfold their charms.

Perhaps no genus, throughout the whole tribe, displays so many lovely species as *Dendrobium*. Their graceful, airy form, the delicate hue and texture of their flowers, and their delicious fragrance, entitle them to a very distinguished place in our esteem. Of all the species, however, hitherto discovered, the one of which a figure is appended is acknowledged to be the finest. The flowers being white, necessarily suffer in a representation on paper, but their unusual size imparts even here an air of superiority, which is fully maintained by their enchanting appearance when depending naturally from the parent stem.

This handsome plant was received at Chatsworth, the seat of His Grace the Duke of Devonshire, in the autumn of 1837, having been collected for His Grace by Mr. J. Gibson, in a district called Pondooah, at the base of the Khoscea Hills, in the East Indies. It is somewhat remarkable, that only one specimen of this fine species was discovered by Mr. Gibson throughout the entire range of country he explored. The specimen alluded to was found growing on a tree, and brought safely to Chatsworth, where it flowered in the spring of 1838, at which time our present drawing was taken.

Copious directions for the cultivation of Dendrobiums have been given in the last volume of this Magazine, and there is only one point to which we need here advert. It is that of withholding water during a certain period, for the purpose of inducing them to flower more abundantly. In their native localities, they blossom in the dry season; and when this circumstance is imitated in their artificial treatment, it has a signally beneficial effect in stimulating their floriferous organs to finer and more liberal production.

The species of drought here recommended is a peculiar one. It does not consist in a suspension of heat, but merely of moisture. It should be commenced in the house employed for this purpose on the approach of winter, and may be allowed to last for one or even two months. During this time no water must be administered, and the atmosphere kept perfectly dry. The leaves of the plants will probably wither, and many of them fall; but, at the termination of this epoch, humidity should again be freely applied, and a most luxuriant growth, together with an extraordinary profusion of flowers, will speedily ensue.

By attention to the above hints, Dendrobiums may be rendered as much superior to what they have heretofore been in this country, as they now are to the majority of other Orchidaceous Epiphytes. The importance of having one or more small houses which can at any time be appropriated to this object, will be duly felt by the cultivator when these circumstances are considered, and we may now reiterate that such structures are highly useful, if not indispensable appendages to an orchidaceous house.

An explanation of the generic name has before been furnished in vol. iii. p. 77.

The specific designation refers to the transcendant and delicate beauty of the flowers of this plant.

Rudbeckia Drummondii

RUDBÉCKIA DRUMMÓNDII.
(MR. DRUMMOND'S RUDBECKIA.)

CLASS.	ORDER.
SYNGENESIA.	FRUSTRANEA.

NATURAL ORDER.
COMPOSITÆ.

GENERIC CHARACTER.—*Flowers* rayed, ligulate. *Calyx* in a double row, many-leaved, nearly equal, spreading. *Seed* with a broad border at the summit; margin membranaceous, four-toothed. *Receptacle* conical.

SPECIFIC CHARACTER.—*Plant* perennial, herbaceous. *Stems* numerous, radical, roundish, slender. *Leaves* pinnate; lobes linear-lanceolate, slightly jagged, acute. *Calyx* five-leaved; segments oblong, obtuse, recurved, bright orange, deeply stained with dark-brown at their base.

IN what may appropriately be termed the natural sciences, and especially in that of botany, so many new subjects are continually occurring, many of which exhibit such close affinity to other species, and are so utterly destitute of prominent distinctive characters, that, in order to establish their identification and recognition, it is found necessary to have recourse to commemorative names. This practice is not only employed as a *dernier ressort*, but, in many instances, is highly useful and laudable in perpetuating the memories of individuals who have in various ways aided in the advancement of science, and whose services would probably be otherwise unknown, or speedily pass into oblivion.

There is, however, a danger of encumbering and tarnishing botanical science by the too frequent use of such appellations; and now that they are becoming so extremely common, a wise and judicious jealousy should be exercised by those with whom they originate, otherwise one grand design of such designations will obviously be frustrated,—the transmission to posterity of worthy names; these being altogether lost sight of among the ignoble and indiscriminate crowd. It is well and desirable that those persons who are immediately instrumental in the introduction of new plants to this country, should have their names thus immortalised; and equally so that yet humbler contributors to the furtherance of the interests of science generally, should be similarly noticed. But there is a class of individuals who are the prime movers of such importations,—furnishing at once the means for effecting them, and for cultivating the plants so imported,—

to whom such factitious aids to reputation are wholly unnecessary, and often unacceptable. The exalted and munificent patron of floriculture is far above the influence of such trifling distinctions, and his name, by being embalmed in the gratitude of his country, is transmitted to future ages by a worthier, nobler, and less meretricious impulse.

We have said that the collectors of plants are principally entitled to have their names embodied in the specific designations of those they discover; and the plant depicted in our present plate, will furnish an instance in which we consider the practice has been legitimately adopted. The person after whom this showy species is named, and by whom, we believe, it was first introduced, but who was subsequently removed by death ere the completion of his valuable labours, merits distinguished notice. To Mr. Drummond we are indebted for many, very many, most ornamental plants, and although several others bear his name, they are not so numerous as to forbid its present application.

Of the era of introduction of this handsome plant, we have been unable to glean any particulars. It is most probably a native of North America, and has perhaps been known in British collections for some years. Our attention was first attracted to it flowering in a frame in the nursery of Messrs. Rollison, Tooting. It is certainly an interesting species, and far excels most other herbaceous plants of a similar character, in the rich colour of its flowers.

The plant which furnished the sample for our present drawing having been kept in a pot, and beneath a frame, it is natural to suppose its character is not fully exhibited, and that, if planted in the open border, the flowers would be much finer. There can be little doubt that it is perfectly hardy, and in such case, its treatment is of the most simple description. It is not at all adapted to the greenhouse, as its herbaceous character, and long slender stems, are only suitable to the flower-border.

An increase may be obtained by dividing the roots in the spring season. We are not aware that it ripens seeds in this country, but this may very possibly prove the fact when more generally cultivated, and placed in more favourable circumstances.

The drawing here given was made in Messrs. Rollison's nursery, in August, 1838. This species grows from eighteen inches to two feet in height, and flowers usually in July and August.

The genus *Rudbeckia* was originally created by Linnæus, and named in honour of Olof Rudbeck, once professor of botany at Upsal, who died in 1702.

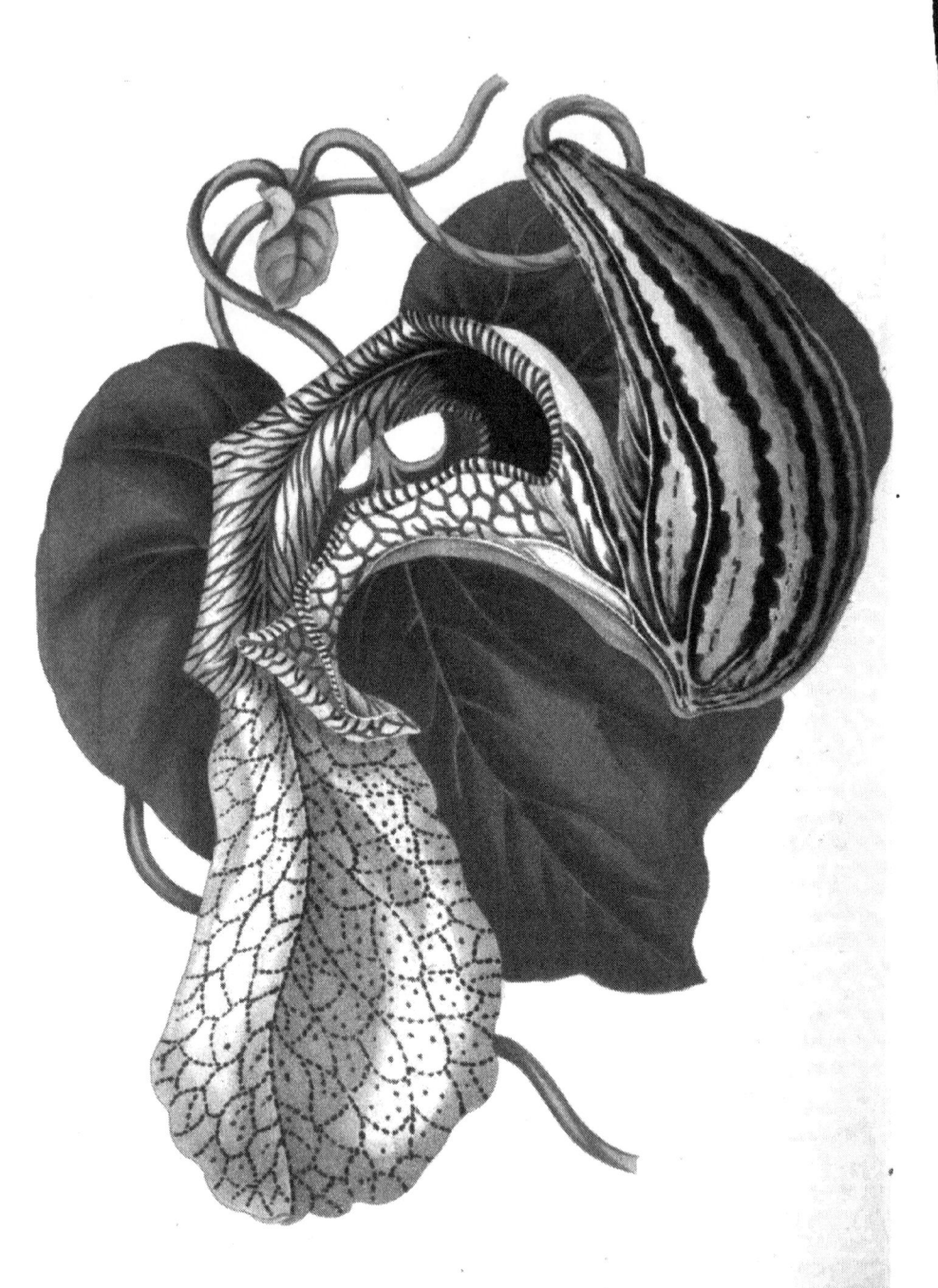

Aristolochia hyperborea

ARISTOLÒCHIA HYPERBÒREA.

(NORTHERN BIRTHWORT.)

CLASS.
GYNANDRIA.

ORDER.
HEXANDRIA.

NATURAL ORDER.
ARISTOLOCHIÀCEÆ.

GENERIC CHARACTER.—*Vide* vol. iii. p. 2.

SPECIFIC CHARACTER.—*Plant* a climbing shrub, evergreen. *Stem* twining, slightly tortuous, branching, the older parts with a rugged surface. *Leaves* large, petiolate, cordate, deep green above, lighter beneath, acute. *Stipules* amplexicaul, oblong, acute, light green. *Flower-stalk* from three to four inches long, curved, axillary. *Perianth* tubular, tube oblong, tapering towards the base, curved upwards towards the extremity, and divided into two lips; lower lip short, upper one spatulate, slightly crenate, emarginate, pendulous, generally six inches in length.

AMIDST the endless diversity of structure and colour which flowers, the fairest of nature's productions, present, some command our admiration by their superlative beauty, while others arrest our attention by the singularity of their form. It is difficult to ascertain which awakens the most pleasing emotions, since, notwithstanding man's universal, perhaps intuitive, love of beauty, his unconquerable love of novelty is frequently paramount, and a curious object is often valued more highly than one truly graceful.

In the very remarkable plant which is represented with great fidelity in the annexed drawing, the curious and the beautiful are admirably blended. Each of these qualities is discernible at a single glance; and the more closely the flower is examined, the more obvious do they become. Its large and richly-mottled tube, the elegant continuous curvature of which ultimately expands into a thin, slender, flowing lip, together with the exquisite markings around the orifice of the limb, are features on which the beholder may gaze for a considerable time without weariness. We may here remark, that the flowers are frequently much larger than the scale given in our figure.

Nor must the habits of the plant, its handsome foliage, and the happy disposition of the flowers, be left unnoticed. By being trained to the roof of a stove, these latter hang pendulously from the stem in such a manner as to exhibit all their beauty. This would be in a great measure concealed, were they not produced in this position, as their exterior surface is almost destitute of the rich stains which characterise the interior. Its habit may be seen from the subjoined woodcut.

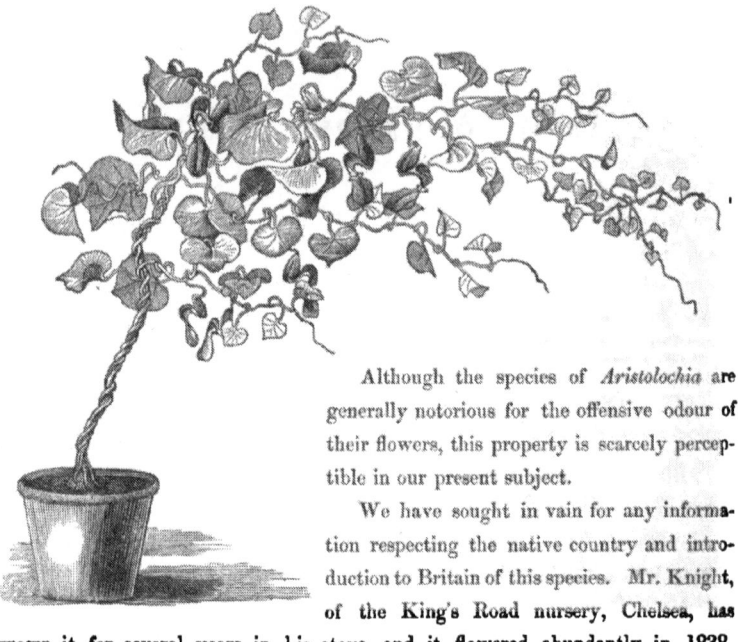

Although the species of *Aristolochia* are generally notorious for the offensive odour of their flowers, this property is scarcely perceptible in our present subject.

We have sought in vain for any information respecting the native country and introduction to Britain of this species. Mr. Knight, of the King's Road nursery, Chelsea, has grown it for several years in his stove, and it flowered abundantly in 1838. That gentleman presumes that it was obtained from one of the northern districts of India, and there is great probability of this proving correct. So far as we have been able to ascertain, it has never before been published, and we have reason to believe it a new species.

It requires the usual treatment of climbing stove plants. A shaded situation, such as is afforded in an orchidaceous house, would be the most suitable; and it should be trained to the rafters of the roof in preference to a wall, as the flowers are displayed more advantageously in the former position. A rich loamy soil, and abundant syringing, are the principal points to be attended to in its further management. Propagation may be effected by cuttings.

In the exotic nursery of Mr. Knight, Chelsea, this species blossomed in the month of May, 1838, and that gentleman kindly permitted our artist to execute a drawing at that period. We have since been favoured with a beautiful figure of the same plant from Messrs. Ronalds, of Brentford.

The derivation of the generic name will be found in vol. iii. p. 2.

Malva Creeana

MÁLVA CREEÀNA.
(SHOWY RED-FLOWERED MALLOW.)

CLASS.
MONADELPHIA.

ORDER.
POLYANDRIA.

NATURAL ORDER.
MALVACEÆ.

GENERIC CHARACTER.—*Vide* vol. iv. p. 269.

SPECIFIC CHARACTER.—*Plant* shrubby, deciduous. *Stem* erect, branched; branches nearly erect, covered with short stellate hairs. *Leaves* petiolate, three-lobed, lobes toothed, deltoidly ovate, sparingly covered with stellate pubescence; entire at the base. *Flowers* axillary, solitary, rose-coloured. *Petals* obcordate, slightly crenate. *Peduncles* shorter than the petioles. *Involucre* of three filiform leaves.

THERE exists in British collections an extensive class of plants, a peculiar feature in the cultivation of which is of comparatively recent adoption. The group to which we allude is comprised in the phrase half-hardy herbaceous plants and shrubs, and the treatment is that of growing them in the flower-beds and borders in the open ground. If we revert to the last century, such a tribe is scarcely recognizable; while, in the present times, their numbers receive immense yearly augmentations.

Half-hardy plants, especially dwarf shrubs, are perhaps even more interesting and valuable than those which are thoroughly hardy. As ornaments either to the greenhouse or the flower-garden, they are alike available; and many of them, if removed from the open air at a sufficiently early period, prove lasting attractions to the greenhouse when they could no longer be retained in the borders. By transference to the open ground during the summer months, their growth is also invigorated, and their appearance improved to such a degree, that when returned to the house in the autumn, they produce a manifest and delightful variation from the general comparative sickliness of other plants.

As being at once an illustration and an evidence of the propriety and force of these observations, we may introduce to the notice of our readers the subject of the accompanying figure. This charming plant is a half-hardy shrub, flourishing most vigorously in the open border through the summer season, and continuing to flower profusely when removed to the greenhouse upon the approach of autumnal frosts. Such treatment not only ensures the greatest duration of its beauty, but is at the same time the most congenial to its nature.

Several very showy species of Mallow have recently been introduced to this country, of a similar character to that here figured. *M. Creeana* is certainly inferior to none of its congeners; while its fine foliage, luxuriant but not straggling habits, and especially its sweet rosy blossoms, entitle it to pre-eminence over at least many others. It has appeared in several of the English nurseries, and we noticed it first in that of Messrs. Low and Co., Clapton, in 1837; since which time its character has been much more perfectly developed in the Epsom nursery. Further than this, we have nothing to communicate respecting its introduction, as this occurrence is yet involved in obscurity.

Whether grown in a pot in the greenhouse, or planted in the open flower-border, it is a most interesting plant; but when these modes of treatment are combined, an extraordinary improvement in its appearance is manifested. If retained perpetually in a pot, it exhibits a stunted and unhealthy aspect, and seldom thrives vigorously even under the most favourable management. Full exposure to the atmosphere, and an unrestricted medium for the extension of the roots, are the circumstances in which it appears to delight. Two or three months of such indulgence, however, will enable it to endure confinement during the remainder of the year without the least injury, and when it is professedly cultivated as a greenhouse plant, this should always constitute an item in its treatment.

It would doubtless form a beautiful object if planted in the border of a greenhouse, although its dwarfness precludes such a practice, unless when the house is of small dimensions. Placed in the open ground it requires no attention, as it will flourish in any loamy soil. Care must be exercised in removing it before the occurrence of frosts to a greenhouse or frame, and it will suffer little from having its roots cramped through the winter, provided it be again planted out in the early part of the succeeding spring.

Cuttings of this species strike freely with ordinary attention, and seeds vegetate readily when they can be properly matured.

Our figure was taken from Messrs. Young's nursery, Epsom, in the month of August last. It commences flowering about June, and continues for an indefinite period, or till checked or destroyed by frost, attaining generally the height of two feet.

An account of the source of the generic name will be found in vol. iv. page 270, of this Magazine.

VEGETABLE PHYSIOLOGY.—No. II.

We resume our notice of this elegant branch of science at the point where we left it, (see No. LXI., p. 10,) and shall now pave the way to serious investigation, by an attempt to elucidate terms, and thereby facilitate the progress of the student. Nothing tends so effectually to *fix* the mind, as a perfect comprehension of scientific phraseology; and nothing more clearly marks and distinguishes the ardent student, than that restless earnestness which seeks the knowledge of principles. The memory always retains those facts which the understanding comprehends.

Referring to our former article, we perceive that there are two or three terms which require explication. They are in the mouth of every one; but, like the phrases of botany, are too often mere sounds which convey no definite or intelligible meaning. The *alburnum*, or sapwood of trees, as we have shown, was by Mr. Knight pronounced to be the channel of the sap, through the medium of its cells.

The term *alburnum* is purely Latin; derived *ultimately* from *albus*, white. It was employed by Pliny to express that white and tender tissue which exists, and is *yearly* produced, between the bark and the wood. By citing the following passage (we believe from the pen of Professor Lindley), it will appear that physiologists now ratify the hypothesis of Mr. Knight.

"It is the principal channel through which the crude sap is conveyed from the roots into the leaves. It consists of little besides vegetable tissue, in which respect it differs from *heart-wood, or duramen*," (*dura*, Latin; hard, or hardened wood,) "which is vegetable tissue *combined with solid secretions*."

The cellular organs of this tissue abound with juices; but the incipient fibres, which finally harden and solidify, are comparatively dry and juiceless: the presence of sap in the cells, therefore, affords a strong argument in favour of the theory.

Associated with the term *alburnum*, we meet with another—*liber*, which may now be explained. It was used by Virgil, and in its original sense, applied solely to that loose, delicate substance, which is interposed between the alburnum and the proper bark. The ancient Romans made use of this inner bark (*liber*) of certain trees for their manuscripts, as they did not possess paper. Hence, we gather that *liber*, when its meaning is confined to *a book*, is a term of comparatively modern acceptation.

In common with that of the alburnum, a layer of liber is deposited yearly; the latter being closely contiguous to, but exterior of the former. Thus the layer or soft tissue of liber, invests that of alburnum; both the one and the other are vehicles of vital fluids, though of a different character; and both are annually separated and thrust apart by the interposed developments of each succeeding year.

At this point, a very momentous inquiry suggests itself: it is one which the human faculties may never be permitted to determine; yet it is perfectly legitimate, and must conduce to admiration, if not to actual discovery.

Every vegetable being may be referred ultimately to a *seed*. Does this seed—this embryo of a mass of perfected organization—comprise within itself all the rudiments of every *future development*, or not?

Here we must take a retrospective view of a work which was published some years since, wherein this great question was embodied into an hypothesis, that merited far more consideration than it appears to have received. We allude to Mr. James Main's Treatise on Vegetable Physiology; a book not in our possession. But fortunately we possess an original letter by the respectable author, from which some extracts will here be given, that, we hope, may rivet the attention of many who are not under trammels to received authority, however it may occupy "high places."

Mr. Main assumes, as his basis, the fact which all analogy bears out; that *a being is originally perfect in all its parts*, and that development and nutrition are not in any way identical with a production of *new parts*. Thus "vegetables have an organic frame, containing specific qualities: the former is *rudimental;* mutable in texture, and expansible under the action of air, heat, light, and water: the latter are *accretive*, in consequence of accessions of vegetable food received from the earth and atmosphere. As the frame is extended or expanded, additional food is required to fill up and distend the swelling vessels, whereby the whole is enlarged in bulk and weight; this process being continued till the plant arrives at maturity, if an annual, or for ever if a perennial. Now, I hold it questionable whether any of the food goes to *generate organization!* That it fills, distends, supports, and is in fact in connexion with the inherent qualities of the plant,—the cause of its growth or amplification, is perfectly obvious: but, that fluids, whether aqueous or gaseous, however gross, can *be changed into organic structure*, or even into a single cell of that structure, is beyond the powers of my comprehension.

"I admit that my ideas pre-suppose that the *oak once reposed in the acorn:* but how much more rational and easy of belief is even this notion, than that it came into existence without a rudiment or nucleus of organization!"

Mr. Main then adverts to his theory of a *vital membrane*, which he termed, subsequently, *Indusium;* and views it as the organ which develops annually the new layer of alburnum and liber. The prepared, and fully elaborated sap, called *Cambium*, had been considered as a substance capable of *becoming organized* under the stimulus of the vital principle; and its situation between the new yearly layers warranted the assumption with those who could believe that new vital parts were *bonâ fide* produced.

But, observes Mr. Main—"Organization must exist before any expansion can take place; and I must still doubt whether vegetable organs can originate in any combination of nutritive elements." He adds,—"There is a distinct member situated between the liber and alburnum, so that if waxed paper be placed within this member, the new alburnum will be formed on the outside; but if placed on the exterior side, the new deposite will be invariably formed within it; and just where it would have been had no paper been inserted."

These remarks are very striking; but if any one start an objection of the infinite minuteness of parts, he may be reminded of the small *dust* of the fern-tribe, every particle of which contains the rudiments of a plant, and many species assume a gigantic growth. Be the fact what it may, it certainly appears most philosophical to conclude that the annual layers are strictly *developments*, and not new creations; and that the enlargement of organs is a process of nutrition, not of abstract production.

INFLUENCE OF CLIMATE ON PLANTS.
SOLAR HEAT.
(*Continued from page* 37.)

From the general principles already premised respecting the agency of heat on vegetation, we proceed to specify a few of its more particular effects; interspersing our remarks with plain and practical hints relative to the instances in which their knowledge is useful in artificial cultivation. They may be comprised in three principal divisions: *viz.* the degree in which the geographical diversity of plants is affected by heat, the influence it exercises upon their functions, and the extent to which adventitious circumstances, such as elevated tracts, valleys, forests, extensive collections of water, &c., modify and regulate its diffusion and intensity. An inquiry into these several subjects will be, we conceive, not only interesting in a physiological point of view, but afford ample data whereon to attempt a system of acclimatizing plants, and supply authoritative bases for any future observations on the regulation of artificial temperature.

That heat is eminently instrumental in the geographical distribution of plants, by assigning and restricting those of a certain habit and character to special districts, is indisputable. Almost every climate on the surface of our globe has a vegetation more or less peculiar to itself; and although various circumstances concur to effect this limitation, temperature is unquestionably the chief. Indeed, not only does heat, by its presence in different degrees, determine the localization and range of plants of particular and kindred habit, but it is exceedingly plausible and probable that the modification of heat has tended much to create the diversity of habit in different zones. Thus, the vegetation of each zone exhibits its own peculiarities and characteristics; that is, we meet with plants of a certain habit in their appropriate region, not only because the mean temperature is propitious, but to a certain extent, and in the lapse of ages, it is extremely likely that the temperature has conduced to the causation of the distinguishing habit existing in such clime.

In endeavouring to ascertain the influence which heat possesses and exercises in the general dispersion of plants, M. de Candolle has very appropriately suggested the following particulars for inquiry; and we shall here follow the arrangement of that distinguished botanist. First, it is necessary to acquire a knowledge of the mean temperature of a country throughout the year. Secondly, the extremes of heat or cold to which it is subjected at any and what seasons. And thirdly, the degree of temperature prevalent in each of the different months.

A knowledge of the mean temperature of any country is only valuable to the cultivators of its vegetable productions, when not deduced from contrary extremes. If the climate be liable to any very great depression or elevation of temperature at different periods of the year, the average, amalgamating these vicissitudes, would be quite useless, with regard to its guidance in cultivation. But, where a nearly equable degree of temperature is maintained throughout the entire year, the variations on either hand being trifling and unimportant, such data would be of the highest possible utility. For instance, in tropical regions the derangement of temperature is never great; since, during the period at which the sun's rays are vertical, the density of the atmosphere is so much increased by evaporation, that a very slight difference of the thermometer is indicated, on its removal from a shaded to an exposed situation. We shall hereafter show, that on no other part of the earth the same uniformity of temperature exists; but, even in this case, general information is insufficient for practical purposes; and nothing but minute and careful observation, from residence or sojourn in or near the particular locality wherein a plant is found, can furnish proper materials for its cultivation.

So far, then, as those climates are concerned in which there is the nearest approximation to equability of temperature, vegetation is found to maintain in some degree a similar uniformity of habitude and aspect, and, with the exception of a brief period, exhibits a constant appearance of verdure and luxuriance. Perennial herbaceous plants, with soft and succulent stems, trees with evergreen foliage, and very generally destitute of mucilaginous or resinous juices, in short, nearly all the shrubby or arborescent forms, and a great proportion of the herbaceous species of monocotyledonous or endogenous plants, inhabit those districts possessing the above character. On the other hand, annual plants are, we believe, nowhere seen; deciduous trees, likewise, and those which form thick and numerous concentric layers of bark, are almost exclusively confined to regions which present a greater diversity of temperature.

Valuable, however, as is a knowledge of the mean temperature of certain portions of our globe, with reference to its influence on vegetation, inasmuch as it teaches that the plants thereto indigenous cannot be cultivated with us unless some artificial means be employed for imitating their native climate; correct information respecting the extremes of temperature to which any country is subjected is of far greater importance, since it embraces a much wider field of observation, and affords more comprehensive and appreciable results. To know that certain tracts are periodically exposed to great alternations of temperature, is to become acquainted with the fact, that the native vegetation of those tracts is capable of supporting and resisting the extremest degree of heat or cold which there occurs.

If the observer allow his inquiries to cease here, they will be found essentially defective when the theory which may have been founded upon them is reduced to practice. The state of their functions at the time when these changes take place, and the usual duration of the hot or cold season caused by such alterations, yield only in importance to the extreme degree of temperature. Thus, if a plant be removed from its native climate to one in which the extremes of temperature are nearly correspondent, but occur at different periods, it must by no means be supposed that it will accommodate itself to the latter, until, by a gradual and natural adaptation, assisted by artificial shelter at particular seasons, a total change in the era of its periodical functions is effected. Again, there are peculiar districts within the tropics, which, on account of their great elevation, are annually exposed to a considerable diminution of temperature; but though, in some such cases, the thermometer ranges equally as low as in the winters of temperate climates, the cold season is by no means so protracted. In attempting, therefore, to acclimatize plants from the former regions in those last mentioned, some protection must be afforded them on the approach of winter; otherwise, their shoots not having been allowed the natural period to mature themselves, will be liable to serious injury from early attacks of frost, even though they should be less severe than what they are accustomed (but prepared) to endure with impunity in their native climes.

More fully to illustrate our meaning, we may instance those countries which lie antipodes to us, and whose summer season consequently occurs at or nearly the same time as our winter. It is obvious that plants obtained from such places will not at once conform to the inversed epochs of our climate; and that the greatest attention is necessary to inure and accommodate them. Nor is the period at which they are removed from their native soil, and their management during the voyage, of trifling importance. Plants taken from such districts at the commencement of their winter would arrive in this country at the same rigorous period, and thus have to linger through that unfavourable season during their usual stages of growth and development, and immediately after being subjected to all the debilitating circumstances of a sea voyage. This would certainly be prejudicial to them. The best time, therefore, for shipping them, would be the decline of their winter, when we should receive them towards the commencement of our spring.

In introducing any kind of plant from the tracts above-mentioned, the advantage of importing seeds in preference to living specimens will be clearly evident from the preceding remarks. Seeds will not only endure greater extremes of temperature during the voyage without injury, but they require no attention, and may be germinated at any desirable period after their arrival. Hence, if received during the autumnal or winter months, they may be safely kept till the ensuing spring before excitation.

On the germination of the seeds of exotic plants at a favourable season, we are inclined to believe that much of their subsequent capacity for naturalization depends. If stimulated in the latter part of the autumn, or during the winter, they acquire a great degree of weakness and sickliness, and what is still worse, an unnatural habit of commencing their growth at an unsuitable period. This will be in some measure retained for a considerable time; and will inevitably retard, if not (by exposing their young shoots to early spring frosts) wholly subvert, all attempts to acclimatize them. On the contrary, by judiciously selecting that month for inducing their vegetation, at which they should afterwards commence their annual development, it appears most probable that they will immediately, and without thereby suffering any debilitation, accommodate the exertion of their functions to the vicissitudes of our climate.

With those countries which are situated in low latitudes, it is more important that the lowest degree of temperature which they ever experience should be ascertained; while, in proportion as they recede from the equator, a knowledge of both extremes is equally essential. Throughout the temperate zones, and as far as vegetation extends towards the polar circles, but more especially in those portions of the former which are considerably elevated, and where powerful but transient summer heat prevails, it is advantageous to know the highest rate of temperature that exists as well as the lowest; for in many Alpine districts it is occasionally found to exceed the usual heat of the valleys of the same latitude. In such cases, vegetation having only a certain interval wherein to perfect its growth, progresses with amazing rapidity; and plants spring up, mature and scatter their seeds, and decay, in an astonishingly brief space of time.

Climates of very variable temperature naturally produce plants to which an intense degree, whether of heat or cold, is either not injurious, or decidedly beneficial. Annuals are peculiarly adapted to countries of this description, as they perform the necessary offices for the propagation of their species in a summer, and the oleaginous matters with which their seeds abound, together with the hard integument or rind in which they are enveloped, enable them successfully to withstand the most severe frosts. These, and such deciduous trees as are well coated with bark, or evergreens in the wood of which resinous or oily juices abound, the buds of both being protected in a very similar manner to the seeds of annuals, or by tough, viscid sheaths, form the principal features in the vegetation of those divisions of the earth which are subjected to great alternations of heat and cold. Herbaceous plants are also abundant, but they assume a very different habit to those of tropical countries; as their stems and leaves annually decay, and those of the succeeding year are duly protected in embryos of a form and nature precisely analogous to those of trees and shrubs.

But the best and safest data whereon to found a proper estimate of the influence of temperature on botanical geography, and especially to establish a code of cultivation for any particular species of plants, are accurate observations with respect to the ratio of heat or cold which prevails in any province throughout each month of the year. By this means, not only are the mean temperature and either or both extremes obtained, but the periodical duration or prevalence of the several modifications is indicated; and we are enabled to arrive at correct conclusions relative to the capability of the vegetation of that province to naturalize itself in any others of which we possess a similar knowledge. Other information is useful, but this alone is entirely divested of vagueness, and reduced to an appreciable and available form. Even in this case, however, we shall be liable to error if we neglect to take into consideration the difference between the diurnal and nocturnal temperature, and the average duration of each.

Few travellers seem to have thought such information worth acquirement; and probably still fewer have ever allowed their observations to transpire. This is perhaps owing, in some degree, to the little attention hitherto bestowed upon the subject by those to whom such communications would alone be valuable—the cultivators of plants. Strange as it may and does appear, the latter class prefer ascertaining the constitution of a plant, with regard to its capability of enduring cold, by experiments requiring years of tedious investigation, and which frequently occasion disappointment by the repeated destruction of their subject, to a few hours' study of the memoranda of travellers on the temperature of its native climate.

It is true that we are at present destitute of the requisite intelligence concerning many districts; but if cultivators would evince greater aptitude to appropriate and employ what we already possess, and thus stimulate collectors to furnish more ample accounts of the variations of temperature in every district from which they procure specimens, it is confidently believed that the practices both of acclimatation and general cultivation might be based upon such solid and unwavering principles, that there would not be an explored tract throughout the entire globe, on the vegetation of which we should not know precisely what treatment to bestow, the moment the plant and the description of its parent country were received.

We entreat attention to these statements from all persons interested in the promotion of either horticultural or agricultural art; and call upon them to assist, by every means in their power, in the attainment of the desideratum herein displayed. Our expectations from this source may appear too sanguine to some, and perhaps altogether chimerical to others; but we are thoroughly persuaded that authentic accounts of the particular atmospheric mutations in every district to which plants cultivated or wished to be cultivated in this or any other country are indigenous, would, if properly estimated,—carefully compared with the known peculiarities of the climate in which they are desired to be grown, and judiciously appropriated and applied,—at once put an end to all uncertainties and conjectures that are now entertained respecting their habits, and effect little less than a complete revolution in the culturist's interesting and important practice.

(*To be continued.*)

LOUDON'S ARBORETUM ET FRUTICETUM BRITANNICUM.

SELDOM do we encumber our pages with notices or reviews of any horticultural works, unless they contain some facts, precepts, or suggestions, of a highly interesting and valuable nature. In the volumes we have now the pleasure of introducing to the attention of our readers, all these recommendations are combined; and that in a comparatively unexampled degree.

Much as we admire and prize many of the previous publications of this estimable and talented author, we know of none in which he has so successfully fulfilled the task undertaken, as in the one now under consideration. It is composed of four octavo volumes of letter-press, and an equal number filled with octavo and quarto engravings of the principal exotic trees described. It would be tedious, as well as useless, to enumerate the various articles, in the history, description, and culture of ligneous plants, which are treated of in this comprehensive work. We will merely observe that every particular which the most devoted patron of arboriculture, or the most ardent admirer of trees could desire, is therein faithfully, fully, and graphically detailed. Of all the more valuable species, an excellent engraving either of the whole tree, a branch, a leaf, or the fruit, is inserted, from which their general character may be ascertained; while the admirable portraits of entire trees which appear in a detached portion of the work, will tend to establish the high character of the artists by whom they were delineated, and greatly enhance the utility and interest of the whole.

As a work of general reference for the culture of indigenous and hardy or half hardy exotic trees and shrubs, but especially the two latter; as a guide to the selection of the most ornamental, the means for procuring them, and the appropriate method of treatment; as an invaluable preceptor in planting, thinning, pruning, and otherwise managing, all kinds of shrubberies and forests; in short, as a compendious cyclopædia of every thing pertaining to these, the most gigantic, durable, and useful of animate but non-locomotive natural productions; the *Arboretum et Fruticetum Britannicum* stands unrivalled. We refrain from offering any remarks on the subject generally, as we propose inserting a few observations in a subsequent number.

It is impossible to give any extract from the body of the work without, in some way or other, mutilating it and impairing its interest; so that we shall merely append the following judicious suggestions on hybridising and grafting arboreous plants, with a view to render them more ornamental, and refer the reader to the book itself, particularly that section of it under which Coniferous plants are arranged. The following passage is taken from the Introduction to the work, the whole of which is written in the author's usual perspicuous and spirited style, and in which the superlative merits of trees and shrubs, as objects of ornament, are rendered apparent.

"It should not be forgotten that all our most valuable plants, whether in agriculture, horticulture, or floriculture, are more or less indebted for their excellence to art. Our cultivated fruit trees are very different from the same trees in a wild state; and our garden and field herbaceous vegetables so much so, that, in many instances, not even a botanist could recognise the wild and the cultivated plant to be the same species. There is reason to believe that the same means by which we have procured our improved varieties of fruit trees will be equally effective in producing improved varieties of timber trees. A few species, such as the oak, the elm, the magnolia, &c., have had improved varieties raised from seed by accidental crossing, or by the selection of individuals from multitudes of seedlings; and variegated varieties, and varieties with anomalously formed leaves, or with drooping or erect shoots, have been procured from the sports of parts of different plants. But the mode of improvement by cross-fecundation is yet quite in its infancy with respect to timber-trees; and to set limits to the extent and beauty of the new varieties which may be produced by it is impossible. There is no reason why we may not have a purple-leaved oak, or elm, or ash, as well as a purple-leaved beech; or a drooping sweet chesnut as well as a drooping ash. The oak is a tree that varies astonishingly by culture; and, when the numerous American varieties that have been introduced into this country shall have once begun to bear seed, there is no end to the fine hybrids that may be originated between them and the European species. In short, we see no difficulty in improving our ornamental trees and shrubs to as great an extent as we have done our fruit trees and shrubs; though we are as yet only procuring new species from foreign countries, which may be considered as the raw material with which we are to operate."

We subjoin the hints on grafting, which almost immediately follow, and from which a few of the objects of the work will be seen.

"Every proprietor of a landed estate is either a planter, or possesses trees already planted. If he is in the former case, he will learn from this work to combine beauty with utility, by planting, in the outer margins of his natural woods or artificial plantations, and along the open rides in them, and in the hedgerows of his lanes and public roads, trees which are at once highly ornamental and more or less useful—in some cases, perhaps, even more useful—than the common indigenous trees for which they are substituted. If, on the other hand, his estate is already fully planted, he will learn from this work how he may beautify his plantations by a mode which never yet has been applied in a general way to forest trees; viz., by heading down large trees of the common species, and grafting on them foreign species of the same genus. This is a common practice in orchards of fruit trees; and why it should not be so in parks and pleasure-grounds, along the margins of woods, and in the trees of hedgerows, no other reason can be assigned than that it has not hitherto been generally thought of. Hawthorn hedges are common everywhere; and there are between twenty and thirty beautiful species and varieties of thorn in our nurseries, which might be grafted on them. Why should not proprietors of wealth and taste desire their gardeners to graft some of the rare and beautiful sorts of tree thorns on the common hawthorn bushes, at intervals, so as to form standard trees, in such of their hedges as border public roads? And why should not the scarlet oak and the scarlet acer be grafted on the common species of these genera, along the margins of woods and plantations? Such improvements the more strongly recommend themselves, because, to many, they would involve no extra expense; and, in every case, the effect would be almost immediate. Every gardener can graft and bud; and every landed proprietor can procure stock plants from nurseries, from which he can take the grafts; or he may get scions from botanic gardens, the garden of the London Horticultural Society, that of the Caledonian Horticultural Society, or the Dublin Gardens at Glasnevin."

SUGGESTIONS FOR DETERMINING THE MERITS OF FLOWERING PLANTS.

It is by no means an uninteresting or useless occupation, to inquire into the nature and causes of the pleasure or indifference begotten in us when witnessing different kinds of plants in a flowering state. By so doing, we are led at once to discard all those vague and ambiguous notions which are frequently induced by extrinsic circumstances or personal infirmities, and to establish definitive rules for our future regulation and guidance. What is termed taste is, we know, exceedingly varied and capricious, but there are even in this certain essential principles which may be easily reduced to some degree of order, and rendered generally available.

The first thing which attracts the attention of the observer of a flowering plant is its blossoms. If these are very numerous, conspicuous, and of a brilliant colour, all other characters are sometimes forgotten, and it is pronounced valuable. But, when the flowers have faded, the plant occasionally proves to be a meagre or even unsightly object, and in this state it continues throughout the greater part of the year. This is a case in which the impropriety of judging the merits of a plant by its flowers alone, is evident. Instances of a contrary nature might be adduced to show that where the flowers are small and inelegant, the general appearance of the plant may yet be ornamental, and remain so perpetually. Again, if the foliage be taken as a criterion in the absence of flowers, similarly erroneous conclusions may be deduced.

To determine with any degree of accuracy the general character of a plant, every feature must be strictly scrutinised. A really beautiful object of any description, is one in which all the parts are in some measure conformable to each other, and this is precisely the case with plants. Symmetry and harmony of outline, though essential, are quite insufficient to constitute beauty, unless every component part contribute distinctly and individually to create that harmony. A large, gross, and uncomely flower surmounting a slender and naked stem, is certainly far from being a graceful object. In the same manner, an insignificant blossom, buried beneath a dense mass of noble foliage, excites feelings completely adverse to those of admiration. Utility is not a constituent of beauty in plants; therefore, our considerations of this quality must be wholly banished when viewing them.

Next to the general conformity of the different members of a plant, and the adaptation in the size and contour of their particular organs, their surface and colour may be examined. These apply principally to the foliage and flowers. Leaves are technically termed *coarse* when they are large, with great and numerous inequalities on their surface, and covered with strong hairs, bristles, or aculei. Neither of these characteristics are independent criteria; and size, especially, is frequently co-existent with real beauty, when unaccompanied by any other detractive quality. Unitedly, however, they constitute the coarseness above mentioned; while precisely the contrary properties are necessary to true elegance, or handsomeness. Their colour, whether it be of a light or deep shade, should be lively and clear; and this is particularly desirable when the plants are what is termed evergreen.

As the appearance of flowers is considerably deteriorated by association with insignificant or slovenly foliage, so, in a much greater degree, fine foliage alone can never compensate for the absence or inferiority of blossoms. Flowers are and must be regarded as the greatest ornaments of a plant, however fugitive they may be. It is important that they stand out boldly and advantageously to view, that their form be somewhat symmetrical, (though this must be taken in a very latitudinarian sense,) but chiefly that their colours should be clear, bright, and agreeable.

Nothing, we believe, determines so much the opinion of an observer of a plant, as the colour of its blossoms. But this, when viewed apart from other considerations, proceeds from an erroneous and puerile taste. Hence, so many shabby-looking, and really uninteresting plants, acquire a degree of notoriety purely artificial, and which invariably subsides when the novelty of its object has ceased. By this means, also, persons of correct taste wholly disregard popular declarations, and many highly valuable plants are thus retained in that state of obscurity which their injudicious and incompetent appraisers alone merit.

The preference for certain colours is a question which individual taste can decide; although some are almost unanimously voted vulgar; but the characters herein depicted are essential to real beauty. If the persons who cultivate plants for sale, and those who in any way describe them, would bear these principles continually in mind, their opinion would be regarded with greater deference and confidence, and the diffusion of floricultural taste and practice would be greatly facilitated. Nor could it be otherwise than useful to the general cultivator, particularly to those who are frequently called upon to decide the merits of plants at horticultural exhibitions, as they would thus acquire that stability and assurance of judgment, which would ensure a cheerful acquiescence in their award.

FLORICULTURAL NOTICES.

NEW AND RARE PLANTS, FIGURED IN THE LEADING BOTANICAL PERIODICALS FOR MARCH.

CLASS I.—PLANTS WITH TWO COTYLEDONS (DICOTYLEDONEÆ).

THE FIGWORT TRIBE (*Scrophulariàceæ*).

TORÈNIA CORDIFÒLIA. Heart-leaved Torenia. A neat and somewhat interesting little annual, with numerous, small, lilac-coloured flowers. It inhabits moist pastures in the Northern Circars of Eastern India, and in this country requires to be grown in the stove. The very branching nature of its stems, which, by producing flowers at the summit of each ramification, cause a pleasing profusion, renders it worthy of cultivation; otherwise the individual appearance of the blossoms is not sufficiently striking to invest it with any attraction. Its flowering season is the month of October. *Bot. Mag.* 3715.

CLASS II.—PLANTS WITH ONE COTYLEDON (MONOCOTYLEDONEÆ).

THE NARCISSUS TRIBE (*Amaryllidàceæ*).

ALSTROMÈRIA LÍGTU. The Ligtu. One of the most beautiful species of this extremely handsome genus. The great size and delicate hue of its flowers constitute it a truly ornamental and delightful plant. Although occasionally cultivated in our gardens, it is far from being so common as its merits deserve; and we agree with Dr. Lindley that, notwithstanding the general neglect of Alstromerias, "there is no genus more likely to reward the care of a skilful gardener." The present species is a native of Chili, South America, and blossoms with us in the month of June and July. These plants may be retained through the winter in the open ground, with a trifling degree of shelter from wet and frost; but the Hon. and Rev. W. Herbert recommends strewing the ground around them with sawdust or peat in the Spring, as they are extremely liable to attacks from slugs, and these insects generally avoid a surface composed of such materials. *Bot. Reg.* 13.

THE CORNFLAG TRIBE (*Iridàceæ*).

MÀRICA GRÀCILIS. Slender-stemmed Marica. In this new and elegant species, the principal distinctive character is, as its name denotes, the gracility of the stem. It approximates most closely to *M. Northiana*, from which it differs in being "much slenderer in every part; the partial spatha particularly long, narrow, and acuminated, the flower smaller, and the outer sepals narrower." The larger petals of the flower, are of a pale lead-colour, but the inner ones are beautifully streaked with yellow and blue, thus rendering it a really admirable object when in blossom. This plant was imported by His Grace the Duke of Bedford, from Brazil, to Woburn Abbey, where it has been kept in the greenhouse. *Bot. Mag.* 3713.

THE ORCHIS TRIBE (*Orchidàceæ*).

ONCÍDIUM LÙRIDUM; *var.* GUTTÀTUM. Mr. Boyd's Oncidium. This charming variety is supposed, and with justice, to rank only inferior to *O. Lanceanum* and *Forbesii*. In general appearance and structure, it has no particular features; but the flowers are liberally and pleasingly stained with red, this colour being of various shades on the different members, and becoming deeper towards the base of the labellum. Messrs. Rollison received this plant from Jamaica, and it is believed by Dr. Lindley to be the *Epidendrum guttatum* of Linnæus, but has not been previously cultivated in this country. It is said to prefer the warmest part of the stove, requiring an abundant supply of moisture, and growing either in a pot or on a piece of wood. *Bot. Reg.* 16.

MAXILLÀRIA VITELLÌNA. Yellow racemose Maxillaria. A small, but pretty species, imported from Brazil by Messrs. Loddiges, in whose collection it blossomed in June, 1838. It has neat, one-leaved, conical pseudo-bulbs, and the flowers, which are produced in erect racemes, are small, and of a deep yellow colour, the labellum having a rich brown spot in the centre, and being slightly undulated. A long period of rest or drought is recommended for this species, as a means for increasing its subsequent luxuriance, and promoting the development of its blossoms; it being retained, at other times, in a humid stove. *Bot. Reg.* 12.

HÙNTLEYA MELEÀGRIS. Speckled Huntleya. So rare is this handsome epiphyte, that Dr. Lindley states he has seen no specimen, except the one which we have before had occasion to notice as flowering with Messrs. Rollison, Tooting. It is a strong growing species, with large, luxuriant foliage, and disposed to bloom frequently, but seldom producing more than two or three flowers at the same time. These appear on solitary peduncles, and are of a yellowish white colour, freely blotched with brown, and having a glossy surface. "This charming plant is found in gloomy damp woods, on the banks of the Rio De Pirapitinga, in the district of Bananal. It is scentless, and flowers in June." It appears to succeed best when grown in a pot, and a large supply of water is necessary. *Bot. Reg.* 14.

NEW, RARE, OR INTERESTING PLANTS IN FLOWER IN THE PRINCIPAL SUBURBAN NURSERIES.

CŒLÓGYNE BARBÀTA.—Our collections of orchidaceæ have recently been aggrandized by several very beautiful species of the genus *Cælogyne* from the East Indies, and the present plant, though less showy than others of its allies, is a highly interesting species from the same prolific region. Its pseudo-bulbs are ovate, tapering slightly towards the apex, and much more thickly arranged along the rhizoma than is the case with *C. nitida* and those of similar habits. The leaves, which are produced in pairs from the summit of the pseudo-bulbs, are oblong and acuminate. The floral racemes are terminal, and grow erect to the point from whence the first flower proceeds; after which they become pendent, bearing an indefinite number of delicate blossoms, the sepals and petals of which are pure white; the labellum is also white, but agreeably streaked with stains of bright yellow, and internally relieved towards its base with pink. It is now finely flowering in the nursery of Messrs. Loddiges.

DENDRÒBIUM TERETIFÒLIUM.—A singular little species of this charming genus, widely differing from the usual habit. Though not of recent introduction, it is, we believe, a scarce plant, and forms a very pretty object when suspended on a fragment of wood from the roof of the house. It has diminutive, cylindrical foliage, which is gradually attenuated to a point, and from within a sheath at the base of which a solitary flower-stem arises, surmounted by a single blossom. The form of the flowers is rather peculiar, all the outer members being inferior and deflexed, while the labellum is ascending. The latter is white, and beautifully fringed, and the sepals and petals are of a greenish yellow colour, faintly striped with purple. The collection of Messrs. Loddiges contains flowering specimens of this species at the present time.

DEÙTZIA CANÉSCENS.—Although very nearly allied to *D. scabia*, the plant here mentioned is perfectly distinct, and of a neater character. In the greenhouse of Messrs. Rollison, Tooting, it is now expanding its attractive blossoms, which closely resemble those of the species just alluded to. The chief point of distinction is in its foliage, which is somewhat downy, ovate, and serrated. From the appearance of the specimen under notice, it would likewise seem to be a particularly dwarf species; and, if this be a permanent characteristic, it will unquestionably enhance its value. The principal merit of the plant, however, resides in its flowers, the fragrance of which is most delicious.

EPÀCRIS COCCÌNEUS.—The name of *Copelandii* having already been affixed to the subject of these remarks, it is with some reluctance that we attempt any alteration. But, as the plant has not yet become publicly known by that appellation, and the bestowal of such designations is much to be deprecated by all lovers of the science; as the name, likewise, which we now suggest accurately expresses the character of the plant, and is alone sufficient to ensure its recognition, we venture to presume that the gentleman in whose collection it was raised will cheerfully be disposed to relinquish the petty notoriety which the attachment of his name would have procured, and we have accordingly concluded to renounce it. This plant is a seedling, raised casually in the garden of Alderman Copeland, Leyton, Essex. It assimilates to *E. impressa* in habit, but has flowers of a brilliant scarlet hue. In the nursery of Messrs. Low and Co., of Clapton, it is now blossoming most beautifully, and will doubtless prove a very splendid ornament to the greenhouse in the spring season.

EPIDÉNDRUM SCHOMBÙRGKII.—The caulescent species of *Epidendrum* are now so very numerous, that a superficial observer experiences considerable difficulty in their discrimination. Many of them are also wholly unworthy of cultivation, except where a complete collection is desired. Neither of these objections applies to our present plant. It is an extremely beautiful species, with bright scarlet flowers, the labellum of which is tipped with orange. It may likewise easily be identified by the abundance of dark brown spots on its stems, and by its emarginate foliage. In the orchidaceous house of Messrs. Loddiges it is now exhibiting its showy blossoms.

HÒVEA PÚNGENS.—With the graceful habit of an *Epacris*, this handsome plant possesses all the beauty for which its congeners are so deservedly admired. It has small, linear, thickly-set foliage, which terminates in a sharp point; and the flowers, with which its stems are profusely studded, are of a deep and brilliant blue colour. It is destitute of all that dulness of hue, both in foliage and blossoms, which detracts from the interest of some other species, and in this respect is equal to any previously known, being, however, more diminutive in all its parts. Messrs. Rollison possess a plant of it now blooming in their greenhouse; and it is admirably suited for mingling with the species of *Epacris*, or other early flowering plants.

PIMÈLEA INCÀNA.—We again request attention to this plant, which is also known under the name of *P. nivea*, on account of its remarkably ornamental habits. It is well known that most species of this extremely interesting genus, by producing their flowers only from the summits of the stems, become unsightly after they attain a certain age, and cannot be employed effectively unless so placed among other plants as to conceal their naked stems. A very extraordinary specimen of the present species is now in flower at the nursery of Messrs. Low and Co., Clapton, which, although more than ten feet high, is covered with foliage, branches, and blossoms, down to its very base. The branches being of a half-pendent nature, exhibit their terminal clusters of beautiful white blossoms most favourably; and it has rarely fallen to our lot to witness a more attractive object than the plant, thus in full blossom, presents.

OPERATIONS FOR APRIL.

IN all extensive collections of plants, there is generally a certain period, at the opening of the spring season, set apart for shifting those of them which are cultivated in pots. Some have thought fit to decry this practice, as being inconsistent with that discriminative treatment which plants of such varied habits require; and undoubtedly there are a few species to which the operation at the present time is wholly needless, indeed detrimental. These instances apart, the fact of vegetation renewing its growth at this period, is alone sufficient to warrant the prevailing system, and to prove its propriety.

The precise time at which potting should be commenced, is too frequently determined by the date of the month, instead of the peculiar progress of the season, and the consequent state of vegetation. Whether artificial heat be employed to induce growth, or whether, as is much better, where practicable, plants be allowed to remain till naturally excited, it is an infallible maxim that they should not be repotted till some enlargement or development of their organs is apparent. This would certainly render the operation somewhat more desultory, but the principal deviation from the usual system would be in the week of its commencement.

Many cultivators pot the major portion of their plants in the decline of February; others not till March; but there are few who have not completed this process before the present month arrives. Early potting is manifestly injurious to plants. No sooner is it effected, than watering is commenced to a liberal extent, and many of them are thus supplied with a large quantity of liquid food while wholly unprepared for its absorption. A saturated soil is inevitably the consequence; turgidity and disease are engendered in the plants; and their growth (if death do not intervene) is invariably unhealthy. This is not an imaginary case. Thousands of tender exotic plants are annually destroyed by such treatment; while the gardener, blind to the cause, still pursues the same routine, and of course similar results as regularly follow.

Now, if the operation of potting were always deferred till vegetation had commenced its annual growth, the above catastrophe would be wholly averted. Water might then be safely applied, as the plants would imbibe and evaporate it with all requisite facility. Nor would they receive any check by disturbance at this period, if the removal were skilfully and judiciously executed, and the congeniality of attendant circumstances regarded and secured.

Another disadvantage which accompanies early potting, is the absence of any criterion for adapting the size of the pot to the future necessities and extension of the plant. A healthy-looking plant is generally placed in a large pot, and before it has begun to grow, the water which is administered accumulates about its roots, and causes sickliness; while the large quantity of soil only aggravates the evil, and continues so to do until the whole of it is removed, and the plant placed in a smaller pot. By potting at the period we recommend, the appearance of the plant will pretty accurately indicate the nature and extent of its subsequent growth, and the size of the pot can be varied accordingly.

Plants intended to adorn the beds and borders of the flower-garden during the summer, must now be reared, if the supply obtained by propagation in the autumn is inadequate. The employment of active heat for this purpose, has a decided tendency to cause deterioration; but, at the same time, many plants will not flower sufficiently early, unless such means are adopted. Keeping both these circumstances in view, some modification of the usual degree should be effected, that either extreme may be equally avoided. Those shoots which are produced without any stimulus, will always form the handsomest plants; and where no heat is employed to strike them, their beauty will be decidedly augmented.

The multiplication of all exotic plants may be commenced this month. The spring is the best season for propagating plants by cuttings for three reasons. First, because the young shoots are at this time in the most favourable state. Secondly, they do not require any artificial excitation. And thirdly, they are thus allowed the whole summer for development and maturation. Where, therefore, healthy and vigorous plants are desired, and economy is any object,—two points which must certainly rank conspicuously in every cultivator's attention,—the work of propagation should be entered upon immediately.

Coelogyne Gardneriana.

CŒLÓGYNE GARDNERIÀNA.
(LARGEST CŒLOGYNE.)

CLASS.	ORDER.
GYNANDRIA.	MONANDRIA.

NATURAL ORDER.
ORCHIDÀCEÆ.

GENERIC CHARACTER.—*Vide* vol. vi. p. 25.

SPECIFIC CHARACTER.—*Plant* epiphytal. *Pseudo-bulbs* bottle-shaped, slightly channelled. *Leaves* lanceolate, five-ribbed, acuminate. *Racemes* pendent, many-flowered, terminal. *Bracts* deciduous, *Sepals* and *petals* oblong. *Labellum* denticulate, pouch-shaped at the base; middle lobe divided into three segments, lateral ones smallest.

THIS is undoubtedly one of the finest species of *Cœlogyne* yet introduced to British collections; although, from the whiteness of the flowers, and their comparatively compressed nature, it is less showy than some of its allies. Being a rapid-growing plant, of easy culture, and flowering most abundantly under congenial treatment, it is a valuable acquisition to the tribe.

Dr. Wallich originally discovered *C. Gardneriana* during his tour through India, but we believe it was not then forwarded to this country. In 1837, Mr. J. Gibson brought living specimens for his Grace the Duke of Devonshire to Chatsworth. They were obtained from near the summit of the Khoseea Hills, in the East Indies, where it flourishes upon trees and rocks, in moist, shady woods.

Its favourite locality, and that in which it appears most to luxuriate, is the immediate vicinage of a water-fall. The spray which is generated by the volume of precipitant waters during the rainy season, supplies a constant moisture to the roots, besides sprinkling the entire surface of the leaves; from the extremities of which, indeed, it is usually seen depending in small pellucid globules. This fact is noticed for the sake of showing the abundance in which water is furnished throughout the period of the plant's growth,—a particular of some importance to the cultivator.

At Chatsworth, this species is grown in a soil composed of three-fourths partially decayed leaves, and one of very turfy loam, to which a small portion of river-sand or reduced sand-stone is added, to promote drainage. It will also thrive in moss which has been well broken and separated, if this be mixed with heath-soil and potsherds. While growing, it must be watered liberally, and daily syringed over the leaves. The temperature of the house will guide the cultivator in the performance of this operation; as it must always be considered that only by being subjected to an adequate degree of heat, is any injury from the large quantity of water received by it in its natural circumstances averted.

When the flowers have faded, and the leaves are beginning to wither, repose ensues in the usual order of vegetable existence, and this must not be disturbed by either atmospheric or more palpable applications of water. Heat, however, will not injure the pseudo-bulbs, provided it be not too intense; in which case, it might greatly debilitate or wholly destroy them. It commences its periodical development about the month of December, by evolving new shoots, from the summits of which the large pendulous racemes of flowers are produced. These appear while the leaves are exceedingly small, and it is not till the blossoms have fallen that the foliage is fully elaborated, or the pseudo-bulbs perfected.

The specimen here figured flowered at Chatsworth in the month of December, 1838. In India, it blossoms under the influence of almost incessant rains, and the appearance of its flowers, hanging as they do from the branches of trees, is said to resemble floating garlands of snow, interwreathed with the golden colour of the bracts, and the vivid green of the pseudo-bulbs and leaves.

For an account of the origin of the generic name, see No. lxii. p. 25.

Balsamina Mastersiana

BALSAMÌNA MASTERSIÀNA.
(MR. MASTERS' BALSAM.)

CLASS.	ORDER.
PENTANDRIA.	MONOGYNIA.

NATURAL ORDER.
BALSAMINACEÆ.

GENERIC CHARACTER.—*Anthers* five, two-celled. *Stigmas* five, distinct. *Capsules* ovate; valves at maturity bending inwards elastically at the apex. *Cotyledons* thick. *Pedicels* always flowered, solitary or aggregate. *Capsules* puberulous.—*Don's Gard. and Botany*.

SPECIFIC CHARACTER.—*Plant* annual. *Leaves* opposite, linear-lanceolate, with remote, pointed serratures. *Flowers* large, purple, axillary, solitary; spur curved, nearly the length of the flower.

EVERY one is familiar with those common but charming varieties of Balsam which are now cultivated to such extraordinary perfection by a few enthusiastic amateurs. There are few, also, except botanists or gardeners of eminence, who do not greatly admire the beautiful symmetry of their form, and the enchanting loveliness of their blossoms.

Perhaps, upon a due consideration of all its features, a well-cultivated balsam may be pronounced the most perfect model of real beauty which the vegetable kingdom can produce. Delicacy, gracility, elegance, richness,—in short, every trait which can be desired by persons of the most refined vision, is admirably concentred and blended in these delightful objects. Notwithstanding this, however, they are grossly neglected by the higher classes of the floricultural world, and by some individuals actually despised.

Nothing exhibits more clearly the factitious taste of the present age, than the disposition to discard these splendid plants. What might be rendered the most brilliant ornaments of the greenhouse, are disregarded, simply because they are becoming vulgar: the term *beauty* may therefore be expunged from the vocabulary of the fashionable floriculturist, to be supplanted by *novelty*. Botanists, again, manifest unequivocal aversion to all plants which produce new varieties from seed; and hence their discouragement of the growth of balsams.

If facility of procuration and erratic propensities are to be deprecated, and the contrary characters esteemed, we imagine that the present new species will prove a favourite; for it is certainly yet extremely rare, and we are not aware that its seedlings vary in colour. Nor is it inferior in beauty to any of its congeners, since, though the flowers present less diversity of hue, they have brilliancy and intensity sufficient to compensate for any monotony in that particular.

We received this species at Chatsworth in the autumn of 1837. Mr. Gibson first found it growing on the Khoseea Hills, and brought home seeds at the period just stated. Plants raised from these, flowered profusely during the whole of the summer of 1838, at which time our drawing was executed.

In its cultivation, the same treatment may be pursued as is generally bestowed on common balsams. A light, rich soil, frequent shifting, a generous supply of water, due exposure to light, and a slight, moist bottom heat, are the chief requisites, previously to the appearance of the flowers. When these, however, begin to exhibit themselves, the plants should be removed to the greenhouse, placing them first in a house of an intermediate temperature, and accustoming them gradually to that of the structure just named. Unless this caution is exercised, their appearance may be greatly injured; for a sudden change of such a description would be in the highest degree prejudicial. The advantage of this transference will be apparent in the larger size, deeper colour, and greater duration of the blossoms.

The main art in cultivating balsams to perfection, is to keep them continually growing after the seeds have germinated. This can be easily effected by affording every kind of aliment which Nature teaches to be essential. We have above stated what are the principal of these, and the cultivator must apportion them to the state of the atmosphere, or the peculiar circumstances in which the plants may be placed.

Although a decided annual species, and capable of multiplication by seeds, cuttings of this plant root with great readiness, and it may thus be perpetuated as a perennial. Plants obtained by this method in the autumn, and retained through the winter in a stove, or a house with a temperature a little above that of the greenhouse, will flower most beautifully in the early spring.

Where specimens of extraordinary size or beauty are desired, the first flower-buds which present themselves should be carefully removed, as they are seldom so perfect as those of subsequent expansion, and would therefore exhaust the plant to no purpose.

Balsamina is derived from *balsamum*, balsam; a preparation of the original species being supposed to possess healing properties. Professor Don, however, suggests that *balassan*, the Arab term for the balsam, is the proper primitive.

We have named this species in honour of Mr. Masters, head gardener at the Hon. East India Company's Botanic Garden, Calcutta:—an individual highly deserving of commemoration.

Schleumeume speciosa.

SPHENÓGYNE SPECIÒSA.

(SHOWY SPHENOGYNE.)

CLASS.	ORDER.
SYNGENESIA.	FRUSTRANEA.

NATURAL ORDER.
COMPÓSITÆ.

GENERIC CHARACTER.—*Receptacle* with distinct paleæ. *Pappus* chaffy, simple. *Stigma* enlarging at the apex, nearly truncate. *Calyx* imbricated; innermost scales, or all of them, dilated at the summit, and scarious.

SPECIFIC CHARACTER.—*Plant* annual, growing about one foot high. *Stems* roundish, slightly declinate at the base, ascending, branched, smooth. *Leaves* twice pinnate, sessile; leaflets linear, acute, somewhat recurved. *Rays* of the flower somewhat lanceolate, bitten at the extremities, bright orange.

IT is somewhat remarkable, that by far the greater portion of hardy herbaceous and annual plants comprised in the natural order *Compositæ*, produce flowers in which some shade of yellow is the predominant colour. This, combined with the popular prejudice against yellow blossoms, has tended considerably to limit the number of those who regard them with due attention, and many beautiful plants of the above description are now scarcely to be found in British gardens.

While, however, variety continues to be considered essential to the appearance of the flower-garden, (and we presume this will be the case as long as the tasteful art of gardening is cultivated; or, in other words, till the human race ceases to exist,) flowers of every diversity of hue will be employed in the decoration of this most interesting department, and those of a yellow tint will be held in equal requisition with their more pleasing rivals of other colours. Annuals, especially, and still more particularly such as are of dwarf habits, and flower freely, will never lack either admirers or cultivators.

The showy annual, a drawing of which furnishes the occasion of these remarks, is one that cannot prove otherwise than an acquisition to any collection. Whether in its finely-cut, and gracefully undulating foliage, or its large and handsome blossoms, it is eminently worthy of admission to all well-arranged flower-borders. The colour of its flowers is far from being vulgar, and its strange variation on the same plant is peculiarly pleasing. With regard to the latter particular, it will be seen by our plate, that some of the blossoms are pale yellow, while others are of a rich orange. The rays of dark spots which encircle the centre of the flower, are also of a most lustrous hue, resembling polished metal, and contributing materially to enhance its beauty.

From what precise district this beautiful plant was obtained, we are yet uninformed. It was introduced to this country in 1836, as some assert from the South American continent, but as others are led to believe, from the Cape of Good Hope. We are not acquainted with a more ornamental annual of the same character, or one better adapted to the formation of groups in the flower-garden. Seldom growing more than one foot high, it may, if considered desirable, be rendered still dwarfer, by securing its shoots to the ground with small pegs at an early period of its progress. It will thus form a most gorgeous display; contrasting admirably with *Verbenas*, and other similar plants.

As this is a rather tender annual, its seeds should be sown in pans, or in a prepared bed, and subjected to a trifling degree of bottom heat. It will not endure much disturbance, and should therefore be potted while very young; and in its subsequent removal to a larger pot, as well as in its final transplantation to the destined situation, great care must be exercised, as its roots are somewhat slender. Seeds sown in February, will produce plants fit for transferring to the open ground in May; and these will flower vigorously during June and July. For the greenhouse it is not at all calculated, and should be cultivated solely for the flower-garden, in which a succession of flowers may be maintained by a variation in the period of sowing.

A considerable advantage will be gained by pegging down the shoots of the plant. No support for its stems will thus be needed, nor will they be so liable to be broken or injured by wind. Its flowers will likewise be brought closer together, and produce, collectively, a more striking effect.

This species flowered most profusely in the collection of Messrs. Young, Epsom, throughout the months of July and August, 1838. Our figure was obtained at this period, and from this as well as most other nursery establishments, seeds may be procured.

Of the generic name, the origin will be found in *sphen*, a wedge, and *gyne*, a female; the stigma of the florets in this genus being wedge-shaped.

Amphicome arguta

AMPHÍCOME ARGÙTA.

(FINELY-CUT LEAVED AMPHICOME.)

CLASS.
DIDYNAMIA.

ORDER.
ANGIOSPERMIA.

NATURAL ORDER.
BIGNONIÀCEÆ.

GENERIC CHARACTER.—*Calyx* campanulate, five toothed, the inner parts exposed. *Corolla* funnel-shaped; limb five-lobed, two-lipped; lobes nearly equal. *Stamens* didynamous; anthers in pairs, pressed close to the style. *Rudiment* of the fifth stamen awl-shaped. *Disc* hypogynous, cup-shaped. *Ovarium* one-celled; placentæ two, linear, parietal, many-seeded. *Stigma* two-plated. *Capsule* pod-shaped, opening by either suture; dissepiments free. *Seeds* protruding, hairy on both sides.

SPECIFIC CHARACTER.—*Plant* perennial, herbaceous. *Stems* subterranean, rooting. *Branches* smooth, from two to three feet high, deep green. *Leaves* dark green, smooth, pinnate; leaflets ovate-lanceolate, acuminate, sessile, rarely without a row of serratures on each side, entire at their summits, terminal one frequently three-lobed: stem-leaves composed of two pairs; lower ones of four. *Racemes* terminal, inclining to one side, few-flowered; peduncles filiform, slender, drooping. *Calyx* campanulate, slightly ciliated, five toothed; lobes awl-shaped. *Corolla* smooth, light rose-coloured, funnel-shaped; lobes of the lower lip rounded, those of the upper one partially truncate. *Ovarium* linear, placentæ likewise linear. *Capsule* filiform, smooth, becoming plaited at the extremity.

PERHAPS a more truly elegant plant, or one more likely to prove permanently valuable, has not been introduced to this country for many years than the one here represented. There is a beauty, a bewitching gracefulness in its appearance, which at once allures the eye of the observer, and elicits his admiration; while no feature in its character has the slightest tendency to depreciate its interest.

For the addition of this lovely plant to British collections, we are indebted to Dr. Royle, by whom seeds of it were sent to the London Horticultural Society. It was collected on the Himalayah mountains, at an elevation of from 6000 to 8000 feet; inhabiting chiefly the valley of the Buspa, and the country near Turanda, in Kunawur. A solitary specimen was raised in the gardens of the Horticultural Society, which blossomed in August, 1837. Subsequently, it has been freely propagated, and distributed amongst various individuals.

Examined botanically, this plant is highly curious, the structure of its flowers presenting some remarkable characters. These we have not attempted to portray, well knowing that its general appearance is chiefly regarded by the cultivator. Of this latter, our plate will convey a correct idea; and we may here state that the flowers remain expanded a considerable time, and appear in continued succession from the month of June till September, inclusive. When the blossoms fade, they are immediately succeeded by the seed-pods; which, from their long, slender, and graceful form, render the plant interesting till the leaves decay.

A sufficient degree of experience has not yet been afforded, to enable us to state confidently what degree of cold it will endure; but it is the opinion of those who have hitherto been engaged in its culture, that, with partial shelter during the winter, it will be found hardy enough to sustain the rigours of our climate without injury. In a greenhouse, it thrives luxuriantly under judicious treatment; this being comprised in the very cautious administration of water, and an unrestricted transmission of light. An open loam, mixed with a small portion of heath-soil, is the most suitable compost.

Whether retained in the greenhouse, or planted in the open ground, the principal subject for attention in the winter is the due regulation of the supply of moisture. Being naturally torpid at that season, this plant is peculiarly susceptible of damage from any superfluity of the element just mentioned. It is more than probable that, if placed in a dry situation in the open border, and protected with some trifling awning which would divert the rain, it would be impervious to at least a considerable degree of cold. Water should therefore be regarded by the cultivator as scarcely less dangerous than frost; becoming increasingly prejudicial in proportion to the amount of its application. Frost, in fact, acquires all its virulence from the quantity of fluids involved in any plant, since it is through these alone that it can operate upon the substance of vegetation.

Either seeds or cuttings will produce young plants; although they grow rather tardily by each of these methods. Unless a great number of plants is desired, only the latter mode should be adopted, as the seeds are some time in vegetating, and the plants thus obtained seldom flower till the second year after semination. Old specimens are likewise greatly weakened by allowing them to ripen their seeds.

In the greenhouse of Messrs. Rollison, Tooting, the plant which furnished the subject for our drawing, flowered in great perfection during the months of July and August, 1838; and there can be no doubt that the flowers would have been still finer if the specimen had been grown in the open air. These gentlemen possess a stock of young plants, as do also most of the principal nurserymen.

The generic name is from two Greek words, alluding to the hairy covering of the seeds.

ON ARRANGING AND PLANTING HARDY ORNAMENTAL TREES AND SHRUBS.

Trees and shrubs may be said to hold precisely the same rank in the vegetable kingdom, with regard to external circumstances, as man in the animal. They are alike superior in their structure, more symmetrical in their form, and less evanescent in their duration. To their nourishment, also, their more volatile allies contribute by their death, since they feed, as it were, on the gases generated from their remains.

It is not surprising, then, that their skilful and judicious cultivation should be regarded as the noblest occupation of the horticulturist; or that a fine specimen of a rare exotic kind should be viewed with the proudest and most pleasurable emotions. The human mind is naturally impressed with grandeur; and it has been well remarked:—

"Than a tree, a grander child earth bears not."

By certain situations, however, and under different treatment, the appearance of these monarchs of vegetation is most powerfully affected; and our present object is to institute a comparison between the method of arranging them in what are termed *Arboretums*, and that of planting them singly or grouped, without any regard to botanical order, in conspicuous parts of the pleasure ground. In so doing, we propose to examine the merits of each of these systems, and endeavour to show which is the most appropriate and ornamental.

An arboretum, vaguely considered, is merely a collection of indigenous and exotic trees, disposed according to the taste of the proprietor; and either scattered over an estate of twenty acres, or congregated on a superficies of one tenth that extent. This, however, is not the general acceptation of the term. In modern arboretums, every genus or tribe of plants is grouped together, more or less densely, and the whole collection arranged with some degree of order and regularity; so that a connecting link of natural affinity may be discovered between immediate neighbours throughout. In estates of considerable circuit, or in botanical or other public gardens, such departments create a variation, and sometimes a pleasing one. They also furnish the beholder, at one gaze, with a knowledge of the hardy ligneous species of every genus, tribe, or order of plants, and their position in the natural system of botany.

Arboretums are thus exceedingly advantageous to the scientific student, or to any individual anxious to acquire an extensive acquaintance with the aspect, habits, varieties, and affinities of arboreous plants. Thus arranged, also, a more specific and discriminate cultivation can be afforded, with much greater convenience and certainty. Indeed, perhaps, this is the only mode whereby a *complete* assortment can be conserved, which in many respects is most desirable. But when this is stated, there remains nothing more to be said in their praise. With beauty, with ornament, with the proper development or exhibition of the character of a plant, they are entirely incompatible. We look upon them as mere living descriptive catalogues,—observative and experimental departments,—and not properly features of limited pleasure grounds.

The practice of attempting to arrange plants of any description according to their natural affinity, or their position in any system of classification, is radically erroneous, when the charms and beauties of vegetation are wished to be exhibited. It creates both a dull monotony, and a slovenly, displeasing irregularity; two extremes equally to be deprecated in landscape gardening. Paradoxical as this may appear, it is not the less correct. The uniformity alluded to is local, differing widely from comprehensive unity; it is confined to the particular beds or plots set apart to the species of certain genera or tribes. These frequently assimilate so closely to each other in appearance, that in one place will be seen a bed of trees, all evergreen; in juxta-position a cluster of dwarf shrubs, perhaps all flowering at the same time; and equally near, but in the opposite direction, a group of the largest kind of deciduous trees. All these are monotonous in themselves; while, viewed in connexion and comparison with each other, they present a total lack of congruity.

Nothing can be more adverse to the genuine principles of landscape disposition, than the system above described. Diversity of outline, of the form, colour, season, and duration of the foliage and flowers, is absolutely essential to the beauty of any scenery. Without this it appears sombre, formal, constrained; in one word, *unnatural*: and much as the imitation of Nature has been despised by mere theorists, it is and must be the system pursued by all who would attain any eminence in this art.

On the other hand, let it not be forgotten that a garden is the medium which associates artificial with natural objects; the dwelling with the surrounding country. In precise accordance with this design, therefore, should be its arrangement and appearance. Trees growing in extensive groups, *en masse*, or even arboretums, planted without regard to the size, the appearance, or the general character of the plants, are inadmissable and intolerable where all is required to be harmonious, and to a certain extent, conformable.

In planting *ornamental* trees and shrubs, (and no others should be allowed a place in the pleasure garden,) they should if possible be so arranged as to stand quite distinct from each other, that every one may be witnessed and examined apart from the rest, without suffering any detraction from having all parts of its surface exposed. They must likewise be so blended, associated, and intermingled, that, when viewed at a distance, they may present the appearance of an agreeable and diversified mass of verdure. These two apparently remote objects may yet be concurrently accomplished. In parterres or shrubberies, of whatever dimensions or extent, a due regard to the known character or habits of the plants employed, will enable the gardener to place them precisely at such distances as will allow them room for their full and complete extension, without becoming entangled with other plants. Or, if the smallness of the plot, or the diminutive size of the plants, preclude this arrangement in the first instance, without derogating from the appearance of the group they can be planted so as to admit of any subsequent thinning, to the required extent.

Shrubberies thus planted with exotic trees only, would be in themselves arboretums; and if that charming variety which can alone please the eye be consulted and effectuated, none of the objections we have before urged against those departments would apply in this case. It is true that species, and even genera, would thus be separated and scattered promiscuously throughout the group, so that it would be almost impossible to trace their associations. Pleasure gardens are not, however, nurseries for botanists; at least, we imagine, few proprietors of them would entertain and follow out such an idea, at the expense of everything that would render them attractive and picturesque. Such information can almost as readily be obtained from books; and the attempt to illustrate it, or facilitate its acquirement, by planting or disposing any kinds of plants according to any other system than that which taste, sense, and nature dictate, is a gross outrage on all the acknowledged principles of beauty, and a complete perversion of the science of landscape gardening, from its original and evident intention.

Of all modes of planting trees and shrubs, none is so well calculated to display the perfection of their character, as that of placing them singly in conspicuous situations, on lawns, or in the centre of small parterres. Unfortunately, it is only certain portions of the pleasure ground which will admit of this system being practised; nor would it, indeed, be pleasing if carried to too great an extent. The most symmetrical, beautiful, and rare kinds should therefore be chosen for this purpose. The advantages of this method are not confined to the opportunity it affords of examining the plants on all sides. Being perfectly isolated, air and light are freely admitted to all parts of their surface, and from the unmitigated operation of these, can they alone attain that admirable symmetry of form which all plants in such situations are known to exhibit.

Our opinion on the different methods of arranging ornamental ligneous plants with the best effect, has thus been unhesitatingly declared. That arboretums in which the plants are disposed systematically, may be rendered in some degree ornamental in very extensive domains, we are prepared to admit. We cannot, however, desire the extension of this system. It is defective in principle; and these defects are most strikingly manifested in practice. All, therefore, who would seek to embellish and adorn their pleasure garden; to heighten instead of disparage its natural beauties; and to steer with such precision between the rules of nature and art, as to avoid the blemishes of either, and rise superior to both; must plant their trees in such a manner as to present, individually and collectively, the greatest diversity, and yet the most delightful harmony.

INFLUENCE OF CLIMATE ON PLANTS.*
SOLAR HEAT.

CLIMATIC differences of temperature, independently of exercising a most important influence on the geographical assignation of plants, essentially affect the various phenomena of their functions, as is illustrated and exhibited in their growth and products. That heat is indispensable to the excitation of vegetable life, is sufficiently attested by the fact that those members of plants which remain exposed to the chilling atmosphere, are invariably torpid during the winter season; and although fluids are absorbed from the earth throughout even the severest winters, it is only by those roots which are far enough removed from the surface to enjoy the degree of temperature necessary for rarefaction, and they can circulate only through those parts which are duly preserved from radiation by the bark.

Vitality itself—that mysterious principle—though apparently an inherent property of vegetation, is dependent on heat for its continued existence. The power of, and proneness to procreation, may likewise be supposed to increase in the same ratio as the temperature; for, in those countries where the highest temperature prevails, plants are met with in greatest abundance; while, in proportion as the degree of latitude increases, vegetation is propagated much less profusely, and, as far as the researches of man can determine, disappears entirely on approaching the poles.

Changes of temperature affect the substance and functions of plants in various ways; but in none is their influence so conspicuous as in the expansion, extension, and dissolution of their structure. Development and decomposition are alike the consequences of heat, and vary in their progress and extent in precise accordance with the existing degree of temperature. It is the former of these that we propose now to explain. A moderate temperature will cause a gradual elongation and enlargement of all living vegetable substances, by inducing the imbibition and circulation of nutritive fluids. By a considerable elevation of this temperature for any length of time, results of a directly contrary nature are experienced, and a perceptible contraction occurs. This is caused by excessive evaporation; which expends too prodigally the vital juices, impoverishes the plant, and thus collapses its tissue.

Heat incites the functions of all kinds of plants in the same manner, though by no means in an equal degree. The axiom that "habit is second nature," applies not more truly and appropriately to man than to vegetation. By long-continued habit, the faculties of all plants are so conformed and adapted to their native climate, that removal to countries of a much higher or lower temperature is always highly detrimental, and frequently fatal. It is possible, however, to effect a change in their habits, and nothing but perseverance in a judicious course of treatment is required to compass this end. Where the change is from a colder to a warmer climate, this is especially practicable.

* Continued from page 63.

Plants, like animals, are supposed specifically to possess a distinct and definite constitution, requiring either particular kinds of food, or that their nutriment shall be attempered, prepared, and transmitted in and by particular modes and media. This is certainly characteristic of some species; but, applied generally, it appears far from accurate. The majority of plants exhibit the same radical organization, have correspondent functions, and are regulated in the exercise of those functions by the same agents. Of these agents, heat exercises the most extensive and manifest jurisdiction. Indeed, so influential is its operation, that vegetation must either adapt itself to its various modifications, or become extinct.

To afford a clear view of the offices and effects of heat on the functions of plants, it will be necessary to trace its agency through the different stages of their growth. The circulation of fluids, the accretion and secretion of new matter, and the process of evaporation, are all mainly referable to the action of solar heat. From the time of the first expansion of their seed-lobes, to the period when their fruit and seeds attain their utmost perfection, none of the above particulars can be accomplished unless the temperature is sufficiently high.

Heat is material, indeed essential, to the germination of all descriptions of seeds; and when we consider that moisture and air (the other necessary concomitants towards inducing this process) are generated, or reduced to a proper rarity of consistence, almost entirely by this agent, we shall perceive that heat is principally instrumental in producing this first and most important of vegetable metamorphoses. No sooner does the vital lymph begin to flow, and the seed-leaves appear above the surface of the ground, than another evidence of the influence of heat is elicited. A system of transpiration commences from their surface, which increases as the plant progresses and the leaves are formed; this being the means whereby the superfluous moisture imbibed from the soil is evolved, and the plant preserved from turgidity, with its inevitable consequence—disease.

In the incipient vegetation of the seed, as well as in the subsequent enlargement of the plant, accretions are continually accruing to its substance, in the form of new strata or elaborations of matter, similar in character and disposure to those which constituted its original organization. These additions, whether longitudinal or horizontal, internal or exterior, are the result of the propulsion of fluids from the soil by heat. The secreted deposites by which they are afterwards surrounded and consolidated, are occasioned principally by the action of light upon the surface beneath which the circulating fluids are spread; but partly, also, by the external agency of heat, which operates upon those fluids through the medium of the pores, and abstracts their more aqueous constituents by exhalation.

Botanists almost unanimously admit the existence of pores in the cuticular membranes of plants, although some deny their visibility. These pores are orifices of various sizes, extremely diverse in number in different plants, provided for the effluence of redundant moisture, and perhaps, also, for the inhalation of genial gases or the dissipation of impalpable excrement. The transpiration of fluid, of gas, or of caloric, appears to be their principal office, as plants seldom absorb nutriment in this manner, unless they fail in obtaining an adequate supply from the soil.

Natural evaporation is undoubtedly due to solar heat; and although it is augmented when the plant is subjected to the rays of light, this latter agent can only be regarded as an auxiliary in its promotion, since it proceeds unrestrainedly when a due degree of heat is present, even though the plant be enveloped in total darkness. The effects of this evaporation are somewhat remarkable. In tropical countries, it is periodically so profuse, as to suspend the functions of vegetation, and occasion a season of repose. The water which is vaporized during this period, descends again upon plants after a certain time, and causes them to resume their growth with renewed vigour.

The vegetation of temperate climes experiences a still greater degree of benefit from this source. Saturated with the fluids absorbed during winter, the genial warmth of the sun in the spring calls these into admirable avail, in the development of stems and foliage; by which, also, it simultaneously provides an immediate exit for their redundant inhalations. As the young branches, too, approach maturity, the higher temperature which prevails at this season increases the exhalations from their surface to such an extent, as to dry and concrete their newly-formed substance and cuticle; thus enabling them to combat successfully the rigours of the succeeding winter.

Frost is found to be particularly destructive to plants in the spring, after they have commenced growing. This is owing, in a great degree, to the protracted interruption of the process of transpiration which has preceded that period, and its aggravated suspension when absorption and circulation have been increased. Hence, the newly-formed leaves and shoots, being the media through which this accumulated moisture is exhaled, are so completely charged with it, as to be highly susceptible of injury from cold. The tender, nascent state of the new developments, and the total absence of cuticle, or its amalgamation with the cellular tissue,—forming, in fact, a similar aggregation of cells, filled with fluid matters,—increase the liability to derangement from such circumstances.

To the same source may be traced the frequent detriment which the young shoots of plants receive, on a severe winter succeeding an unusually cold summer and autumn. Being unable to rid themselves of the refuse portion of the moisture they abstract from the soil, without a sufficient stimulus, their parts remain succulent, flexible, and incapable of repelling frost. It would appear from these facts that water or any other fluids radiate heat much more readily than dry and solid substances; and such is really the case: therefore it may be affirmed as a fundamental principle in cultivation, that the less moisture a plant is allowed to absorb during the autumnal months, the better will it be prepared to retain its needful temperature through the winter.

Extreme cold is, as stated before, much more injurious to plants in the early stages of their periodical growth; and, as analogy teaches, while experience attests, young trees are generally tender, and particularly pervious to frost: whereas, in proportion as they become older, evaporation is increased,—their tissue is consolidated and protected by a thicker and tenser cuticle,—and they are thus rendered far more secure from any danger arising from a decrement of temperature. The tenderness in this instance proceeds from the same cause as that of the newly-formed wood previously noticed: *viz.*, an undue propulsion of fluids into the young shoots at a period when they are only partially organized, and consequently, when the texture of their vesicles is not sufficiently rigid to resist the pressure of the accumulated sap, during the interruption of the transpiratory process.

Young plants have generally a larger absorbent superficies on their roots, till these have become fully hardened, than they present relatively to the atmosphere for ensuring the necessary exhalations and concretion; and their supply of fluids is thus much greater than they can dispose of, if at all checked by cold. The short distance at which their roots lie from the surface of the soil, may also be assigned as a reason for their peculiar susceptibility; because, when their rootlets have penetrated to a considerable depth, they are enabled to imbibe fluids from the lower strata of a much higher temperature than those of the surface, and these, by their ascension, necessarily tend to preserve a due degree of warmth and vitality in the plant. By a parity of reasoning, those plants whose roots extend themselves horizontally, cannot possibly be so well prepared for sustaining cold, as others, the roots of which strike downwards in a perpendicular direction.

As a brief account of the manner in which frost operates so inimically on vegetation, cannot prove otherwise than interesting, it may here be attempted. The substance of plants is mainly composed of cellular and vascular tissue, the individual vesicles and vessels of which are filled with fluids. By the congelation and consequent expansion of these fluids, the membrane which envelops and confines them is ruptured, and disorganization is thus effected. The subsequent action of heat upon the parts affected, causes an increase of evaporation commensurate with its intensity; and this, having then nothing to oppose or regulate its progress, continues till decomposition and volatilization are thoroughly completed.

When the degree of frost is very trifling, and no derangement of the organic structure of the plant occurs, there are means of modifying or even counteracting its prejudicial influence. Every gardener is cognizant of the fact, that the external application of cold water to a plant newly frozen, will, in cases where the organization is uninjured, prevent fatal consequences. It is upon the same principle that snow, applied freely to a frozen member of the human body, restores life and animation. In both cases, the vital fluids are congealed, and a rapid thaw, such as the action of heat will induce, would have a similar effect to that of a more intense degree of frost, *viz.* expand too precipitately, and cause a disruption of the membraneous covering of the tissue. On the other hand, by immediately washing or sprinkling with cold water the part frozen, the thaw is rendered more gradual, and circulation is afterwards recommenced.

There are two important principles in the treatment of plants affected by frost, which should never be forgotten by the cultivator. First, they must not be subjected to a higher temperature till the frost is expelled; and secondly, this expulsion must be effected in the gentlest manner, and by the tardiest means, which can be conceived. To allow the vital fluids of plants to remain congealed for any length of time, is highly dangerous; and to dissolve them too rapidly, is equally so. No restorative, therefore, can be efficient, unless promptly applied; and none is so appropriate as *cold* water. When this fails, it must not thence be supposed that it is useless, but that the frost had been too violent and destructive to admit of reparation.

(To be continued.)

FLORICULTURAL NOTICES.

NEW AND RARE PLANTS, FIGURED IN THE LEADING BOTANICAL PERIODICALS FOR APRIL.

CLASS I.—PLANTS WITH TWO COTYLEDONS (DICOTYLEDONEÆ).

THE INDIAN FIG TRIBE (*Cactáceæ*).

EPIPHÝLLUM RUSSELLIÀNUM. The Duke of Bedford's Epiphyllum. There is little to distinguish this most interesting new species from the well known *E. truncatum*. It is rather more slender in habit, and has flowers of a somewhat deeper hue, but the principal difference is in the structure of the blossoms, which, in those of the present plant, is perfectly regular, consisting of an imbricated series of equal petals. The colour of the anthers is also dark red, those of *E. truncatum* being white. On the Organ mountains of Brazil, this species was discovered by Mr. Gardner, and forwarded to the superb collection of His Grace the Duke of Bedford. It grows on the branches of trees, or upon rocks, and would appear to be somewhat more hardy than *E. truncatum*, as it is found at a much greater altitude. *Bot. Mag.* 3717.

THE MEZEREUM TRIBE (*Thymelàceæ*.)

PIMÈLEA HENDERSÒNII. Of the many lovely species of *Pimelea* which adorn our greenhouses, this seems to be the most ornamental, with regard to the size of the head of flowers, and their rich rosy-pink colour. The leaves are small, linear-lanceolate, smooth, and mucronulate, but apparently placed at a great distance from each other, thereby leaving the stem too bare. Though a strong-growing plant, it flowered in great profusion, when only eighteen inches high, in the month of July, 1838; having been raised by Messrs. Eagle and Henderson, near Edinburgh, from seeds sent to them by Captain Cheyne, from King George's Sound. *Bot. Mag.* 3721.

THE EPACRIS TRIBE (*Epacridàceæ*).

EPÀCRIS IMPRÉSSA; *var.* PARVIFLÒRA. Small-flowered pitted Epacris. A neat, showy, and abundant-flowering variety of a plant which all acknowledge to be the most attractive greenhouse shrub that the spring develops. This variety differs from *E. impressa* in the size and form of its flowers; in the latter particular greatly resembling *Fuchsia microphylla;* that is, having an expansive, laciniated limb. Seeds of it were sent from New Holland by Mr. James Backhouse, to his residence in Yorkshire, where it flowered in the early part of last spring. Although then denominated *E. ruscifolia*, Dr. Lindley considers it a variety of *E. impressa*, and adds, that seedling plants are disposed to vary greatly in colour. *Bot. Reg.* 19.

THE COMPOSITE-FLOWERED TRIBE (*Compósitæ*).

CALLICHRÒA PLATYGLÓSSA. Golden Callichroa. A slender, yellow-flowered annual, with pinnated or toothed foliage. Dr. Fischer of Petersburgh, who founded the genus, transmitted seeds of the present species to the Glasgow Botanic Garden, where it flowered in the open border, in September, 1836. Its large flowers, and graceful habits, render it an engaging object; but we presume it requires to be planted in groups or beds, and its stems secured to the ground, in order to preserve it from having a straggling and unsightly appearance. Its native country is Ross, in New California, a colony under the government of Russia. *Bot. Mag.* 3719.

THE ASCLEPIAS TRIBE (*Asclepiadàceæ*).

HÓYA CORIÀCEA. Thick-leaved Hoya. We have previously spoken of this curious plant, as flowering on a block of wood in the stove of Messrs. Loddiges, when we surmised that it might prove a species of *Asclepias*. Its dwarf nature, large, deep-green foliage, and clusters of white blossoms, constitute it a most enchanting plant. Mr. Cuming forwarded specimens of it from Manilla to Messrs. Loddiges, with whom it blossomed in August, 1838. These gentlemen have cultivated it in the orchidaceous house, retaining it on the log of wood into which it was naturally growing when they received it. Cuttings or layers (and perhaps leaves) root tardily but successfully, with care. *Bot. Reg.* 18.

THE FIGWORT TRIBE (*Scrophulariàceæ*).

PENTSTÈMON BARBÀTUM; *var.* CÀRNEUM. Although this delightful plant would be almost universally referred to the genus *Chelone*, yet Dr. Lindley concurs with Mr. Bentham in placing it and all other supposed species of that genus (except *C. lyonii, glabra, obliqua,* and *nemorosa*) in *Pentstemon*. The plant under notice has beautiful flesh-coloured flowers, with a delicate beard in the orifice of the corolla. Notwithstanding its being of Mexican origin, it is found to be a hardy perennial in the latitude of London, and flowers during July and August. G. F. Dickson, Esq. presented seeds of it to the Horticultural Society, in whose garden at Chiswick it first flowered. Growing usually from two to three feet high, it forms a charming feature in the flower border, requiring some protection from excessive dampness in the winter, and increasing readily by cuttings or seeds. We believe this to be identical with the *Chelone Mexicana* of nurseries. *Bot. Reg.* 21.

THE JUSTICIA TRIBE (*Acanthàceæ*).

RUÉLLIA CILIATRIFLÒRA. Fringe-flowered Ruellia. Seeds of this handsome plant were sent to the Glasgow Botanic Garden, by Mr. Tweedie, of Buenos Ayres; but Sir W. J. Hooker supposes that they were collected from some interior country. With apparently luxuriant habits, it has not yet exceeded eighteen inches in height in the stove of the above establishment, and blossoms in September. The foliage is large, and of a most vivid green; the flowers being blue, with a purple throat. These latter have all their segments ciliated at the margin. *Bot. Mag.* 3718.

PLANTS WITH ONE COTYLEDON (MONOCOTYLEDONEÆ.)

THE ORCHIS TRIBE (*Orchidàceæ*).

DENDRÒBIUM AÚREUM; *var.* PÁLLIDUM. Golden-flowered Denbrobium; pale variety. A charming Epiphyte, with white or cream-coloured blossoms, and remarkable for its agreeable fragrance. Mr. Macrae first discovered this plant growing upon trees near Nuera Ellia, in Ceylon; and the variety here noticed, flowered in the collection of Messrs. Loddiges in March, 1838. The original species has dark, golden-coloured flowers, while those of our present subject are, as above stated, nearly white. The labellum, however, is very richly marked with orange towards its base. *Bot. Reg.* 20.

DENDRÒBIUM CRUMENÀTUM. Another white-flowered species of this genus, though less interesting than the former. The pseudo bulbs are terete and furrowed, the leaves small, oblong, and emarginate; and the flowers are produced in long terminal racemes. "According to Blume, it varies with white and pink flowers, and with leaves more or less oblong and coriaceous." Like the species last alluded to, it is delightfully fragrant. It has been found in various parts of the Indian Archipelago, and a specimen flowered in the garden of His Grace the Duke of Northumberland, at Sion, in August, 1837; having been sent thither by Mr. Nightingale from Ceylon. *Bot. Reg.* 22.

NEW, RARE, OR INTERESTING PLANTS IN FLOWER IN THE PRINCIPAL SUBURBAN NURSERIES.

CAMARÒTIS PURPÙREA.—*Orchidaceous* plants naturally arrange themselves in two divisions, viz.—such as have their stems compressed into the form of a bulb, and those which approach nearer to the habits of shrubs, and are continuous; the former class being termed pseudo-bulbous; the latter caulescent. It is undeniable that the caulescent tribes comprise the most beautiful objects, and that their appearance generally is of a more interesting character. Of this statement, the enchanting little plant whose name prefaces the present notice is an excellent attestation. With its graceful stems, and long pendent roots, which are fully exposed to the atmosphere, it appears perfectly independent of the soil, and seems to derive almost all its nourishment from aerial elements. Messrs. Loddiges imported specimens from Sylhet, a district in the East Indies, and it is now, for the first time in Britain, flowering in the Orchidaceous house of these gentlemen. It has the habit of a *Vanda* or *Ærides*, but is of more slender growth than most of the species comprehended in those genera. The leaves are alternate, linear-lanceolate, and much bitten at the extremities. The floral racemes are pendulous, and many-flowered; the sepals and petals of the flowers being similar in size and form, and of a bright purplish-lilac colour, while the labellum is deep purple, ascending, and attached to the margins or the two upper sepals. It is a lovely plant, and appears to continue flowering for a long period.

CORBULÀRIA TENUIPÒLIA.—An exceedingly pretty bulbous plant, and undoubtedly a very scarce one also. We observed it blossoming in the nursery of Messrs. Young, Epsom, a few days since, and were much arrested by its simple beauty. With the general aspect of a dwarf *Narcissus*, it is decidedly more graceful and ornamental, the foliage being longer and more attenuated, and the flowers larger, more expansive, and of a richer yellow colour. It is probably only a half-hardy plant; as, although at present growing in the open air, it is in a very sheltered situation. In height it does not exceed three inches, and is peculiarly suited for planting on choice and elegant rock-work where it would receive proper attention, as it evidently requires to be kept dry in the winter season.

DENDRÒBIUM PULCHÉLLUM.—A magnificent specimen of this delightful plant, in the collection of Messrs. Loddiges, is at present displaying from fifty to a hundred of its exquisitely beautiful blossoms. Being a very dwarf species, and the flower-stems being likewise extremely short, the plant presents a dense mass, about a yard in diameter, of stems, foliage, and flowers, altogether forming one of the most superb objects imaginable. This specimen affords additional evidence of the very appropriate treatment of the genus *Dendrobium* in this establishment.

DENDRÒBIUM ———?—A new and somewhat remarkable species of *Dendrobium* has recently bloomed at Messrs. Loddiges', the flowers of which resemble those of *D. nobile* in colours, are equally handsome, and of considerably greater dimensions. The lip of the flower is more attenuated, curled, pointed, and contracted, than that of the species just named; and the habit of the plant is very distinct. Besides having smaller, darker, and more rigid foliage, the stems are more slender, less moniliform, and, when old, are enveloped in a whitish, dry, membranous sheath. From the size of the flowers, it would seem to be superior to any other species. It is not yet named.

EPIDÉNDRUM DICERÀTUM.—One of the most slender species of that division of *Epidendra*, with elongated stems, and slightly resembling *E. elongàta*. Specimens were received by Messrs. Loddiges from Guiana, through the medium of Mr. Schomburgk, and it is now producing its pretty blossoms in the Hackney nursery. The leaves are ligulate and mucronulate, being likewise rather small; while the flowers, which appear in dense clusters at the extremities of the shoots, are of the usual pink colour of those species with which it is more nearly connected. The petals of the flowers are, however, much longer than the sepals, and have deeply-indented margins; the labellum is attached to the column, standing erect in the centre of the flower, and expanding into a rich purple and delicately fringed lip. A succession of flowers has continued unfolding for nearly two months, and the beauty of the plant is not yet in the slightest degree diminished.

GÚNNIA PÍCTA.—A very interesting little orchidaceous plant from New Holland. Its diminutive size, so far from decreasing its attraction, appears only to enhance it; and, when grown on a log of wood, as is the case with a plant at Messrs. Loddiges', it having been retained on the block to which it was attached naturally when imported, it has a most pleasing appearance. The flowers are produced in pendulous racemes, and assimilate to some species of *Oncidium*; they are pale-yellow, but most extensively and prettily spotted with reddish-brown. The leaves are rather more than an inch long, and the length of the racemes is not more than three inches.

ONCÍDIUM STRAMÍNEUM.—Inferior in richness and brilliancy of hue to some other species, this is, nevertheless, a very neat plant, and constitutes an acceptable feature in the orchidaceous house. The flowers are of a pale straw colour, and are produced numerously on erect spikes; the sepals, besides being concave and entire, are shorter and darker than the petals, which have undulated margins, and emarginate extremities; the labellum is furnished with two crescent-shaped lateral appendages, and is liberally spotted with reddish-purple. Its leaves are remarkably thick and fleshy, ovate, acute, and about nine inches long. Messrs. Loddiges, we believe, imported this plant from Mexico, and in their collection it is now exhibiting its flowers.

WITSÈNIA MAÚRA. This singular plant appears to have been introduced to Britain from the Cape of Good Hope, so early as the year 1790. It has, however, been almost lost since that period, and we have now, for the first time, witnessed a specimen of it flowering in the nursery of Messrs. Rollison. It is altogether stronger and less branching than *W. corymbosa*, growing also to a greater height, and generally retaining its foliage throughout the entire length of its stems. But the flowers are its more remarkable features. These are large, of a deep blackish-purple at the base, and with bright yellow segments. They evince no disposition to expand, which may probably be owing to the unfavourableness of the season. They remain in a full-grown but contracted state for nearly six weeks.

Erratum.—In page 69 of our last number, for *Cælogyne barbata* read *Cælogyne ocellata.*

PECULIARITIES IN THE CULTURE OF ORNAMENTAL PLANTS.

ON GRAFTING RHODODENDRONS, CAMELLIAS, AND OTHER EXOTIC SHRUBS.—The propagation of plants, although pre-eminently the province of professional nurserymen, and chiefly conducted in their establishments, is a practice in which all cultivators are more or less interested, and of the speediest and most efficacious means for effecting which, it is highly desirable that all should be informed. Many processes are devised, and quietly pursued in nurseries, of which the majority of amateur cultivators remain ignorant for a very considerable period; and equity demands that those with whom they originate should alone reap the fruit of their skill, at least for a season. When, however, they are known and adopted by other nurserymen, they become public property, and should be rendered generally useful through the medium of floricultural publications.

In accordance with this apprehension, we intend laying before our readers some information concerning the grafting of exotic shrubs; a method of propagation which is now most extensively employed in a few of the metropolitan nurseries. For increasing many of those plants which were previously multiplied by inarching, by layers, or even by cuttings, the method in question is, to a great extent, now substituted. Its advantages over propagation by layers or cuttings will be readily perceived, because specimens may be obtained in a few months, to obtain which would require as many years by either of those modes. To inarching, it evidently assimilates more nearly, and the only reasons why it should be preferred are, that far less room is necessary, and, consequently, less heat and attention; and that, moreover, the plants from which the young scions are procured, are not subjected to the stimulating and weakening circumstances attending that process. It will be admitted that the attainment of these objects is of great importance; but the system under discussion presents other advantages to which we shall hereafter advert.

Grafting has, till within the last few years, been almost wholly confined to hardy trees; and even of these, with the more tender and valuable kinds, inarching has invariably been preferred. It seems not censorious to say that we have been heretofore lacking in a knowledge or appreciation of convenience, economy, and efficiency in the propagation of plants; for all these consequences are certainly entailed by this system in a greater degree than by any other.

It is more convenient. By inarching (with which alone grafting can be compared) the plant to be increased has to be surrounded with the stocks on which the operation is to be effected, thereby occupying a considerable space; these having likewise to be elevated to a certain height, and the specimen plant distorted and bent in various directions, so as to bring it in contact with the stock. Perhaps, also, the elasticity of the latter will derange the operation; and, however trifling this disturbance may be, the process will inevitably be nullified. Shading or protection has also to be afforded, and, of course, in proportion to the extent of surface occupied.

Again, grafting is more economical. It requires less time and labour in its preparatory procedure, in effectuation, and in subsequent attention. It is performed with far less injury to the parent plant, whether from inappropriate treatment, from distortion, or from actual amputation; since, in the latter point, a much smaller portion of a branch is requisite, and frequently a mere bud. Where heat is required, (and this is generally necessary,) a less amount of it will suffice, as the plants may be stowed in a much more limited area.

Lastly, the method here advocated is more efficient. Grafting, according to the plan yet to be detailed, is very rarely unsuccessful. This may be attributed to the greater precision with which the operator is enabled to fix the scion in its proper position, and the certainty of its maintaining that position undisturbed. Besides, when a failure occurs, nothing is lost or injured but the mere scion; the parent plant being wholly unaffected, because entirely unconnected with the operation.

Having thus shown the superiority of this system, we shall briefly state the manner in which it is effected, and the plants to which it is applicable. Stocks of the more common species of the genus are always kept in readiness for the purpose, and these are obtained either by germinating seeds, or striking cuttings. They may be of any desired height; but those whose stems are rather less than a quarter of an inch in diameter, are the most appropriate, and they should be reduced to within five or six inches of their base. In some cases, where it is desirable to conceal the union, they may be decapitated to about an inch from the ground, and the point of junction can be concealed beneath the soil, after it is properly established. Young plants are decidedly preferable for stocks, as the two surfaces will sooner unite if their texture and the condition of their functions are congenial.

It appears to be almost essential to the success of the operation that the scion should be a terminal one; *i. e.*, taken from the extremity of a shoot, so that its inner substance may not be exposed to the influence of the atmosphere in a defenceless state. Whether it is better to insert the graft in the side or on the summit of the stock, must be decided by the nature of the former. If only a bud, it must necessarily be placed in the side, as in the ordinary case of budding, from which this process differs only in the time of its performance, the circumstances attending it, and the external application of a composition which we shall presently describe. The buds, however, should be placed as near as possible to the extremity of the stock. Budding of this description may be effected at any time, although the spring season is undoubtedly the best. It is only practised with very scarce plants, and they are immediately placed in a gentle heat, in which situation they soon make satisfactory progress.

Where terminal shoots can be procured, be they ever so short, they should always be attached to the summit of the stem, as its erectness will not thus be interrupted, and the junction will, after a time, be almost imperceptible. Any mode of grafting may be adopted, and that in which the operator has had the greatest practice will certainly succeed best. After securing the graft with matting in the usual way, the whole surface of the matting is enveloped in a glutinous covering, composed of pitch, turpentine, bees-wax, and grease. With the exact proportions in which these should be compounded, every gardener must be familiar, and they form a substance quite impervious to air and moisture; hence their utility.

Plants thus grafted, are placed in a frame or house where a gentle bottom heat is kept, and covered with hand-glasses, which serve the twofold purpose of retaining a proper atmosphere around the plants, and of affording means whereby they may be shaded with facility. Not only those genera mentioned at the head of this article, but almost all other shrubs of that description, and also the rarer species of *Pinus*, and their allies, are propagated in this manner with extraordinary celerity and success; and the revival of the application above mentioned, is found to be of the greatest possible service in preventing failures.

OPERATIONS FOR MAY.

As the most striking and important developments of vegetation occur in this celebrated vernal month, while the physiologist is conducting his inquiries into their character, the practical cultivator must evince his assiduity in affording that aid and encouragement by which alone they can be healthfully promoted and maintained. Heat and moisture—the latter for the solution of aliment, and the former for inducing the absorption of such sustenance—are now in extensive requisition by all plants. Nature will most probably duly provide these essentials for all that are under her immediate surveillance; but to those which pertain to other climes, and are here grown in an artificial condition, the care and attention of the gardener is necessary ordinately to supply these indispensable offices.

Some hints were inserted in our Number for March with regard to the propriety of elevating the temperature of plant-houses as the season advances. To this subject we may here recur; since, during the present month, the adoption of such a practice is particularly desirable, at least with the denizens of the stove. There will now be little necessity for fire heat, except through the night, as the confinement of the house, combined with the influence of the sun, will be sufficient to create a due degree of temperature. It is important, however, that fires should be employed during the night; otherwise plants will experience an injurious chill in the early part of the morning, before the solar beams are powerful enough to restore the heat dissipated by radiation.

It will hereby be apparent that we deprecate the practice of admitting air to the stove at this season; for, however useful it may be in promoting the health of vegetation, its advantage is more than counteracted by the attendant diminution of temperature, which renders its impolicy obvious. In these observations we do not, of course, include those occasions on which the temperature is increased to such an extent, as not only to justify, but imperatively require the introduction of air. This must be regulated by the judicious cultivator. We only wish to subvert the system, so generally practised, of attempting to maintain an equability of temperature throughout the year, by the too copious admission of air in the summer, and the employment of powerful artificial heat during winter.

The principles to be regarded in watering plants have been frequently inculcated in this Magazine, and their repetition here would be useless. *Discrimination*, or the adaptation of the quantity administered to the actual necessities of plants, is what the cultivator should especially exercise. Each individual subject must be examined, and watered separately and distinctly, according to its apparent appetences.

Transplantation is a prominent item in the management of the flower-garden this month. Annuals, and half-hardy herbaceous plants, are now to be removed to their summer stations. Of the former, we may remark that, with the exception of a few particular sorts, all will derive great benefit from being transplanted. It will check the natural exuberance of their growth, and promote the production of flowers, at the same time furnishing the plants with a greater number of fibrous roots, and, by consequence, an increased capacity for enduring drought.

Physiologists concur in the opinion that the roots of plants can absorb moisture or nutriment only by their extreme points or spongioles. The importance, therefore, of preserving these uninjured in their removal, will be at once perceived. With annuals, an especial necessity exists for exercising this care; as, unlike trees and shrubs, they have a very brief period to form new ones, and unless this be effected with great rapidity, their season of development and display passes before they are prepared for its commencement. Many of them, however, possess a long, tapering, central root, that has rarely more than one point, and by the abscission of the lower part of which, the plant will not be materially injured, while the operation will cause the emission of a great number of smaller and more useful lateral rootlets from all parts of its surface.

Before any half-hardy annual or other plants are placed out in the open border, every precaution should be taken to render them capable of sustaining the depressions of temperature, or even frosts, which frequently occur in this month. The best mode of effecting this, is to expose them to the atmosphere for a considerable time previous to their being planted, merely sheltering them from excessive rains or cold when requisite. Besides ensuring their safety, this practice will render their growth more healthy, and thus tend to stimulate or strengthen their productive organs.

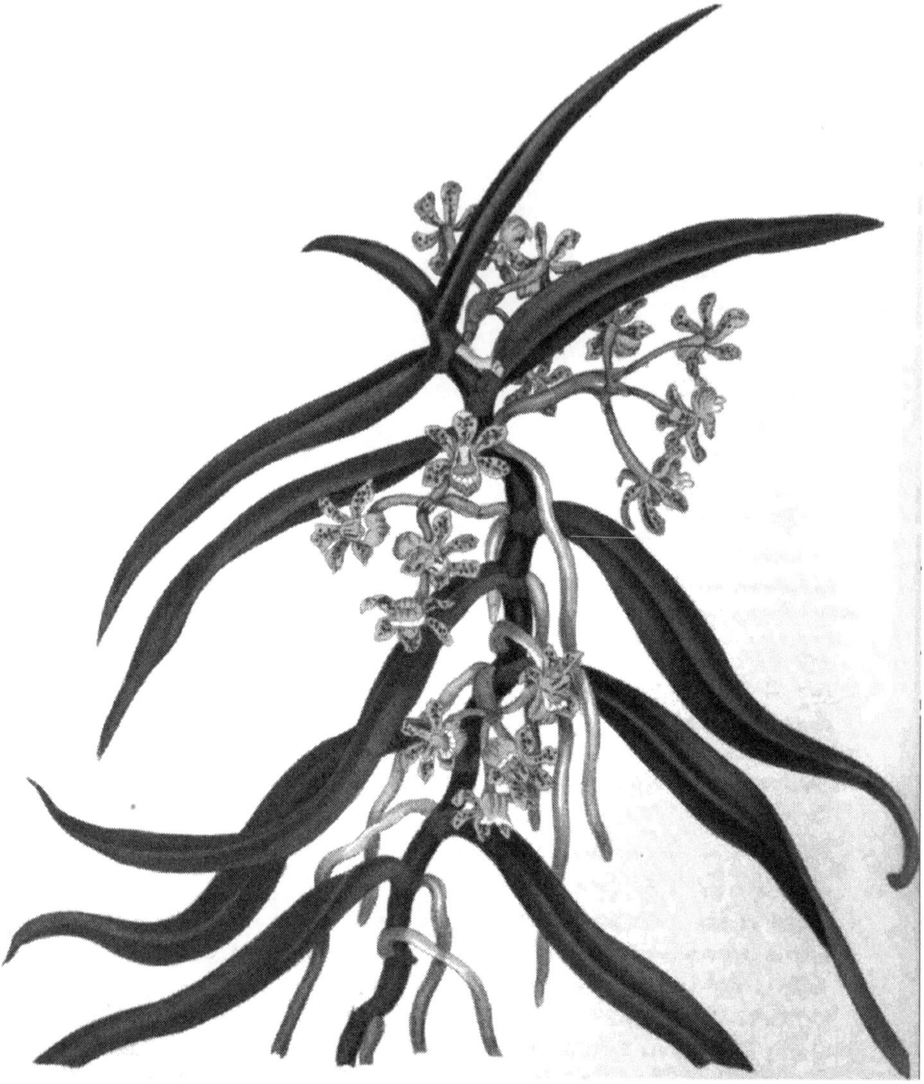

SACCOLÀBIUM CALCEOLÀRE.
(SLIPPER-SHAPED SACCOLABIUM.)

CLASS.
GYNANDRIA.

ORDER.
MONOGYNIA.

NATURAL ORDER.
ORCHIDÀCEÆ.

GENERIC CHARACTER.—*Perianthium* smooth, spreading. *Sepals* and *petals* equal, lateral ones sometimes larger. *Labellum* undivided, spurred, growing to the base of the column. *Column* erect, half-rounded, with an awl-shaped beak. *Anthers* half two-celled. *Pollen-masses* two, roundish, with an elongated appendage, and a minute gland.

SPECIFIC CHARACTER.—*Plant* epiphytal, caulescent. *Leaves* strap-shaped, acuminate, obliquely two-toothed at the summit, spotted at the base. *Corymb* many-flowered, shortly pedunculate. *Sepals* and *petals* obovately oblong, obtuse, yellow, marked with roundish purple spots. *Labellum* with an inflated spur, nearly circular, with a crescent-shaped ciliated plate.

DIMINUTIVE as are the flowers of this pretty orchidaceous plant, it is so exceedingly interesting in habit, and its blossoms exhibit such a charming combination of showy hues, that it will certainly win a place in the esteem of all who delight to worship at Nature's shrine, and to feast their vision on its gems, with the exalted view of eliciting some new benevolent and benign trait in the character of its divine Founder and Upholder.

There can be few well-regulated minds but have derived exquisite gratification from a survey of the wondrous variety of attractive features which the vegetable kingdom presents. An entirely new field, however, has recently been opened to their gaze, by the introduction to Britain of so many members of the remarkable tribe *Orchidaceæ*. Some of the choicest and most ornamental of these species we have from time to time figured in our Magazine, and although the subject of our present remarks has not the splendour of many others, it possesses several truly excellent and admirable characteristics.

We have latterly had frequent occasion to record the results of the exploratory tour of his Grace the Duke of Devonshire's botanical collector in the East Indies; and the plant now noticed furnishes a renewed instance of its success. Mr. Gibson brought specimens of this species to Chatsworth in 1837, which flowered, and one of which was figured as here represented, in August, 1838. It occupies a range of country on the Khoseea Hills, about 4000 feet above the level of the sea. In this locality, it is found depending from the branches of trees, in confined humid forests, where it appears to shrink from the immediate influence of the solar beams.

Like the majority of other *Vandeous Orchidaceæ*, it is an Epiphyte, and thrives most luxuriantly when treated as such. A log of wood, of almost any dimensions, should be employed for its support, and to this it may be secured with wire or matting, merely surrounding the lower roots with a little moss. It may here be remarked that the size of the block selected should in all cases be somewhat conformable to the height of the plant intended to be attached; and, in the present instance, a piece of about six or nine inches long, and an inch or rather more in diameter, will be most appropriate. The cultivator need scarcely be reminded that it is in a great measure by the roots which are evolved from various parts of the stem, and not alone by those which are enveloped in the moss at the base, that nourishment is obtained. By a proper consideration of this fact, and an enlightened reference to the conditions in which *S. calceolare* naturally flourishes, as before stated, it will be seen that *atmospheric* humidity, and a protection of some thin material which will refract the sun's rays, are the most necessary constituents of its cultivation.

The statements just delivered apply solely to the management of this plant while growing. As it flowers during the months of July and August, its growth is fully completed before the commencement of the winter, and during this latter season it should be retained in a dry and cool atmosphere, apart from all exciting circumstances. Being naturally a pendent species, it should either be allowed to hang very loosely from the block of wood, suspended perpendicularly from the roof of the house, or the block should be placed horizontally during its growing stage; as, if made to assume an erect position, water would accumulate in the nodes of the young shoots, and probably promote their decomposition.

If desirable, it may be planted in a wire or rustic wooden basket, filled with moss, and hung from the rafters of the house; but this treatment is not so suitable as that before recommended.

For propagation, the young shoots may be broken carefully out when the plant is dormant. It is advisable that the branches thus detached should be of two or three years' growth, and have one or more small lateral shoots. By placing them in a shady situation till they evince signs of withering, and afterwards treating them as the old specimens, they will almost invariably succeed.

The term *Saccolabium* is derived from *saccus*, a bag, and *labium*, a lip; the labellum of the flowers of this genus being pouch-shaped.

In our present species, the lip is fancied to bear some resemblance in form to a slipper; hence the name *calceolare*.

Gladiolus ramosus.

GLADIÒLUS RAMÒSUS.
(BRANCHING CORN-FLAG.)

CLASS.	ORDER.
TRIANDRIA.	MONOGYNIA.

NATURAL ORDER.
IRIDÀCEÆ.

GENERIC CHARACTER.—*Vide* vol. ii. p. 197.

SPECIFIC CHARACTER.—*Plant* a corm. *Stem* erect, four to five feet high, branched; branches ascending. *Leaves* entire, long, lanceolate, acuminate, five-nerved, whitish green. *Flowers* terminal, spicate, sessile, alternate, large. *Bracts* ovate, acuminate, striated, enveloping the tube of the perianth. *Perianth* composed of six segments; upper three broadly oblong, obtuse, deep blush colour; lower three narrower, emarginate, rich sanguineous red towards the base. *Stamens* three; filaments distinct. *Anthers* attached to the filaments by their middle, blue. *Style* longer than the stamens, three-lobed.

THE splendid genus of which the present plant forms a distinguished feature, is far from being regarded with the attention it deserves. In many collections, and even among those of the highest order, its most showy species are scarcely allowed a place; while it is only in a few isolated instances that they are cultivated in an appropriate manner, and attain that degree of perfection which, when once witnessed, invariably secures them from further neglect.

G. *ramosus* is a rare and highly valuable plant, introduced to this country from Holland about three years since, but a native of the Cape of Good Hope. In the size and beauty of its flowers it yields to none of its congeners; and on account of its peculiarly branching habit, it may be considered the most ornamental species of the genus. By the possession of the character just referred to, it is enabled to produce a much greater number of flowers, and these are arranged with much better effect than those of the species with simple stems.

Messrs. Lucombe and Pince, nurserymen, Exeter, kindly forwarded to us the accompanying drawing of this plant in the autumn of 1838. It flowered most profusely in the garden of those gentlemen in the month of July of that year, having been planted out in the open ground in the early part of the preceding spring.

Of the practice of transplanting *Gladioli* to the open border, we wish here to record our decided commendation. No other mode of treatment will be found so suitable; and we can only account for the little esteem in which these superb plants are held, by supposing that this system is very rarely adopted. Thus treated, our present subject will grow to the height of four or five feet; and, with three or four lateral spikes of flowers considerably larger than that shown in our figure, presents an almost unexampled picture of magnificence.

Should wet weather ensue for any lengthened period after this plant has ceased flowering, it will be advisable to protect it with a hand-glass or some other covering that will divert the rain. This is of great importance, as it would otherwise continue growing throughout the autumnal season, to the almost inevitable suppression of flowers in the succeeding year. When the leaves have entirely decayed, the corms may be taken from the ground, and kept in a dry situation till the month of October, at which time they should be placed singly in pots of a moderate size, filled with light rich compost. A cold frame, from which frost is thoroughly excluded, will be the most favourable position for them during the winter, and they may be transferred to the open ground about the latter end of the following May.

In propagating this plant, no other trouble is required than the separation of the young corms when the old ones are taken from the ground. They should be managed according to the preceding directions, except that several of them may be placed in one pot, and they can be planted out in groups or beds for the first year. Removal to the flower-border is indispensable to their rapid development, and a situation fully exposed to solar influence should invariably be chosen for this purpose.

In vol. ii. p. 197, is an explication of the generic name.

Ixia pungens

HÒVEA PÚNGENS.

(POINTED-LEAVED HOVEA.)

CLASS.	ORDER.
MONADELPHIA.	DECANDRIA.

NATURAL ORDER.
LEGUMINOSÆ.

GENERIC CHARACTER.—*Vide* vol. iii. p. 241.

SPECIFIC CHARACTER.—*Plant* shrubby, growing from eighteen inches to two feet high. *Stem* roundish, erect, branching, covered with long brown hairs. *Leaves* linear, pungent, sessile, convolute at the margins, indistinctly reticulated, smooth. *Flowers* solitary, axillary. *Corolla* papilionaceous; wings bright blue, keel purple.

AMONG the vegetable tribes, the instances are by no means common in which such a striking uniformity of colour exists in the species of a genus as in *Hovea;* and still more rarely is that colour an agreeable one. Blue flowers, of various shades, sometimes containing a combination of red, and thus forming purple, and again occasionally approaching to grey, characterize the whole of the species of *Hovea* that have yet been introduced to British collections.

It need scarcely be added to the above statement, that this genus is accounted a peculiarly interesting one. Some of the species (for example, *H. Celsii*, a figure of which appeared in vol. iii. p. 241) having flowers of a much brighter blue than others, are universally esteemed and cultivated. With this class may be ranked *H. pungens*, the blossoms of which are of even a deeper hue than that just mentioned, while its slender and graceful habit contributes greatly to exhibit them to advantage.

The remarkable similarity in the colours of the flowers, renders it necessary to refer to the leaves for specific marks of distinction, and the greater number of species are consequently named in accordance with the form of these organs. In the species now under consideration, the foliage is particularly short and narrow, but its prominent feature is the stout, pointed prickle by which it is terminated. In other respects it resembles some of the rest of this family, but is dwarfer, more compact, exhibits a greater tendency to branch, and has somewhat smaller flowers.

In conjunction with most other Australian plants, this species delights in a situation well exposed to light and air. A compound of loam and heath soil, in which the former is allowed to preponderate if a luxuriant growth is desired, with a trifling quantity of sand or reduced stone, forms an excellent and appropriate compost. When the specimen is inclined to manifest an extraordinary degree of exuberance, the quality of the earth may be modified by employing a larger portion of heath soil; and if its growth continues of too straggling a character, pruning should be resorted to in the autumnal months.

Those who wish to cultivate *Hoveas* to any remarkable degree of perfection, should use a rather rich compost, allow the roots due liberty to extend themselves, and occasionally reduce the plants. The larger kinds may be advantageously planted out in the border of a conservatory, and, with proper attention to pruning, they would there constitute most superb objects. The species here figured is, however, too dwarf for this purpose; but a few months in the open ground during the summer season would unquestionably be found beneficial.

These plants frequently suffer greatly, even to the loss of all their foliage, from careless watering; extreme moisture or drought being alike inimical. If potted in a suitable soil, and a sufficiently large pot, they will seldom be subjected to injury from drought; but these circumstances will of themselves render them liable to be damaged by a superfluity of water. The constant care of the cultivator is therefore requisite in the application of fluid.

Messrs. Rollison, of Tooting, received this species, in 1838, from Baron Hugel, of Vienna, and with these gentlemen it flowered in the month of March of the present year. Our drawing was made at this latter period.

For the origin of the generic name, see vol. iii. p. 242.

Gesneria oblongata.

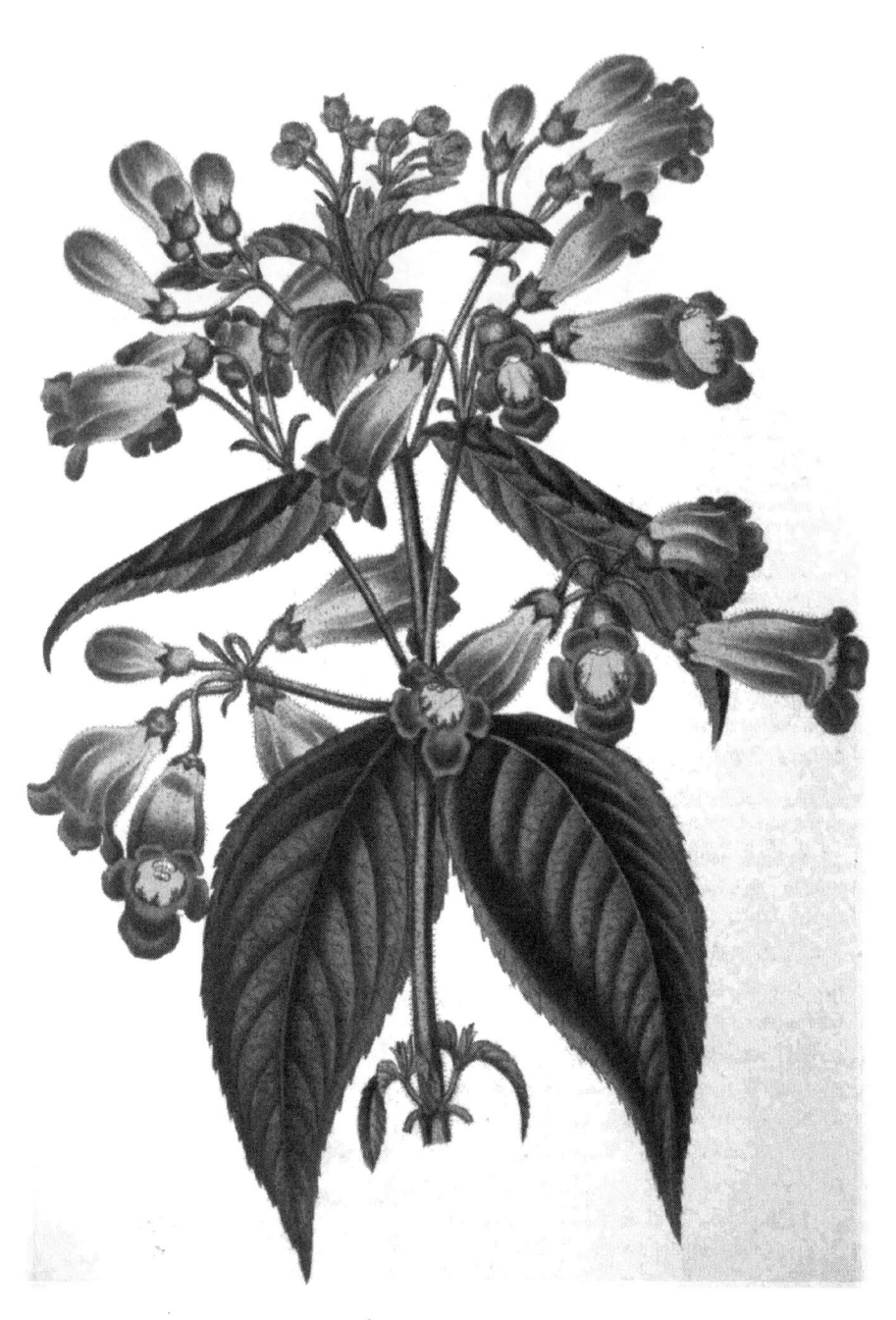

GESNÈRIA OBLONGÀTA.

(OBLONG-FLOWERED GESNERIA.)

CLASS.
DIDYNAMIA.

ORDER.
ANGIOSPERMIA.

NATURAL ORDER.
GESNERIÀCEÆ.

GENERIC CHARACTER.—*Vide* vol. i. p. 224.

SPECIFIC CHARACTER.—*Plant* villous. *Stem* (five feet high) shrubby, much branched; branches ascending. *Leaves* (three to six inches long, one and a quarter to two and a quarter broad) opposite and decussating, petiolate, lanceolate, acuminate, neatly and subequally serrated, somewhat harshly pubescent and bright green above, white with soft tomentum below. *Umbels* four-flowered, villous, shorter than the leaves; peduncle shorter than the petiole; pedicels about two thirds of the length of the peduncles; bracteæ two, opposite, lanceolate at the subdivision of the umbel. *Flowers* unilateral. *Calyx* with small, spreading, ovato-subulate segments. *Corolla* (one inch long, half an inch across) tubular, clavato-ventricose, dilated and somewhat fleshy at its base. *Stem* contracted, and after being dilated again slightly contracted at its mouth, villous on the outside, glabrous within; limb spreading, lobes subequal, rounded, crenate. *Stamens* inserted into the base of the corolla, and rising to the throat; *filaments* pubescent, anthers divaricated at the base, where the connective is dilated, cucullate and fleshy; fifth stamen rudimental. *Pistil* pubescent; *stigma* minute, truncated; *style* bent at its base, compressed; *germen* more than half embedded in the adhering calyx, and surrounded at its free apex with five glands. *Ovules* numerous and minute.—*Dr. Graham* in *Bot. Mag.* t. 3725.

SYNONYM.—Gesneria elongata; *var.* fruticosa.—*Bot. Mag.* 3725.

By far the greater portion of the Gesnerias cultivated in our collections have tuberous roots, and produce their flowers in a cluster or spike at the extremity of the stems. Their number and the duration of their flowering season are consequently limited. In the present species, the flowers appear at the axils of the leaves, and as the plant is shrubby, facility is thus afforded for illimitable production.

But it is not in the above character that the superior merit of this plant alone resides. It manifests a striking disposition to branch laterally, and the leaves being likewise elegantly formed, and happily disposed, when well grown, the plant has a most symmetrical appearance. This quality, as most of our readers must be aware, is not common to its allies. In the regular structure of its flowers, it assimilates to *G. elongata*, and several others; and Dr. Graham (see *Bot. Magazine*, as before quoted) considers it a mere variety of that species. Without disputing the propriety of this, or the resemblance our plant bears to *G. elongata* in some respects, we had previously adopted, and therefore here retain, the name by which it has long been known in the London nurseries, humbly conceiving that the points of difference are sufficient to constitute it a distinct species.

In its capability of accommodation to variable temperature, this species is as far removed from most others as in its general structure. We have witnessed specimens flowering with almost equal vigour in the stove, the greenhouse, and a house of intermediate temperature. In the former case, the blossoms unfolded themselves more rapidly, and the leaves maintained a more vivid verdure, but this appeared to be solely owing to its greater exposure to light in the greenhouse. It rarely exceeds two or three feet in height, and is invariably handsomest when not suffered to grow too luxuriantly.

If placed in a house appropriated to Camellias, and having a western aspect, it would doubtless develop itself as perfectly as if retained in a stove. By this means, those individuals who do not possess a structure of the latter description, might easily cultivate this plant; and, as it will continue blooming for three or four months incessantly, this period being also the least favourable to the production of any other kinds of flowers, we regard it as indispensable to the smallest collections, and cordially recommend its extensive culture. To the cultivator of tropical plants it is especially acceptable, as the treatment usually bestowed on these is undoubtedly the most congenial, and therewith it would supply a brilliant profusion of its showy flowers during the entire duration of the most gloomy season of the year.

With regard to soil, and other particulars of culture, there is nothing peculiar to our present plant, and it may be managed as the rest of the genus. Being a kind of under-shrub, and an evergreen, it will not endure the drought and dormancy to which tuberous species are subjected, although a partial rest is requisite after it has ceased growing. When the stems grow too straggling, they may safely be pruned to within a few inches of their base.

Cuttings strike freely at any time when young shoots can be obtained. Their extraordinary propensity to flower must be duly checked during the enactment of this process, by the removal of the flower buds on their first appearance.

Several years have elapsed since its first introduction to this country, and it is now comparatively common in nurseries, from whence it may be procured for a very trifling charge. We believe it to be a native of South America.

To Messrs. Rollison, of Tooting, we are indebted for the specimen from which the accompanying drawing was made. These gentlemen possess a considerable number of plants of various sizes. It begins to expand its flowers in the month of October, and there yet remain a few scattered blossoms on some specimens. Our figure was taken last January.

The generic name has been explained in vol. i. p. 224.

THE PERIODICAL REPOSE OF PLANTS.

PLANTS, considered as animate substances, and endued with the power of extension and enlargement, are supposed to require a certain period of complete torpidity, to enable them to mature their recently developed members for further elaboration. This axiom now forms a stated item in most works on practical botany, and the cultivators of plants are likewise beginning to regard it with some degree of requisite attention. In its support, it may be alleged, that the continual exercise of the growing functions is unnatural; that plants are unable to endure an uninterrupted circulation and distension, without suffering debilitation; and that an analogical reference to animals evinces and confirms its propriety.

To the validity of the principle, *per se*, we can have no possible objection. Both nature and experience prove to demonstration, that, with existing circumstances, rest is essential to all plants. Writers on this subject (as far as our observation extends) have, however, failed in tracing this principle to its legitimate and proper origin. It is therefore left for us to expose the fallacy of the general impression, and to attempt to establish the hypothesis on a rational and satisfactory basis.

That plants require a season of repose to consolidate their newly acquired substance, perfect its mechanism, and concoct its juices, or slowly to prepare and distribute their resources for future growth, is, we humbly conceive, neither plausible nor demonstrable. Such an opinion, if entertained, would involve a complete inversion of natural order. Were we to admit any theorem of so questionable a character, we must also allow that variations of climate were created to suit the constitutions of certain plants: whereas, sense and reason concur to assure us that plants are distributed over those climates, the peculiarities of which are most favourable for their sustenance and development. It must be obvious that plants are allotted to those districts the climate of which is most congenial to them; and not that the climate of any region is modified and adapted to the wants and necessities of certain kinds of plants. The peculiar season of rest, therefore, its duration, and particular mode, or characteristics, are also regulated by climate.

Perpetual excitement is, we concede, neither natural nor practicable with any degree of safety. But, to the notion that plants are incapable of sustaining it, if the necessary concomitant circumstances could possibly be furnished, we cannot so readily subscribe our assent. On the contrary, it appears highly probable that, by subjecting plants to a continuously high temperature, could this be accompanied with a due proportion of light and moisture, they might be maintained in a state of constant verdure and luxuriance, and that their produce, whether flowers or fruit, would not thereby be deteriorated, nor in the slightest degree prejudicially affected. While, therefore, unintermittent stimulation is to be deprecated because it is contrary to nature in existing climates, the physiologist who is anxious to know why it is so, will not find a correct solution of this question by referring to the capacities of any kinds of plants, but in the variation of seasons peculiar to each district over which those plants are scattered.

The opinion that continued excitation weakens and enervates the energies of the vegetable tribes, must be viewed in precisely the same connexion as that to which we have just alluded. In temperate climes, vegetation is dormant during the winter season, because neither heat nor light is sufficiently intense and durable to maintain vital action. Tropical regions, on the other hand, preclude unvarying verdure, since moisture is almost if not entirely evaporated at certain periods of the year. The winters of some countries (Great Britain for instance) are supposed to be necessary to plants; because they imbibe at this season a quantity of liquid food, wherewith to enable them to repair the effects of anterior exertion, and furnish means for their future development. The supply of fluids thus obtained is not, however, circulated through the entire substance of plants till the return of vernal suns and increased temperature; and as heat alone can render them capable of appropriating those fluids, by the prompt application of moisture when necessary, no scarcity can ever be experienced: so that the store received during their torpidity is by no means essential, or even useful, to the succeeding progress of vegetation.

Of the analogy between plants and animals in this particular, a very few observations will suffice to show that the sleep of the higher orders of the latter is of a totally different nature to the repose of plants; while those instances of periodical dormancy which occur in the lower classes of animals, may be distinctly traced to the same cause as is here assigned for that of vegetation generally. Animals sleep,—not to enable them to grow with greater rapidity and vigour, but to furnish them with a renewed capacity for the active exertion of their locomotive powers. Plants, on the contrary, not having any such functions to exercise, have all their energies concentrated in the growing process. So long therefore as they can absorb a sufficient quantity of nutriment, and at the same time be subjected to the elements which will induce them to appropriate and as it were digest it, they need no such suspension of their faculties.

These observations must not be misunderstood as implying the unimportance of a periodical cessation of growth. We hold it to be an indispensable feature in the cultivation of all plants; but previously to adopting any particular system of treatment, we deem it necessary that its applicability and suitableness should be distinctly and clearly understood. Some cultivators of Orchidaceæ, being deeply impressed with the propriety of affording them a season of repose, and not knowing that this occurs in their native localities on account of the peculiarities of the climate, commit great and dangerous errors. Thus, we have seen many of these plants placed in a dry cool house for repose during the summer, and removed to a humid heat towards the approach of winter, because they are inert in the hot and dry season in their natural state. By this practice, their functions are forced into action by an artificial stimulus, which being alike difficult to maintain, and almost destitute of that *sine qua non* to the healthy growth of all plants, light, causes a weak, partial, deformed, and immature development, and where the plant is of a delicate nature, sometimes terminates in its total destruction.

We are aware that much difficulty attends the management of orchidaceous plants in this respect; and that a great diversity of treatment must be practised. The natural habits of these and all other plants should not only be studied, but to them the treatment must be conformed, as far as is consistent and practicable. Summer repose, and winter excitation, however, are too grossly absurd, and too fatally prejudicial, to be long followed in this country. Orchidaceous, stove, greenhouse, and all other tribes of plants, must have rest *when the climate in which they are cultivated renders it necessary;* and, according to the principles herein inculcated, in Great Britain that period is the winter season.

INFLUENCE OF CLIMATE ON PLANTS.[*]
SOLAR HEAT.

Pores, besides fulfilling the office of respirators, are likewise the chief vehicles of the radiation of heat. It has been frequently stated that radiation and evaporation are reciprocally dependent or concurrent; the exhalation of fluids either causing or resulting from a simultaneous effusion of heat. In proof of the former of these positions, it is said that frost is never hurtful to plants, till evaporation has succeeded; and that the abstractions of temperature which accompany such evaporation are mainly productive of the injury. But a more mistaken hypothesis could not possibly be imagined.

We have already described the action of frost upon the structure of vegetation. The increased escape of fluids which follows a renewed application of heat, so far from being the operating cause of the damage sustained, is merely one of its effects, and that by which it is made manifest. Indeed, it is ridiculous to suppose that radiation can be a consequence of evaporation; because external heat, the agent which induces the latter, would evidently repress the former.

Nor can it be acknowledged that evaporation accompanies radiation, except in a very trifling degree. For, although it is remarked that dew is formed on the under surface of leaves, it seems to have been forgotten that the vapour of which dew is composed by condensation, has so slight a specific gravity, that it is diffused through, and held in suspension by, the atmosphere; and does not therefore necessarily descend perpendicularly, but may be deposited upon a cooler substance, in almost any position. Before we can admit that these processes are simultaneously effected, we must assume that they are produced by the same or coincident agents; a theory wholly at variance with existing facts.

[*] Continued from page 88.

Plants, it is well known, have a temperature altogether peculiar to themselves. This does not arise so much from the elicitation of latent heat—although, probably, internal chemical combinations may tend to increase it—but is acquired chiefly by the admission of warmer fluids from the soil into the roots, and their transfusion throughout the entire plant by the vessels. The power of retaining this temperature depends entirely on the stage of the plant's progress, and the consequent density or porosity of its cuticle. Unless duly preserved by a perfect epidermis, the extent of radiation will be equal to the difference between the temperature of the plant and that of the atmosphere. This will at once account for the effects of cold on the imperfectly developed or incompletely matured substance of plants.

A knowledge of the laws and process of radiation, is of the greatest value to the cultivator of exotic plants; as the safety of all the objects beneath his care is almost wholly dependent on the manner in which the reduction of temperature is prevented. Protection of all kinds may be said to consist in the effectuation of this simple object; and so far only as it is conducted with that specific end in view, can it be either suitable or successful.

Radiation, as we have shown, is transacted from the surface of plants, and caused by contact with, or exposure to, a colder atmosphere. If, then, we envelop tender plants in an atmosphere of their own, or obviate the transit of heat to the external air, by interposing some material of slow radiating power, we effectually preserve them from injury by frost. When cold is not very intense, but vegetation extremely susceptive, as, for instance, in the spring and autumnal seasons, at which times the frosts are trifling, and the substance of plants only newly developed, or but partially organized, more especially in the latter case, a covering of any slight material will be sufficient to restrain radiation from proceeding too rapidly, or to too great an extent. The screen, however, must always be perfectly detached from the plant which it surrounds, otherwise conduction will be substituted for radiation; a consequence by which the remedy will be nearly nullified.

Attempts to naturalize any exotic plants, can only issue in the desired result when active attention is bestowed upon the particular just named. The most careful preservation during the winter will be of little avail, unless a similar protection is nightly afforded in the decline of autumn, and the commencement of spring; at least, when the atmosphere is clear, or there is any indication of frost. It would be difficult to decide at which of these seasons defence is most requisite. Although a slight consideration would lead us to declare that the greatest necessity existed in the spring months, because vegetation is then in a highly excited and impressionable condition, further investigation establishes an equal need for it in the fall of the year.

In the autumn, both the soil, and the plants growing on it, are more highly imbued with heat than the atmosphere; and hence, the excessive radiation which takes place during the cool night hours of that season is, on account of its abruptness and violence, very injurious to the members of the vegetable world. The abstractions of winter leave them in a completely inversed condition in the spring; and their average temperature is decidedly below that of the atmosphere in the day, so that they are the less able safely to part with any caloric at night. We conclude, therefore, that shelter is equally essential to tender plants at both these epochs; but that a much thinner covering is required in the autumn than in the spring, because vegetation is thoroughly furnished with internal heat in the former, and retains a small amount only in the latter season.

Inferior only in degree to the radiation from plants fully exposed to the atmosphere, is that of the more delicate kinds which are confined in houses. Glass has been before declared to be a most liberal radiator of heat; and hence, the greater the amount of glazed surface a house presents, the more speedy and perfect will be its radiation. The temperature of a plant-house being diminished, that of the plants will rapidly be reduced likewise; and as vegetation is always more or less susceptible according to the circumstances to which it has been habituated, those plants which are kept in an artificial condition will suffer considerably from the most trifling degree of radiation to which they may be subjected.

To retard radiation in hot-houses, and prevent it from entailing any injurious consequences on the plants which they protect, recourse is generally had to the introduction of artificial heat. In this respect, cultivators err most egregiously. Radiation is effected from the *external* surface of the house, and the means professedly employed to counteract it are usually arranged near or beneath the *lower* surface. Notwithstanding the lightness and ascension of heated air, the porosity of the glass combined with the numerous fissures which occur at the junction of the panes, invariably maintains the superior stratum of atmosphere at a low temperature. The upper, and *most tender* portions of plants, thus come in contact with the *coldest* air; and these, being rendered more susceptive by the excitation of heat from below, are kept in a perpetual state of conflicting exertion and endurance.

Did plants require to be supplied with a uniformly high temperature throughout the winter season, the practice here denounced would be in some measure defensible. But this is not the case. We hesitate not to affirm, that the total exclusion of frost is all that is desirable with even tropical species. How much more easily, safely, and effectually, then, could this be ensured, by an exterior covering to the roof! This appears to us the only rational mode of procedure, seeing that it is through the roof alone that frost can be admitted, or, more strictly speaking, heat dissipated. And though we grant the utility and propriety of applying fire heat in extreme cases, it should never be regarded otherwise than as an inevitable auxiliary.

If it be urged as an objection to the above method, that such a measure would exclude light as well as frost, the torpidity of the plants under the circumstances recommended will render the continued action of light unnecessary. Complete dormancy, and partial darkness, are by no means incompatible; nor is the latter, when coincident with the former, at all detrimental. When maturation is duly effected, and circulation has entirely ceased, the absence of light is rather to be desired than deprecated. These qualifications must, however, be regarded with the greatest accuracy; and every precaution taken to produce and maintain the state herein described. A departure from this would counteract the good effects of the system, endanger the health of the plants, and engender prejudice.

To these observations on radiation, we may be allowed to request more than ordinary notice. The cultivator who is anxious to obtain celebrity, and is yet unacquainted with the principles and influences of this process, is pursuing an uncertain route to a goal which nothing but a rare concatenation of fortuitous circumstances can enable him to reach. But, enlightened on this point, he may continue his progress without a doubt of ultimately obtaining satisfactory and honourable success. It is to this, and principles such as this, that the horticulturist must alone look for advancement in his art, and these it will ever be our object to elucidate and establish.

Inferences of a practical nature are also deducible from the fact of fluids circulating only when rarefied by heat, and of the same agent acting as the prime causative of accretions to the substance of plants. Since heat alone can induce an upward flow of sap, it is clear that the supply must be apportioned to the demand; or, in other words, that heat must accompany moisture in equal proportion. A continued application of water in a low temperature would speedily surfeit plants, and either obstruct or rupture their vessels. Injury of a much more serious nature, or at least more immediately perceptible, follows a contrary course of treatment: withering and contraction are soon apparent, and the plant rapidly decays.

Healthy developments are the consequences of appropriate excitation; and the only method of ascertaining the degree of temperature required to render them of such a character, is by accurate observation of the habits of the plant. Either too great or too limited a supply of heat, or its employment at an unseasonable period, will produce similar results;—sickly, imperfect, degenerate growth. In the practice of acclimatation, therefore, the *gradual* adaptation of plants to the climate, or of the climate to plants, should be the first and greatest, indeed almost the only concern of the cultivator.

(*To be continued.*)

ON THE PROPAGATION OF CAMELLIAS.

Since the paper on this subject which appeared in our last number was written, we have been favoured with the following communication. As the process of grafting Camellias is here minutely detailed, and some excellent directions given for their management during that trying period, it will, we have no doubt, be found highly useful. We again commend the practice to all who estimate duly the value of improvements, or who would wish to avoid superfluous trouble and expense.

If we refer to the comprehensive article on the *culture of the Camellia*, commencing vol. i. p. 33 of the Magazine of Botany, it might appear superfluous to make any further observations on the subject. But nevertheless something may be added, and a few inaccuracies, or at least inadvertencies, corrected. We shall attempt to render that able paper more complete, and hope to point out one method of propagation which is very little known.

First as to stocks, it is unquestionable that the single red Camellias usually make the best stocks, as asserted at No. 16, p. 35; it is true, also, that *Cuttings* of the young ripe wood can be put in, either in the spring, in heat, or in the cold frame, in November, when a callus is gradually produced which is the precursor of roots that, by the aid of a little moist heat in March, or April, following, will be developed. But a great improvement appears to consist in rejecting pots altogether for striking Camellias.

A gentle hotbed, or the bed of a small propagation-house, wherein a heat of not more than 60 or 63 degrees, by fire or hot-water, is maintained, offers the best means to raise a stock of young Camellias. We prefer the latter, and shall attempt to describe what we witnessed. The house is about fifteen feet long, and ten feet or more wide; it has a front and *one* end light; the slope of the sashes is not above 25 degrees by the French scale, or 65 degrees by that of the English gardeners, (see vol. i. p. 257). In this house there is a central pit, to contain four feet of tan, or hot leaves. One end abuts against the north wall—a walk goes round the back, front, and south end of the pit; the aspect of the house appears to be about east, and it is heated by hot-water pipes. Over the tan of the pit, earth is placed of a quality suited to the nature of the plants to be raised; for the Camellia, reduced turfy loam, and sandy, black heath mould, mixed in the proportion of two parts of the latter to one of the former, form the best medium, and should be laid at least three inches deep, and covered with an inch of pure white siliceous sand. Nurserymen thus raise Camellias from cuttings by hundreds; but we will presume that the amateur propagator has two or three dozens of cuttings to operate upon; and that he possesses a propagation-house constructed in a way not remotely different in principle from that we have alluded to.

A clean and well-glazed hand-glass, quite free from flaw or crack, should be pressed on the sand, so as to leave its mark; the sand being previously made compactly firm with water. A number of cuttings, of the ripe young wood, are then to be made ready, and inserted at convenient distances, two points deep, holes being made and nearly filled with writing sand. Each cutting is to be fixed very firm by working about its heel and pressing with the setting-stick. No leaf is to be let into the earth, but not one is to be removed the base of whose footstalk will remain above the surface. Water must then be given freely through a fine rose, or by flirting it on with a hair-brush, and when the leaves become rather dry, the hand-glass is to be placed over the cuttings, pressing it down, so that its lower edge may pass into the wet sand, and completely exclude the air. Success will mainly depend upon the closeness of the covering, shading from mid-day sun, and a moist soil. The growth of the cuttings, and the firm adherence of the leaves, will indicate the development of roots; and not a plant should be moved till it have made some inches of fine young wood, and borne exposure to the air of the house. The glass will of course be removed cautiously, and, for many weeks, only while it is cleaned and made dry.

There is nothing new in raising young stocks by this method, neither is it at all strange to meet with fine plants of the *double* varieties which have been raised from cuttings; but there is a prejudice against the latter, it being a received opinion that such plants are short-lived, and little to be depended on. We have, however, a double white kind now in flower: it is altogether the prettiest specimen that we possess; and we know it to be at least four years old from the cutting. But *inarching* on the *red stock*, is a process at once so easy and successful, that it ought never to be lost sight of by those who are not adroit grafters. This mention of grafting brings us to the point which is the chief object of the present article.

Very few persons succeed in their attempts to propagate by independent grafting. Notwithstanding the utmost caution to adapt the bark of the scion to that of the stock, to secure the junction by ligature, and to prevent access of air by covering the graft with clay, or wax, the leaves fall, and the scion perishes. The cause of failure is to be traced to the length of the scion; which, with wood so hard and comparatively void of sap as is that of the Camellia, almost invariably prevents the interflow of the vital juices of the two members at the first critical period. The Camellia has great facility in forming a junction with its congeners, provided its wounded surfaces can retain their sap; hence the almost certain success of the inarching process. Therefore, if independent grafting be aimed at, both stock and scion must be brought to a state of activity by a gentle heat of 60°; and just when the buds of the stock swell, and those of the plant to be propagated enlarge and draw out to the length of half an inch, *one single bold eye* (generally selected from those at the tops of the shoot), with an *inch* only of ripe young wood, is to be cut sloping, in the same way as the shoot of an apple scion, when prepared for whip or tongue grafting. Here, however, the cut will extend the *whole length* of the wood, and the scion thus prepared will resemble the *bud* or shield of a fruit tree, saving only that the wood is not removed from it. The *stock* is next cut off so as closely to match and correspond with the sloping cut of the scion, at a part of the stem not more than an inch above the surface of the soil.

The utmost care and adroitness to secure adaptation of parts must be exerted; and then a small tongue may, or may not, be made; for if the bark fits perfectly on both sides, the success will not be affected thereby: still, we would recommend those who are not adepts, to make a very minute incision and corresponding tongue in stock and bud, in order to assist them in tying the members together. The parts being correctly fitted, a narrow but strong and flexible *new* shred of bass matting, wetted, is to be passed firmly around the scion and stock, thus securing the perfect junction of the two surfaces, without pressing or disturbing the growing bud.

The operation being completed, the plant is to be covered closely with a bell-glass, to exclude the air completely. The soil is to be kept freely moist, but not wet, and the sun is to be warded off by a paper shade. All depends upon the due regulation of heat, shade, and protection from the *dryiny influence of air*. *This one bud* in a state of luxuriance, seated upon a young and active stock, at a point where it can receive all the ascending sap, and commanding the entire energies of the roots, must possess every advantage; and we were assured, while inspecting a set of plants so raised, that rarely one instance of failure occurred among forty or fifty operations. Another great object is gained; for not only is the success prompt and speedy, but from the position of the bud, a fine green plant is formed at once from the very surface, and if the knife be from time to time properly used, the juncture of the parts becomes so true as scarcely to be observed.

FLORICULTURAL NOTICES.

NEW AND RARE PLANTS, FIGURED IN THE LEADING BOTANICAL PERIODICALS FOR MAY.

CLASS I.—PLANTS WITH TWO COTYLEDONS (DICOTYLEDONEÆ).

THE NETTLE TRIBE (*Urticáceæ*.)

GALACTODÉNDRON ÙTILE. The Cow Tree. Figures of the leaves, wood, and fruit, the natural size, accompanied by a coloured engraving of the tree on a reduced scale, are given in the *Botanical Magazine*, p. 3723-4. To these is appended a long and most interesting account, composed partly of an extract from a work by M. de Humboldt, and partly of an original communication from Sir Robert Kerr Porter, Consul-General at La Guayra, interspersed with some remarks by Sir W. J. Hooker. Of the excellent quality of the milky juice which exudes from the bark when punctured, and its admirable adaptation to the sustenance of animal life, conclusive evidence has been afforded. It is a native of various parts of Caraccas, and grows at an elevation of nearly 3000 feet. The leaves are large and handsome, and the bark of the older branches has a peculiar yellow colour. It is imagined by the natives of the district in which it is most abundant that the tree never flowers; but Sir W. J. Hooker explains this notion by the probable fact of the flowers being exceedingly minute. The following extract from the letter of Sir R. Kerr Porter will furnish an idea of the character of this remarkable tree:—"The trunk of the *Palo de Vaca*, from which the drawing was made, measured somewhat more than twenty feet in circumference at about five feet from the root. This colossal stem ran up to a height of sixty feet, perfectly uninterrupted by either leaf or branch; when its vast arms and minor branches, most luxuriantly clothed with foliage, spread on every side, fully twenty-five or thirty feet from the trunk, and rising to an additional elevation of forty feet, so that this stupendous tree was quite a hundred feet high in all. I saw *others still larger*, but the state of the weather drove us from our position. The leaves, when in a fresh state, are of a deep dark and polished green, nearly resembling those of the laurel tribe, from ten to sixteen inches long, and two or three inches wide."

THE AMARANTH TRIBE (*Amarantdceæ*).

TRICHÍNIUM ALOPECUROÌDEUM. Foxtail Trichinium. This is a half-hardy annual species of a curious, though not very ornamental genus. Seeds of it were collected in the Swan River colony by Captain James Mangles, R.N., and it flowered in this country for the first time in the garden of R. Mangles, Esq., of Sunning Hill. The flowers, which are greenish yellow, and deeply tinged towards their summits with pale purple, are produced in long, dense, terminal spikes. They are thickly covered with long hairs, and, when faded, they incline towards the axis of the stem, presenting the appearance of a fox's tail. It is said to blossom very abundantly in the open border during the summer, and the flowers are interesting on account of their glossy hue. *Bot. Reg.* 28.

THE MINT TRIBE (*Labiàtæ*).

SÁLVIA CONFERTIFLÒRA. A really showy species of *Salvia*, with lengthened terminal spikes of rich orange-red-coloured flowers, which appear in dense whorls of less than an inch apart. It was first discovered by Mr. Macrae, near Rio Janeiro, that individual being then in the employment of the Horticultural Society. A plant was subsequently presented to that society by John Dillwyn Llewellyn, Esq., and this has flowered profusely. A house of a temperature intermediate between the stove and the greenhouse is recommended as the best situation for this plant, but it appears to thrive also in the greenhouse, or even if planted out in a rich border in the summer, and removed to some protective structure on the approach of autumn. The flowers are short and woolly, but the leaves are large, deep green, rugose, and serrated; the stem being also pleasingly marked with bright brown. *Bot. Reg.* 29.

PLANTS WITH ONE COTYLEDON (MONOCOTYLEDONEÆ).

THE ORCHIS TRIBE (*Orchidaceæ*).

LOÈLIA PURFURÀCEÆ. Scurfy-stalked Lœlia. Very nearly allied to *L. autumnalis*, which is also figured in the *Botanical Register*, p. 27, but of which a drawing is prepared for the ensuing number of this Magazine. The colours of the flowers of the present plant appear to be less brilliant and abundant, the habit being much more slender, and the pseudo-bulbs essentially different. These latter are shorter, more compressed, and rounded, and have deeper furrows. They appear also to produce only one short leaf, which is quite erect, "the petals are so much more undulated as to appear lobed; and the ovary is closely covered with black mealy glands. It would seem, moreover," adds Dr. Lindley, "that the scape does not bear more than one flower, instead of several, but of this I cannot so well judge." This species was imported by G. Barker, Esq., of Birmingham, with whom it flowered in November 1838. It was originally found by Count Karwinski, near Oaxaca, and is now supposed to be frequent in collections. Like most of its allies, it is a very beautiful plant, and requires a less degree of moisture and temperature than many other orchidaceæ. *Bot. Reg.* 26.

THE ARUM TRIBE (*Aroídeæ*).

CALÀDIUM PETIOLÀTUM. The remarkable structure of the plants of this tribe is in all cases interesting, and in the present species, combined with the striking tints, is peculiarly so. It has a long and curiously mottled stem, or petiole, surmounted by a pair of large pinnate leaves; and from its base the flower-scape arises. This latter generally attains the height of one foot, and on its summit the flower appears, enveloped in a large, rich purple, and very ornamental spathe. Tubers were first discovered by Mr. Boultbee jun., in the island of Fernando Po; these were transmitted to Joseph Boultbee, Esq., Springfield, Knowle, Birmingham, in whose stove they flowered in 1832; since which period it has blossomed in the Glasgow Botanic Garden. It usually flowers in June, and thrives best in a rich loamy soil, with a plenteous supply of water while growing. *Bot. Mag.* 3728.

NEW, RARE, OR INTERESTING PLANTS IN FLOWER IN THE PRINCIPAL SUBURBAN NURSERIES.

BORÒNIA CRENULÀTA.—A very pretty species, slightly inferior to *B. serrulata*, from which it is distinguished by its shorter, darker green, and crenated foliage, and deeper coloured flowers; these latter being also axillary and solitary, (instead of in terminal clusters), and much more expansive. It is figured in the fourth volume of this Magazine, and is now flowering most abundantly in the greenhouse of Messrs. Loddiges, Hackney. By its less straggling habit, and the stems being well covered with leaves, it is rendered very nearly equal to *B. serrulata*.

BURLINGTÒNIA VENÚSTA.—Messrs. Loddiges possess a handsome specimen of this extremely elegant and little orchidaceous plant, in flower at the present time. It grows most successfully on a piece of wood, producing its long, channelled, and deep green foliage in a similar direction on either side of the stem, this being occasionally interspersed with small, attenuated roots. The flowers are protruded in half-pendent racemes; they are numerous, comparatively large, and pure white, with a slight tinge of yellow down the centre. Its native country is Brazil.

CHORIZÈMA VÀRIA.—Decidedly the finest species of this highly interesting genus yet introduced. It has recently blossomed in great perfection at the nursery of Mr. Hally, Blackheath. In the size and brilliant colours of its flowers, it is certainly surpassed by no other species; while the leaves and habit are of a remarkably ornamental character. Growing with great rapidity and vigour, it yet maintains a symmetrical form, and the leaves are large, ovately-cordate, and liberally studded with prickles round the margins. In the hue of its blossoms, it resembles *C. ovata*.

DILLWYNNIA SPECIÒSA.—As an ornament to the greenhouse during the early spring months, this beautiful plant will doubtless be considered valuable. The abundance and density of its terminal clusters of yellow and brown flowers, contrasted with its graceful character and slender foliage, render it a most attractive object. It has been received by Messrs. Rollison and Low, from Baron Slugel of Vienna; and, in the establishments of these gentlemen, is now blooming profusely. It is eminently worthy of extensive cultivation.

GOMPHOLÒBIUM POLYMÓRPHUM.—Two charming varieties of this splendid plant, together with the original species, are expanding their flowers in the nursery of Messrs. Henderson, Pine Apple Place. They differ chiefly in the colour of their blossoms; those of the new varieties being of a much lighter hue, and one of them approaching to yellow. Though this circumstance obviously renders them less showy, they are otherwise quite as interesting as their parent, and constitute a very pleasing diversity.

PÆÒNIA PAPAVERÀCEA RÙBRA.—This superb plant is flowering simultaneously in the nurseries of Messrs. Low and Co. Clapton, and Messrs. Young, Epsom. Its principal distinguishing character is the rich purplish-red colour of the flowers, the base of the petals of which is also deeply stained with a still intenser hue. In both instances, it is kept in a greenhouse, but is most probably half hardy.

PÆÒNIA TENUIFÒLIA PLÈNA.—An almost equally splendid variety to that just noticed. It has flowers of a deep sanguineous red, and quite double. In other respects, it is similar to *P. tenuifolia*.

PECULIARITIES IN THE CULTURE OF RARE AND ORNAMENTAL PLANTS.

CLÉMATIS CŒRÙLEA and C. SIEBÓLDII. It will doubtless be generally admitted, that the two handsome plants whose names introduce the present article, are unequalled in beauty by any of their allies. Although, in the extensive genus *Clematis*, many very ornamental species are to be found, the subjects of this notice have received a greater share of popular admiration than any of those previously discovered.

To such of our readers as have yet had no opportunity of examining flowering specimens, we may refer to the figures of these species given in the fourth volume of this Magazine. These will be found both accurately delineated and faithfully coloured. Being then unacquainted with any authentic particulars respecting their cultivation, a few additional remarks—the result of subsequent observation and experience—may perhaps prove serviceable.

Many may deem it unnecessary to advert to the management of any species of *Clematis*, so obviously simple is their cultivation, and so familiar to most practical individuals. Seldom, however, do we traverse anew a beaten track; and never, unless for the elimination of obscurities, or the completion of our observations by appending some newly-acquired particulars. In the present instance, the course of culture we have seen pursued, and which we intend recommending, is not generally practised: we shall therefore escape any accusation of needless repetition or useless detail.

The species of *Clematis* now under notice, are neither of them so thoroughly hardy as to be preserved successfully with the attention bestowed on the common kinds. *C. Sieboldii* has certainly been proved capable of sustaining a considerable degree of frost; but it will nevertheless long rank as an appropriate and valuable ornament to the greenhouse. *C. cœrulea*, on the other hand, is not near so hardy; and its great scarcity, as well as the imaginary difficulties connected with its cultivation, will also operate effectually in perpetuating its confinement to the greenhouse.

We have repeatedly heard it produced as an objection to *C. cœrulea*, that it is apt to grow weak and sickly, and is likewise, while in this unhealthy state, liable to great injury, and even destruction, from ordinary moisture. Now, as this is by far the most beautiful species, and cultivators are generally open to prejudice from such reports, we are anxious confidently to affirm that such a condition can only be produced by injudicious treatment. An insufficient supply of air or light during the growing stage, or the employment of any artificial heat, would undoubtedly occasion such debility; but the prudent culturist is as anxious to ascertain and shun the cause of this evil, as he is piqued at its presence and consequences.

In the culture of *C. cœrulea*, particular care should be taken that its growth, from the commencement to its conclusion, is purely natural. Every stimulating application or circumstance must be avoided as prejudicial. Retaining it constantly in a cool house or frame, from which only the more severe frosts are excluded, the first motion of the sap in spring should be left to the excitation of solar heat, and it must be kept in a situation where the light is refracted as little as possible, and around which air can be unrestrainedly circulated at every period when its temperature and hygrometrical condition are favourable. Some caution is requisite in applying water to the roots, particularly in cloudy or misty weather, and when the plant is not growing vigorously. When both these circumstances are reversed, a gentle syringing over the leaves in the evening of the day will be of great advantage in promoting its luxuriance.

Favoured with the treatment thus imperfectly described, and potted in a slightly enriched loamy soil, somewhat elevated in the centre, we have seen specimens of this plant flourishing in extraordinary perfection, and bearing flowers of considerably more than four inches in diameter, with leaves which, for the brightness of their colour, and their peculiar vigour, surpassed all our previous and most sanguine hopes.

To *C. Sieboldii*, this minuteness of attention appears scarcely necessary, as it is not so easily injured by improper treatment. But, when it is considered that both of them are of similar habits, and that *C. cœrulea* is only more tender on account of its flowering rather earlier in the season; or, that this susceptibility has been preternaturally induced by the extrinsic conditions in which it has been kept; it will be seen that the nearer approach is made to the adoption of the above directions in the management of either of these plants, the more perfect will be their developments and production.

All plants, be they ever so hardy naturally, may be reduced to a state of tenderness by subjecting them to artificial circumstances. How much more marked therefore will be the results of such treatment, when its subject is originally only half-hardy! If *C. cœrulea* had been grown according to the principles herein set forth, instead of being rendered less hardy, as is the consequence of a contrary practice, it would most probably have been by this time capable of enduring, without shelter, any change of temperature that occurs in our climate. Nothing tends more powerfully to demonstrate this assumption, than the fact of *C. Sieboldii* being now nearly as hardy as any other exotic species.

Whether trained to the rafters or back of a greenhouse, to a trellis beneath its roof, or to a conservative wall in the open ground, both these plants have a very showy appearance for the first two or three years; but, after this time, the lower part of their stems becomes denuded, and they lose thereby much of their interest. This is equally the case with all the species of *Clematis*, and, wherever they are cultivated, they should be trained in a peculiar manner. It is of little consequence whether they be kept in a greenhouse or in the open air, provided the preceding hints on their general cultivation and the following observations on training be practised.

These kinds of climbing plants produce long straggling shoots, the newly-formed parts of which, whether terminal or lateral, alone bear flowers. To ensure a uniform distribution or a pleasing display of these flowers, the shoots must be arranged spirally round a circular, square, or triangular trellis. The two first of these forms are preferable; and they may either be affixed to the outside of a pot, or inserted in the soil, if the specimen is growing in the open ground. By this method, young shoots can easily be trained over the old ones that are bare, and a symmetrical mass of verdure and beauty will be the consequence. Each coil may be kept at about two inches from the one below it, either closer or wider if necessary. Messrs. Young, of Epsom, possess some splendid specimens, disposed in this manner, which, when in flower, are unrivalled by any other greenhouse plant with which we are acquainted; the blossoms being regularly arranged over the whole plants, from the extremities to the base.

The most common mode of propagating these species is by layers. By securing each bud of the shoot to be layered at a trifling distance below the surface of the soil, they will after a time project roots; and, by the severance of the shoot between the buds, a quantity of plants, equal to the number of buds, will be obtained.

This is, however, a tardy process. Attempts to multiply these plants by cuttings of the young and immature shoots, very frequently prove futile, as they are extremely prone to decay from damp. The most successful and expeditious method is that of grafting, in the same manner as has been recommended for Camellias. A bud or a young shoot inserted into a vigorous stock of one of the common species, will form a tolerably large specimen in an incredibly brief period; and this practice is especially deserving of universal adoption.

OPERATIONS FOR JUNE.

In the management of tender exotic plants this month, there is one point which is too frequently overlooked, but which is of the greatest importance to their maintenance in a healthy condition. We allude to the necessity of placing them at such a distance from each other, throughout their season of growth, that they may be perfectly accessible to light and air on all sides. Unless this is properly attended to, it is impossible that their developments can be of the proper consistence and strength. Cultivators are very generally accustomed to arrange their plants too closely at this season, that each specimen may afford umbrage to the roots of its neighbour, and thus tend to preserve it from drought. This, however, is an inconsistent method, by no means calculated to effect the object for which it is adopted, and peculiarly prejudicial to the plants so treated.

To carry into execution the measure above recommended, many persons remove a portion of their greenhouse, and even of their stove plants, to the open air. Those of the latter description are incalculably injured by such treatment, as the majority of them prefer a shaded house to one entirely uncovered, and consequently cannot, under any alleviating circumstances, endure the unchecked intensity of solar light. It matters not how congenial the climate may otherwise be, a great degree of light will inevitably wither or destroy their foliage, and with the loss of this, not only the beauty, but sometimes the vitality, of many species is sacrificed.

Greenhouse plants are certainly not so greatly endangered by such circumstances as those just mentioned. Still they suffer materially under a clear sky, when surrounded by an arid and burning atmosphere. This is chiefly attributable to the confined range of their roots, and their inability to imbibe and supply moisture commensurate with the extent of the abundant exhalations from all parts of the plant's surface. By planting them in the open ground, therefore, this objection would be surmounted; and by a proper selection of plants, their acquired habits would not be outraged.

Now, we would suggest, that only the sickliest and weakest specimens of those kinds which are known to affect exposed localities, should be taken from the greenhouse. In most collections there will be found a sufficient number of these to admit of the remainder being placed at proper distances, and a twofold object will thus be

gained; viz. that of affording each of these kinds of plants its requisite treatment. By retaining the healthy and more delicate sorts in the house, they will be spared many injuries to which they must necessarily be subjected in the open air; and the transplantation of the weakly ones to the flower border, will have the effect of restoring their relaxed energies, and infusing into them new luxuriance and vigour.

Cactaceous plants, particularly the Epiphyllous sorts, derive considerable advantage from summer exposure. We have recently had an opportunity of observing that those individuals who succeed best in flowering these plants, annually place them in the open air, for two or three months subsequent to the cessation of their growth. In most cases, this will cause them to assume a somewhat brownish hue, which, however, entirely forsakes them when again excited, and does not permanently detract from their appearance. The result of this system is also more than equivalent to the temporary deformity it occasions; for the flowers produced are far more splendid and profuse than those of the plants which are kept continually in the house.

The flower garden and borders being now thoroughly furnished with ornamental plants, primary attention must be bestowed upon the operation of training and supporting them. Next to the disposition of a pleasure garden, and the arrangement of the plants, nothing tends so much to embellish it as a neat and judicious method of staking each object that requires it. Amateurs, especially, are particularly neglectful of this, or perform it very unskilfully; in which last case, the aspect of the plants is decidedly worse than if they were left to grow naturally.

To render the practice of staking effectual in fulfilling the desired end, without at the same time exhibiting prominently the materials used, it is incumbent on the cultivator to apply stakes to all those plants which may be supposed to need them, at a very early period of their growth. "As the twig is bent, the bough is inclined," is an aphorism familiar to every one, and as literally true in its direct sense, as in a moral one. Upon this then every cultivator should act. By supporting a plant in its required position, when only about four or six inches high, no difficulty will be afterwards experienced in retaining it there; neither will its foliage have to be inverted or disturbed for this purpose, as is very frequently the case.

Where plants have more than one stem, each should be the subject of a separate ligature, unless they can be collectively secured, without exposing the band employed, or confining or deranging the leaves, or any portion of them. Care should always be exercised in keeping all parts of the leaves and lateral branches perfectly free, as well as in their natural position. If this particular be efficiently performed at the present time, the only other attention of the kind that will be requisite throughout the ensuing summer, will be the occasional application of an additional band of matting as the plants advance in height, or the substitution of a larger one in those instances where they increase considerably in diameter.

Lælia autumnalis.

LÆLIA AUTUMNÀLIS.
(AUTUMNAL-FLOWERING LÆLIA.)

CLASS.	ORDER.
GYNANDRIA.	MONANDRIA.

NATURAL ORDER.
ORCHIDÀCEÆ.

GENERIC CHARACTER.—*Vide* Vol. iv. p. 73.

SPECIFIC CHARACTER.—*Plant* epiphytal. *Pseudo-bulbs* ovate, terete, ribbed, attenuated towards the summit, two or three leaved. *Leaves* oblong-linear, spreading, much shorter than the flower scape. *Scape* cylindrical, bearing six or more flowers. *Bracts* oblong, membranaceous, acute. *Sepals* lanceolate, acuminate, spreading. *Petals* oblong-lanceolate, undulated. *Labellum* three-lobed, two-plated, lateral lobes erect, rounded, truncate, middle one oblong-lanceolate, reflexed at the point. *Ovarium* smooth.

One of the most charming features in orchidaceous plants, is the peculiar delicacy and transparency of their flowers. In many kinds, this is so remarkable as to present a vitreous appearance, which, in the absence of colour, might easily be mistaken for a production of art, or, if the tenuity of their texture were not so perceptible, a genuine crystallization.

Lælias, in common with Cattleyas, and some species of Dendrobium, possess this character in a distinguished degree; and amongst these, our present subject occupies a prominent station. The different members of the flowers, especially the exterior ones, such as the sepals and petals, seem to be thickly studded with minute, glassy, and shining specks, which are apparently slight indentations, and impart to them, when viewed obliquely, a most interesting and strikingly lustrous surface. These lucid and colourless spots, by being intersected with a pale blush, pink, or lilac tint, as is the case with *L. autumnalis*, in which all these shades are present, and gradually merge into each other, are exhibited more vividly, and by their contrast render the blossoms additionally attractive.

The lovely plant now figured is a native of Mexico, from whence it was received in this country a few years since. Although a great number of specimens are said to have been distributed by the Horticultural Society, it certainly at present is far from common in collections. Perhaps it is slightly inferior to *L. anceps* in the hues of its flowers, but in their mode of production and greater abundance, we deem it decidedly superior. Instead of appearing in pairs, upon a long, slender, half pendent peduncle, and widely dispersed over the plant as the flowers of the species just named, those of *L. autumnalis* are borne on erect spikes, which have from four or five to twelve and twenty blossoms on each, according to the age and strength of the specimen.

Some very judicious remarks on the cultivation of Lælias are given in the superb work of J. Bateman, Esq. on the Orchidaceæ of Mexico and Guatemala, which we here take the liberty of inserting :—" Being found at a considerable elevation, they all thrive best in a moderate temperature, and require to be high potted, as by that means the roots are more likely to be retained in a healthy state, and are better able to withstand the extremes of heat and moisture, which will sometimes occur, and which we have found excessively injurious to Lælias, Cattleyas, and species of some allied genera. In winter they should be very sparingly watered, and kept in almost a dormant state."

We obtained our drawing from a specimen which flowered in the splendid collection of Messrs. Loddiges, in the month of October 1838. As its name implies, it blossoms in the autumnal season, continuing in perfection for several weeks; it is altogether one of those truly valuable plants of which all cultivators should be possessed. We presume it may be procured from most nurserymen who grow this extraordinary and fascinating tribe.

L. anceps has been figured at page 73 of the fourth volume of our Magazine. By comparing that figure with the above woodcut of *L. autumnalis*, the difference in habit will be seen.

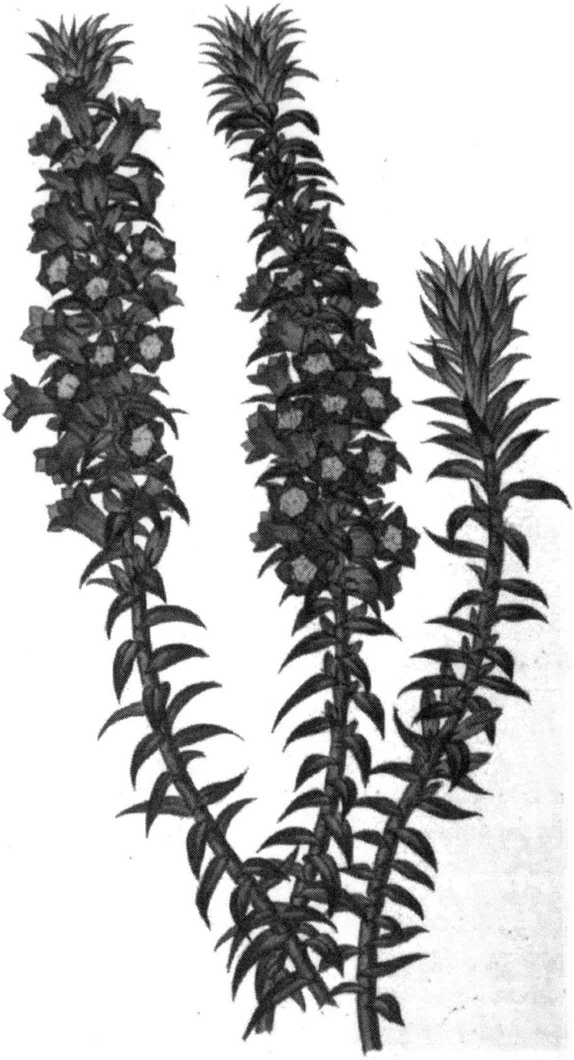

EPÁCRIS COCCÍNEUS.

(SCARLET-FLOWERED EPACRIS.)

CLASS.
PENTANDRIA.

ORDER.
MONOGYNIA.

NATURAL ORDER.
EPACRIDACEÆ.

GENERIC CHARACTER.—*Vide* vol. i. p. 52.

SPECIFIC CHARACTER.—*Plant* a shrub, usually growing from eighteen inches to two feet high. *Stem* roundish, erect, branching. *Leaves* ovate-lanceolate, pungent, sessile, thickly-set, somewhat recurved. *Corolla* shortly campanulate, expanding into five short, broad, acute segments; deep scarlet. *Stamens* situated round the mouth of the corolla. *Anthers* yellow, distinctly visible.

To a genus like Epacris, the species of which are so highly valued, both for their graceful beauty and the early period at which they flower, the addition of any novelty, from whatever source, must be considered as a boon by all the lovers of exotic floriculture. No striking deviation in form or habit from the species and varieties at present known would, we conceive, be so acceptable as a species with blossoms of a more brilliant and showy colour, and a correct drawing of such a plant we have now to introduce to our readers.

The subject of this figure has been before noticed by us as a seedling raised in the garden of Alderman Copeland, Leyton, Essex, under the management of Mr. Kynoch. It flowered in the collection of that gentleman in the early part of the present year, and was then purchased by Messrs. Low and Co., of Clapton, in whose establishment we were favoured, towards the conclusion of last February, with an opportunity of obtaining the annexed plate.

Since that time, a variety of *E. impressa* has been figured in the Botanical Register, with the remarks accompanying which, Dr. Lindley furnishes an extract from a communication of Mr. Gunn, a respectable traveller and botanist in New Holland, the purport of which is, that seedling Epacrises vary so considerably in colour in their native districts, that it is impossible to establish specific distinctions, or even varieties, upon the hue of the flowers alone. Were we to act in accordance with this statement, we should be constrained to consider our plant a mere casual departure from the usual colour of *E. impressa*. In bestowing upon it a specific designation, therefore, we are bound to declare upon what we believe its claims to that position to rest.

Specific names are obviously and confessedly given for the purpose of distinguishing certain allied plants from all others of the same genus. As far as we are aware, no characters essential to constitute a species are recognized, and we might bring forward almost numberless instances in which the colour of the flowers of plants denominated species alone entitles them to that rank. If it be said that *E. coccineus* will not reproduce plants of a similar colour from seeds, the same may be urged against *E. impressa*, and probably many others, not to mention species of other genera. Assured, then, that no *Epacris* has ever before been seen in this country with flowers similar to the present, and that the colour is so very distinct as well as so imposing, we unhesitatingly deem it worthy of the situation to which it is here elevated.

Besides the colour of the blossoms, this species differs from *E. impressa* in its stronger and more luxuriant habit, in its denser and larger foliage, in the corolla being much shorter, more truly campanulate, and having smaller, broader, and less acuminate segments, and in the flowers protruding themselves either horizontally or in a partially erect position.

The cultivation of Epacrises has been repeatedly discussed in this Magazine, and we need only refer to former volumes for all needful information on this point. It may suffice here to state that they should be managed precisely as Cape Heaths, not requiring a rich soil, but perfect drainage and a good supply of water. They are less liable to be destroyed by bad treatment than Heaths, but the careful culturist is always liberally rewarded by a more dense and charming profusion of flowers.

Tweedia caerulea.

TWEÈDIA CŒRÙLEA.

(LIGHT BLUE-FLOWERED TWEEDIA.)

CLASS.
PENTANDRIA.

ORDER.
DIGYNIA.

NATURAL ORDER.
ASCLEPIADÀCEÆ.

GENERIC CHARACTER.—*Calyx* five-parted. *Corolla* campanulate, throat crowned. *Petals* five, fleshy, retuse or bifid, exserted. *Crown of stamens* none. *Anthers* terminated by a membrane. *Pollen-masses* ventricose, adhering by the summit, attenuated, pendulous. *Stigma* elongated, acuminate, two-parted.

SPECIFIC CHARACTER.—*Plant* densely clothed with downy white hairs. *Root* perennial. *Stems* twining, herbaceous, filiform, nearly simple, varying from a foot to three feet high. *Leaves* opposite, stalked, cordate-lanceolate, mucronulate, entire, even, about an inch and a-half long, and half an inch broad; posterior lobes rounded, connivent, frequently overlapping each other. *Inflorescence* interpetiolary, composed of three or five-flowered umbels. *Pedicels* filiform, about three inches long, densely hairy. *Petioles* short, semicylindrical, woolly. *Calyx* five-partite; segments lanceolate, acuminate, interiorly glabrous. *Corolla* rotate, five-partite, blue, the base furnished with five nectariferous cavities; segments elliptical oblong, obtuse, densely hairy beneath, nearly glabrous above. *Corona* simple, five-leaved; segments ligulate, obtuse, fleshy, about half the length of the corolla, revolute at the apex. *Stamens* five, monadelphous. *Filaments* membranous, white. *Anthers* yellow, crowned by a broad, oval, retuse, membranous appendage. *Pollen-masses* clavate, compressed, amber-coloured, pendulous; each of the pedicels furnished with a sharp recurved tooth. *Gland* linear, obtuse, erect, channelled exteriorly, of a dark chocolate colour, glossy, longer than the pollen-masses. *Ovaria* two, smooth, ventricose. *Styles* shorter than the ovaria. *Stigmas* compressed, acute.—*Don's British Flower Garden*, t. 407.

THIS handsome climbing shrub was first discovered by Mr. Tweedie, in Buenos Ayres, and seeds of it were sent by that gentleman to Scotland, the plants raised from which flowered in several collections in the vicinity of Edinburgh and Glasgow in 1836. It is yet scarce in English gardens, although its merits are sufficient to obtain for it a very extensive dispersion. The extreme caution of cultivators has, however, by keeping it in too high a temperature, prevented it from exhibiting hitherto its true character.

Perhaps no plant loses more of its beauty by confinement in a stove, greenhouse, or intermediate house, than *Tweedia cœrulea*. In the first and last-named of these structures, especially, the colour of its flowers is deteriorated to a pale bluish grey; and those who have only seen it in such situations, would be perfectly justified in regarding it as a plant of little value. But, when transplanted to the open border in the summer months, and trained to a detached trellis, a pole, or a wall, the blossoms assume a most lively azurean hue; and, being exceedingly numerous, produce a highly ornamental effect.

From these declarations, it will be seen that summer exposure is the most appropriate treatment which this plant can receive. Indeed, it is quite essential to the proper development of its natural characteristics, and its investiture with sufficient interest to render it deserving of general cultivation. As this mode of culture is likewise the most convenient, and attended with the least amount of trouble, another cogent reason is afforded in favour of its universal adoption.

Specimens of this species may be planted at the base of pillars, pedestals, or any kind of trellises, about the beginning of the month of June; and here they should either be protected during the following winter, or pruned and removed to a greenhouse towards the decline of autumn. Trained against a conservative wall, where it can be effectively preserved from winter winds and frosts, *T. coerulea* would form an attractive feature, and doubtless thrive with great vigour, as well as blossom abundantly. Little danger could attend this management, as, if the shoots were annually destroyed, new branches would be formed at the commencement of each succeeding year. It has usually been considered an herbaceous plant; but, as we are assured that it exhibits a shrubby habit when kept in a stove, it is most probably a decided shrub.

Its propagation is easily effected by cuttings of the young shoots, and large specimens may perchance produce seeds; but we have not yet seen the latter supposition realized.

The plant from which we procured our drawing bloomed in the nursery of Messrs. Rollison, Tooting, in October, 1838. It is again flowering at the present time in the same collection. We believe the months of July and August to be its natural flowering season.

Professor Don states that the genus *Tweedia* is nearly allied to *Sarcostemma*, being principally distinguished by the absence of the exterior crown, by the form and length of the pollen gland, and by the presence of a tooth to each of the pedicels. It was named after Mr. James Tweedie, by whom, as before stated, it was originally found, and transmitted to this country.

Lilium aurantiacum.

LILIUM AURANTIACUM.
(ORANGE-COLOURED JAPAN LILY.)

CLASS.	ORDER.
HEXANDRIA.	MONOGYNIA.

NATURAL ORDER.
LILIACEÆ.

GENERIC CHARACTER.—*Vide* vol. v. p. 1.

SPECIFIC CHARACTER.—*Plant* bulbous, growing about three feet in height. *Stem* erect, roundish, smooth. *Leaves* oblong, lanceolate, acute. *Perianth* composed of six broadly oblong, acute segments, deep orange-red, liberally striated. *Stamens* dark brown. *Ovarium* oblong, three-ribbed, pale green.

From the earliest ages, lilies have been assigned an exalted rank among herbaceous plants, and there has been a species of rivalry between the admirers of the Lily and the Rose, as to which of these favourites is entitled to the distinguished designation of the floral queen. A very worthy and eminent poet has, however, endeavoured to adjust the matter by awarding to each of them a regal crown, considering most truly that their beauties, when associated, and exhibited in harmonious opposition, respectively shine out the more conspicuously.

Lilies are generally remarkable for their stately aspect, and, in the case of the common species, (*L. candidum,*) the subject of the contest above mentioned, as well as some other similar ones, for the stainless purity of their noble white flowers. In the last volume of this Magazine, we figured two extraordinarily beautiful sorts, introduced to Europe by Dr. Siebold, from Japan. The plant here represented was obtained from the same source by the gentleman just alluded to; and though much less showy than either of those to which we have referred, it will be received as a welcome addition to the rich store already collected in this country.

The only plant of this species we have yet had an opportunity of seeing in flower, produced two comparatively feeble blossoms in the nursery of Messrs. Young, Epsom, during the summer of last year. From this our figure was taken, in the month of July. As the plant was confined to the greenhouse, and in a pot, being at the same time of weakly habit, it may justly be supposed susceptible of great improvement under more generous treatment. Nevertheless, the flowers were, with all these detracting circumstances, highly ornamental, presenting a delicacy of colour and texture really admirable.

Little doubt can now be entertained of the capability of the Japan Lilies for existing in the open ground, if properly sheltered in the winter; and still less can it be questioned that such a situation would be perfectly congenial. The tendency they manifest, when kept in a house, to commence their growth so early in the season, would be overruled by the natural coldness of the external soil and atmosphere, as such early excitation is obviously occasioned by the artificial temperature of these media in all plant structures. This, therefore, need not be considered an impediment to their more decided naturalization. Besides, a hand-glass would be alone sufficient to preserve them from spring frosts, and this could very easily be furnished.

We are the more urgent in our recommendation to adopt this mode of treatment, because fully convinced of its appropriateness. Lilies, by being naturally dormant in the winter, and having no part of their substance exposed to the action of frost, are far from yielding so readily to injury as shrubs, or even fibrous-rooted herbaceous plants. They are likewise much more conveniently protected, because the spot they occupy might be covered with a close wooden case, without depriving them of any of the influences necessary to their health. Indeed, a covering of the description here suggested would be the most suitable, as it would exclude both wet and frost; the absence of the former always being a more effectual barrier to cold.

An excellent method of propagating these plants, has been described in Vol. V. p. 273. We witnessed, last year, the performance of an experiment for increasing Lilies, adopted simultaneously in two celebrated nursery establishments, which was conducted with the view of inducing the emission of buds or bulbs from the axils of the leaves. The plants operated upon were *L. speciosa*, and *L. aurantiacum;* but although every necessary attention was bestowed, it utterly failed in both instances. This is mentioned, partly to eulogize the ingenuity displayed in the execution of these processes, and particularly to apprize our readers of the futility of making similar attempts.

We refer to Vol. V. p. 2, for the origin of the generic name.

BOTANICAL CLASSIFICATION.

The science of botany is naturally separable into two departments; the one comprising the physiological and functional processes and products of plants, the other arranging and classifying them according to their structural affinities. It requires no ingenuity to show that the former of these is immeasurably the more interesting and useful; and that an acquaintance with the latter, obtained only from the names and superficial appearance of the more prominent organs of vegetation, is little better than a knowledge of the simple alphabet of a language, without the capacity for understanding the meaning of the letters when connected into words and sentences.

If it be asked, What then is the real utility of botanical systems?—the answer is easy. The present age is notoriously a systematizing one. Its laws, its agricultural, commercial, and financial polity, its education, its very literature, are all valued or despised, successful or abortive, in the attainment of their ultimate design, as they develop a certain degree of natural order and arrangement. This is especially the case with sciences. By collecting into groups those objects which bear the nearest resemblance to each other, by again uniting these groups to such as assimilate most closely to them in character, an unbroken chain is formed, by which the student may proceed from link to link in the examination and comprehension of the whole, or at once discover any desired subject, on referring to the division wherein its characteristics are embodied.

Let us not be mistaken, however, to imply that the study of systematic botany should be preliminary to the acquirement of some knowledge of the common mechanism of the organs and offices of plants. This latter is indispensable to the most consummate tyro in botanical classification; for unless the structure of a plant is understood, no system in which the peculiar features of that structure form the distinguishing characters, can possibly be otherwise than abstruse and unintelligible. We are aware that the course here advocated is contrary to the general practice, but are nevertheless satisfied of its propriety.

Various arrangements have been successively devised by the greatest masters of botany, and these, as in most other sciences, have generally been modifications or improvements of those which preceded them. Only two at present survive,—the Linnæan and Jussieuan,—respectively founded by the individuals whose names they bear. Of these, the former may be considered as almost exploded, since nearly all the most distinguished botanists of Europe have avowedly renounced it. It is still retained by a few individuals, who value it solely on account of its simplicity, and the facility with which it may be acquired.

From the classification of Jussieu being disposed according to the natural affinities of plants, it has received the designation of the Natural System, and several recent changes in its arrangement have given a colouring of justice and meetness to this title. Botanists of the Linnæan school vehemently affirm that it is an inapplicable epithet; while its advocates, admitting that the system has yet numerous anomalies and defects, explain its appellation relatively to the arrangement of Linnæus.

In laying the foundation of some future remarks on the Natural Orders, it may be well to state the advantages of either system. By the Linnæan method, vegetation, as all our readers are probably aware, is divided into twenty-four prominent Classes, these being subdivided into an irregular number of Orders. The Classes (excepting the twenty-fourth, which is comprised of flowerless plants) are founded on the number and position of the stamens, and the presence or absence of the other sexual organs: the Orders represent the number of pistils, up to the nineteenth Class, the divisions of which are more purely natural; and those of the remaining Classes, (excluding the twenty-fourth) are distinguished, some by the number of stamens, others by peculiarities in the disposition of stamens and pistils. This, then, is a fair outline of the system. It has no details, unless it be the enumeration of genera and species, which are arbitrarily and desultorily composed; and its basis may be comprehended at a single glance.

Far different is the case with regard to the Natural arrangement. It is complex in its nature, abounds with explanatory particulars, and requires considerable exertion to grasp and remember its numerous and comprehensive divisions. But when thoroughly known and understood, the student has the whole vegetable kingdom within his power, and may at once satisfactorily assign any plant its peculiar and distinguishing properties. Its characters are not illusory, because minute, permanent, and invariable; the object of research may immediately be traced to its proper position: the reverse of which is amongst the most glaring defects of the system of Linnæus. The opposition to the Natural method may therefore appropriately be stigmatised as an array of indolence against industry.

We are far from desiring the abolition or disparagement of the arrangement of the immortal Linnæus. Let it still exist for those who wish to profess a rudimental knowledge of botany, without ever penetrating deeper than the examination of the few organs on which that classification is founded. It is an admirable stepping-stone; but, if the student who attains this position do not feel desirous of advancing higher in the scale of information, the inference is natural that he has not even mastered the elements of the science; for it is one of its distinctive characters to impart an eager desire for further acquisitions, which is never satisfied till its extreme boundaries are fully explored.

It is much to be feared that the existing antipathy to the Natural method, arises chiefly from the prevailing ignorance of structural botany. Were young gardeners and botanical students better informed on that subject, the mastery of this system would only be a question of memory. The titles of its various orders are nearly all modifications of the names of one of the principal genera of which each is constituted; their essential characters may be easily remembered by connecting them with the most peculiar or extraordinary plant which they contain; and the properties of the genera compiling them may likewise be impressed upon the mind in a similar manner, by associating them with the species in which they are most perceptible.

Considering the universal, nay instinctive, love of natural order which exists among mankind, it is really astonishing that any attempts should be made to check the progress of a botanical system, of which that is the most remarkable recommendation. What would be thought of a valuable narrative, the events of which were connected only by the similarity of one or two of their features, without any regard to the period of their occurrence, or their relative position towards each other? We may reasonably infer that every person of sense would discard and contemn it; while the individual who undertook and accomplished its proper arrangement, would be regarded with respect and honour. Analogous to this, was the classification of Linnæus. The greater part of the plants composing his Orders have no real relation to each other, while the Classes are of course still more heterogeneous. How, therefore, the obloquy that has been heaped on those who have defended, elucidated, and improved the system of Jussieu, can be reconciled with the rational feelings of mankind generally, we are at a loss to divine. It is certain that future ages, at least, will appreciate their labours, and we cannot but hope that the present will evince a greater disposition to avail themselves of their results.

After the declaration we have already made, that the study of structural botany must precede any efforts to compass the Natural system, our object in the future attempts we may make to simplify this method, cannot be misapprehended. A loose acquaintance with the organs of plants, affords nothing more than a general idea of their functions; to obtain, therefore, an insight into their more particular and individual nature and offices, or to illustrate and confirm the description of their ordinary organization propounded in botanical works, the species must be examined; and to effect this easily, some classification is necessary. The Natural system can alone impart these requisite facilities; and in furnishing the means for research, it very generally supplies likewise the object of that investigation; thus fulfilling much more useful ends than any other arrangement has the slightest pretensions to accomplish.

To present the non-professional portion of our readers with an opportunity of obtaining a knowledge of this system, without encountering unaided its technical difficulties, or wading through the tedious formulæ of botanical publications, we propose occasionally to insert articles explanatory of its basis, principal divisions, and most extensive or interesting orders. In effecting this, we shall illustrate our subject by the most characteristic or familiar plants, and endeavour to divest the science of those impediments to its study that present themselves in the form of scientific details, which, to the uninitiated, are so intricate and inexplicable.

INFLUENCE OF CLIMATE ON PLANTS.*
SOLAR HEAT.

Connected with the growth of plants, and constituting, in fact, an epoch thereof, is the development of their blossoms, and the formation and maturation of their fruit and seed. Heat is essential to the due performance of these functions, especially of the latter, and hence it is that many exotic plants seldom, in this country, produce flowers; the temperature being inadequate, or not sufficiently uniform and continuous.

Various modes of accounting for the infertility of plants have been adopted by different authors, among which, a consideration of the quality of the soil appears to have obtained a prominent place. There can be no doubt that soil exercises a considerable influence on vegetable production; but it seems to have been forgotten that, unless possessing peculiar properties, it is not so much the chemical composition, as the capacity for the retention or circulation of fluids, which renders it inimical or congenial. The importance of light in promoting fertility has before been insisted on; this agent is, however, chiefly requisite for the plants of temperate climates, as the majority of tropical species do not luxuriate beneath the immediate beams of the sun, but have shade afforded them either by surrounding vegetation, or the dense vapour of the superincumbent atmosphere.

Moisture is so intimately concerned with heat in the elaboration and development of the fruitful organs, the degree of each being increased by the absence of the other, and diminished by its presence, that it is absolutely necessary (though contrary to the plan we have proposed to ourselves) to notice the reciprocal operation of both these agents in the present place. We shall not attempt to investigate the different members of flowers, or the manner in which they are formed, but merely state the conditions most favourable to their production. On the former point, physiologists promulge such extremely diverse hypotheses, that the unsophisticated inquirer after truth feels himself strangely confounded and perplexed by perusing the works of antagonist authors.

That flowers are distinct organs, fulfilling definite and necessary offices, appears indisputable. Like all other parts of a plant, they are, however, subject to remarkable changes, according to particular circumstances, and their development is also determined by atmospheric conditions. It is by neglecting to consider, compare, and associate these very palpable positions, or by regarding either of them too exclusively, to the virtual suppression of the other, that the differences of physiological writers on this question have been occasioned.

Growth, and the production of seminal organs, are obviously different processes, and require individually the application of particular agents, or, more strictly

* Continued from page 110.

speaking, a special comparative amount of agency, to render them of a proper character. Without reference to the actual degree requisite for any species, we may state generally that heat, and a copious supply of moisture, will induce a vigorous growth; while a considerably greater relative proportion of heat is necessary for promoting floral developments. It is upon this point that practical men have generally become confused, and stumbled. Being unable to account for the non-development of flowers in otherwise favourable seasons, they have assumed that a period of repose is necessary to consummate and elaborate the embryo fructiferous organs in the year antecedent to that in which they are evolved; the facts of the case being that either the temperature was too low, or moisture too abundant, to admit of maturation being fully performed.

A very luxuriant growth is adverse to the protrusion of flowers, solely because the supply of nutrimental fluids is, in such instances, invariably greater, in proportion, than the degree of heat which attends it. For this reason, the summer immediately succeeding a warm and rather dry one, is always characterized by a fine display of flowers, and an abundant crop of fruit. On the other hand, cold and moist, or even warm and wet seasons, are as certainly and uniformly followed by partial barrenness; because the nucleus for the ensuing year is not sufficiently perfected for the exercise of the fructiferous functions.

In support of the statements we have advanced, several facts, of frequent occurrence, may be adduced. It is an exceedingly common practice in the cultivation of fruit-trees, when their growth is too exuberant, to deprive them of a portion of their roots. This is done professedly with the object of checking their luxuriance, and rendering them more stunted; the latter state being considered the most fruitful. The good consequences resulting from such treatment consist in the imbibition of much less moisture, and a contracted, but especially a *more mature* development; since an equal intensity of solar influence is exerted on the restricted as on the abundant accretions.

On the same principle, annual plants, and nearly all kinds of fruit-bearing trees, are subjected to the process of transplantation. The loss of roots which inevitably accompanies this operation, by suspending, or considerably reducing the absorption of moisture, ensures such an extreme elaboration and induration of what sap is imbibed, that flowers, seeds, or fruits, are ultimately produced more speedily, and in much greater liberality.

The experienced cultivator of exotic plants will likewise be familiar with many instances in which all attempts to flower them have proved futile, until he has adopted the course of withholding water. We refer principally to such as are grown in a lower temperature than they naturally enjoy; as a greater degree of heat is in all cases equivalent to the application of a less quantity of water; and, therefore, this peculiar management is unnecessary if sufficient heat be present.

Those exotics which are grown in the open air of this country, frequently remain for many years without flowering; and this period is always more prolonged in proportion to the higher temperature of their native climes. Still more rarely do plants from such regions ripen their seeds or fruit: the flowers, when they do appear, generally being abortive. This is unquestionably owing to the want of a due degree of heat to evaporate their unnecessary inhalations, and mature their young shoots. The judicious culturist will, however, in some measure supply this lack of temperature, by modifying and diminishing the communication of moisture. If only a sufficient quantity of water is administered, or allowed to be received, to enable them, with the existing degree of temperature, to harden and partially desiccate their annual growth, there will never be any scarcity of flowers after they have attained a proper age and size.

Flowers and fruits appear to be not only the means which Nature has provided for maintaining and increasing the species, but, by assisting materially in abstracting the aqueous fluids of perennial plants, they prepare them for resuming a similar office in the next season. This is clearly proved by the circumstance of exotic plants continuing to blossom annually after they have once been induced so to do, provided external conditions remain suitable. An extraordinary profusion of flowers may, and does, by engrossing too large a quantity of sap, diminish fertility in the subsequent year; an insufficiency of pulp leaving the young shoots in a similar state to that caused by a superabundance of fluids—immaturity. But this extreme degree of exhaustion operates very transiently, as the plant becomes equally prolific after the lapse of another season, if auspicious for the particular kind of maturation required.

Reasoning from similar premises, it is highly probable that seeds, especially those of annuals, will vegetate and fulfil the cycle of their destined offices much sooner, with greater certainty, and with less superfluous development of leaves and branches, if obtained from the plants which yield a great number of seeds, and from which, consequently, they are sparingly supplied with fluids; than from such as grow rankly and luxuriantly, at the expense of flowers and seed. Independently of its being an axiom in vegetable physiology, that the peculiar characteristics of a plant are transmitted to its progeny, there are cogent reasons, derivable from analogy, why this supposition should prove well-founded; one of the chief of which is, that seeds, when, by keeping, they lose part of their constituent moisture, are rendered more immediately and profusely productive. If, therefore, as in the case above cited, this desiccation can be performed naturally, while the seeds are attached to their parent plant, it follows that the consequence will be in all respects similar, and yet more satisfactory. The question is certainly deserving of the strictest investigation.

(*To be continued.*)

BOTANICAL EXPEDITION TO NORTH AMERICA.

MELANCHOLY LOSS OF THE COLLECTORS, MESSRS. WALLACE AND BANKS.

Probably many of our readers remain yet unaware that a mission, for the exploration of an extensive district on the North-West Coast of North America, with a view to the discovery of new botanical treasures, and the enrichment of British collections with the seeds of the rarer kinds of those already obtained from that country, was instituted by subscription in the early part of the last year; two young men being then deputed from Chatsworth to the arduous, and as the event has but too painfully proved, perilous undertaking.

Conceiving that much of the ground traversed by the late Mr. Douglas, with other land on which no English botanist has hitherto planted foot, presented an inviting and prolific field for research; and impressed with the incalculable importance to British arboriculture, and British interests generally, of an extensive accession of valuable forest trees, as well as with the great desirableness of acquiring any other kinds of ornamental plants which, procured from such latitudes, must eventually prove hardy here; we were induced to design an expedition to those regions, the expenses and proceeds of which were to be shared by a select number of subscribers. This project, upon being promulged in November 1837, was immediately countenanced and supported by all the more influential and distinguished patrons of horticulture, to whom application was made.

Under these auspices, and having in great kindness and confidence the whole conduct of the proceedings intrusted to ourselves, we selected and prepared two intelligent, active, and enterprising young men (names; Robert Wallace and Peter Banks) from the gardens at Chatsworth, who left London in one of the Honourable Hudson's Bay Company's vessels for New York, in March 1838, carrying with them every requisite and comfort for their voyage, and every facility for the promotion, as agreeably and successfully as possible, of the objects of their subsequent tour.

We may embrace this occasion to declare publicly, the handsome manner in which the gentlemen officially connected with the Hudson's Bay Company afforded every assistance in their power towards the accomplishment of our enterprise. At all times ready to sanction and further any measure tending to the advancement of science, these gentlemen have manifested a disposition to advance the ends of this expedition which is beyond all praise. We need only cite the following letter of introduction, furnished to its unfortunate members by the governor here, and which we must also state was fulfilled to the last, in its spirit as well as to the letter, by the gentlemen to whom it was addressed, to convey a better idea of their munificent behaviour than any language we can employ.

"*To James Keith, Esq., and the Gentlemen in charge of the District Posts in the Hudson's Bay Company's service.*

GENTLEMEN,—Mr. Banks and Mr. Wallace proceed to Canada, and from thence by the Company's craft to Fort Vancouver, for the purpose of collecting seeds and plants. The Governor and Committee feel much interested in the object of their mission, which is patronised by several persons of high distinction in this country. I have therefore to request that every assistance and facility that may be required by Mr. Wallace and Mr. Banks, towards the accomplishment of the object in view, be afforded them. From La Chine they are to proceed with the Brigade to Norway House, and to be provided with tent, bedding, &c. &c., and to mess, on the voyage and at the establishments, at the officers' tables on the route. And wherever they may be they are to have any supplies they may require, and assistance in men, craft, and horses, in any excursion they may wish to make, within the range of the Company's districts or hunting grounds. Any seeds they may wish to send over-land, are to be conveyed to York Factory; and should they wish to separate at Vancouver, the one to proceed coastwise, and the other to accompany any of our trapping expeditions to the southward, the necessary accommodation is to be afforded them. All necessaries and supplies that may be furnished them are to be charged to the account of Mr. Joseph Paxton, at the usual sale prices, as per the Company's Servants' Tariff. Horses are to be furnished them at the same charge, and the wages of any servants they may require. In short, there is to be an account opened for them in the name of Joseph Paxton, at any establishment where they may require supplies, to which will be charged whatsoever may be furnished them, except for their maintenance while at the establishments, for which no charge is to be made. And I have to beg that they may be treated with every kind attention and hospitality, and that every assistance and facility be afforded them. With esteem, I remain, &c.,

H. SIMPSON.

HUDSON's BAY HOUSE,
London, 12th March, 1838."

Upon the arrival of Messrs. Wallace and Banks in New York, they proceeded by various modes of conveyance, to Montreal; and from thence reached La Chine, a short distance from the last named town, on the 27th of April, 1838. Here they were detained by the ice till the 2nd of the following May, of which opportunity they availed themselves to write home, detailing their journeyings and notifying their safe arrival thus far, testifying to the kindly reception and attentions they experienced, and stating their enjoyment, after recovery from sea-sickness, of "the best of health." On the above day they commenced their route to the Columbia River, and the last letters received from them were dated Norway House (a station of the Hudson's Bay Company referred to by Governor Simpson), July 20th; by which epistles they appear to have been absorbed in the necessary arrangements, and indulging a sanguine anticipation of reaping "a most glorious harvest."

They left this post a few days afterwards, and had descended a considerable distance down the Columbia River, when on the 22nd of October the distressing event occurred which arrested for ever their hopes and exertions, ere they had attained the sphere of their researches. It is thus alluded to in a communication to the authorities of the Hudson's Bay Company, from, we presume, their resident officer at Fort Vancouver, and dated 7th of November, 1838.

"In my letter of the 4th instant, I mentioned the arrival at this place of Chief Trader Tod with a detachment of the York Factory recruits, and noticed the cause which had made it necessary for him to leave the bulk of the party behind.

"A boat which Mr. Tod had sent back from the Upper Columbia Lake left the boat encampment on the 22nd of October, with the last of the party. In the evening of the same day, when running one of the rapids below Dalles des Morts, the boat unfortunately filled, and the following persons perished in attempting to gain the shore.

Mr. and Mrs. Wallace, } Botanists.
Mr. Banks,

Mr. Leblanc and his three children, Keneth M'Donald,
Fabien Vital, J. Bapt. Laliberté, and two children } In the Company's service.
of André Chalifoux,

In all, twelve persons, who have travelled from their distant homes to find an untimely grave beneath the raging waters of the Columbia."

Within a few days' journey of their destination, in perfect health and excellent spirits, these two zealous and qualified individuals were on the point of engaging in efforts, which might have entailed immortal honour on their names, and lasting benefits on their native land, when they were suddenly consigned to a watery sepulchre; Providence thus defeating the scheme on the very threshold of its realization, by a casualty which no human prudence could have foreseen or averted.

It need scarcely be stated, that on account of the expeditious manner of their travel, and the districts through which they passed having been previously rifled of their botanical novelties, they had been able to procure nothing worthy of transmission to Britain.

When time has in some measure allayed the sorrow and disappointment occasioned by this grievous catastrophe, and the affairs connected with the expedition have been fully investigated and adjusted, it will remain for decision whether another attempt to prosecute the design to which these young men have so haplessly fallen victims, shall be hereafter ventured on.

FLORICULTURAL NOTICES.

NEW AND RARE PLANTS, FIGURED IN THE LEADING BOTANICAL PERIODICALS FOR JUNE.

CLASS I.—PLANTS WITH TWO COTYLEDONS (DICOTYLEDONEÆ).

THE CROWFOOT TRIBE (*Ranunculàceæ*).

PÆÒNIA BRÒWNII. Douglas's Californian Pæony. Possessing more attractions for the botanist than the general cultivator, this curious species is yet not altogether unornamental. It is a hardy perennial herbaceous plant, growing about a foot high, with luxuriant foliage, and comparatively small solitary flowers, the chief beauty of which resides in the rich red colour of their disk, and the large, densely-set, yellow stamens encircling five green and prominent carpels. Dr. Lindley mentions it as a novel instance of a *Pæonia* being found in America, this genus having hitherto been supposed to be restricted to the old world. It was first discovered by the late Mr. Douglas "near the limits of perpetual snow, on the sub-alpine range of Mount Hood in North-west America; according to Torrey and Gray it was met with (subsequently) by Nuttall, east of the Blue Mountains of Oregon, not in subalpine situations." It flowers in May, and is treated as the other species. *Bot. Reg.* 30.

THE BEAN TRIBE (*Leguminòsæ*).

LUPÌNUS HARTWÉGII. Mr. Hartweg's Lupin. One of the finest and most handsome Lupins that we have yet seen. With a very robust habit, and attaining generally the height of two or three feet, it produces a long spike of brilliant blue blossoms, equal in splendour to the most showy of its kind. The whole plant appears to be peculiarly hairy, the leaves obtuse, and, in the younger stages of the flowers, they are furnished at their base with attenuated, hairy bracts, more than an inch in length. Mr. Hartweg, botanical collector to the Horticultural Society, found this valuable plant growing in corn-fields, in the Mexican territory, and forwarded seeds to the Society just named, by whom they have been distributed. Being a half-hardy annual, it requires to be sown in heat, and managed artificially till the season permits of its plantation in the open border. *Bot. Reg.* 31.

THE SYRINGA TRIBE (*Philadelphàceæ*).

PHILADÉLPHUS GORDONIÀNUS. Mr. Gordon's Philadelphus. Like most other plants of this genus, the present species has white blossoms, but these are large, exceedingly profuse, and, relieved as they are by the deep green foliage, highly interesting. They are said to lack that peculiar odour, to some persons productive of such unpleasant sensations, which characterizes the rest of the species; being, as Dr. Lindley observes, "nearly scentless." " It is readily known by its small deeply serrated leaves, its nearly superior fruit, its broad-spreading calyx, and by the compact manner in which its flowers are arranged." This is one of the many plants introduced by Mr. Douglas to the gardens of the Horticultural Society; that individual having found it growing on the banks of the Columbia River. On account of its late season of flowering, and the number and size of its blossoms, it is probably the best species known in this country. *Bot. Reg.* 32.

CLASS II.—PLANTS WITH ONE COTYLEDON (MONOCOTYLEDONEÆ).

THE LILY TRIBE (*Liliàceæ*).

BÈSSERA ÉLÈGANS. Elegant Bessera. A singularly beautiful little bulbous plant, a native of Mexico. It was first sent to Britain by John Parkinson, Esq.,

H. B. M.'s Consul in Mexico, and has flowered in the garden of J. Rogers, jun., Esq., of Sevenoaks. It is described as having two leaves of "two feet long, cylindrical, with a furrow on one side, deep green, not glaucous, and about twice as thick as the scape, which is two feet high." The flowers are produced in a terminal cluster, depending very gracefully on all sides from the extremity of the stem; they are bright scarlet on the outside, and whitish within, the stamens being dark green, and forming a cup at their base, which is much serrated. It is an extremely elegant plant, and will probably succeed well with the treatment generally given to Cape bulbs. *Bot. Reg.* 34.

THE ORCHIS TRIBE (*Orchidaceæ*).

ÈRIA FERRUGÍNEA. Rusty Eria. Imported by Messrs. Loddiges from Calcutta, and blossomed for the first time in the orchidaceous house of those gentlemen, in March 1838. The singular coating of thick, shaggy, brown hair which clothes the exterior of the flowers, is its most remarkable character; these members being otherwise very prettily blotched with pink in the inside. Its large and dark green foliage contributes to render it handsome, and it is certainly not one of the least interesting of the tribe. We recently saw it flowering at Messrs. Loddiges under the name of *E. callosa*. *Bot. Reg.* 35.

SCHOMBÚRGKIA MARGINÀTA. This splendid species of a new and highly valuable genus was figured by Dr. Lindley in his *Sertum Orchidaceum*, Part III.; and a handsome variety now appears in the *Botanical Magazine*. The latter differs in having no parti-coloured margin to the flowers, and, as would appear, in this particular alone. It has long been known in collections by the designation of "Spread Eagle," and has, at length, displayed its flowers in the collection of Thomas Brocklehurst, Esq., of the Fence, Manchester. These prove to be of a deep orange-red colour, with a pale lilac labellum, and are very showy. The specimen was obtained from Surinam, and bloomed in December 1838. *Bot. Mag.* 3729.

NEW, RARE, AND INTERESTING PLANTS IN FLOWER IN THE PRINCIPAL SUBURBAN NURSERIES.

ÆRIDES TESSELLÀTUM. Without exception the handsomest species of this very elegant genus at present known in Britain; nor in the slightest degree inferior to *Æ. odorata* in the delicious fragrance of its flowers. In habit, it resembles its kindred species, being, however, somewhat stronger; while the flowers are produced in half-pendent racemes, and are much larger than those of *Æ. odorata*; added to which, they present a most pleasing union of white, light-green, and purple hues. Messrs. Loddiges, who imported this species from the East Indies, have a fine specimen now adorning their orchidaceous house with its charming flowers.

ANIGOZÁNTHOS MANGLÈSII. A very beautiful species, the corolla of which has a green-coloured limb, the lower part of the tube being bright scarlet, and densely covered, besides, with short red hairs. The genus, of which this plant constitutes a conspicuous feature, has, till within the last two years, been much neglected; but the splendid additions received through the disinterested and highly laudable zeal of Captain Mangles, R. N., will assuredly elevate it to its merited rank in greenhouse and flower-garden culture. After the gentleman just named, the species here noticed has been most appropriately designated. Several plants are now flowering plentifully in the greenhouse of Messrs. Henderson, Pine-Apple Place.

CAPRIFÒLIUM *hybrid*. By a cross impregnation between *C. sempervirens* and *C. pubescens*, Messrs. Young of Epsom have obtained an hybrid which is in some respects superior to both its parents. Partaking partially of the large foliage, and entirely of the expansive blossoms of *C. pubescens*, the tubes of the flowers are almost as rich as those of *C. sempervirens*, and have a dark orange-coloured tint. It appears to be one of the most liberal-flowering of all Caprifoliums, as a small specimen not more than eighteen inches high, kept in a pot, and trained closely and spirally around a circular trellis, is almost covered with flowers, and forms a truly charming spectacle. If the adaptation to this mode of training should prove peculiar to this plant, it will be no less valuable as a greenhouse ornament than it is beautiful as a hardy climber.

CATASÈTUM ATRÀTUM. The genus *Catasetum* is perhaps the least interesting, and certainly the least admired, of all the more conspicuous tribes of orchidaceous plants. *C. atratum*, therefore, being a truly engaging species, will be eagerly sought by those who delight in possessing every variety of form consistent with beauty. It is a really handsome Brazilian plant, with flowers in which a very dark brown is the prominent hue, but which is pleasingly blended with pale green and bright yellow. The blossoms are produced numerously on pendulous racemes, and Messrs. Rollison have a well-grown specimen in a flowering state.

CEANÒTHUS COLLÌNUS. In the nursery of Messrs. Low and Co. this pretty species is at present blooming. Although every way less worthy of cultivation than *C. azureus*, it is indispensable to an extensive collection, and may indeed, by proper treatment, be rendered intrinsically valuable. Its ovate, deeply furrowed, and serrated leaves are of a very symmetrical character, and the flowers, which appear in terminal thyrses like those of *C. azureus*, are pure white. It is now growing in the greenhouse, but will most likely be found as hardy as the other species; that is, it will endure our winters in a sheltered situation, if slightly protected in severe weather.

DIPLÀCUS PUNÌCEUS. We have now, for the first time, been gratified by the sight of the flowers of this splendid plant, in the collections of Messrs. Low and Co., Clapton, and Messrs. Henderson, Pine-Apple Place. With the habit of *D.* (formerly *Mimulus*) *glutinosus*, it has very rich scarlet flowers, which have a bright yellow spot in the centre. Seldom have we witnessed a more ornamental plant, and it is easy to predict that it will become universally admired and cultivated.

An early opportunity will be taken for bringing forward a figure that has been prepared for this Magazine.

FABIÀNA IMBRICÀTA. A rare and agreeable plant, nearly related to the genus *Erica*, and having dense, diminutive foliage, with a character very branching and compact. The flowers are long, slender, tubular, and white. When abundant, they make an exceedingly beautiful exhibition, of which the circle of small brown stamens, seated just within the tube of the corolla, is one of the most pleasing features. It is flowering, though rather sparingly, in the Tooting nursery, and has recently bloomed in great perfection in the collection of Messrs. Lucombe and Pince, Exeter.

HÚNTLEYA VIOLÀCEA. Although far deficient in luxuriance to *H. meleagris*, this lovely species is much superior in the colour of its flowers. These are of a hue approaching nearer to violet than those of any other orchidaceous plant with which we are acquainted; so that, if in this respect alone, the plant is deserving of high consideration. But the blossoms are likewise large and showy, with the labellum very beautifully furrowed in a longitudinal direction: they are produced solitarily, on slender pendulous scapes, depending about six inches from the base of the plant. Like *H. meleagris*, it would appear to have no definite season of flowering, but to bloom at the expiration of every two or three months. In Messrs. Loddiges' collection, it is at present exhibiting its charming blossoms, being grown in a pot, and liberally treated with regard to temperature and moisture.

MÓRNA NÍTIDA. One of the most brilliant and beautiful of yellow everlasting flowers, seeds of which were imported from Swan River, Australia, by Captain Mangles, R.N.; and from some of these presented by that gentleman to Messrs. Henderson, plants have been raised which are now finely in flower, at the nursery in Pine-Apple Place. Its mode of growth is extremely graceful and erect, the stems branching freely towards the summit, and bearing a considerable quantity of their delicate shining blossoms. To a greenhouse or flower-garden collection, it is quite essential.

ONCÍDIUM PULVINÀTUM. This scarce species is barely surpassed in elegance and gracility by *O. divaricatum;* while its flower stems are longer, and bear also a greater number of finer blossoms. We presume that the specific name applies to the form of the pseudo-bulb, as this is somewhat flattened, with sharp edges. The leaves are large, rigid, and fleshy; and the flowers of the usual yellow colour, extensively blotched with brown. These tints are, however, exceedingly clear and bright, and the species is remarkable for a large white woolly tuft in the centre of each flower. It is now in great perfection in the orchidaceous houses of Messrs. Loddiges and Rollison.

ONCÍDIUM REIDIÀNUM. Singularity in the structure of the flowers, rather than genuine beauty, characterises this new species; which is also, we believe, on account of the solitary horn that protrudes from the middle of the blossoms, called *unicornutum*. In its pseudo-bulbs, leaves, and the disposition of the flowers, it greatly resembles *O. raniferum ;* the blossoms are, however, larger, more diffuse, and of a pale greenish-brown colour, becoming darker towards the centre, from whence is produced the protuberant horn before-mentioned. Messrs. Rollison have just succeeded in flowering it, and both these gentlemen and Messrs. Loddiges have saleable specimens.

PÉNTSTEMON ABGÙTA. Growing about three feet in height, with an almost innumerable quantity of handsome blue flowers, this fine species is calculated for a prominent position either in the flower-garden or greenhouse. The leaves are from one to two inches long, nearly ovate, smooth, bright green, and deeply indented. at the margins. A slight tinge of purple is perceptible in the flowers, which are large, and rather expansive at the mouth. Flowering plants may now be seen at Messrs. Henderson's nursery, in a high state of perfection.

PERISTÈRIA STAPELIOÌDES. Oval and smooth pseudo-bulbs characterize most of the species of *Peristeria ;* nor does the present plant exhibit any difference in this respect. It belongs to that division with pendent flower-scapes, the flowers being produced on a short scape of about eight inches in length, after the manner of *P. cerina.* They are of a pale yellowish-brown ground, and very closely studded with pretty dark brown spots. We consider it the most beautiful of all Peristerias, and its fragrance is as powerful as it is agreeable. Messrs. Loddiges, in whose collection its flowers are now expanded, received it from the Spanish main.

STEPHANÒTUS FLORIBÚNDUS. A specimen of this highly valuable stove-plant is now exhibiting its fine white blossoms, and exhaling its delightful odour, in the stove of Mr. Knight, Chelsea. With thick, elliptical, deep green, and shining foliage, it combines a graceful climbing habit, and the long white flowers are borne in clusters of five from the axil of each leaf. It appears to be a most vigorous flowering plant, and, both for its ornamental character and fragrance, is entitled to very general attention. The tube of the corolla is about an inch long, rather larger at the base, and becoming more attenuated towards the apex, where it dilates into a five-parted, spreading limb.

STYLÍDIUM FASCICULÀTUM. Seeds of this species were received by Messrs. Henderson, from Captain Mangles, R.N. having been obtained by that gentleman from the Swan River colony. Although not new, it is at present somewhat rare, and, in the establishment of Messrs. Henderson, is blossoming abundantly. It is a dwarf shrub, not more than three inches high, with a loose fascicle of flowers extending six or eight inches above the woody stem. In the colour of its flowers, it assimilates to the other species, but has a yellow spot in the centre, which is quite peculiar. The leaves are long, closely set, and narrow, and the plant is altogether a truly interesting one.

THYSANÒTUS PROLÍFERUS. Few plants have ever received a more significant and applicable specific name than that under notice. More than a hundred buds are visible at the same time, and in sunny weather, the plant is so thickly covered with its rich blue blossoms as to render it too dazzling to be long gazed on. The exquisitely beautiful and finely-woven fringe of the flowers insensibly but decidedly enhances their charms, and it is, without doubt, a most desirable acquisition to the greenhouse or frame. The specimen in which we observed its extraordinarily prolific nature, is yet blooming in the nursery of Messrs. Low and Co., Clapton.

VÁNDA LAMELLÁTA. Among the first importations of the orchidaceous plants collected by Mr. Cuming, in Manilla, most persons will remember a Vanda-like Epiphyte, with close, rather long, and attenuated leaves. This having produced its flowers with Messrs. Loddiges, proves to be a *Vanda*, and is called *V. lamellata*. The colour of the flowers is chiefly brown, with a trifling admixture of yellow. They are exceedingly pretty, and the plant is certainly a worthy addition to the genus.

OPERATIONS FOR JULY.

A LIBERAL supply of heat, light, and water, is, at the present period, a desideratum for nearly every kind of plant. The former of these influences is universally requisite; the two latter must, in some instances, be greatly modified. Active developments being by this time almost concluded, it is of the first importance that they should be duly ripened, and the flower-buds of the ensuing season efficiently organised, and prepared for expansion at the natural time.

Plants, of whatever description, that are cultivated in pots, will now require a more than ordinary quantity of moisture; but this should nevertheless be applied cautiously, as it is only necessary to preserve them from actual withering, comparatively little extension being now effected. It is not, therefore, the real demands of the plant for appropriation, as the necessity for counteracting the action of a hot and arid atmosphere that calls for an increased command of water.

Solar light is of the highest possible advantage, during this and the two following months, to those plants which can endure its immediate rays. Succulents, greenhouse plants, and nearly all hardy, or half-hardy herbaceous species, delight in its unmitigated influence; although the two former classes, from being treated artificially, must be very gradually (if at all) introduced to the open air. On the other hand, most stove-plants and orchidaceæ thrive best in a partially shaded house, since the epidermis of their organs is too delicate and sensitive to receive the direct rays without experiencing irreparable injury.

With the single exception of shade, the whole of the plants comprised in those groups which are kept in houses may be similarly treated. They should be regularly and freely syringed in the evening of each day, and only as much air admitted as will prevent the temperature from becoming too high. In this suggestion we must be understood to mean, that a free circulation of air should, if possible, be generally maintained, but that ventilation should not be had in requisition unless the atmosphere of the house is too hot.

Daily syringing, at this dry season, is, we believe, much more beneficial to plants than most cultivators imagine. By thus applying water to their evaporating surface, that excessive transpiration which occurs at this period is seasonably repressed, and the processes of nutrition and secretion are enabled to proceed, sufficient succulence being by this means preserved, without the absorption by the roots, and consequent circulation through the entire system, of crude sap, which would considerably interfere with the consolidation and maturation of the newly-formed wood.

In favour of this practice, it may also be mentioned that, to plants in the open ground, rain or heavy dew is always more propitious and useful than a much greater artificial administration of fluids to their roots. The succeeding day's sun has thus, for a while at least, a moist surface to act upon; and, on the failure of this, there is always a supply that has been absorbed by the leaves, which diverts that powerful agent from sapping so extensively the substance of the plant. It follows, in natural coincidence with these facts, that gentle syringing would be of great advantage to plants in the open border, when any artificial watering is considered needful.

In watering plants in pots, particularly those whose roots are very much compressed, or much exposed to the action of the sun, it is advisable to thoroughly wet the pots themselves. This may appear a superfluous or whimsical hint, but its adoption is of some value. Most of the more tender roots and their spongioles are situated near the sides of the pot, and these being of the most highly susceptive nature, are frequently damaged, or even destroyed, by the intense and dry heat conducted through the substance of the pot to the surface with which they are in contact. It is this, as well as the copious exhalations from so large and exposed a superficies, that makes some covering for the pots, or some medium in which to plunge them, so essential to those kinds which are placed in the open air.

The young shoots of all exotics are now, perhaps, in the very best condition for propagation by cuttings. Being in some slight degree hardened, they are not so liable to decay as when much younger; while they unquestionably form roots sooner than the more matured branches. We have before recommended the spring as the most suitable epoch for increasing plants in this manner; and, for the reasons then expressed, we still adhere to that opinion. But there are some exceedingly delicate species which, owing to the weakness and succulence of their new developments, could not then be successfully struck; and for such the present is the preferable season. They should only be allowed to grow just sufficiently to establish themselves before winter, and on no account must they be vigorously excited, except for a very brief time.

Dendrobium amarantum

DENDROBIUM AGGREGATUM.

(AGGREGATE-FLOWERED DENDROBIUM.)

CLASS.	ORDER.
GYNANDRIA.	MONANDRIA.

NATURAL ORDER.
ORCHIDACEÆ.

GENERIC CHARACTER.—*Vide* vol. iii. p. 77.

SPECIFIC CHARACTER.—*Pseudo-bulbs* cæspitose, one-leaved, ovate, furrowed, stipitate, with an ash-grey cuticle. *Leaves* oblong, emarginate, coriaceous, nerved. *Racemes* lateral, partially drooping, many-flowered. *Flowers* with two ovate petals, which are generally longer and broader than the sepals. *Labellum* nearly entire, broader than long, concave at the base, pubescent.

THROUGHOUT the vast continent of India, which is well known to be peculiarly opulent in floral beauties, the genus *Dendrobium* is most extensively diffused, forming one of the gayest of its numerous natural charms. Our pages have already been enriched by plates of some of its superlatively attractive species; and while the one now brought forward is equal to almost any we have yet published, we possess drawings of others, still superior to the present, which will appear at no distant period.

In an extensive group like *Dendrobium*, it might be expected that a considerable variation in structure and habit would occur. This is not, however, the case to any great degree. The majority of species are decidedly caulescent, differing only very slightly in size and form. We use the word *slightly* in a qualified sense, meaning that they exhibit a kind of structure which, in its leading features, is common to all; but which is, nevertheless, so modified in certain species, as to render the whole of them easily distinguishable by an experienced eye, even though destitute of flowers.

There are a few comparatively insignificant species with terete, leaf-like stems; but the other main type besides the caulescent, and that to which the subject now illustrated belongs, has pseudo-bulbous stems, which are more or less encircled with nodular rings: in some, however, these latter peculiarities are entirely wanting. *D. aggregatum* is perhaps the finest of this class; its brilliant flowers being very similar to those of *D. densiflorum*, and somewhat larger. It is worthy of remark, that the flower-scapes emanate from the sides of the pseudo-bulbs, at the point where the circular sections exist. Many of the caulescent species are known to protrude their flowers in a similar manner from that part of the old stems whence the leaves have fallen, so that the two divisions are not far removed from each other in character.

British collections are mainly indebted for this, as well as innumerable other orchidaceæ and Indian plants, to Dr. Wallich, by whom it was found on the banks of the Chappadong river, near the Gulf of Martaban. Mr. Pierard also discovered it on the northern border of Arracan, where it inhabited exclusively the trunk of *Lagerstrœmia Reginæ*. Specimens were brought by Mr. Gibson from the Calcutta botanic garden, but it was not met with in any of the districts which he traversed. From one of the plants thus obtained, which bloomed at Chatsworth in the spring of 1838, the accompanying figure was prepared.

The epiphytal character of all *Dendrobia* suggests the propriety of attaching them to short pieces of wood; nevertheless many of the larger species attain a higher standard of excellence, both as regards luxuriance and beauty, when cultivated in a well-drained and loosely-placed compost of heath-soil, potsherds, and sphagnum. Our present plant, on account of its pseudo-bulbous habit and consequent proximity to the soil, which is apt to become too moist at certain seasons, should be grown on a block of wood, merely securing it thereto, and enveloping its principal roots in moss or lumps of very fibrous heath-soil.

Its specific designation serves more to distinguish it nominally than to express its particular characteristics, the term being so nearly synonymous with *densiflorum*, (the name of another species,) that the only difference is the still closer aggregation of the flowers on the racemes of the last-named plant.

Thunbergia Hawtayneana.

THUNBÉRGIA HAWTAYNEÀNA.

(HAWTAYNE'S THUNBERGIA.)

CLASS.	ORDER.
DIDYNAMIA.	ANGIOSPERMIA.

NATURAL ORDER.
ACANTHACEÆ.

GENERIC CHARACTER.—*Vide* vol. ii. p. 2.

SPECIFIC CHARACTER.—*Plant* climbing, shrubby. *Stems* numerous, round, smooth, usually slender. *Leaves* opposite, sessile, oval, acute or terminated by a small obtuse protuberance, of a lighter green beneath than above, liberally and distinctly veined, perfectly smooth. *Flowers* axillary, pedunculate, generally appearing opposite each other, one at the base of every leaf. *Calyx* composed of two parts, sheathing the base of the corolla tube, pale green. *Corolla* bluish-purple, with a yellow tube nearly an inch and a half long; limb divided into five nearly equal bifid segments.

We owe our permission to publish a figure of this very splendid species to the courteousness of Mrs. Lawrence, Drayton Green, Middlesex, in whose select and valuable collection,—comprising such numbers of the choicest plants, and in which so many rare specimens are cultivated with marked success, frequently blossoming before they fall into the possession of scarcely any other amateur,—it developed its showy flowers early in the month of June last.

No other *Thunbergia* within the range of our knowledge is at all equal to the present in genuine beauty and sterling worth. Even *T. grandiflora*, although its flowers are likewise blue and somewhat larger, is deficient in habit, in the depth, intensity, and brilliancy of the hue of its blossoms, and in its remarkable infertility, the flowers being rarely produced in abundance, and occasionally not appearing throughout the whole season. Of *T. Hawtayneana*, on the contrary, a specimen of tolerable size blooms in unbounded profusion, and in this respect rivals the universally cultivated species *T. alata*.

Dr. Wallich, superintendant of the Calcutta botanic garden, has sent plants of this species, which were collected in Nepal, to several British gardens; and Messrs. Rollison of Tooting have had it in their possession for two or three years. Mrs. Lawrence's specimen is, however, the first, indeed we believe the only one, that has flowered in this country. It is a plant of great luxuriance, and exhibits striking traces of good management; for in all other establishments where we have yet seen the species, it has invariably been in a weakly state, the leaves not more than half as large, and of a much paler green.

To grow it to a similar degree of perfection to that just noted, it should have a loamy earth, with only a small quantity of heath-soil incorporated, must be kept in a rather shady part of the stove, and ought especially to have the pot in which it is placed plunged to the rim in bark, or otherwise secluded from the action of the sun. Until brought to a thoroughly healthy condition, the above system of operation must be carefully watched, that no superabundant dampness accumulate about the roots, there being great danger from this source when the specimens are very young or sickly. But, if once fairly established, its culture ceases to be troublesome, and it will flourish with extraordinary vigour.

As this plant throws up a considerable number of stems from its base, there is no difficulty in procuring cuttings, but these are generally far from easy to strike. The extreme points of the shoots should be wholly discarded if they can conveniently be dispensed with, because they will inevitably form slender, straggling, and unhealthy plants, on account of their remarkable tenuity. Stronger portions of the young wood should therefore be chosen, and these may be treated according to the general practice, planting them in sand, covering them with a bell-glass, and preserving them cautiously from injurious moisture.

Those who desiderate strong plants must not subject them to too high a temperature during their propagation, or they will induce in them that tenderness and weakliness of habit which always follow the too profuse application of artificial heat in the early stages of the plant's progress.

For the derivation of the generic name, the reader may revert to vol. ii. p. 2.

Potentilla Hopwoodiana.

POTENTÍLLA HOPWOODIÀNA.
(MR. HOPWOOD'S CINQUEFOIL.)

CLASS.	ORDER.
ICOSANDRIA.	POLYGYNIA.

NATURAL ORDER.
ROSACEÆ.

GENERIC CHARACTER.—*Vide* vol. v. p. 223.

SPECIFIC CHARACTER.—*Stems* ascending, clothed with villi; lower *leaves* with five or six leaflets, upper ones ternate; leaflets oblong-cuneiform, coarsely toothed, hairy on both surfaces; calycine segments ovate, acuminated. *Petals* obcordate, imbricated, longer than the calyx.—*Don's Gard. and Botany.*

THERE is a class of plants, certainly not a very extensive one, which, although easily and cheaply acquired, may be denominated permanently valuable, because really ornamental, of which we are anxious to afford occasional figures in this Magazine. Such we are persuaded will be more universally acceptable to our subscribers, particularly when accompanied with plates of new or exceedingly rare kinds, than an exclusive supply of those which are merely novel.

Potentilla Hopwoodiana is a plant which, if sufficiently made known by good cultivation, will be found worthy of ranking in the order above noticed. Viewed at a proper period, and in a position favourable to the abstraction of the mind from every consideration of its comparatively little pecuniary value, we pronounce it one of the most splendid border flowers which have yet been brought to deck our gardens. We have seen single specimens of about three feet in height, presenting a compact mass full four feet in diameter, the entire surface of which has gleamed with the most vivid tints, combining every shade from the richest rose colour to the nearest and most delicate approach to white which it is possible for pink to assume.

Regarded as a hybrid, a *Potentilla*, procurable for a mere trifle, and having been some years in cultivation, many persons will probably despise this charming plant; but if once admitted into collections, and treated in any way accordant with propriety, we are assured that it will not speedily be eradicated or suffered to degenerate.

It was raised about the year 1829 from an artificial impregnation between *P. formosa* and *P. recta*. The flowers will be observed to partake of the colour of the former species, which is scarcely less beautiful, and merits very general attention. Although, during the period which has elapsed between the date just specified and the present time, *P. Hopwoodiana* has become common in gardens, there are many who are yet strangers to its strikingly interesting character, and with such, it is hoped, this recommendation will have due influence.

All that is required of the cultivator of this plant is, to furnish it with a moderately rich loamy soil, and administer a large quantity of water in the summer, should the weather render this measure needful. In some situations, and during particularly severe winters, a covering of dry litter may be requisite for the roots; but, under ordinary conditions, this will usually be superfluous. It is rather too tall for collective display in beds, but where high-growing plants are wished for, or the site admits of their being planted, a large solitary specimen, but more especially a small group, produces a magnificent effect at the time of flowering.

Propagation may be performed in the early part of the autumn, either by taking up the entire roots and dividing them, or by separating the offsets. It is desirable that this operation should be attended to in the autumnal months, because, if not parted till the spring, transplantation then checks them so considerably, that they seldom flower finely in the succeeding summer. A removal of the old plants every two or three years to a different spot is likewise beneficial.

Our drawing of this species was taken in the nursery of Messrs. Young, Epsom, in the month of August, 1838. It commences flowering about the latter end of June, and continues in perfection till the middle of September.

It is named after the individual by whom it was originally raised.

Gompholobium polymorphum.

GOMPHOLOBIUM POLYMORPHUM.

(MULTIFORM-LEAVED GOMPHOLOBIUM.)

CLASS.
DECANDRIA.

ORDER.
MONOGYNIA.

NATURAL ORDER.
LEGUMINOSÆ.

GENERIC CHARACTER.—*Calyx* five-parted, nearly equal. *Carina* of two concrete petals. *Vexillum* broad. *Stigma* simple. *Legume* many-seeded, nearly spherical, very blunt. *Don's Gard. and Botany.*

SPECIFIC CHARACTER.—*Plant* shrubby. *Stems* procumbent, twining, very slender, much branched. *Leaves* digitate; segments five, linear, or oblong-cuneated, mucronate, with recurved margins. *Stipules* very small, resembling the segments of the leaves. *Pedicels* much longer than the petioles, bracteolate. *Vexillum* large, rich scarlet-crimson, yellow at the base. *Wings* purple.

HAVING been known to British cultivators for a considerable time, and thus outlived the usual term of interest in its preservation; being also of an exceedingly delicate nature, this handsome plant was, till within the past few years, nearly lost to our gardens. Seeds of it were, however, copiously imported about the year 1837 by Captain Mangles, R.N.; and that liberal-minded gentleman has the merit, in addition to that of having introduced so many purely new plants, of reviving the cultivation of this deeply interesting species.

From seeds presented by Captain Mangles to Messrs. Henderson, Pine-Apple Place, the plant which supplied the subject of the annexed drawing was raised, and flowered most profusely in the above-named establishment, in the month of May of the present year. Some new varieties, one of which is decidedly superior, were likewise obtained at the same time, and that to which particular attention may be directed, has flowers of a much richer hue than the original species. The rest are chiefly of a lighter colour, and consequently not so showy; still, they are deserving of especial notice, as having all the gracefulness of appearance which *G. polymorphum* so eminently possesses.

Owing to the peculiar slenderness of its stems, and, what almost invariably accompanies such a feature, the similar weakness and scantiness of its roots, its culture must be essentially characterized by attention and care. It is even more gracile, though perhaps not more difficult to manage, than *Chorizema ovata;* a nearly allied plant, on which some lengthened observations were inserted at page 153 of the fourth volume of this work. To these we may now refer the reader, as they comprise many details which it were needless here to repeat, and which are unqualifiedly applicable to Gompholobiums.

The point which we consider to be of greatest moment in the treatment of this plant, is the due preservation of its roots from redundant or stagnant fluids. Proper potting, drainage, and other matters of that kind, are doubtless indispensable to the attainment of this end, and no enthusiastic cultivator will allow these to be performed without vigilant personal inspection. But the period of potting, the condition of the plant at that time, and the size of the pots employed, demand earnest consideration; and even these will subsequently be greatly influenced, if not completely governed, by the manner and degree in which water is actually applied. We merely mention these particulars in this place, as every intelligent individual will understand how to carry out the hints thus desultorily given.

For compost, the usual admixture of light heath-soil with sandy loam is such as will suit this or any species of the genus. It is exceedingly probable that elevation of the soil in the middle of the pot, round the base of the plant's stem, as is frequently practised by experienced Heath-cultivators, would have a beneficial effect; the roots of such plants as that now under discussion assimilating greatly to those of Heaths.

An increase may be obtained by cuttings, which, like the old plants, require great and assiduous regard. They should not be prepared till after the plant has shed its flowers, and the extremities of the shoots are not to be preferred, since they are generally too tender to endure actual contact with a humid soil. To save the plant from mutilation, if seeds can be ripened, they should always be saved for the purpose of multiplication; and we are induced to believe that, by this means, new varieties may occasionally be produced.

Gompholobium is derived from *gomphos*, a club, and *lobos*, a pod; the shape of the seed-pods of the original species presenting some resemblance to that of a club or wedge.

VEGETABLE PHYSIOLOGY.—No. III.

In an article at p. 57-8 of the present volume, allusion was made to Mr. Main's hypothesis of the Vital membrane or *Indusium*; the view taken of it was favourable, as it appeared more philosophical to consider the annual formations of sap wood and liber to be *developments* of parts already existing, than as new *creations*. In order to do the subject all the justice within our power, and to afford the physiological reader matter for reflection and experiment, we feel impelled to offer a few additional observations which have been suggested by facts that have come under notice since the article alluded to appeared in print: however, before we do this, we must refer to Mr. Main's work in further illustration of his views. He observes :—

"There are two states or degrees of vegetable life. The *first* is always present in those members which are capable of amplification, or are in the act of accretion, i. e. expanding from a small to a large volume. The *second* is that state in which it is only conservative, but without the power of a further growth of the members preserved by it. The first it is deemed proper to designate by the name of *vital envelope*, whence proceeds every new member of trees, shrubs, and many herbaceous plants. The second is, that state of the bark and alburnum which, having but recently come into full form and magnitude, serve as conductors of the fluids of the system for a certain time, but from which the actual life has for ever fled.

"Where then does the living principle reside? In the pith? No. In the wood, or in the bark? No, in neither of these; but it is always found, at all times, *between the liber and the alburnum;* slightly attached to both, but united to neither: it is reasonable therefore to conclude that it is a *distinct member* of the system. This slender body of vitality, or *vital envelope*, is constitutionally compound, not simple, as such a thin tissue may be supposed to be, containing the rudiments of both roots and buds; and moreover it is the source of all accretion, whether as to the magnitude, or number of the parts produced."

In the foregoing passage we perceive the *leading principle* of the hypothesis: it presumes that every part and member of a plant are formed and coexist with the rudimental germs of its existence; the absorption of food and the laboration of the juices being processes of nutrition only, while the development and growth of all the members are those of *accretion* and *enlargement*, not of *organization*.

We are far from disputing the existence of an *indusium* or *vital envelope*, which we believe is considered to be identical with the *cambium* of physiologists; but the fact to be established or disproved is simply this :—it may be stated in the form of a question. Is the *cambium* or laborated sap capable of organization? or, with Mr. Main, must we suppose that the *vital envelope* is constructed of an indefinite number of distinct concentric layers, two of which are developed annually and become nourished or enlarged?

The identity of this vital member is, Mr. Main says, visible and palpable during summer in the form of a *white belt*: it is the *swelling cambium*, that ultimately is divided into two distinct layers; between which, "an almost imperceptible membrane or coating of gelatinous matter" is interposed. This is the vital envelope from which "the new growths of *wood* and *liber* of the next and all succeeding years will be produced."—(See Main's *Illustrations of Vegetable Physiology*.)

If the reader appreciate these few detached and abbreviated extracts from a work which ought to be deeply studied, he will be interested in comparing them with the facts which will now be adduced in proof that *organization* may be effected in prepared nutritive fluids.

We are jealous of analogies between animal and vegetable bodies; they mystify and lead to fanciful conclusions: but there is one point wherein a fair analogy may be traced, and that is, that the *vitality of the nutritive fluids* of both the *cambium* or vital *indusium* is the pabulum of *vegetable* organization, just as the blood is the support of animal life and the cause of growth and increase; *and both are endowed with life:* let the annexed truths speak *for themselves*.

"If a living egg be exposed to a degree of heat equal to the temperature at which the egg is maintained during incubation, certain motions or actions are observed spontaneously to arise in it, which terminate in the development of a chick. An analogous process takes place in the blood: if it be effused from its vessels in the living body, either upon the surfaces of organs or into cavities, *it solidifies without losing its vitality*. This is not the same process as the coagulation of blood out of the body; it is a vital process indispensable to the action, and completely under the control of the vital principle. If blood thus solidified within the body be examined sometime after it has changed from the fluid to the solid state, the solid is found to abound with blood-vessels. Some of these vessels can be distinctly traced passing from the surrounding living parts into the mass of the solidified blood: with others of these vessels no communication whatever can be traced. A clot of blood surrounded by *living* parts becomes organized—*no dead* substance thus surrounded by living parts becomes organized; the inference is that the blood itself is alive."

But blood coagulates when drawn from the living body, and separates into two distinct portions. "In three minutes and a half the change is sufficiently advanced to be manifest to the eye; in seven minutes the fluid is separated from the solid portion, while the change progressively advances, until, in the space of from twelve to twenty minutes, the separation may be said to be complete.

"The nature of this curious process is imperfectly understood; it is a process *sui generis*, there being no other with which we are acquainted perfectly analogous to it. It is really a process of death: it is the mode in which blood dies!" (See the able article on *Blood*, in the *Penny Cyclopædia*; the author is unknown to us.)

Analogy exists, therefore, between the *animal blood* and *that fluid* which Mr.

Knight termed the prepared blood of the living plant, in so far as both are nutritive and living fluids. Then if blood be capable of organization, why may not the vital *cambium* also become organized? But the new theory assumes that it *is* the seat of life and of organization; though it admits that not a trace of anything beyond a colourless homogeneous mass appears in the first stage of its existence. Herein, however, we perceive no difficulty; for not the slightest trace of organization can be detected in the white of an egg prior to incubation; yet certain it is that, without access of any nutritive fluid from without, the yolk and white become organized under the stimulus of vital heat alone.

The principle of life resists putrefaction or decay; chemical energy cannot act upon it, nor upon any living body, unless it first destroy the vitality of that body. Now the sap, be the degree of atmospheric heat what it may, never runs into fermentation while the life of the plant which it sustains is preserved; the yolk of the egg undergoes no degree of putrefaction under the high temperature communicated by the breast of the sitting hen; the blood, whether it be fluid or solidified within the *living* body, does not undergo decomposition. It is just therefore to infer, that each of these supporters of life and increase, is itself alive, and endowed with a quality which fits it to become organized. Much more might be said, and indeed may be found in the article to which allusion has already been made; perhaps enough has been advanced to excite deep and earnest reflection. The subject is profoundly mysterious, and we believe that its depths can never be fathomed by the finite understanding.

INFLUENCE OF CLIMATE ON PLANTS.[*]
SOLAR HEAT.

THE facts submitted in our last article justify the inference that before any flowers or fruit can be produced,—at least, any quantity of them,—the plant must undergo a complete process of evaporation, whereby its aqueous fluids will be evolved, and its vital substance matured; but whether it is from its inability at that period to produce real shoots, or contrariwise, by the concentration and consummation of its mechanism to effect this greatest of vegetable efforts, we cannot take upon ourselves to determine. Due maturation, such as the vigorous stimulation of heat, with only so small a supply of moisture as is sufficient to carry on the economy of the system, will induce, is undoubtedly the main process necessary for the extension of reproductive organs. To suppose this a result of repose (as some recent authors have done) is to ascribe the consequences of the exertion of an active agent, to the quiescence of an inert condition.

Many practical directions might be based upon the position we have thus been attempting to establish; a few of the most prominent of which we will here

[*] Continued from page 134.

indulge in. It is scarcely needful to apply them to the common ornaments of the flower-garden and pleasure-grounds, since these are chiefly such as require no artificial treatment to render their flowers more profuse. Nor does the design of this Magazine admit of any particular reference to fruit-trees. Our remarks will, therefore, be wholly confined to the more tender kinds of exotic plants.

In the naturalization of ornamental plants from warmer climates, one of the principal difficulties to be surmounted is, the bringing them to a productive state. Being planted in the open ground, the atmospheric elements cannot possibly be adjusted to them in the necessary manner and degree; other measures must, therefore, be adopted, which will, as nearly as practicable, answer the same purpose. As the class of plants susceptible of acclimatation in this country comprises species which, upon the aggregate, are found in exposed situations, one of the chief designs of the cultivator should be to choose a spot for planting them where they can receive the full advantage of air and solar influence, and yet be partially or seasonably sheltered from cold winds. A position where the action of the sun during summer would be sufficiently strong to ripen the growth of that year, even though artificial protection should be requisite in the same situation in winter, is far preferable to one in which the shelter is permanent, because naturally afforded, and creating shade likewise.

Where the heat, under prevailing climatic circumstances, is not intense enough to occasion a proper and perfect maturation, attention must be directed to the diminution of the sources of fluid sustenance, by remitting its application, or checking its imbibition. This latter may be effected in two different ways. A temporary covering to the soil around and above the roots during heavy or long-continued rains; or a reduction in the number of absorbent spongioles on the roots, according to the vigour of the plant, and the amount of deficiency in solar supplies, will both fulfil similar ends; and either, or both, of these methods may be practised when necessary. That last named is, however, the most efficient, and can more easily be executed.

It is somewhat singular that one or the other of the above systems has not been extensively acted upon in the management of plants of the description now under discussion, where flowers are desired. Their beneficial tendency cannot be doubted: particularly as the means thus employed to facilitate the expansion of the floriferous organs, are precisely those which would assist in rendering the plants impervious to frost; ripe and indurated wood, and the almost total absence of juices, being a state in which frost can inflict little injury.

Greenhouse or stove exotics, or such as are cultivated in pots in any situation, are far more fully beneath the gardener's surveillance, and can more readily be stimulated or restrained in the exercise of their functions, by modifying the conditions of the atmosphere in which they live. Plants which are required to flower freely, are never placed in pots of too large a size, and are watered with the utmost caution. This treatment produces the same effects as the reduction of the roots of those which are in the open ground. In both cases, the amount of moisture received is lessened, and a lower degree of heat is competent to perform nearly the same service as an adequate temperature would under ordinary circumstances; saving, of course, that the accretions are circumscribed in extent, which is of no real importance.

Orchidaceous plants are universally presumed to derive advantage from a few months' repose from active growth; but it may be safely affirmed that it is not rest itself which elicits their dormant disposition to flower, this latter function being made palpable solely by the desiccating influence of heat. The proper nature of this repose is, therefore, evidently a degree of aridity proportionate to the rate of temperature. Where no artificial heat is employed, water may be entirely suspended; and never should there be more applied than will suffice to preserve life. Assuming this opinion to be correct, the natural inference is, that what is called a season of rest should be termed a period of drought or maturation. It seems ridiculous to suppose that actual dormancy can be in any way useful; for this condition can only be beneficial, when so modified that heat may predominate over moisture. And if these two agents were adapted to each other throughout the growing season, maturation would be completed ere the commencement of cold weather, and the plants might then remain in a cool, dry house, and perfectly torpid, during the winter.

With respect to very young exotic plants, of all kinds, it is plain that their treatment should be essentially different from that pursued towards plants which are wished to flower profusely. So far from endeavouring to restrain their growth, every means, consistent with health, should be resorted to, which can in any way facilitate it. Precocious developments are, however, greatly to be deprecated; and (orchidaceous plants excepted) stimulation must not be extended beyond the natural period. By potting them frequently into larger pots, liberally bestowing water, and judiciously increasing the natural heat *in summer* by artificial aids, they may be much more rapidly prepared for a state of vigorous production and beautiful display than is ordinarily the case. After the attainment of this epoch, the policy we have before recommended may be commenced and followed.

When plants have flowered very abundantly, and there is any probability of their relapsing into a state of sterility in the following year, this consequence may be partly averted by the administration of a large portion of nutrimental liquid food, accompanied by a greater ratio of heat, immediately upon the fading of the flowers. Tropical, or other *very tender* species, that are not disposed to flower freely, should never be allowed to bear seed, unless they grow too luxuriantly, or this is indispensable for their propagation; as such a process has a most debilitating effect, and one which *sickly* plants of this kind are unable to endure without injury, on account of their being so unnaturally circumstanced.

The results of many experiments, casually obtained, render it, in our opinion, extremely likely that the capacity of plants for withstanding cold, varies exceedingly according to the temperature of the climate in which the seeds from which they are raised were ripened. This hypothesis, however vague it may seem, is certainly a rational one, and is confirmed by analogy, as well as by the experience of many intelligent cultivators. It is, doubtless, generally known that plants growing in elevated or exposed sites are more hardy, and far more capable of bearing with impunity a transference to a colder country, than those which are luxuriating in every species of atmospheric condition most congenial to their habits. Nor, we imagine, are any ignorant that the longer those of the former class remain in such positions the more hardihood they acquire. The normal organization of the germ being constituted under certain circumstances, it is, by one of the wise laws of nature, adapted for development beneath similar circumstances.

These facts tend greatly to the establishment of the theory in question; since, if individual plants thus differ, the seeds of the hardier specimens must partake of the character of the parent. When germinated, the young plants produced from them will, from that incident, have a yet more robust habitude than their progenitors originally possessed; and, by consequence, will be fitted for more extensive alterations in their capacities, and the endurance of greater climatic rigours.

Within our own knowledge, plants that were once confined to the greenhouse, or even to the stove, have been made to adorn the flower-garden during the summer months; and, in some instances, have also, with a trifling protection, stood through the winter in the open air. Some may attribute this to the well-known fact, that scarce and valuable plants are almost invariably kept in too high a temperature on their first reception in this country, and from thence argue, that they would have been equally hardy at *that* period, had their capabilities of sustaining cold been thoroughly and properly tested. But while we grant qualifiedly the truth and force of this train of reasoning, we cannot coincide in it to the extent it is here carried. There appears to us no doubt that such ability to endure the changes of our clime is due to the circumstance of many of the plants alluded to having been raised from seed ripened in Britain. In every instance, the habits have indisputably been modified, as may be seen by importing and exposing specimens of the same species, which would inevitably be destroyed.

Were the correctness of this theory fully demonstrated,—and we venture to predict that it only needs due investigation to place it beyond dispute,—it would afford most valuable assistance to the cultivator in his endeavours to acclimatize exotic plants. We recommend all individuals of this class to institute immediately a course of experiments with this definite object in view; and however gradual and protracted may be the process by which a plant is thus brought to accommodate itself to our flower-borders, if it should ultimately succeed an inestimable advantage will be gained, and it is impossible to say to what extent the practice may eventually be carried. Collectors should also have this in constant remembrance in their searches; and, when their object is to obtain plants adapted to the climate of the countries for which they are travelling, they should endeavour to procure the seeds from those localities, the temperature of which accords most nearly with that of their own clime.

There is another office performed by heat in maturing fruit, to which it may be well briefly to allude. It has already been asserted to be the prime cause of fertility; but, with pulpy and edible fruits, it is also the main agent in rendering them palatable and agreeable. All saccharine matter is generated by the action of heat, as is proved by the acidity of those fruits which are produced in cold summers, or are insufficiently ripened. It may be assumed, likewise, that though sugar is so abundantly manufactured from the beet-root in France, a remunerative, or at least an equal, return could not be realized in England, even though the price of land and of labour were assimilated.

(*To be continued.*)

ON THE TREATMENT OF GREENHOUSE CLIMBING PLANTS, AS ORNAMENTS TO PLEASURE-GROUNDS.

AMONG the numerous alterations introduced by modern taste and science into the disposition and arrangements of the ornate department of a garden, none is better entitled to be called an improvement than that of transferring tender exotics to the external beds or borders during a few of the more favourable summer months. Exhibiting in general a more graceful character than hardy kinds, there is besides a peculiar charm connected with the appearance of a plant luxuriating unreservedly in the open ground and air, which is well known to belong to a distant and much warmer climate, and to be usually cultivated in our greenhouses. A feeling of delight pervades the mind when such an object is presented to view, which it is almost impossible to delineate or define, but which, we are sure, is participated or experienced by all whose perceptions are in any degree influenced by extrinsic associations.

Self gratulation is very naturally awakened in the human breast on the accomplishment of any object hitherto deemed impracticable, or so unlooked for as never to have excited attention or thought. And perhaps in no instance is this emotion more innocent, or less sullied by ignoble promptings, than when occasioned by the simple, yet, if fathomed aright, intensely profound pleasure, derivable from the superior or novel and successful treatment of any scarce or favourite plant. Nor do we think but that *amor patriæ*, so characteristic of Britons, must glow more warmly when witnessing the capability of their beloved isle to sustain the vegetable productions of far more genial regions.

No situation can be conceived which would be more talismanic in its effect upon an enlightened and sensitive mind than a prospect on British ground bedecked with the blooming beauties of the tropics, revelling under the fostering hand of progressive art in all the splendour and voluptuousness of their native habitats. The associations with which such objects are invested are innumerable: from poetry, from philosophy, from Scripture, they each borrow resplendent robes, and invite as truly the sober eye of contemplation, as they fascinate the more susceptible gaze of the imaginative.

We pass from these cursory suggestions as to the nature of the influences of which every one acknowledges himself a subject when indulged with the spectacle of exotics so far naturalized as to unfold for a season all their beauty in this country, to the more immediate intention of the present observations. Freely as annual, herbaceous, and even shrubby greenhouse plants are now planted in the flower-borders of the leading floriculturists, there is a manifest shyness to venture the exposure of their more interesting climatic congeners—climbing plants. It is true that what are aptly designated conservative walls exist in most extensive establishments, and that, by their protection, many plants are subjected to the natural climate of Britain; but these conveniences are only adapted for the more exuberant of the shrubby species, while by far the most attractive sorts, such as the herbaceous tribes, and slender shrubs, are wholly confined to the greenhouse.

Walls cannot, we must ever maintain, be considered at all suitable for the support of climbing plants; and it is only as they tend to retain heat, and afford shelter from cold winds, or when some agreeable verdure is desirable to conceal them, that the practice of training exotics against such erections can be recommended. And since it is necessary that the plants thus employed should spread over the entire surface of the wall at all seasons, to screen it as much as possible from the observer's gaze, there is thus rejected a number of species which cannot be permitted to enjoy the beneficial action of a pure, unrestricted atmosphere, unless some other mode and different materials be devised and brought into use. Such a method and materials it is the purport of this paper to exhibit and explain.

Arched trellises, constructed of either wood or iron, and generally extended over a narrow walk in the flower-garden, or occupying some smaller plot, intersected with walks, in a retired part of the pleasure-grounds, are now becoming fashionable, and may subserve the purpose of supporting climbers with tolerable effect. An objection, however, attaches to these, which will, we imagine, decide their inferiority to some of another description hereafter to be noticed. No single specimen can thus be trained so as to show any of the particular characters of the species; nor would it produce its flowers on the inner surface of the trellis, from which alone, in many cases, they can be viewed. This would be caused by the universal tendency of flowers to grow upwards, or towards the light. Indeed, were the blossoms all to incline inwards, the space would be too confined, and the light admitted too imperfectly, to expand them finely, or render their display, when at its greatest height, at all pleasing. All the advantage, therefore, that this kind of trellis can be said to afford, is an umbrageous and refreshing retreat from the vehemence of a summer sun; and, where the flower-garden is extremely circumscribed, a mass of showy flowers on their exterior might present a lively picture to some distant point of the pleasure-grounds.

Rustic baskets, with a span of a semicircular outline to represent the handle, likewise supply facilities for introducing a few climbing species. These are still more generally adopted in modern gardens than the form of trellis last alluded to, and have before been described in this work. They will admit, at the most, no more than two climbing specimens, and these are merely conducted over a single hoop across the middle.

It is both just and politic, in mooting a subject of this nature, and proposing a new system of operation, or, what is closely analogous, the extensive adoption of a mode which is scarcely known, and certainly but rarely practised, to point out all the particulars in which old customs fail or are faulty. By this means the standard of propriety is not only set up but established; and it frequently needs but to be ascertained, at once to ensure an advance towards it, or even its complete attainment; for, although this may not be the immediate result, the ultimate tendency of the practice is clearly to accelerate an improvement.

None of the methods on which we have here incidentally touched, are free from great and manifold defects. To form a favourable opinion of a handsome *dwarf* climbing plant, (and it is to dwarf species that these strictures principally apply,) it should stand perfectly detached; be as open as possible on all sides; have erect supporters, which may divaricate according to its habits, and terminate neither pointedly nor abruptly, but with a gentle curve, in the direction of the ground: while, finally, as little restraint as comports with order should be exercised in its management, that its natural character, or one sufficiently irregular to have the appearance of nature, due regard at the same time being paid to real elegance, may be fully displayed and preserved.

To effect at once, and without perplexity or difficulty, these exceedingly desirable objects, plants chosen and prepared for this express purpose should be placed at proper distances and in approved situations,—both as regards the circumstances most propitious to them individually, and their general influence on the landscape,—on any glade of lawn that may be considered appropriate. That immediately surrounding small villa or cottage residences, or, in larger estates, any spot which may present itself eligibly at a sufficient distance from the mansion, may be partly devoted to this end; and, if a tasteful care govern their disposition, the prospect, when all are at their utmost perfection, will be in the highest degree enchanting.

But we have yet to state to what sort of trellis it is best to attach them; and this may be condensed into a few closing remarks. Strong iron wire, for the sake of its neatness, pliability, and power of endurance, is preferable to any other substance that can be employed. It may be bent or twisted into various shapes, to suit the taste of the cultivator or the peculiar habit of the plants. An excellent form for those shrubby species which are capable of being trained with an erect stem, to the production of a drooping, branching head, is to have a strong perpendicular rod of iron, surmounted by a circular convex frame of weaker wire, so as to resemble a parasol in figure. Others will be better exhibited by a frame in the shape of a spirit-flask or a balloon. An infinity of types might be mentioned, or illustrated by engravings, but every needful diversity can be procured at any wire manufactory in the vicinity of the metropolis, and, we presume, at most other large towns. One essential point in their structure should not be forgotten, which is that the summits be always so recurved that the upper shoots of the plants grown upon them may not protrude far above the trellis, but rather depend gracefully on all sides. Perhaps, in a future number, we may furnish a list of such plants as are particularly suitable for this mode of growth, and add some apposite suggestions on the treatment they should receive previously to being thus exposed: on the present occasion, our space precludes further detail.

FLORICULTURAL NOTICES.

NEW AND RARE PLANTS, FIGURED IN THE LEADING BOTANICAL PERIODICALS FOR JULY.

CLASS I.—PLANTS WITH TWO COTYLEDONS (DICOTYLEDONEÆ).

THE BEAN TRIBE (*Leguminòsæ*).

EDWÁRDSIA MACNABIÀNA. Mr. Macnab's Edwardsia. Strongly resembling *E. grandiflora* in general appearance and habit, it is highly probable that this plant is merely a seedling variety; but, says Dr. Graham, "it is instantly distinguishable from the ordinary form of that species, by its nearly equal petals, by the wide separation of the petals of the keel, and by its flowering when in full leaf." No other distinctive particulars are enumerated, nor is the source whence it was obtained known. Having been cultivated for many years in the Edinburgh Botanic Garden, it is found to be somewhat more hardy than *E. grandiflora*; and when trained against a protective wall, forms a really handsome shrub. The profusion of bright yellow flowers is very striking; but, like the species above referred to, it appears deficient in foliage. *Bot. Mag.* 3735.

THE ASCLEPIAS TRIBE (*Asclepiadàceæ*).

CEROPÈGIA VINCÆFÒLIA. Periwinkle-leaved Ceropegia. Of this very curious genus, the present plant constitutes a new and slightly interesting species. Considered as a stove ornament, it presents few attractions; but there is a degree of gracefulness in its general disposition and flowers, the latter being, moreover, prettily spotted, which will render it welcome to the admirers of novelty. It has twining stems, and opposite, ovate leaves, from the axils of which the flowers appear in clusters of four or six. These last are greenish white at the base; which deepens into green towards the middle, and gives place to deep purple at the summit. It was received in the Glasgow Botanic Garden, from Bombay, and flowers most copiously in September. *Bot. Mag.* 3740.

THE GESNERIA TRIBE (*Gesneridceæ*).

GESNÈRIA STRÍCTA. Upright Gesneria. A pale crimson, bilabiate-flowered species, growing to the unusual height of five feet, with slender, erect stems, which are triflingly branched towards the extremities. Mr. Tweedie sent roots of it from Rio Grande in South Brazil, to the Glasgow Botanic Garden, in which establishment its blossoms were produced in July, 1835. "In habit, it resembles *G. Sceptrum* of Martius; but the flowers are very different in shape; the corolla having a remarkable curvature of the upper side, and, following its direction, the style is singularly geniculated at its base: the upper lip too is much longer: the style and anthers exserted." *Bot. Mag.* 3738.

THE BORAGE TRIBE (*Boraginàceæ*).

CYNOGLÒSSUM CŒLESTÌNUM. Blue and white Hound's-tongue. The chief character of this plant is sufficiently expressed by its name; and the pleasing combination of azure and white in its flowers, from which that is derived, imparts to it a very lively aspect. With large, ovately-cordate foliage, its flower-stems rise to the height of from one and a half to two feet, bearing the blossoms in terminal racemes, which are generally bifid. Bombay, or some district in the north of India, appears to be its native country, and seeds obtained from the place just mentioned, produced plants which flowered in the Horticultural Society's Gardens, in August, 1838. Dr. Lindley recommends for it the same treatment as is practised towards Brompton Stocks, sowing the seeds in June and July. *Bot. Reg.* 36.

CLASS II.—PLANTS WITH ONE COTYLEDON (MONOCOTYLEDONEÆ).

THE ORCHIS TRIBE (*Orchidàceæ*).

BLÈTIA PARKINSÒNII. Mr. Parkinson's Bletia. This pretty plant is more unique than ornamental, as the scape is extremely long and slender, and the flowers smaller than those of any other species. Mr. Parkinson, H. B. M. Consul General at Mexico, forwarded bulbs from that country to His Grace the Duke of Bedford, and it bloomed at Woburn Abbey, in January, 1839. No leaves are represented, nor is it said to bear any. The flowers are rose-coloured, with a deep, rich red band round the edge of the labellum, and a fine purple anther-case. The bulbs are terrestrial and nearly round; its nearest affinity is stated to be *B. reflexus*. *Bot. Mag.* 3736.

DENDRÒBIUM JENKÍNSII. Captain Jenkins's Dendrobium. One of the smallest of the tribe, but, at the same time, having large and very showy yellow flowers.

It belongs to the pseudo-bulbous division of the genus, and the bulbs, which are short and tetragonous, are produced very densely on a creeping rhizoma, each being surmounted by a single oblong, obtuse leaf. Its flowers appear solitarily on short, attenuated peduncles, and are very similar to those of *D. aggregatum* in form and colour. Captain Jenkins furnished plants of it to the Calcutta Botanic Garden, having obtained them at Gualpara, India. Some specimens were transmitted by Dr. Wallich to this country, one of which Messrs. Loddiges succeeded in flowering in September, 1838. It should be cultivated on a piece of wood, and the roots surrounded with a little adhesive heath-soil or moss; as it will not thrive if confined to a pot. *Bot. Reg.* 37.

NEW, RARE, AND INTERESTING PLANTS IN FLOWER IN THE PRINCIPAL SUBURBAN NURSERIES.

CALLIPRÒRA LÙTEA. This is an interesting little bulbous plant, producing, from the extremities of slender stems about a foot in height, umbels of deep yellow flowers; which latter are rather more than half an inch in diameter. The leaves are long, narrow, and insignificant; the blossoms alone entitling it to attention: and these have each six light-green streaks diverging from their centres at equal distances. It is undoubtedly allied to the genus *Allium*, and we presume it to be a half-hardy plant, though at present kept in the greenhouse of Messrs. Low and Co., Clapton, who possess flowering specimens. Its native country is California.

CAMPÀNULA CAROLÌNA. In the establishment of Messrs. Henderson, Pine-Apple Place, this exceedingly pretty species is at present most densely studded with pale blue blossoms. It is of a dwarf, suffruticose, and symmetrical habit, the whole plant being covered with a whitish down, and the flowers, which are about an inch in diameter, and expand themselves in a horizontal direction, appear in the greatest abundance. For greenhouse purposes, or for growing in a pot in any situation, we know no species better adapted than the present; and there are certainly not many plants of its class more ornamental when in flower.

CAMPÀNULA PUNCTÀTA. Few gardens contain specimens of this old but most delightful plant. Like that previously noticed, it is best calculated for pot culture, but is much more diminutive in height, and requires to be elevated on a stage or other conspicuous position. Notwithstanding its small size, the flowers are rather more than two inches long, and as they are solitary, pure white, and beautifully spotted with purple on the interior, the leaves being also smooth and bright green, it presents altogether a unique and fascinating appearance. We saw it flowering, about a fortnight since, in the rich herbaceous collection of Messrs. Young, Epsom.

CLERODÉNDRON SQUAMÀTUM. Our reasons for the present allusion to this old but very handsome stove plant, are to commend it to public attention as a valuable feature in a hothouse, and to rectify an error which, we observe, is rapidly gaining credence, that it is identical with the *C. speciosissimum*, figured in the fourth volume of our magazine. It is much inferior to the species just mentioned, both in general character and the size of its blossoms; but these are of a deeper colour, and on this account, as well as from its contracted habits, and the early period of its existence at which the flowers appear, it is deserving of very general esteem. The specimen which suggested these remarks, is now displaying its beauties in the nursery of Mr. Knight, Chelsea.

ECHÌTES SUBERÉCTA. Not presenting the omnipotent claim of being a new plant, though undoubtedly a scarce one, this fine species, again, is barely entitled to notice here. Some of our readers are perhaps, however, unacquainted with its merits, which are those of an elegant climber, with small but neat foliage, and very large, lively yellow, trumpet-shaped flowers, arising in bunches from the axils of the leaves. Allied to it, and alike flowering in the stove of Mr. Knight, Chelsea, is a new species of *Echites*, bearing large, rich, and shining evergreen foliage; but its flowers, though produced in great numbers from the base of the leaves, prove to be puny, pale-brown, and quite unornamental. Being a climbing plant, of vigorous growth, and strikingly promising leaves, it has long excited considerable expectation. It is now found to be utterly worthless, except for the purpose of covering a vacant space in an extensive house, with a pleasing mass of fine foliage.

ERÝSIMUM PEROWSKIÀNUM. Planted in the flower-garden either singly or *en masse*, we have seldom seen a more appropriate plant than that whose name is prefixed to this paragraph. Its general character is that of a common Wall-flower, but it is less straggling, and produces a more regular and unbroken surface of brilliant orange-coloured flowers. Whether it be an annual or biennial, we cannot now state; but it is just such a plant as every cultivator must be desirous of possessing. Specimens in the open border of Messrs. Rollison, Tooting, are blooming most profusely.

GERÁRDIA DELPHINIFÒLIA. It is said to be more than thirty years since this charming herbaceous plant was received in Britain from the East Indies; and yet, at this time, it remains almost unknown. Witnessing, in our late visit, a specimen planted out in the open ground of the Tooting nursery, we were much pleased with its appearance, and are induced to recommend it for summer display. The form of its leaves is well expressed in the specific name, while the flowers are of a delicate blush tint, slightly striped with a darker pink, and much resembling those of some species of *Pentstemon*.

LOBÈLIA ÌGNEA. A very peculiar species, and at once distinguishable from all others by its dark purple stems and leaves. The flowers are of a most dazzling and fiery red, surpassing almost all its congeners in brilliancy, and establishing for it an exalted position in the regard of all admirers of the genus. Its blossoms are just expanding in the collection of Messrs. Henderson, which, so far as relates to the culture of new plants, has recently undergone a rapid and decided advancement.

LOBÈLIA MÍLLERII. Hybridization has now been carried to a great extent with Lobelias, and the species here named is one of the most showy results that we have yet met with. Having long, broad, and excellent foliage, an erect, bold, and luxuriant habit, and rich purple flowers, it forms a splendid object when in full bloom, which is now the case with a plant in the possession of Messrs. Henderson. It is related to *L. speciosa*, (which, indeed, is one of its parents,) and grows to the height of from two to three feet, with an indefinite number of stems.

LOBÈLIA RAMÒSA. Altogether different in character from the two species just registered, this interesting plant is more nearly related to *L. heterophylla*, having flowers of a very similar form and colour. From this, however, it is sufficiently removed by its much more branching tendency, by the leaves being larger and hairy, and the whole plant completely clothed with very conspicuous hairs. It is, moreover, less diffuse than *L. heterophylla*, and better adapted for all kinds of ornamental effect. We believe it to have been obtained originally from the Swan River colony. The Epsom nursery at present contains some very showy flowering plants.

PHÀIUS BÍCOLOR. Like the rest of the genus, this species is remarkable for its deep green foliage, and highly healthy appearance. With the usual form of pseudo bulbs and leaves common to its allies, it is specifically marked by its large yellow flowers, the labellum of which is pure white; thus presenting, as implied by the name, a combination of hue which, though not particularly striking, is not lacking in interest. Messrs. Loddiges have a well-grown plant now blossoming in their orchidaceous house.

PLATYCÒDON GRANDIFLÒRUS. The propensity of botanists to multiply the names of a plant, has been strangely exhibited in reference to our present subject. Primarily it was known as *Campanula grandiflora*, and this is yet the name most usually employed, but it was subsequently constituted a distinct genus under the title of *Wahlenbergia pendula*, and M. de Candolle has more recently bestowed upon it the designation which heads this notice. It is yet much rarer than it deserves to be, seldom being met with in private gardens. The very deep blue colour of its flowers, and their extraordinary size, associated with its dwarf habitude, render it an admirable border plant. Our attention was directed to it in the nursery grounds of Messrs. Henderson, where its splendid flowers are now exhibiting themselves in great perfection.

SÁLVIA CONFERTIFLÒRA. Since the introduction of the much admired *S. patens*, another species, bearing the above name, has been received from Mexico, and a plant in the Epsom nursery is now opening its flowers. Unlike *S. patens*, it appears to produce only a single stem, this being peculiarly exuberant and stately, and the leaves, especially, growing to an unusual size. It is at present nearly four feet in height, and of a particularly handsome character, the stem terminating in a long spike of small scarlet woolly blossoms. These last, though they by no means rival those of the species already referred to in dimensions, are not inferior in richness, and it is more than probable that the plant will become a favourite, at least in those gardens where large plants are desired.

THYSANÒTUS INTRICÀTUS. One of the charming productions of the fertile soil of Australia, obtained by Captain Mangles, R.N., from the Swan River colony. An innumerable quantity of slender stems issue from its roots, and these are so closely and intricately interwoven with each other, as to form an almost inextricable mass, the surface of which presents a brilliant covering of deep blue flowers. These have a stripe of purple down the centre of each petal, and are most exquisitely fringed round the margins. The leaves are narrow, scanty, and scarcely to be distinguished from the stems. It is flowering liberally with Messrs. Low and Co., Clapton.

OPERATIONS FOR AUGUST.

ONE most important design of the cultivator of exotic plants, and especially of those obtained from tropical regions, should be to render the corresponding epochs of the existence of all as nearly as possible simultaneous. In a collection of plants which naturally inhabit such an immense variety of climate, that climate also having its maximum and minimum degrees of temperature at extremely remote or totally reversed periods, this object may be deemed almost impracticable. Experience, however, the only thing by which such a subject can be tested, is in favour of the presumption that this important consummation *may* be attained.

We are extremely desirous of impressing upon the minds of all who have the superintendence of stove plants, the propriety and value of the above practice. Unless every species is induced to conform to a general system of treatment, regulating its development or dormancy according to British seasons, their culture cannot be conducted on any principles which are at all calculated to entail success. We have chosen to allude to tropical species thus distinctively, because every one sees the necessity of managing the kinds requiring less artificial assistance with an eye to this end, and acts accordingly.

Taking this datum, then, as our basis, which, indeed, we have long done, it follows that, in the present month, the temperature of the stove should be maintained at a moderately high rate, but that air should be allowed more freely to circulate through it, and, where shading has been adopted, it ought now to be greatly modified, in order to afford every desirable condition for the thorough maturation of the young wood of the present year's growth. If this latter process be rightly effected during August and September, all kinds of plants may be indulged with a winter of torpidity, without the usual outlay for fuel, and the too frequently concurrent loss of their health and beauty.

These observations include the orchidaceous house as well as the stove; but, if umbrage has been regularly afforded throughout the last three months, it must be removed by slow stages, otherwise the appearance of the plants will be deteriorated. With those which have been permanently shaded, that is, over which the shading material has been retained both day and night, such precaution is particularly required. Although some culturists pursue the method just described for the purpose of saving trouble, it is greatly to be deprecated, since it tends to endue the plants with an unnatural degree of susceptibility, and their first subsequent exposure to the sun's rays inevitably causes the leaves to assume a yellow and sickly hue. If, again, the shading be only partially applied, and allowed to remain constantly on the house, it does not fulfil the end for which it was intended, and by intercepting the light during dull weather, or that part of the day at which the sun is mild and salutary, creates the same state of weakness as that previously mentioned. Only, therefore, at those times when it is quite essential, should any plants be shaded.

In the greenhouse, and also the open ground, all shrubby plants should, if needful, receive a check to their growth at the present time, by curtailing their supply of water. Where any disposition to a remarkable and continued luxuriance is apparent, this measure should be immediately commenced; for it is solely at the present period that the cultivator can interfere with advantage, as, in the ensuing months, solar influence will be so much diminished, that no reduction in the amount of fluid nutriment would render maturation complete, or secure the plants from the danger attending their temporary subjection to casual frosts.

Seeds of many annual plants being now ripe, may be collected according to the directions given in our last volume. On this subject some hints are also thrown out in page 134 of the July number, wherein it is attempted to be shown that those seeds are generally most prolific which are taken from plants yielding the greatest number of them. Cultivators will do well to scrutinize this suggestion, because, to the augmentation of the splendours of the flower-garden, it will, if correct, furnish an infallible guide. We leave it with an urgent recommendation to their notice at a time when the best possible opportunity is afforded for its examination.

Dendrobium Pastoni.

DENDROBIUM PAXTONI.

(PAXTON'S DENDROBIUM.)

CLASS.		ORDER.
GYNANDRIA.		MONANDRIA.

NATURAL ORDER.
ORCHIDACEÆ.

GENERIC CHARACTER.—*Vide* vol. iii. p. 77.

SPECIFIC CHARACTER.—*Plant* epiphytal, caulescent. *Stems* terete, furrowed. *Leaves* ovate-lanceolate, acuminate, or obscurely emarginate at the summit. *Peduncles* two-flowered. *Sepals* oblong, acute, lateral ones a little prolonged at the base; *petals* broader, obovate, acute, serrulate. *Labellum* unguiculated, ovate, concave, undivided, villous, much fimbriated at the margin.

IF the species of *Dendrobium* we have hitherto figured are such as to recommend themselves strongly to the cultivator's favour, every one will admit that the subject now represented is, of all the orange or yellow-flowered kinds, the most magnificent. And when it is considered that no drawing can do justice to the peculiar beauty of the fringed labellum of an orchidaceous flower, and at the same time borne in mind that the present species surpasses any of its allies in that particular, the richness and general accuracy of our plate will still require considerable aid of the imagination to invest it with those charms which nature has so lavishly bestowed upon the living plant.

With many other nearly related species, the pictorial delineations of some of which have so greatly embellished our work, the plant that furnished our drawing was imported from India by His Grace the Duke of Devonshire in 1837. Mr. Gibson originally discovered it growing on trees at Pondooah, a station near the base of the Khoseea Hills, and it flowered at Chatsworth last June. It approaches pretty closely in some features of its character to both *D. fimbriatum* and *D. chrysanthum*. To the former, its stems, foliage, and general habit assimilate, while the flowers are far superior, and these again differ from those of *D. chrysanthum* chiefly in the serratures of the petals and the deeply fringed labellum.

So many and such frequent allusions have been made in this Magazine to the culture of Dendrobiums, that it would almost appear a work of supererogation to insert any further remarks. In our August number (p. 146) we were led to notice a small group which requires little more than aerial support, or merely a slight covering to the roots for the retention of moisture. *D. Paxtoni* belongs to a very different class; and, besides its great height demanding some substance in which to fix the stakes needful for maintaining its erectness, the roots are more tender, and must be completely enveloped in moss or soil.

In the management of this and other similar species, where they can readily be slung from the roof of the house, the practice of placing them in rustic wooden baskets, with openings between the bars both at the sides and bottoms, is eminently calculated to prove successful. These receptacles should be filled principally with moss and such-like matters, because materials of this nature will allow water to pass through more freely, and protect the roots equally as well as heath-soil, without possessing its more retentive properties. By being suspended, and open at the sides, such baskets likewise preclude the accumulation of an undue supply of moisture, and render it much more easy to preserve a proper degree of drought (*i. e.* a medium between excessive aridity and too great dampness) during the annual period of repose.

We have repeatedly advocated the propriety of subjecting *Dendrobia* to an unusual degree of periodical dryness, and there cannot be a doubt that *D. Paxtoni* has been induced to flower so early after its arrival in this country in a sickly state, entirely through the cautious application of that principle. Similar, and even more unequivocal confirmations of the utility of such a course have recently crowded upon our attention, which naturally impart greater force and urgency to our recommendation of it to those who have yet doubted its appropriateness.

Pentstemon speciosus

PENTSTÉMON SPECIÒSA.

(SHOWY PENTSTEMON.)

CLASS.
DIDYNAMIA.

ORDER.
ANGIOSPERMIA.

NATURAL ORDER.
SCROPHULARIÀCEÆ.

GENERIC CHARACTER.—*Vide* vol. iv. p. 243.

SPECIFIC CHARACTER.—*Plant* an herbaceous perennial, evergreen. *Stems* numerous, from two to three feet in height. *Leaves* variable; radical ones spatulate, inclining to the earth; stem-leaves sessile, linear-oblong, obtuse, slightly channelled down the centre, perfectly smooth. *Corolla* bright azure-coloured, with a prominent naked throat, and a sterile, elongated, beardless filament.

PERHAPS the genus *Pentstemon* is, on the whole, one of the greatest boons conferred upon our gardens by the discovery of the New World. The attention of cultivators has however been too long and too exclusively occupied with the hybrids obtained from some of the less showy kinds, to the neglect of such as are more decidedly ornamental. This consideration has caused us to publish the accompanying plate of one of the choicest and most valuable species yet introduced.

P. speciosa was first known to British collections about the year 1826. It is one of the most worthy fruits of the lamented Douglas's labours on the North American continent. From the era of its original appearance in this country, to the present time, many thousand plants have been raised and distributed both by public and private individuals and bodies; but it does not appear to have created that admiration which its striking beauty is calculated to inspire in the breast of every lover of Nature's beauties. In only one nursery establishment (Messrs. Young's, Epsom) have we ever seen it cultivated, either abundantly or successfully, and from the garden of these gentlemen we had our drawing taken in June, 1838.

There are few general culturists able to grow the scarcer species of this genus to any state approaching the perfection they attain under the care of some two or three individuals, who, having investigated their habits, understand their peculiarities, and accommodate thereto the treatment they bestow. It is to this almost universality of failure, that the rarity of these most delightful plants is mainly due; since they are not only reduced in number by actual loss, but, owing to the general impression that they will barely exist under ordinary circumstances, are seldom sought, and still less frequently procured and perpetuated.

Nothing contributes more materially to the maintenance of Pentstemons in health, than planting them in an open and dry situation; while, on the contrary, when placed beneath the shade or drippings of trees, or in any low, damp spot, they invariably perish in the winter season. *P. speciosa* is, we believe, quite hardy, and is not injured by frost, except it be intense; but it will not endure excessive moisture, and cannot be grown in too exposed a position, provided it is not so much above the level of the surrounding parts as to be subjected to extremely bleak winds.

A rather rich loamy soil should be chosen for this plant, especial care being taken to avoid one that is too adhesive. Cultivated in beds, its modest but brilliant-looking blue flowers present a most gorgeous mass: but probably a fine solitary specimen may produce the best effect. It should always be grown in the flower-garden, or in open beds, and never in a border in or near which shrubs or trees exist; these, however, being only inimical as they overshadow the plant, or tend to collect water about its leaves and roots.

It may be propagated by offsets or layers; but, as the seeds are freely ripened, and a greater number of finer plants may be raised from them, it is better to increase it by this means. The seeds can be sown about the month of February in a very slight hotbed, and protected by garden mats thrown over a temporary wooden frame. When planted out in the beginning of June, the young plants rarely require water; and we are informed that, in the Epsom nursery, young plants which were watered suffered considerably, indeed many were destroyed by this treatment; those which were left untended growing vigorously, and speedily establishing themselves.

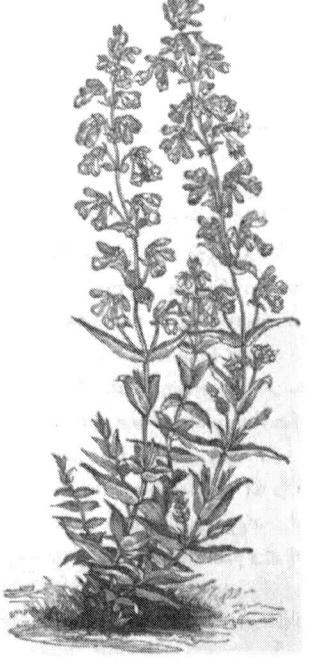

Messrs. Young, of Epsom, possess an extensive stock of this handsome plant. Its habit will be seen from the above engraving.

Nuttallia papaver

NUTTÁLLIA PAPÁVER.

(POPPY-FLOWERED NUTTALLIA.)

CLASS.
MONADELPHIA.

ORDER.
POLYANDRIA.

NATURAL ORDER.
MALVÁCEÆ.

GENERIC CHARACTER.—*Vide* vol. v. p. 217.

SPECIFIC CHARACTER.—*Root* biennial, fusiform, white. *Stem* erect, branched, from a foot to two feet high. *Branches* filiform, sparingly furnished with adpressed bristly hairs. *Leaves*, the radical ones on footstalks of from four to five inches in length, five-lobed, with cuneate-oblong, blunt, lobed, sometimes pinnatifid segments, furnished with a few scattered, adpressed, bristly hairs; those of the stem on shorter stalks, more deeply divided into three or five narrow, linear, acute, mostly entire segments. *Stipules* ovate, acute, fringed, leafy. *Flowers* solitary. *Peduncles* straight, filiform, from three to six inches long, clothed with adpressed bristly hairs. *Calyx* five-cleft, copiously bristly, with ovate, acuminate lobes, and furnished at the base with three linear, acute, spreading, bristly bracts, of about three lines in length. *Petals* five, broadly wedge-shaped, an inch long, somewhat connivent, the upper edge truncate, torn and crenate, of a rich lake, the claws short, white, and fringed at the border. *Stamens* very numerous. *Filaments* united into a column. *Anthers* yellow, reniform, unilocular, composed of two cup-shaped valves. *Stigmas* about twelve, long, filiform, pale purple, spreading, bearded along their upper surface. *Ovaria* about twelve, one-seeded, arranged closely in a circle, glabrous, notched exteriorly.—*Sweet's British Flower-Garden*, vol. iii. p. 279.

ANOTHER and somewhat finer species of this interesting genus was figured in the last volume of this work, under the name of *N. grandiflora*; in preparing the description of which, we indulged in a few remarks laudatory of its generally ornamental character. These may now be enlisted in favour of our present plant; for, though its flowers are not so large, and, by consequence, less showy, it has a beauty and elegance peculiarly its own; and we cannot but lament the little esteem in which both it and the other species referred to appear to be held. Indeed, we may extend our regret to almost all the newer kinds of herbaceous plants, which now but rarely find their way into any collections except those of the more zealous cultivators, or such amateurs as regard them with especial complacency.

The immediate subject of present notice has been known in Britain nearly six years; having been imported from Louisiana, in the United States, about 1833. Being a half-hardy plant, it is not often seen in a high state of cultivation; most individuals thinking the trouble of keeping it through the winter greater than its summer appearance will fully compensate. With respect to this species, however, and many others of like habits that require the same temperature, such an inference is unjustifiable and erroneous. They are much more easy to preserve than half-hardy shrubs, and, in the case of *N. papaver*, a sufficient number of seeds are annually matured to enable the culturist to manifest a degree of indifference as to whether the old specimens are preserved or destroyed.

Plants raised from seeds sown as early as possible in the spring beneath some protective awning, will have every opportunity of developing their flowers in the same season, because the species does not naturally blossom till the commencement of autumn. The surest method of protecting them in the winter, where frames exist in abundance, is to place the plants in pots, and retain them constantly in frames. If this system be practised, every pains must be taken to prevent them from becoming too tender, by completely exposing them whenever the weather is at all propitious. Extreme humidity must also be guarded against, since, to plants of this description, it is exceedingly prejudicial.

When a stock of young plants is possessed, and these are properly housed, or where no frame or greenhouse can be conveniently spared, the old plants may be covered, to the depth of four or six inches, with decaying bark, or some substance of a similar nature. But the best mode of preserving all plants of this kind in the open ground, is to prepare a number of small wooden covers, constructed in the form of pyramids or hand-glasses, and place one of them over each plant needing shelter, filling up the interior with dry hay or litter. These would exclude both rain and frost, and could be employed or taken off at pleasure, according to the state of the atmosphere. The expense of such covers would be very trifling; their appearance, if neatly painted, far from unsightly; and, with a little attention, they would also be found durable.

For our drawing of this species, we are obliged to Messrs. Young, of Epsom; from whose establishment it was obtained in August, 1838.

The specific designation explains itself; applying almost exclusively to the flowers.

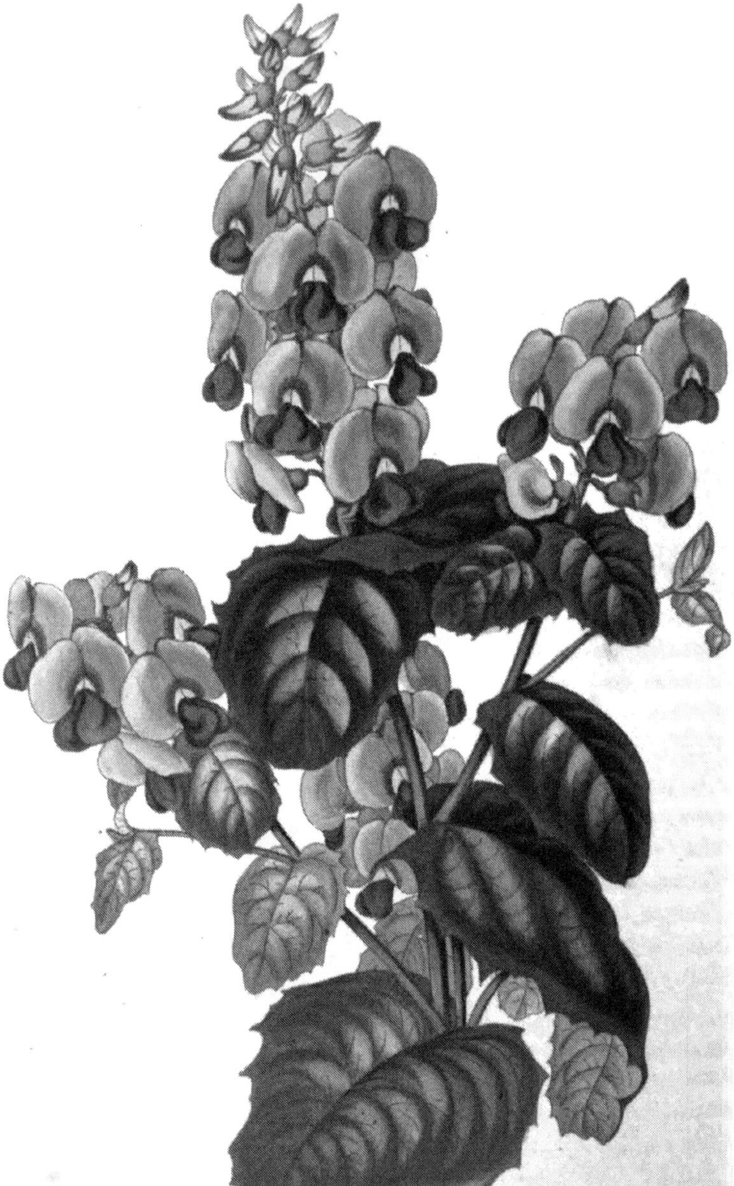

CHORIZÈMA VÀRIUM.

(VARIOUS-LEAVED CHORIZEMA.)

CLASS.	ORDER.
DECANDRIA.	MONOGYNIA.

NATURAL ORDER.
LEGUMINÒSÆ.

GENERIC CHARACTER.—*Vide* vol. iv. p. 153.

SPECIFIC CHARACTER.—*Plant* shrubby, growing from four to six feet in height. *Stems* erect, strong, slightly downy, branching. *Leaves* nearly sessile, roundly-cordate, undulated, with regular, entire serratures, which terminate in spines, pubescent. *Racemes* erect, many-flowered, terminal, short, and densely covered with flowers. *Calyx* tubular at the base, with obtuse, pilose, sub-equal teeth. *Flowers* reddish yellow.

BEFORE the seeds of this remarkably handsome species were germinated in England, the genus *Chorizema* was composed of plants which, without reference to the flowers, were comparatively worthless. So much indeed was this the case, that when we published a figure of *C. cordata*, we particularly noted its great superiority over its allies in habitude and foliage. We are now compelled to qualify very largely our encomiums on that plant, as a more mature acquaintance has convinced us that the rapidity and extent of its growth are far from desirable characteristics, prolonged, as they generally are, into a most displeasing laxness and diffusiveness, with the usually attendant paucity of leaves.

To *C. varium* we are fully persuaded none of the above objections will ever apply. Its habit is totally the reverse of straggling; extraordinary luxuriance, combined with strength and robustness of stems, and particularly large, conspicuous, and well-formed foliage, being its prominent and invariable features. To maintain these in their natural vigour, it is of course necessary that judicious treatment be afforded; but less mischief follows a departure from such a course to this plant than to any of those with which it is directly associated, on account of the greater number, consistence, and native energy of its roots.

During the years 1837 and 1838, seeds of this plant were received by many individuals from the Swan River colony, Captain Mangles, R. N., having probably distributed the greatest quantity. We cannot with confidence affirm, but are led to believe that its flowers first expanded in the nursery of Mr. Halley, Blackheath, through whose kindness we were favoured with an opportunity of having our drawing executed from a specimen which bloomed in the month of June last. That gentleman had been furnished with seeds of this, and a variety of other supposed new Australian plants, from a friend connected with the Swan River district, and these having vegetated in great abundance, as well as the specimens thus raised having been subsequently multiplied, there is a copious and valuable stock in his nursery at the place above-named.

Regarding its cultivation, we have few suggestions to offer beyond those recorded in our previous volumes. There is one point which will not fail to impress itself upon the mind of every enlightened grower, which is its obvious need of more liberal treatment, both as relates to the quality of the soil and extent of pot-room, than *C. ovata* or even *C. cordata*. The *apparent* constitution of a plant will almost always determine this consideration, and that of *C. varium* may be confidently depended upon. Rich soil for strong-growing species, with a much less generous and nutrimental compost for the weakly kinds, is a principle that holds good throughout the entire vegetable kingdom, with some slight restrictions and modifications in unusual cases; and, in exact accordance with this datum, the subject now under deliberation should be tended. Abundance of light is likewise an essential condition, and should be duly supplied. In a small conservatory, where it would be sufficiently near the glass, it would most probably thrive more vigorously, and form a more signally beautiful object if planted in a prepared bed or border. But this should not be attempted unless proximity to the light can be ensured.

Cuttings, taken off while in a half-ripened state, will strike without the least difficulty if attended to in the usual manner. It would appear almost politic to prepare these from the leading shoots, or at least the central one, as the plant is disposed to grow too much to a single stem, without branching enough to render its outline compact and symmetrical.

The specific name was applied by Dr. Lindley in reference to the variable character of its foliage. It has been known in nurseries by the title of *C. latifolia*, and likewise, we suspect, *C. elegans*.

RUDIMENTS OF THE NATURAL SYSTEM OF BOTANY.

Lord Bacon, the brilliancy of whose philosophic genius has shed its rays upon even our enlightened era, is reported to have destroyed the whole of the works on gardening with which his library was furnished, because the subjects were too superficially or dogmatically treated. Since that period, the British nation has been continually advancing in intelligence, and yet, at the present time, the demand for philosophical literature is, in this department, far from being fully met and satisfied. Botanical science, rather than horticultural art,—comprehensive principles in preference to individual experience,—are now, we believe, almost universally sought.

In endeavouring to gratify this pleasing propensity, we have been among the first to abandon the old and still frequently-practised system of conducting floricultural works; and while, in express elucidation of vegetable structure and processes, a greater or less number of our pages are monthly occupied, we are led to conceive that some simple observations on systematic arrangement, in which likewise a popular account of the organs of plants is embodied, will meet with acceptance. Few in the more respectable classes of society will now be found who are not in some way aiming to obtain a knowledge of botany. This taste—at once worthy of the noblest minds, and innocuous and elevating to the feeblest—is rapidly spreading. It reckons among its followers the inmates of palaces, and is not unknown to simple hearts in cottage shades. It establishes a communion of sentiment between individuals whom pecuniary circumstances would otherwise separate, and invariably brings in its train social and domestic order and comfort. We therefore hail its extension as a national blessing, the token and evidence of peace and refinement, and the precursor of honour and prosperity.

To those who shrink from the effort to master the natural system of botany, on account of its extent, intricacy, and, in some parts, apparent anomaly, we here intend to supply a sketch of its main principles, preparatory to a more enlarged or particular display of the different orders. It will soon be seen that we do not contemplate any tedious prolixity of description, nor the employment of many technical terms. Whatever may have before appeared in our Magazine connected with this subject, there exists an absolute necessity for laying a proper foundation in this place, by declaring and illustrating the first great divisions which botanists recognise. We shall avail ourselves, in matters of detail, of the works of Dr. Lindley, who, in this country, may be said to have taken the lead in the improvement and explication of this system.

Two prime divisions, termed classes, serve to embrace the entire vegetable world. These are designated by botanists VASCULARES and CELLULARES. *Vas-*

culares, called by some *Phænogamous*, or flowering plants, are those which, while they possess a cellular tissue in common with *Cellulares*, have also a system of tubular, longitudinal, and straight or spiral vessels. *Cellulares*, on the other hand, are composed of cells alone, the form of which is always some modification of round, the angular corners being caused by compression. These are the most important distinctions; and while it is more easy for the learner to consider the former as *flowering*, and the latter as *flowerless* plants, it is highly useful to fix in the memory the scientific appellations of each, because these afford an excellent key to their structure.

In the class *Vasculares*, nearly all the plants which possess any interest to the cultivator are arranged; *Cellulares* being, for the most part, inconspicuous and worthless. *Vasculares* will, consequently, claim primary and most extensive consideration. They are first divided into two *sub-classes*, respectively denominated EXOGENÆ and ENDOGENÆ, to which the terms DICOTYLEDONEÆ and MONOCOTYLEDONEÆ, are concurrent. The titles first mentioned refer to the mode of growth; the stems of *Exogenæ* enlarging exteriorly, and those of *Endogenæ* towards the centre. The two other terms contain an allusion to the number of seed-lobes, *monos* and *dis* signifying one and two.

Exogens principally inhabit temperate climes, and are much more numerous than Endogens. In the absence of seeds, they may be known by their stems being branched, and having both pith and bark. With herbaceous plants, or even trees, a more simple method of determining their class is an examination of the leaves; those of Exogens being reticulated, that is, having a great number of irregular transverse or divergent veins. It should be remembered, however, that many Endogens have *parallel* veins to their leaves, and that it is only when these branch laterally, and ramify themselves throughout the entire leaf, that they are to be regarded as characteristic of Exogens.

The common trees of our own climate may be mentioned as examples of this sub-class. In the centre of all these, especially while young, a greater or less circular deposite of pith may be found. This is composed solely of cellular tissue, and may also be distinguished by its remarkable elasticity, by its susceptibility of compression, and, compared with the surrounding wood, its extreme softness, while, after the wood is duly formed, the substance in question ceases to contain fluids, and is, in fact, a mere mass of cellular integument. That, in such a state, the pressure of exterior deposites of wood should contract its bulk, is not at all surprising; particularly if, as physiologists assert, a horizontal communication, for the conveyance towards it of annual secretions, is constantly maintained in Exogenous plants. Accordingly if a tree is examined at different epochs of its age, the observer will discover that the volume of pith is gradually lessened, year after year, till, in old trees, it is scarcely perceptible.

Let it not be supposed that this information is misplaced or superfluous. One of the acknowledged tests of Exogenous plants is the existence of pith; and, as every criterion of this kind should be rendered worthy of trust, it is of advantage to the student to know that, in the trunks of very aged trees, this is not to be traced. Such knowledge will very naturally lead the intelligent investigator to the young branches, in all of which he will not fail to detect an internal layer of pith.

Some botanists of considerable eminence have wholly denied the contraction of pith; but the universal observation of practical gardeners is opposed to this conclusion: and, from close scrutiny, we unhesitatingly affirm that, within four or six years, the pith of a vigorous elder shoot will decrease to half its original size. We are the more tenacious of this position, because it involves one of the fundamental characters of Exogens; and, unless the solidification of pith be admitted, its presence as a mark of distinction falls to the ground; as every one must have witnessed trees in which the pith was entirely obliterated.

Immediately surrounding the pith of Exogenous plants, is that portion which is known by the name of *wood*. It is the structure of this member that brings them beneath the class *Vasculares*, while the manner in which it increases alone determines it Exogenous. Wood is formed of various kinds of longitudinal vessels and fibres, intersected by horizontally disposed cells. It differs from pith, not only in figure and position, but also in its capacity for induration and enlargement. Pith, indeed, may be regarded merely as a provision of Nature for the support and development of the first layer of wood; and being by this drained of its fluids and vitality, it is ever afterwards virtually dead, and quite useless to the vegetable. Wood, on the contrary, yearly gives birth to, nourishes, and matures an additional layer of the same nature and consistence as itself; which new deposite performs the same office in each succeeding year, perhaps by exudations from its surface, which the action of the atmospheric elements solidifies and hardens.

Numberless theories respecting the formation of wood in Exogens have, at various times, been propounded by botanists. In support of all these, both arguments and facts have been brought forward. It still remains a doubtful and disputed point; and is one of those intricacies, to unravel which, great ingenuity, labour, and time are required. Whether each new deposite of wood possesses the power of exuding a fluid, which, though at first apparently homogeneous, is ultimately converted into the different forms of cell and vessel, of which the vegetable body is constructed; whether this fluid is imbibed from the soil, and, by being subjected to the action of influences peculiar to each tribe of plants, is thus transformed and assimilated to the plant's own nature; or whether, further, the leaves are the grand laboratories in which fluids extracted from the earth are changed in quality and substance, and thence dispersed as secretions and deposites throughout the vegetable frame, we cannot pretend to decide.

Based on the above three hypotheses, as well as on others we deem it unnecessary to adduce, philosophers and theorists have been prodigal of their suggestions as to the process by which wood is elaborated. During the spring of the present year, we examined the growing wood of several trees, for the purpose of satisfying ourselves on this subject. The results, however, were by no means so conclusive as we desired, probably because we had not provided magnifying-glasses of sufficient power, and other necessary auxiliaries. In the young shoots of the Horse Chestnut, (which is an excellent object for exhibiting the organs clearly,) we found a decided fibrous communication between the old wood and the leaves. The petiole of each leaf contains a quantity of fibres, visible to the naked eye, which envelop the growing stem, and may be traced down it, at regular distances from each other, till they are covered by the next layer of fibres, which issue from the leaf immediately below the one examined; nevertheless, this structure, so far from sanctioning the supposition that such fibres are originated in the leaves, appears to favour a directly contrary assumption. If the fibres emanated from the foliage, it is most reasonable to imagine that those proceeding from the uppermost leaf would, by being last formed, maintain their exterior position throughout their whole extent; since it is extremely unlikely that they should be capable of penetrating beneath all the other layers, and preserving their contiguity to the pith of the new shoots, and the wood of the previous year. And yet this last is undoubtedly the case; so that the theory which attributes to the leaves the generation of woody tissue, must be received with some degree of reserve.

Besides being essentially characterised by wood which enlarges from the outside, the stems of Exogens are invariably encompassed by a cuticle or bark. This bark, like the pith, is composed of cellular tissue alone; but an annual layer is deposited in the inside, which seems to have the same origin as, or one very similar to, the woody layer; and, by its proximity to the atmosphere, the pressure of this latter, combined with the outward pressure, indeed, enlargement of the wood, causes it to assume a compactness of appearance resembling the woody tissue itself. When neither bark, wood, nor pith, are present to assist the student, he can refer to the leaves; and from the description of them we have already given, the sub-class of any plant may be discovered.

Such is a very brief delineation of the prominent distinguishing traits of Exogens. The reader who has by this means made himself acquainted with that first and greatest sub-class, will be prepared to follow us, at some subsequent period, into the further subdivisions of this arrangement; from which we shall endeavour to conduct him, by a regular and pleasing route, to the lesser orders for a more minute inquiry into the peculiarities of individual plants. If we sometimes depart from the beaten path, to illuminate its obscurities by a borrowed light from other departments of botany, we hope, by accomplishing the design of those digressions, to conciliate the most captious, and inform those who have never had sufficient time, means, or inclination, to thread the mazes of botanical science.

INFLUENCE OF CLIMATE ON PLANTS.*
SOLAR HEAT.

COULD we have entertained a well-grounded opinion that popular desires are always guided by permanent advantage, and directed towards the emolument of science, we might have felt ourselves justified in multiplying these papers to an almost indefinite extent; so comprehensive and transcendently important is the subject of which they treat. But, impressed with the conviction that, to the majority of our readers they must now be growing tedious; and in accordance with the saying of one possessing deep penetration and knowledge of human nature, that "variety's the spice of life;" for we believe that this applies with no less force to literary and scientific recreation than to the meaner occurrences and engagements of general society; we shall speedily close this series, by portraying some of the most striking effects on vegetation of the varied climate attendant on different zones, altitudes, and other circumstances which influence the temperature of a locality.

On a mountain of sufficient size and height within the tropics, the whole of the vegetable species inhabiting our globe might have assigned to them a climate whose temperature would be exactly such as they naturally experience in their respective degrees of latitude; these embracing all that man has yet been able to explore. However startling this assumption may appear, it is confirmed by indubitable facts. The proofs of its verity are profusely furnished by nature's great Architect, since, on the most insignificant hills, many plants that would flourish in the valleys can scarcely be preserved; while, on the summits of the former, other plants are found which, still farther north, seek a lower and more retired position. Cases are by no means rare, even in Britain, where, in ascending a hilly range, or isolated mountain, the limits of distinct groups of native vegetation may be discovered, each possessing a hardier character than the one beneath it, till we arrive at the point, beyond which, during the severe months, continued snow performs the part of a protector, and the plants, consequently, are less hardy.

Let us, however, as collectors and cultivators of the vegetable productions of all countries, carry our researches beyond this comparatively diminutive, ocean-encircled spot, and contemplate, for instance, that incomparably vaster range of mountains—the enormous Himalayah. Here is a tract, from the study of which great practical assistance and instruction may be obtained. Many thousand feet above the base of these mountains, the ordinary tropical plants are met with in the greatest vigour; while below their summits trees are found which will thrive, without shelter, in the open ground of Britain. The same phenomenon prevails, though to a smaller extent, throughout every elevated region in the world. As the sea, with reference to the earth's centre, is at all points nearly on the same level, it is very properly chosen as a universal standard from which to calculate the

* Continued from page 159.

height of any eminence; and the higher we ascend above the surface of this immense plane, the greater degree of settled coldness the atmosphere assumes.

Commencing, therefore, with the position that a certain degree of increased elevation is commensurate with an infinitely greater advance towards the polar circles, or that the temperature undergoes a similar but much more rapid and sensible diminution, we need not stay to expose the inutility of acquaintance with the native country of a plant, while the height of its actual haunts is unknown; but will at once urge the direct bearing of the question, and strive to show how this apparently lax and broad principle can be brought to regulate common cultivation on British soil. It might be imagined that in an island, the face of which is so little diversified, the temperature could not, on the highest of its puny hills, be palpably depressed. Those who yield to this supposition, will, however, by a little observation, find themselves strangely in error. There is not a hill, how limited soever may be the space it occupies, or the height it attains, which affects not the condition of the plants growing upon it. In a few instances, this influence is beneficial, and these we shall hereafter enumerate; but, with regard to exotic plants generally, it only tends to augment the cultivator's difficulties, retard the progress of his charge, or facilitate their destruction.

To prevent any unnecessary cavil at the foregoing statement, we will add that it refers solely to an unsheltered hill; where the danger to tender plants would increase in proportion to its height, on account of the additional cold to which they would be exposed. On very trifling eminences, however, this would perhaps be more than counteracted by circumstances which will subsequently be noticed.

Hills are not necessarily improper situations for the plantation of exotic species; nor are valleys, as might be mistakenly inferred from what we have just declared, always the most appropriate. The suitability of either depends entirely on local considerations, and the nature of their surface. The summits of extensive but not very high hills, which present a considerable and tolerably uniform superficies, may probably be the best sites for half-hardy shrubs; because, in such localities, the desired degree of aridity is usually preserved about the roots, and the thorough exposure to sun and air that is afforded, is exactly such as will give firmness and maturity to every annual development. Imperfect protection from cold wintry winds would not, in this case, be followed by the usual injury; as sufficient natural preparation would be made during the summer to enable the plants to dispense with the greater portion of such assistance.

A position on the sides or slopes of hills, though in some respects eligible, affords much more doubtful security for the maintenance of tender plants, unless it be open alone to the south or south-west. In all other aspects, no valuable trees or shrubs can be planted without incurring great risk. The reason of this is perfectly clear. Very little direct light, and much less heat than is supplied to the opposite side, ever reach such spots; while, at the same time, they lie completely open to the most inclement winds which our climate experiences. We may add, also, that, owing to the former of these causes, (lack of light and heat,) the escape of water is, in cold, wet weather, much impeded, and stagnates about the roots of plants, to their great detriment.

Valleys, to be perfectly adapted for growing exotic plants, must not be circumscribed, especially if traversed by a river or stream. No spot can be less fitted for conducting the more refined part of floriculture, than a narrow valley, through which a river flows. The constant exhalations from water are calculated not only to saturate the leaves and branches of plants, but, by remaining in the lower stratum of the atmosphere during a frosty night, in many instances occasion all the consequent destruction. All who have had an opportunity of observing the injury sustained by plants in dales from a slight hoar-frost, must have noticed that in those districts which were above the low-lying vapours, similar plants have wholly escaped its effects. This simple circumstance casts much valuable light on the subject of the present article.

Wherever water exists, it has a constant tendency to lower the temperature; and the vicinities of places wherein it abounds most, suffer the greatest reduction of heat. The sea may, however, be considered an exception to this, since its immense and continuous expanse of water retains through the winter a higher temperature than the superincumbent and surrounding air. Plants growing within a few miles of the sea coast, (at least of that portion of it which is not swept by the icy blasts from colder regions,) may therefore be presumed to enjoy an increased degree of heat at that season, on account of the incessant radiation from so large a body. On the other hand, by absorbing more rapidly than land the superior heat of the atmosphere, it materially reduces the temperature in summer, and thus maintains a comparative equability.

With rivers and all smaller channels of water, it is wholly different. The mists which are perpetually arising from them, if confined between two ranges of hills, having no room to disperse, are condensed and precipitated to the earth in cold evenings, and, by their deposition upon plants, affording as it were an attraction to frost, subside into globules of congealed fluid, the mischief occasioned by which is soon exhibited after the first action of the sun. But where the valley occupies a broad district, these vapours, possessing like heat a diffusive power, are dispersed throughout even its most remote parts, and their density, with its concurrent effect upon vegetation, is proportionately lessened.

Having stated thus cursorily the changes in the temperature of a climate which the altitude of a spot or its proximity to water will produce, we will now, lest any misapprehension should arise, add our own deductions and conclusions. All low marshy places should be particularly avoided, as containing within themselves elements which, if not counteracted, inevitably cause or lay the foundation of disease and death. We here include those tracts in which any disposition (although only periodical) to particular dampness is apparent. Whatever may be the impressions or desires of cultivators, nothing is more certain than that the production of a stunted habit of growth is the surest method of acclimatizing plants. If once the natural luxuriance of any species is attempted, whether immediately or within several years after its being planted, its wood will never be ripened, in a few years it will become weak and sickly, and there is every probability of its ultimate loss, because in such a state, it will require greater and more durable protection than can possibly be afforded.

All the bad consequences here specified inevitably attend a too humid situation and soil. A less moist compartment in a wide-spreading vale, but effectually sheltered and shaded either by trees or artificial erections, is equally inappropriate with that to which we have just objected; and from the same as well as additional causes. Besides giving encouragement to excessive moisture, it deprives the plants of a condition which is quite essential to their perfect development. Nearly all half-hardy shrubs flourish beneath a far more vigorous emanation of both light and heat from solar sources, than we could allow them in our most prominent and unincumbered districts. By contracting, or in any way infringing this supply, we of course, and to precisely the same extent, diminish their produce, and prejudicially affect their health.

Notwithstanding, then, the too frequent practice of forming plantations to shelter tender plants, we would press upon all who are desirous of naturalizing the most beautiful of European, Australian, and other exotics, to place them where nothing can impede or subdue the action of any atmospheric elements, rain and its various modifications alone excepted. Permanent shelter of every kind is injudicious, unnecessary, and even hurtful. That effected by plantations of trees is the more common mode; but, as many of these must be deciduous, the plants are most protected at a time when there is not the slightest need for any such interference. And in the winter, if frosts are so severe as to occasion danger, it is as easy to apply artificial shelter according to our proposed system, as it would be in the case of which we have been complaining; nor, all circumstances duly weighed, would there be any greater necessity for it, or for a more abundant application.

While we denounce so unqualifiedly the general method of providing any fixed material for averting cold, we must cautiously guard against the opposite extreme, for reasons heretofore delivered. The top of an extremely elevated piece of ground, unless it be of considerable circuit and tolerably free from irregularities, would be a highly dangerous spot for cultivating tender species. The upper verge of any declivity, however slight, is equally objectionable. In short, a nearly level, dry, thoroughly exposed plot, of only a moderate altitude, and, if on a plain, at a proper distance from rivers, lakes, or other large bodies of water, will, with regard to temperature and its dependent or concomitant conditions, furnish a situation wherein any kinds of plants may, if anywhere, be fully acclimatized.

(*To be concluded in our next.*)

FLORICULTURAL NOTICES.

NEW AND RARE PLANTS, FIGURED IN THE LEADING BOTANICAL PERIODICALS FOR AUGUST.

CLASS I.—PLANTS WITH TWO COTYLEDONS (DICOTYLEDONEÆ).

THE BERBERRY TRIBE (*Berberàceæ*).

EPIMÈDIUM MUSSCHIÀNUM. White-flowered Barren-Wort. With small and almost colourless flowers, this new species is of very little value, unless it be for the delicacy and abundance of its foliage, and its hardy character. Dr. Siebold has added *E. Musschianum* to many others of much greater beauty, transmitted by him from Japan, some of which we have before noticed and figured. It blossoms about March in the greenhouse of the Glasgow Botanic Garden; but at Messrs. Young's, Epsom, we have seen it flowering in the open ground through the months of May and June. Pale greenish white blossoms, which are comparatively diminutive, are its principal points of distinction. *Bot. Mag.* 3745.

THE BIRTHWORT TRIBE (*Aristolochiàceæ*).

HETEROTRÒPA ASAROÌDES. Messrs. Morren and Decaisne have thought it necessary to form a new genus of this plant under the above title, on account of the different disposition of the stamens and structure of the anthers, from the established character of *Asarum*. We have previously described it as *Asarum japonicum*. The leaves resemble, in variegation of hue, those of some species of *Cyclamen*; while the flowers are contracted pitcher-shaped, dark-brown, with a purple and yellow centre, and exceedingly curious. It was forwarded to Europe by the same gentleman and from the same empire as the preceding, and plants may be obtained from the Epsom Nursery, where it blooms in the greenhouse in the early part of March; the flowers lasting for several days. *Bot. Mag.* 3746.

THE BEAN TRIBE (*Leguminòsæ*).

INGA HARRÍSII. Mr. Harris's Inga. Handsome leaves, curious as well as showy blossoms, and an apparent disposition to bear a considerable quantity of them, render this species a worthy remembrancer of the horticultural zeal of Thomas Harris, Esq., of Kingsbury, by whom it was imported from Mexico, and after whom Dr. Lindley has named it. The peduncles of each leaf seem to separate into pairs at a short distance from their base, and on both of these divisions three hairy leaflets, about an inch and a half long, are produced. The short pink corollas, which appear in clusters, and are tipped with green, are surmounted by bunches of long pink filaments, with yellow anthers; and these have a most interesting appearance. A rich soil, and a medium temperature between that of the greenhouse and stove, are recommended for its cultivation. Being a climbing shrub, it may be trained to the rafters of the house. *Bot. Reg.* 41.

BAUHÍNIA FORFICÀTA. By a remarkable coincidence, the genus *Bauhinia*, whose species invariably bear twin leaves, commemorates two brothers, John and Gaspar Bauhin, who distinguished themselves as botanists in the sixteenth century. The present plant is a native of Brazil, and though long cultivated in the Glasgow Botanic Garden, did not flower there till July, 1837. It is a climbing plant, with long pendent branches, short spines in pairs at the bottom of the petioles, and large white flowers, which are divided into five narrow expansive segments, from the common bases of which, and in the centre of the flower, the extended, recurved stamens gracefully protrude. It requires the atmosphere of the stove, and is doubtless an ornamental species, though rather straggling in its habits. *Bot. Mag.* 3741.

GOMPHOLÒBIUM VERSÍCOLOR. Changeable Gompholobium. The elegant *G. polymorphum* which we figured last month is, we think, outrivalled by the subject of these remarks, both in the richness of the tints of its flowers and the greater strength of its stems; although this opinion is founded solely on the drawing of *G. versicolor*, as we have not yet seen living specimens in bloom. Its native country is the vicinity of Swan River, and it was introduced as well as first flowered, by R. Mangles, Esq., of Sunning Hill. Dr. Lindley states that it approaches very nearly to *G. tenue*, differing from that species " in its shorter petioles, and subracemose dark flowers; and from *G. sparsum* in the leaflets not being at all veiny, and all equal sized." The leaves are divided into three linear mucronate segments, and the flowers are bright yellowish brown. It may be treated as *G. polymorphum*. *Bot. Reg.* 43.

THE BUCK-WHEAT TRIBE (*Polygonàceæ*).

POLÝGONUM AMPLEXICAÚLE. Stem-clasping Polygonum. A very pretty herbaceous plant, which, with its numerous spikes of red flowers, and noble foliage, forms quite a desirable feature in the flower border. It is said to be common in Nepal, and from being distributed over an extensive tract of country, varies so much in its appearance as to have led some botanists into the mistaken application of more than one distinct specific name. These variations are, however, not apparent in plants growing in the same conditions; since a number of specimens raised in the garden of the Horticultural Society from seeds obtained in India, are perfectly uniform in their character. Dr. Lindley proposes for its culture a spot on the bank of a lake or pond, as it prefers a situation where the roots can extend themselves into water. Increase is effected by division of the plant or by seeds; the former method being the most speedy. July and August are its seasons of flowering, and it grows to the height of three or four feet. *Bot. Reg.* 46.

THE GESNERIA TRIBE (*Gesneridceæ*).

GESNÈRIA MÁRCHII. Mr. March's Gesneria. Under this title, a species of a very extraordinary character has been imported and flowered by G. Wailes, Esq., of Newcastle, which may be expected to eclipse all our old inhabitants of the stove belonging to the same genus. Mr. Wailes describes the root as "a large, roundish, depressed tuber, measuring more than three feet in circumference, and about an inch and a half thick." From this immense body, there appears to issue a profusion of stems, about two feet and a half high, with short, infertile, lateral shoots, but terminating in a spike thickly covered with beautiful red flowers, the form of which is nearly regular, though considerably swollen at the base. The number of flowers which one plant is capable of developing is really astonishing. The species was collected on the estate of George March, Esq., in the Organ mountains of Brazil; and, in consideration of that gentleman's kindness to botanical collectors, it has been appropriately designated by his name. It has hitherto flowered in October. *Bot. Mag.* 3744.

CLASS II.—PLANTS WITH ONE COTYLEDON (MONOCOTYLEDONEÆ).

THE ORCHIS TRIBE (*Orchidàceæ*).

! BURLINGTÒNIA MACULÀTA. Spotted-flowered Burlingtonia. In the superb collection of Messrs. Loddiges, this novel species was induced to disclose its flowers in May, 1838. They are of a yellow ground, prettily and irregularly blotched with brown, thus introducing quite a new trait to the genus. The small and slender habits to which it seems naturally inclined, render its attachment to a block of wood indispensable, while the drooping nature of its floral racemes alike requires its suspension from the roof of the house to exhibit them properly. Brazil is its native country; and the pleasant scent of its blossoms is not the least powerful of its recommendations to amateurs of Orchidaceæ. *Bot. Reg.* 44.

CÀTTLEYA CITRÌNA. Yellow-flowered Cattleya. We are always rejoiced in hearing that orchidaceous plants of distinct character and peculiar form have been blossomed in this country, and it is with high gratification we now witness a figure of this handsome Cattleya, prepared from a blooming specimen in the possession of His Grace the Duke of Bedford, at Woburn Abbey. The smallness, shortness, and semi-rotundity of its pseudo-bulbs afforded but indifferent promise of its flowers; but these have proved of a highly ornamental character. They are large, solitary, half-pendent, and of a deep and brilliant yellow colour. It was sent from Oaxaco, Mexico, by Robert Smith, Esq., and flowered in April of the present year. It may at once be known by the glaucous hue of the bulbs, of which also the leaves in some degree partake. *Bot. Mag.* 3742.

NEW, RARE, AND INTERESTING PLANTS IN FLOWER IN THE PRINCIPAL SUBURBAN NURSERIES.

ÆRIDES ——— ? All who are acquainted with this most lovely genus, would doubtless receive with delight any new accession; but when a decidedly distinct species is introduced, rivalling even *Æ. odoratum* in beauty, and of a still richer fragrance, it may be presumed to excite particular attention. Such a plant has been blooming for several weeks in the orchidaceous house of Messrs. Loddiges, and its charming blossoms have not yet withered. In habit, it is not unlike the species above referred to; though the foliage is apparently larger, and the mode of growth stronger. The flowers are produced from the sides of the stem on half-pendulous racemes, which are usually about six inches in length. In an immature state, the horn or spur of the labellum is deep-green, but this gradually changes to a cream-colour as the flowers expand; and over the centre of the prominent concavity of this spur, is a beautifully fringed purple arch, which adds greatly to the interest of the blossom. At the tip of each sepal and petal, there is a large blotch of purple, and many minute purple spots are scattered over the remaining parts of these members, which are otherwise cream-coloured. As above hinted, its odour is most delicious. It was, we believe, imported from India.

ANGRÆCUM CAUDÀTUM. To the admirers of the curious in nature, orchidaceæ present an endless variety of pleasing objects; and amongst these, none is more remarkable than the plant now beneath our notice. Those who are familiar with *Angræcums*, need not be informed that this species is caulescent. It is a plant of luxuriant growth, with very handsome foliage; and the singular flowers are protruded from the stem in extensive drooping racemes. A glance at their form at once fixes the eye of the beholder on the erect, pure white, and spatulate labellum; from which it descends to that much more extraordinary feature, the spur, or tail. This latter is more than nine inches long, tortuous, and pale-green. The other parts of the flowers are greenish-yellow, which merges into brown towards the centre. With Messrs. Loddiges, in whose house it is at present blossoming, it is an acknowledged favourite, on account of the great singularity and beauty of its structure.

BOUVÀRDIA ANGUSTIFÒLIA. The old *B. triphylla* is, we presume, universally known and cultivated. From that plant the present species does not differ very greatly, and is quite as ornamental. It has narrow, rather rough, ovate-lanceolate leaves, grows to about two feet in height, and bears its flowers in clusters at the extremities of the branches. As with those of *B. triphylla*, scarlet is the distinguishing colour of its blossoms; but in this plant, the upper surface of the limb of the corolla has a tendency to turn purple, which seems peculiar to the species, and is by no means uninteresting. It is now finely in flower in the greenhouse of Messrs. Low and Co., Clapton. There is every probability of its being capable of thriving in the open border in summer weather.

CATTLÈYA HARRISÒNIÆ; *var.* ÁLBA. In Messrs. Loddiges' collection, a very interesting white *Cattleya* has just expanded its blossoms. Both the flowers and general character agreeing most perfectly with those of *C. Harrisoniæ*, it is considered a variety of that species. The flowers lack the airy elegance of *C. crispa*, as well as the richness of its labellum; but, being white, they are novel and exceedingly attractive, and their appearance is enhanced by the pretty, lilac-coloured lip.

CLEISÓSTOMA RÒSEA. An unpractised observer would at once assign this little plant to the genus *Vanda;* but besides the difference in the form of the flowers, it has longer and more attenuated stems, the leaves are alternate and distant, and the flowers burst forth in bunches from the side of the stem, without any visible peduncles, and leaving a perceptible aperture at the point from whence they protrude. It has very small, but neat brown and yellow flowers, and a pink labellum; the whole texture of the blossoms being exceedingly transparent and delicate. Messrs. Loddiges, who are now flowering it abundantly, received it from Manilla, through Mr. Cuming.

CYCNÒCHES VENTRICÒSUM. Inferior in beauty to *C. Loddigesii,* and with much less flowers than *C. chlorochilon,* this species is nevertheless sufficiently showy to recommend itself to all who wish for perfect collections. The flowers are greenish-yellow in all parts, but their large size and peculiar form compensate for the deficiency of brilliant colours. Messrs. Rollison, Tooting, have a specimen now developing its flowers. With the rest of its allies, it is kept in a pot filled with heath-soil and potsherds, and cultivated in a similar manner to *Catasetums.*

GENTIÀNA GÉLIDA. If the species of this most valuable genus could be grown and preserved without difficulty, they would form some of the richest ornaments of the flower-garden. *G. gelida* is both rare, and one of the most splendid of the tribe. It grows about six inches high, with a great number of stems, on the summits of which the charming flowers appear. These are of an intense cerulean hue, with a handsomely bearded throat, the hairs of which are slightly tinged with white. It appears to be far more hardy than most of the other species, grows more vigorously, flowers more abundantly, and is altogether one of those plants whose worth seems to us inestimable. Messrs. Young, Epsom, with whom it is now flowering, succeed to admiration in cultivating alpine plants of this nature; and we are happy to observe, that they have imported a large quantity of seeds from Switzerland, many of which have already germinated, and among which several novelties exist.

LÍLIUM LANCIFÒLIUM RÒSEUM. Two specimens of this extremely fine variety, planted in a rich compost of loam and decayed wood, in the centre of one of Messrs. Loddiges' greenhouses, have attained the height of six feet, with leaves from seven to eight inches long, and are now magnificently in flower. The centres of the flowers are thickly studded with delicate filamentous processes, which resemble an exquisite fringe, and the whole of the petals (with the exception of the rose-coloured spots) are of a pure, transparent whiteness, quite enchanting. A singular *lusus naturæ* is observable in one of the flowers; a petal having become united to a stamen, the straight direction of the latter, opposed by the naturally recurved position of the former, has rent the petal into a number of narrow fragments, which have a very peculiar appearance. The system of culture pursued by these gentlemen, viz., that of planting the bulbs in an unconfined bed, or border, and supplying a nutritive soil, appears to be decidedly the most congenial, except that it may be questioned whether, at such a distance from the glass as they must necessarily be when they commence growing, they are not deprived of a degree of light which, if afforded, would contract their growth, and render them more prolific of flowers. The open air will ultimately, we conceive, be found in all respects most suitable for their culture.

MAXILLÀRIA LENTIGINÒSA. Although orchidaceous plants rarely ripen their seed in this country on account of the artificial nature of the climate in which we cultivate them, and we have in consequence been unable to hybridize any of the species, it is more than probable that cross impregnation, followed in the progeny by an actual intermixture of the parent's qualities, is frequently performed in their native localities. This supposition, besides being feasible and natural, is strongly corroborated by several instances of plants which have fallen beneath our notice, in which the character of two well-known species seems combined. The subject which has elicited these suggestions is allied to *M. stapelioides* and *M. Rollisonii;* and either they are variations of the same species, or *M. lentiginosa* would seem to be a hybrid between the other two. The leaves of all are very similar, but the blossoms of *M. stapelioides* are very profusely spotted with brown, those of *M. Rollisonii* scarcely at all, and those of our present plant are intermediate with regard to spots. It was first bloomed at Messrs. Loddiges, and the flowers are yet in perfect preservation.

NUTTÁLLIA MALVÆFLÒRA. An entirely new and very pretty species of *Nuttallia*, with digitate, hairy foliage, and pale pink flowers. It has been most correctly named from the general similarity of the latter members to those of some species of *Malva*. The petals are narrow, about an inch long, and unequally serrated at the summits. The plant grows about eighteen inches high, and although retained in the greenhouse of Messrs. Young, Epsom, where it is now blossoming, will most likely prove as hardy as *N. grandiflora*, or *N. papaver*. Probably the flowers would be much darker if the plant were exposed.

ŒNOTHÈRA PARVIFLÒRA. As with the preceding plant, the name of this species conveys an accurate idea of its character. Its habit is dwarf, as it seldom grows higher than eight or nine inches, while both the flowers and foliage are smaller than those of the majority of its congeners. It ranks among the species which produce yellow blossoms, these being likewise numerous, and rather rich. In the fine herbaceous collection of Messrs. Young, Epsom, we saw it blooming most freely about a week since, but are unable to state whether it is annual or perennial, though we presume the former. It is a native of North America.

ONCÍDIUM TRULLÍFERUM. Of all the numerous kinds of *Oncidium*, the present species has decidedly the largest, finest, and most imposing pseudo-bulbs. Previously to seeing its flowers, we imagined it would create quite a new feature in the genus; but now that these have been unfolded, both with Messrs. Loddiges and Messrs. Rollison, our opinion of it has been considerably lowered. It has very long and large pseudo-bulbs, but the flowers are borne on short spikes, not more than a foot high, and are very small when compared with its general character. Yellow, brown, and greenish-white, are the predominant colours in them. The species is only worthy of cultivation where all the others are possessed, and a careful selection of the best kinds is not attempted or desired.

SÁLVIA LINARIOÌDES. This new species is blossoming in the collection of Messrs. Henderson, Pine-Apple Place. With small and slightly glaucous foliage, it has light blue flowers, the centre of which is of a nearly white ground, very neatly spotted with blue. It is a dwarf greenhouse shrub, about a foot in height, and bearing a profusion of flowers on short, terminal spikes. As an autumnal-flowering plant, for placing on a stage, it will be highly useful in the greenhouse.

OPERATIONS FOR SEPTEMBER.

AN attempt to cultivate plants at any season, irrespective of the particular circumstances in which they have been placed during a shorter or longer period immediately preceding, would be in the highest degree absurd. So, in affording monthly suggestions relative to the manner in which plant culture should be conducted, it is important, when any remarkable deviation from the ordinary course of nature occurs, to take a retrospective glance at its actual influence at the time, and endeavour to estimate the future consequences to which it is likely to lead.

The heavy rains and general gloominess of atmosphere experienced in most parts of the country towards the end of July, were calculated greatly to affect all those plants at that time in any way exposed, and to render some kind of treatment corrective of their effects absolutely necessary. We have before attempted to show that sunshine and partial drought are the most congenial autumnal influences for plants grown in temperate climates. When, therefore, nature reverses these conditions, it is the province of art to employ every possible means which will control or counteract her agency.

Both in plant structures and the open ground, (for even in houses plants are all more or less prevented from ripening their wood and buds by unfavourable weather, although certainly not liable to that extensive injury from wet, to which such as remain unprotected are subjected,) some method which will exhaust the supply of fluids should be immediately adopted. It cannot be too often insisted upon that a quantity of water disproportionate to the temperature, not only checks the flowering propensities of the most healthy plant, but leaves it much more open to the action of frost. During such weather as that already recorded, fire heat should be applied to the stove, while the greenhouse should be kept closely shut, provided always the rains continue so long as to occasion injury, either palpable or perspective, to the objects of the culturist's attention. No other intervention than that of covering the earth around the roots can be afforded to plants in the open borders; but this, if effectively accomplished, will be of immense benefit to half-hardy exotic shrubs and trees.

As at this season, more than at any other, the less hardy sorts of border plants produce their flowers, those persons who are anxious to hybridize any choice species, will now be on the alert to watch for a period favourable for the accomplishment of the process of inter-impregnation. Most individuals are doubtless aware that a shower of rain, or the contact of liquid in any manner with the pollen, within a certain time after its application to the stigma, will completely nullify the operation. For this reason, then, as well as on account of the crosses frequently occasioned by bees, it is most prudent to retain the plants intended for hybridization in frames, pits, or greenhouses. The desired result will thus be more unerringly insured, and much disappointment averted.

Propagation by cuttings is now again beginning to arrest the consideration and engage the skill of the flower-gardener; such a mode of increase, at least of the established species, being generally suspended through the hottest part of the summer season. All those tender plants which are at present decorating the flower-borders, can and must be forthwith multiplied in this manner. Particular directions, or lists of species, are not needed here; the general terms we have used having rendered sufficiently obvious the subjects and objects of our remarks.

For striking cuttings during the summer months, some of the most celebrated nurserymen plant them in pots in the open air, merely placing them on the north side of a wall for shelter, and securing due preservation from rain by a hand-glass, or shelving piece of slate. In the spring and autumn, they are always kept in a propagating house, and the pots plunged in heating bark or manure, or simply in sawdust, beneath which flues or pipes, supplied with artificial heat, are conducted. Perhaps the latter is the better system, since the degree of temperature is thus more easily regulated, and the atmosphere never impregnated with those rank or extremely moist fumes, which are so frequently fatal to slender plants, and particularly to unrooted cuttings. A proper moisture can always be maintained, by watering the material used for surrounding the pots, whenever it indicates too great dryness.

September is likewise the month in which budding is performed on standard roses, and other similar plants. It is indispensable to success, that the buds inserted, and the wood of stocks employed, should be in a mature state; otherwise the former will wither under the influence of an autumnal sun, and a vital union will never be effected. Those who wish to have more than one or two kinds budded on the same stock, should be careful to choose sorts resembling each other in habit. Nothing tends more powerfully to destroy the beauty and symmetrical effect of a standard rose, than an unnatural combination of luxuriant and weak, vigorous and stunted growing varieties on one stock; and yet this is the inevitable consequence of introducing buds of an indiscriminate mixture of sorts. Where, however, the habit is known to approximate, a diversity of colour is rather to be wished than deprecated.

Phaius Wallichii.

PHÀIUS WÀLLICHII.

(DR. WALLICH'S PHAIUS.)

CLASS.
GYNANDRIA.

ORDER.
MONANDRIA.

NATURAL ORDER.
ORCHIDACEÆ.

GENERIC CHARACTER.—*Vide* vol. v. p. 125.

SPECIFIC CHARACTER.—*Plant* stemless. *Leaves* oblong-lanceolate, acute, very long. *Sepals* and *petals* lanceolate. *Labellum* cucullate, entire, very acuminate, with a curled margin; spur curved, emarginate. *Bracts* acuminate.

THE remarkable habits of most orchidaceous plants naturally render them of very humble stature, and, indeed, preclude the possibility of their ever attaining any considerable height. Nevertheless, there is a division of them, which, attaching themselves to the ground, and striking their roots into the soil, have very properly been termed terrestrial. Among these some are found which grow three, four, or even six feet high, though this must be understood as referring solely to their flower-stems or foliage.

Phàius Wallichii is a plant of extremely vigorous habits, as its stems, and even its leaves, sometimes reach the height of four feet. A glance at the flower-spike exhibited in our drawing will at once show its extraordinary luxuriance, and, by comparing that with the very reduced engraving of the entire plant, given in the ensuing page, a faithful idea of its character may be obtained.

This handsome species had not, we believe, been cultivated in British collections, till it was imported to Chatsworth by His Grace the Duke of Devonshire, in 1837. It was met with by Mr. Gibson on the Khoseea range of hills, where it luxuriates beneath a densely umbrageous covering of trees, on such portions of rock as are partially covered with vegetable soil. Those crevices and fissures in which leaves or moss have fallen and decayed, afford a locality and soil especially preferred by this plant, and in such situations it arrives at its greatest perfection.

Since its reception at Chatsworth, it has flowered very abundantly, and in the manner here represented. The individual subject of our figure blossomed in May of the present year. To the *P. grandifolius* of Loureiro it is most nearly allied, and Dr. Lindley at first thought them identical; "but upon more full consideration," he adds, "I have come to the conclusion that *P. Wallichii* is to be distinguished by its very acuminate bracteæ, sepals, and petals, and also by the labellum not only gradually tapering into a long point, as in *Brassavola nodosa*, but being also destitute of the rich yellow and red marking of the Chinese species."

Those who cultivate *Peristerias* successfully, will find the treatment bestowed upon them perfectly adapted to this plant. A rather rich turfy loam, amongst which broken free-stone, or any thing of a similar kind, is freely mingled, will furnish an excellent compost. It should be supplied with every necessary stimulant or auxiliary to its growth in the summer, but preserved as dry as practicable in winter. Indeed, at all times, stagnant water about its roots, or too great atmospheric moisture, must be carefully guarded against, for it is highly impressionable to injury from this source.

One feature in its natural condition is worthy of the cultivator's remembrance and imitation. It is the occurrence, in the soil in which it flourishes, of a large proportion of nearly but not thoroughly decayed leaves or wood. By attending to this point, we have observed that the plants at Chatsworth derive a very perceptible advantage.

Aeschynanthus ramosissimus

ÆSCHYNÀNTHUS RAMOSÌSSIMUS.

(MOST-BRANCHING ÆSCHYNANTHUS.)

CLASS.	ORDER.
DIDYNAMIA.	ANGIOSPERMIA.

NATURAL ORDER.
CYRTANDRÀCEÆ.

GENERIC CHARACTER.—*Vide* vol. v. p. 241.

SPECIFIC CHARACTER.—*Stem* much branched, radicant. *Leaves* narrowly oblong, acuminated, slightly recurved at the extremities, smooth, with small indistinct protuberances along the edges, obscurely veined. *Umbels* terminal, many flowered. *Calyx* with five subulate segments, hairy, yellowish-green. *Corolla* tubular, an inch long, enlarging and curving downwards towards the apex; upper lip with two, lower lip with three obtuse, unequal segments, clothed with short downy hairs. *Stamens* inserted in the tube of the corolla, about half-way down; *filaments* longer than the style, slightly downy. *Stigma* clavate, convex at the summit; style much thicker and more downy than the filaments. *Seeds* sometimes terminated by two bristles at their apex, these uniting into one towards the base.

By a slight inspection of the accompanying plate, most of our readers will probably be enabled to remember the superb species of this genus, a figure of which adorned our pages some months since. Lest memory should in any case fail, we beg to refer them to page 241 of the preceding volume, because, from the general resemblance of the two species, it is important, where living specimens are not possessed, that the drawings should be brought together, and the particular characters of each plant accurately noted.

It is unnecessary to mention that *Æ. grandiflorus* is far superior to our present subject, and that, consequently, it is useful to be able to recognise and distinguish each of them, both for the purposes of purchase, and also to prevent disappointment should only *Æ. ramosissimus* be received. The latter is, however, apart from its more showy congener, a highly ornamental and valuable plant, possessing, in the richness and profusion of its flowers, the vivid verdure of its elegant and shining foliage, and its graceful mode of growth, many real and sterling attractions.

Compared with *Æ. grandiflorus*, it will be seen that its foliage is much narrower, smaller, and of a deeper green, while the flowers are likewise more diminutive;

but the principal distinctive test will be found in the peculiarly branching nature of the stems of the plant now more immediately under examination. Before any specimen has grown a foot in height, this character will be easily discerned. Within a few inches of the soil, it will begin to send forth a number of lateral shoots, and as these usually take an ascending direction, the plant becomes particularly dense about this part of its stem. This affords an unerring criterion for the determination of its specific name, as the term itself applies to that feature alone.

At the same time, and through the same medium as the finer species already noticed, this beautiful plant was introduced to Chatsworth, where the sample of our drawing flowered in June last. On the trunks and branches of trees, in moist shady woods, it was found by Mr. Gibson, near the summit of the Khoseea hills, at an elevation of about four thousand feet. Messrs. Loddiges and other cultivators have had thriving specimens for several years, but the plant at Chatsworth was, we presume, the first to unfold its flowers.

A reference to the great height of the tract it inhabits, would seem to favour the opinion that the extreme heat of many orchidaceous houses must be unfavourable to the development of its flowers, and that in a somewhat lower temperature it would succeed better. But we imagine the best means of inducing it to flower are to refrain from stimulating it too much through the winter season, by diminishing very greatly the supplies of both heat and water. Doubtless a trifling degree of cautious exposure to the sun would also accelerate the production of blossoms.

It may be cultivated and propagated precisely as *Æ. grandiflorus*, succeeding quite as well as that species, if potted in moss, or some very light material of a similar kind, with the stems attached to a block of wood; around which, if assisted by a little sphagnum, they will speedily form roots, and by this means may be increased. Soil, especially such as is calculated to retain much moisture, should never be made use of in its cultivation, for it is to the employment of this, and not to its natural constitution, that the character it has obtained of not flowering freely is to be entirely ascribed.

Lobelia heterophylla.

LOBÈLIA HETEROPHÝLLA.

(VARIOUS-LEAVED LOBELIA.)

CLASS.	ORDER.
PENTANDRIA.	MONOGYNIA.

NATURAL ORDER.
LOBELIÀCEÆ.

GENERIC CHARACTER.—*Vide* vol. ii. p. 52.

SPECIFIC CHARACTER.—*Plant* annual, smooth. *Stems* angular, nearly simple. *Leaves* thick; inferior ones pinnatifid, toothed, upper ones linear, entire. *Corolla* with the lower lip jagged in the middle, obcordate; lateral lobes unequal; bright blue.

WERE it possible for any coloured figure to do justice to the exquisite beauty and richness of the flowers of this deeply-interesting little plant, we are convinced that those of our subscribers who have not yet seen it in a growing state, would entertain towards it the same attachment which we now profess. There is certainly a gracility in the stems, and an extraordinary diffusiveness of habit, which, when delineated on paper, have a tendency to depreciate its merit; but these are chiefly produced by a particular course of culture, and if viewed as characteristic of the living plant, so far from diminishing, actually increase its charms.

The discovery and colonization of Australia has, among other and greater benefits conferred upon the mother country, enriched our gardens with an immense number of almost invaluable plants, so excellently adapted are they to the mode of management which we practise in our greenhouses. Nor are our flower-borders lacking in ornaments from the same region, as the many delightful annuals recently procured from the Swan River Colony sufficiently prove. *Lobelia heterophylla* is, however, a product of Van Diemen's land: and were there no other annual to testify of its fertility in the generation of floral gems, this alone would be sufficient to compel us to regard it with honour.

Seeds appear to have been received in this country about the year 1835, as it blossomed in several collections at different periods of 1836. Mr. William Shenton, of Winchester, and Mr. Veitch, of Exeter, were among the first individuals with whom it flowered in that year. Owing to the liberal manner in which its seeds are produced and ripened, it has subsequently been distributed most extensively, and there are few nurseries from which it may not be procured. That it may soon become equally common in private collections, we have been urged to publish the drawing here given, which was executed from a plant that bloomed at Chatsworth in the summer of 1837.

Hitherto this plant has been almost exclusively confined to the greenhouse, having been generally considered a half-hardy species. The latter opinion is evidently correct; but it will, notwithstanding, be found quite hardy enough for summer display in the flower-garden, of which it would form a most brilliant ornament. Such a situation would also better elicit its native colours, and prevent it from straggling, which last propensity is merely a consequence of being screened from the direct rays of solar light, by growing beneath glass, and at a considerable distance from it.

Wherever cultivated, it should always, if possible, be sown where it is desired to flower. By this practice, singular as such results may seem, the stems are repressed, and hindered from assuming that length and tenuity which by some cultivators is deemed unsightly. They can likewise be made to flower in a much shorter time, if this method is adopted. Seeds may be sown at almost any season, according to the period at which the flowers are required. The earliest month in which they can with safety be sown in the flower-garden is April. Single specimens, grown in pots in the greenhouse, will require some training and support; but if the seeds are scattered rather sparingly over the soil in a moderate-sized pot, and the young plants thinned as they appear, a much better effect will be ensured, and no other trouble will be necessary.

We have still to record a quality of the flowers, which, if anything yet be wanting to guarantee the species a lasting esteem, will effectually supply the deficiency. Dr. Lindley, in allusion to specimens of this plant recived from Mr. Veitch, nurseryman, of Exeter, states that they were accompanied by "a memorandum that the plant *had been hung up in the stove for more than a month, without the least soil, and without ceasing to flower;* — a very singular fact, and quite new in plants of this description."

For the derivation of the generic title, the reader may revert to vol. ii. p. 53. The specific name obviously applies to the difference in form between the upper and lower leaves.

Tcoma jasminoides.

TECOMA JASMINOÌDES.

(JASMINE-LIKE TECOMA.)

CLASS.
DIDYNAMIA.

ORDER.
ANGIOSPERMIA.

NATURAL ORDER.
BIGNONIÀCEÆ.

GENERIC CHARACTER.—*Calyx* campanulate, five-toothed. *Corolla* with a short tube; throat campanulate, limb five-lobed, each two-lipped. *Stamens* four, didynamous, with the rudiment of a fifth. *Stigma* two-plated. *Capsule* pod-shaped, two-celled; partition opposite to the valves. *Seeds* imbricated, winged, disposed transversely.

SPECIFIC CHARACTER.—*Plant* a climbing shrub. *Branches* terete, glabrous, green. *Leaves* pinnate, with two pairs of leaflets; leaflets ovate, smooth, shining, bluntly acuminated. *Calyx* crenately five-toothed. *Panicles* terminal, trichotomous. *Corolla* funnel-shaped, downy, and slightly bearded in the throat; limb nearly equally divided into five jagged, undulated segments.

For specimens of this strikingly beautiful *Tecoma* we have to thank Mr. Webster, gardener to Mrs. Huskisson, of Eartham, Petworth, Sussex, by whom they were communicated in August 1838. He informs us that it was raised from seeds sent thither from Moreton Bay, in New South Wales, and had flowered in the conservatory at Eartham for two years. On first examining it, an impression arose in our mind that it might at least be considered a new variety of *T. jasminoides*, the flowers being so much finer, and of a far richer colour than those of the plants of that species we had previously seen. Subsequent investigation has, however, shown beyond a doubt that it is only *T. jasminoides* in a superior state of cultivation, and perhaps the species may naturally be inclined to vary its hue.

It is quite impossible that the enchanting delicacy and loveliness of its blossoms can fail to arrest the attention of every observer. They combine a degree of elegance so truly fascinating, with such a depth and brightness of colour in the throat, (neither of which can be fully portrayed by art) that the beholder is conscious only of admiration and delight. Our drawing is doubtless sufficiently correct to create these feelings, though necessarily to a much less extent than its beauteous original. Besides the pleasing character of the flowers, the plant itself is a very handsome climber, of an exuberant mode of growth, and with noble evergreen foliage. We trust it will therefore no longer remain a scarce object, but contribute to the gaiety of every greenhouse which is large enough to admit of its being grown to its proper size. Most extensive nurserymen have, we should think, saleable plants, though we have only noticed it in the greenhouse of Messrs. Chandler, Vauxhall.

But all plants of the kind we are now describing, however beautiful their flowers may be, can so rarely be induced to develop them, that they are very frequently discarded from this cause. We have no hesitation in saying, that in the majority of such cases the culturist alone should be blamed. Without directing a thought to the roots, on which, of course, the condition of the plant entirely depends, the branches are pruned, and as fast as new ones succeed, these are likewise shortened or removed. The result of such treatment, when pursued independently of attention to other circumstances, is never satisfactory.

Mr. Webster, following the course which philosophy and experience suggest, confines the roots of this plant in a small pot, and by thus effectually checking its growth, as well as providing against an undue lodgment of fluids in the soil, easily surmounts the difficulties above hinted at, and brings his plants into flower as soon as they have attained a productive age. In this simple fact lies the whole art of flowering plants perfectly; and nothing can be more prejudicial to a species like the present, which is constitutionally disposed to grow exuberantly, than planting it in a bed or border, where its supplies of fluid cannot be completely controlled, and its roots judiciously limited.

As it produces a great number of lateral shoots, by taking off these at a proper period, and tending them carefully, according to the general mode of managing cuttings, any quantity of young plants can with the greatest facility be struck. Perhaps, likewise, the seeds may occasionally be matured, but these should be disregarded, except for hybridization, since plants raised from cuttings invariably flower sooner.

Tecoma is a contraction of *Tecomaxochitl*, the Mexican name for one of the species. The genus comprises many plants that formerly belonged to *Bignonia*, to which, indeed, it is closely related.

THE ADVANTAGES OF GROWING GREENHOUSE PLANTS IN FRAMES.

No one accustomed to visit collections of plants, either in the neighbourhood of London or of any large provincial towns, can have omitted to note the remarkable superiority of appearance which the same species assume in different places. The regular attendants on horticultural exhibitions must likewise have remarked that, with reference to ornamental plants of certain classes, the prizes for well-cultivated specimens are nearly always shared among a limited number of exhibitors. This has, without doubt, created considerable jealousy in the minds of some unsuccessful competitors; who are apt, generally without good foundation, to impugn the impartiality of the judges.

For the honour of the science, and the promotion, not only of good feeling, but of a better system of treating plants, we intend showing, as the result of personal investigation, the manner in which the excellence above mentioned is usually attained. We also hope by this means to supplant that discreditable spirit of envy which is now extant, establishing in its place a generous emulation and rivalry, more worthy of the members of our fraternity, and especially adapted to further their common wishes and interests.

The only purposes to which greenhouses, constructed according to the present prevailing mode, should be devoted, are those of displaying plants during the period at which their flowers are opening or expanded, and preserving them in the winter season. If we could convince every cultivator of this incontrovertible truth, what a perfect paragon of concentrated beauty might such a structure become! The flowers which unfold themselves in each month of the year would thus be brought together, unmingled with anything to detract from their loveliness; and when the winter denies all floral charms, there would still be the admirably formed and healthy specimens to gaze upon, which, in the opinion of the floricultural devotee, are only surpassed in interest by the addition of the blossoms themselves.

Greenhouse plants, and a number of tender annuals, which, although belonging to intra-tropical countries, constitute some of the principal ornaments of our conservatories in the summer, are too seldom grown with such success as to appear to advantage from any and every point of view. Deficiency of air and light is doubtless the cause of this inferiority. In the greenhouse, notwithstanding all the cultivator's efforts to place the plants so as to leave a proper space between each, this is confessedly impracticable, without transferring a large proportion of them to the open air. For such as happen to be removed to the latter situation, necessity enjoins that they should be crowded together as closely as possible, in order to screen each other from the powerful rays of the sun, as well as from its evaporating action upon the soil in which they are potted.

Various objections might be brought forward against both the greenhouse and the open air, for the summer growth of the hardier kinds of plants requiring artificial culture. Only a few of those which refer to the former of these positions need here be urged. What we have already said respecting the insufficiency of solar light, must, with regard to some plants at least, be slightly modified. Heaths, for instance, appear to want occasional shading, when the sun's rays are very violent. But most other greenhouse plants would endure, and flower more freely under, a far greater degree of light, provided their roots were sufficiently excluded from the influence of the sun, and prevented from becoming too dry. It is their confinement in pots, the exposure of these latter to the solar beams, and the inability of the culturist to keep them duly moist under such circumstances, that causes the plants to look yellow and sickly; and not, as is frequently presumed, the agency of light, except where this is poured upon them suddenly after they have been confined for some time in comparative darkness. To render as much protection as possible to the roots, plants of this nature should all stand on the same level, and their individual growth should be such as to secure the necessary umbrage to their own roots. Neither of these ends could be accomplished in the greenhouse; for even a level stage placed near enough to the glass, would have an extremely unsightly effect, and materially check the circulation of air.

From considerable experience, and attentive observation, we have found that the surest way of obtaining perfect specimens of greenhouse plants, is to place them, during their growing season, within a foot of the roof of any glass erection, to remove entirely, but temporarily, the lights or sashes of that structure, merely replacing them in cold weather, or when heavy rains are falling or expected to fall, and throwing a covering of thin canvass over the frame-work of the house when the sun is particularly fierce. This last operation would not be requisite to the plants in a natural state, but, from being long kept in pots, their acquired habits would, under the treatment above named, demand this or some similar precautionary measure in the early stages of their development. Such canvas would mitigate the sun's influence fully as much as the thickest glass, while its perviousness to air at once decides its greater suitability. Further, each plant should be elevated on an isolated pinnacle, at least two feet above the floor, stage, or other uniform surface. This is perhaps one of the most strikingly beneficial systems of management which the aspiring cultivator can follow. Assuming that the house in question has front and end moveable lights, when these are thrown open, it is not easy to conceive a more thorough circulation of air between, around, and through all parts of the plants, than would thus be ensured.

Frames, besides being better adapted for carrying out this plan and supplying much greater facilities for its execution than greenhouses, are infinitely more economical, and can be kept in any private part of the garden; or the mere fact of having to look down on the tops of the plants will effectually divert the eye of the spectator from the materials on which they are elevated. They would thus, even in the more obscure departments of the pleasure-grounds, be objects of delight rather than disgust; whereas, in the greenhouse the plants, by their nearness to the roof, would be too distant from the walk to be advantageously seen, and their pots, with those upon which they are raised, would be most displeasingly conspicuous.

On a recent call at the gardens of Sir Edmund Antrobus, Bart., at Cheam, we saw, under the skilful care of Mr. Green, a frame appropriated to Heaths, and apparently managed precisely on the principles we have here laid down. In the first place, the four corners of the frame were equally raised on bricks, to about a foot from the surface of the ground; thus leaving a large open space for the admission of air beneath. Where wood is abundant, four posts of any kind, about four or six inches in diameter, on which the bark is retained for the sake of its rusticity, may be driven into the ground at the proper points, and they will form a substitute for bricks in all respects preferable. Next, the plants were elevated on inverted pots till the tips of their branches nearly reached the top of the frame. And lastly, the extremities of the lateral shoots of each plant were from four to six inches from all the others by which it was surrounded. By keeping the ground moist in the inside of the frame, a most refreshing humidity is maintained about the plants in the hottest weather; and the symmetry of their form combines with the intense verdure of the foliage to impart to them an air of beauty very triflingly remote, and that solely as regards size, from the *ultimatum* of perfection.

With some slight alterations, this mode of procedure is applicable to all the plants that are ever grown in a greenhouse. And as there are few cultivators of these plants who do not possess frames, these being also very generally unemployed during the summer months, no inconvenience will be created by the plan we have proposed; but, contrariwise, a saving of trouble, on account of frames requiring less attention, and being altogether easier to manage,—and what is of still greater importance, the attachment of a very considerable additional value to the plants,— will undoubtedly attend the application of a system having the preceding hints for its basis.

Such plants as Cockscombs, Balsams, and Amaranths, not only thrive best with, but actually require frame culture. That humid heat, constant proximity to the glass, and frequent shifting, in which they delight, cannot so well be supplied and attended to in any other situation. Frames, indeed, should be regarded as summer nurseries for the greenhouse, to which last structure no plant should be introduced that has not gone through a regular preparation in the first. When this method is brought more generally into vogue, then alone may we expect to see both plants and houses exhibiting those attractions of which the major part of them are so susceptible.

INFLUENCE OF CLIMATE ON PLANTS.*
SOLAR HEAT.

WHILE describing the manner in which water lowers the temperature of any tract in its vicinity, we must not omit to mention, in connexion therewith, the similar effects of forests or other extensive groups of trees. Wherever the superior kinds of vegetation abound, to that spot a large quantity of moisture is attracted, for the purpose of administering to their necessities. This is an essential feature in the economy of nature; and such fluid, accumulating both in the soil and plants, cannot pass off so rapidly as if the surface of the ground were completely open to the atmosphere. A more than usual stagnation, proportionate to the limits and closeness of the forest, is the consequence.

We have previously stated, that whenever the atmosphere is highly charged with moisture, it is always at an inferior rate of temperature than when less humid. Taken in conjunction with the above observations, this will explain the reason why woods contribute to render any country colder.

North America presents an excellent illustration of the influence of both these peculiarities. Traversed throughout by huge rivers and lakes, which are subdivided towards their origin into an innumerable quantity of lesser streams; and covered in its less cultivated parts with dense and boundless forests; its climate, in the same latitudes as those of Britain, or any of the more southerly countries of Europe, is uniformly less genial.

There can, moreover, be no doubt that the burning deserts of Africa derive an inconceivable degree of the intensity of heat to which they are subjected, from the almost total absence of vegetation. We do not here allude to the grateful shade which trees would furnish to the traveller, for this could at the utmost be merely temporary; but assume that masses of trees, if even growing at considerable distances, would, from the causes before pointed out, so modify the general temperature as to make it far more easily supportable.

Fully persuaded of the accuracy of these declarations, we may, by applying them practically, go on to exhibit the fallibility of such practices as are sanctioned only by general adoption, and the hallucinations into which persons may be led, by adhering to universally admitted rules, without inquiring whether they can be supported by reason and philosophy. Perhaps there is not a gardener but will assert, as a fundamental and indisputable dogma, that any site which may be chosen for the cultivation of plants that are not thoroughly hardy, and which may happen to lie particularly exposed to the quarters from whence cold winds are usually expected, should be defended by a plantation of trees. And where that plantation can be kept at a proper distance, such a system merits nothing but approval. But when such a species of shelter is brought within a few feet or yards

* Concluded from page 184.

of where the plants are to be grown, or is rendered unnecessarily extensive in order to fulfil some other design, the object of the planter is more than counteracted, and a positive evil is entailed.

Few can be unapprized of the fact, that from every leaf of the minutest vegetable an insensible moisture is constantly being exhaled. Let but this circumstance be considered, in connexion with the immeasurable surface which a large tree presents, and, again, with the augmented evaporation of a considerable number of them, and it will be confessed that the quantity of fluid evolved cannot be trivial. Further, instead of this vaporised fluid ascending into the higher regions of the air —at least on those occasions when its influence can be injurious—it is wafted over the superficies immediately beneath it, and there suspended, till the action of cold precipitates it to the earth, or condenses it on the vegetation that may intervene.

For those who have witnessed the additional violence with which frost acts upon plants saturated with moisture, (and by the least scientific cultivator this circumstance cannot have been unobserved,) it will be needless to add, that the increase of fluid just noticed, cannot, when succeeded by frost, prove innocuous. But atmospheric and external moisture are even more prejudicial in such a case, if the vessels of the plant are likewise moderately filled with liquids, than any internal and inherent repletion would be. Vapour spread over the surface of any vegetable substance, actually serves as a conductor for the transition of latent heat; and a plant is much more speedily and dangerously deprived of its temperature by this means, than it could be if suffering under extreme saturation, provided, at the same time, its surface were kept comparatively dry.

Many may think the mode we have taken for demonstrating this point far-fetched and abstruse; some will probably also consider our conclusions hyperbolical. If, however, great masses of trees can be proved (and none, we imagine, will deny this) to diminish the temperature of an immense district, there can be no question that the causes which operate in this instance will, when more circumscribed, produce within an equally limited area precisely the same effects. The purport of these remarks has not the most remote reference to the prejudicial shade which would be afforded by large trees, this latter particular being a distinct and powerful objection to their employment as materials for shelter, and one which we have heretofore discussed.

What we have now to adduce may, to some minds, appear completely to nullify the suggestions already advanced; though we think it will be easy to enlist it in our train of argument against the plantation of trees for the defence of tender exotics. Strong currents of air, and even the slightest breezes from certain quarters, are known materially to decrease the temperature. Particular localities, and especially elevated spots, suffer the greatest reduction of heat from this source; while, as winds are proverbially changeable, and their effects on the temperature appear or vanish with their mutations, such sudden transitions are exceedingly likely to prove hurtful to vegetation. Some artificial provision to check their violence would therefore seem indispensable.

But besides generating cold, winds are strikingly productive of drought. By their continued action upon the earth and its vegetation, they entirely remove all superficial moisture, and thus prepare plants for enduring a much greater degree of even actual frost. It becomes, therefore, a consideration of great practical import, whether the cold which accompanies winds is not at least counterbalanced by their tendency to aridity.

Having, in a former paper, demonstrated the great value of a certain degree of dryness to exotic plants, we affirm, with unwavering confidence, that all winds, except such as occur during the brief period immediately succeeding the development of young shoots, (these latter being extremely susceptive of injury at that season, not only on account of the imperfection of their structure, but also because they need copious and perpetual supplies of fluid,) are rather beneficial than otherwise. The keen easterly winds generally experienced in Britain during the early spring months, are, consequently, alone to be diverted; and all who are conversant with horticultural pursuits, must sooner or later be convinced that nothing but a covering or protective screen to each individual plant, will effectually guard them from the withering influence of these pernicious blasts.

Even spring gales have, however, one good effect, which renders it doubtful whether it is most prudent to allow them to take their natural course, or to offer them every possible resistance. They unquestionably mitigate the severity of the night-frosts which always attend them; and which, in not a few instances, would inevitably destroy all the young developments of tender plants, were it not for the preparative action of those agents. Viewing this question, then, in all its relations, we arrive at the following results. Where foreign plants, and those from warmer regions, are wished to be acclimatized, a too open spot, with regard to both artificial and natural incumbrances, buildings and trees, cannot be selected. If it is discovered (as in most cases it ultimately will be) that protection is essential in either winter or spring, let each specimen have a portable covering to itself; or, where the species are allied, and the nature of the ground, the nearness of the specimens, and the convenience of the proprietor admit of it, a large screen can be constructed of any required dimensions, and employed whenever circumstances may dictate.

Should these hints be deemed irrelevant and foreign to the asserted subject of this dissertation, we beg most distinctly to avow that, in conjunction with those of a like nature which have preceded them, and which will be found interspersed throughout the whole of these papers, it has been our principal object to inculcate and display all such practical deductions. Whatever scientific disquisitions we may have attempted, have all been made, either by direct inference or implication, subservient to the promotion of floricultural art. This is the great work in which we are continually engaged, and to which we hope ever to be found ready, with our utmost abilities, to lend a helping hand.

We cannot allow this occasion to pass, without exhorting all our readers to whom these articles have possessed the slightest interest, to gratify us with their ideas on any portion of the subject which we may inadvertently have omitted. Our pages may always be regarded by the enlightened culturist as a faithful vehicle for the transmission to the world of whatever opinions may be entertained. But, whether our Magazine or other journals may be the favoured medium of communication, we would earnestly entreat every individual who has bestowed any attention on the points we have thus so largely discussed, to digest and mature his opinions, and commit them to some channel whereby they can be made publicly beneficial and available. By an undisguised declaration of the views current among the leading members of any community, these being understood to combine the lesser differences of their more humble compeers, errors are speedily eliminated, and sound philosophical principles elicited and established.

FAMILIAR HINTS TO YOUNG GARDENERS ON MENTAL IMPROVEMENT.

Every thing that tends to ameliorate the mental condition of gardeners, by burnishing their intellectual faculties, and prompting them to judicious exertion, must eventually prove instrumental in advancing the interests of horticultural science, and elevating and ennobling its sister art in the estimation of the higher orders of society. With this impression deeply graven on our minds, we have penned the following hints to the junior branches of our profession, in the hope of inciting them to a greater degree of vigilance and ardour in the cultivation and development of their thinking and reasoning powers.

It is an established and incontrovertible axiom in educational philosophy, that youth is the season for study and improvement. Nor must this be misunderstood as restricted to the term usually devoted to scholastic acquirements. It is alike applicable to the states of adolescence and early manhood, and extends even to the meridian of life. On the young gardener, especially, a heavy responsibility devolves, to devote this period to a constant and steady application to his vocation, and the general enrichment of his mind; for according to the proficiency he attains in these conjoined particulars, his ultimate promotion entirely depends. Seldom sufficiently educated in mere rudimentary knowledge, all his leisure moments require to be devoted to self-instruction; while the more vividly he perceives the importance of this duty, and the more faithfully he acts in conformity to such apprehension, the greater will be his own subsequent happiness, usefulness, and honour.

All real friends of mankind must have observed with pleasure the spirit of progression that is now abroad, and the anxious concern manifested by operatives of every description to exalt to a much higher degree their intellectual standard. That this impulse may be imparted to the members of the gardening profession we cannot but most fervently desire; and if the suggestions we may now furnish shall in any measure conduce to this desirable consummation, we shall have abundant cause to rejoice in our labours.

There are a variety of means of self-improvement available to the youthful gardener, to the principal of which we shall briefly advert. Individual application, oral communication with fellow-workmen, careful observation, and frequent experiment, are the modes to which our remarks will be restrained. The first of these — individual application — is, without question, the most important, and includes several branches of study. If his rudimentary education has been but superficial, primary and chief attention should be devoted to its completion. Reading, composition, and drawing, should then occupy his leisure hours. Reading, if judiciously conducted, is calculated to prove immensely beneficial; but much depends upon the choice of books, the manner in which they are perused, and the methods adopted for impressing their contents on the mind. Many young gardeners meet only with those works which detail the procedure of cultivating all kinds of plants, but in which the science and principles of horticulture are rarely referred to. These, notwithstanding every effort to keep alive attention, become insipid and wearisome, and are soon discarded, as utterly devoid of interest. A disposition to loathe and despise gardening publications is thus engendered, which, if not timely subverted, frequently proves fatal to further progress and future prosperity. Others obtain works of a directly opposite nature, wherein the style and mode of treating the subject are so abstruse, that they speedily meet with a similar fate (and for the same self-evident reasons) to those already mentioned.

Removed alike from either of these, however, there is a class of works precisely suited to the circumstances of the individuals in question. These are such as combine principle with practice, which illustrate science with familiar and interesting exemplification, and are explicable to the weakest understanding, while they convey knowledge needful to the most capacious. To peruse them with advantage, every sentiment advanced must be subjected to the strictest scrutiny, and no opinions imbibed but such as are consonant to reason, and, as far as they can be tested, to truth. We would say—always read with a view not only to receive information, but to discover error. Do not imagine, however, that you have detected an erroneous opinion or deduction, unless you can demonstrate it to be such by fair confutation. Neither let any proposition be considered unworthy of credence because you cannot comprehend it. Much as a cavilling spirit is to be deprecated, it is far preferable to a simple and credulous disposition, which receives every assertion for fact, because it will not take the trouble to investigate it.

An excellent method of reading with profit, is for two individuals to choose a volume, and peruse it simultaneously, appointing certain periods at which they can meet, and discuss the merits of the different theses as they proceed. By this means, they may confirm or rectify each other's opinions; and the difficulties which one may experience, the other may probably be able to unravel. Subjects on which they disagree will thus be canvassed, to their mutual benefit; and if the arguments, *pro* and *con.*, are committed to writing, distinct ideas will be elicited and incorporated, the matter in dispute will be more thoroughly investigated, and they will thus be led to practise another species of improvement—composition.

Literary composition is invaluable to the gardener; and if it were universally practised, and properly pursued, would have an unequivocal tendency to augment his abilities, and refine and exalt his whole intellectual character. By this practice he is led to examine attentively and critically the productions of others, to digest them fully, and what is of much greater value, to think for himself. His ideas are expanded and embodied, an impetus is communicated to his mental exertions, he matures and appropriates whatever information he can procure, and, finally, succeeds in amassing to himself a treasure, which neither wealth could have purchased, nor of which penury or time can deprive him. Notwithstanding the incalculable benefit to be derived from this pursuit, it is one from which the young gardener almost instinctively shrinks. We think this may be traced either to indolence, to the fear of encountering ridicule, or the lack of any distinct knowledge how to commence. The former of these are very unworthy influences, requiring nothing but a due sense of the vital importance of the undertaking to overcome; for the latter we shall endeavour to suggest a remedy.

Persons who have been engaged in active manual labour during the day are, we know, unable to write with great facility in the evening; but this is a very trifling impediment, compared with the advantage of having the whole day to select and ruminate upon a subject. The young gardener's first attempt at composition should be made while reading. He may begin with a work which is written in simple language, and is easy of comprehension. A pamphlet will be the most suitable, as he can then easily interleave it with writing-paper, which would be a decided convenience. As he reads, he should study closely the subject, the mode of treating it, and the style; and on the paper which he has inserted, note down any preferable variations, or correct any errors in the language, that may suggest themselves, at the same time marking where the subject has been fully discussed, and where further elaboration seems necessary,—in the latter case endeavouring to follow out the author's ideas,—and thus proceeding till he has carefully revised the whole. It should then be left unnoticed for a few days, when, upon reverting to it, some new alterations or additions may appear desirable; and those previously attempted should undergo a rigid examination, for the purpose of making other emendations or improvements.

The process we have detailed may be thought tedious, but it is one which is employed upon their own manuscripts by the best authors, previous to publication;

and when the review and analysis are completed, the student will have gained an important step towards acquiring a knowledge of composition, besides having learned to read with greater attention, relish, and benefit. His next effort may be of a similar nature, but on a work of a higher class; and if fewer grammatical errors or improprieties occur, he may yet endeavour to divide long periods, to find happier and more significant modes of expression, to introduce relevant arguments, or elucidate obscure statements; and, should the work be of a scientific nature, to insert illustrations from his own observation or experience, or from the combined opinions of other authors, reduced to a concise and original form. By the time this and other similar engagements have been accomplished, and carefully revised for at least the sixth time—cotemporaneously with the epistolary disquisitions before proposed, and which should be conducted with equal diligence and care—the individual will be able to write with accuracy, perspicuity, and some degree of energy, upon any subject that may present itself, and of which he may possess a competent knowledge.

Neither in the performance of the above initiatory operation, nor in the exercise of reading, would we recommend the student of horticulture to confine his attention to professional works. Books on any branch of natural or moral philosophy should be perused with equal avidity, and the best poetical works may likewise be advantageously indulged in or consulted, as nothing is more calculated to improve and refine the imaginative and inventive powers.

In composing any essay, however brief, or upon what subject soever it may be, the principal art consists in committing the ideas to writing at first in as simple language as possible. By so doing, the train of thought is not interrupted to search for expressive phraseology; and when the task is completed, the style may be refined, and polished, and elevated to any desired extent. Recurring to it occasionally, during a period of several weeks after first inditing it, will enable the writer to effect an astonishing improvement; and this practice should never be neglected.

Our observations on composition have been extended further than we had designed; but the great importance of the subject, as affecting the character and prospects of the gardener, and, indeed, the interest and gratification of the whole horticultural world, will be a sufficient justification of their otherwise unwarrantable length. Of drawing we need only remark, that it is a peculiarly useful, in fact an essential, qualification to the gardener, and every opportunity should be embraced for its practice. The subject of oral communication will be included in a future article on Gardeners' Societies; but some further suggestions, in continuation of our present paper, will appear in the ensuing Number. We cannot for the present conclude better than in the following appropriate words of Lord Bacon—" Reading makes a full man, writing a correct man, and speaking a ready man."

FLORICULTURAL NOTICES.

NEW AND RARE PLANTS, FIGURED IN THE LEADING BOTANICAL PERIODICALS FOR SEPTEMBER.

CLASS I.—PLANTS WITH TWO COTYLEDONS (DICOTYLEDONEÆ).

THE POPPY TRIBE (*Papaveràceæ*).

PLATYSTÈMON LEIOCÁRPUM. Smooth-fruited Platystemon. Very little difference is discernible, except in the smoothness of its seed-vessels, between this species and the pretty *P. californicum*. The latter is, indeed, decidedly more interesting, as the flowers are larger, and of a pleasing uniform colour; whereas those of the present plant, judging from the figure before us, are pale green at the base of the petals, above which they are nearly white, and again quite yellow at the tips. It is an annual plant, a native of Ross, in New California, from whence seeds were transmitted to St. Petersburgh. From the Imperial Garden of this last city some were forwarded to the Glasgow Botanic Garden, where the plant flowered in August and September, 1836. *Bot. Mag.* 3750.

THE BEAN TRIBE (*Leguminòsæ*).

BAUHÍNIA CORYMBÒSA. Corymb-flowering Bauhinia. A very showy, and remarkably free-growing species, long since introduced into this country, from China; but, through some strange neglect, or other more inexplicable circumstance, it had never blossomed till September, 1838, when its fine clusters of delicate pink flowers expanded in the greenhouse at Redleaf. It is described as being naturally most prodigal of blossoms; and Dr. Lindley plausibly presumes, that the specimen which has thus flowered will, with the progeny that may be raised from it by cuttings, henceforth continue to display its beauties annually. In a rich soil, and a temperature a little higher than that of the greenhouse, it will succeed admirably, being apparently of a luxuriant habit. *Bot. Reg.* 47.

ZÌCHYA TRICOLOR. Three-coloured Zichya. From the genus *Kennedia* a small section has been detached by Baron Hugel, and formed into a distinct group, under the above generic title. *Z. tricolor* approaches the old *Kennedia* (now *Zichya*) *dilatata* in some particulars, but differs from it in the rounder margin and more obtuse extremity of the leaves, and in the flowers not being of one colour, since "the keel is deep purple, the wings are bright rose-colour, and the vexillum is a bright brick red." It is a charming addition to this elegant genus of climbing plants, being fully equal in beauty to *Kennedia coccinea*, although of a rather more spreading character. The drawing in the *Botanical Register* was obtained from Mr. Young, of Milford Nursery, near Godalming. In conjunction with its allies, it should be kept in a partially dry situation, and never subjected to artificial heat. *Bot. Reg.* 52.

THE BEGONIA TRIBE (*Begoniàceæ*).

TOURRÉTTIA LAPPÀCEA. Bur-fruited Tourrettia. There is much more to engage the attention of the botanist than of the cultivator of flowers in this curious plant, as it is an isolated species, and possesses very little beauty. It is a climbing plant, with slender, succulent, square stems, which support themselves by the tendrils of the leaves, these latter being thrice pinnate. The flowers appear in erect spikes, are small, red, and much resemble those of some leguminous plants. M. Dombey originally found it in Peru, and sent it, many years since, to the Paris Royal Garden. It was recently furnished to the Glasgow Botanic Garden by John M'Lean, Esq., of Lima; and flowers in the greenhouse during the autumnal months. Being an annual, the approach of winter invariably destroys it. *Bot. Mag.* 3749.

CLASS II.—PLANTS WITH ONE COTYLEDON (MONOCOTYLEDONEÆ).

THE ORCHIS TRIBE (*Orchidàceæ*).

ONCÍDIUM CÓNCOLOR. One-coloured Oncidium. Sir W. J. Hooker expresses some doubt with regard to the genus to which this plant should be assigned, *Miltonia*, *Cyrtochilum*, and *Odontoglossum*, being so nearly related to *Oncidium*. It is a very handsome plant, has small furrowed pseudo-bulbs, encased in large brown scales, an erect, slender flower-spike, and fine yellow flowers. It is sufficiently distinguished from all other Oncidiums by the pure and entirely yellow colour of its blossoms, in which the large labellum is a prominent object. Mr. Gardner discovered this plant on the Organ Mountains of Brazil, in 1837; and plants consigned by him to the Woburn collection have since bloomed. *Bot. Mag.* 3752.

ODONTOGLÓSSUM RÓSSII. Mr. Ross's Odontoglossum. Mr. Ross, the botanical collector of George Barker, Esq. of Birmingham, introduced this charming plant from Mexico, and after him it has been named. With diminutive pseudo-bulbs, which appear to be smooth in the early stages of their growth, but become channelled when old, it has solitary and strongly-nerved foliage, and produces its blossoms on erect racemes, each of which usually bears two flowers, one situated about an inch below the other. The sepals are greenish-yellow, blotched with brown; the petals white, with purple spots at their base; and the labellum pure white. Altogether, it is a most beautiful species, and must be greatly valued by the cultivator. *Bot. Reg.* 48.

CORYÁNTHES MACULÀTA; *var.* PÁRKERI. The only character by which this variety is distinguishable from the original species, is the dark brownish purple colour with which the base of the labellum is tinctured, and, as Sir W. J. Hooker believes, the smaller size of the spots on the other portion of it. C. S. Parker, Esq. imported from Demerara the specimen figured. The colour of the labellum would greatly resemble that of *C. macrantha*, were it not deeply tinged with a dingy brown, which renders it far less rich. These plants thrive well on a block of wood, and to this treatment their natural habits seem to adapt them; but they will also flourish in a pot, filled with heath-soil, and potsherds, or broken stones. *Bot. Mag.* 3747.

NEW, RARE, AND INTERESTING PLANTS IN FLOWER IN THE PRINCIPAL SUBURBAN NURSERIES.

ÆSCHYNÁNTHUS ROXBÚRGHII. In the commencement of the present Number, a figure and description of *Æ. ramosissimus* will be found. To that species, *Æ. Roxburghii* is much more nearly allied than to *Æ. grandiflorus*. Having recently flowered with Messrs. Loddiges, we are enabled to state that it is a distinct species, with paler green and broader foliage than *Æ. ramosissimus*, and flowers of a light orange colour, each having five dark purple stripes extending from the summit of the corolla about a quarter of an inch down its tube. Like the rest of its congeners, it is an importation from India, and thrives in the stove or orchidaceous house, under the treatment already recommended.

ANGRÆCUM ARMENIACUM. Far from being a showy plant, this little species is decidedly new, and derives its name from the dark orange or apricot hue of its blossoms. In Messrs. Loddiges' extensive collection it is now flowering; and may be recognised by the paucity, length, and narrowness of its leaves, these being also very unequal at the extremities. The floral racemes appear on the old and lower part of the stem, are not more than three inches long, and are densely covered with their small but interesting blossoms. The chief peculiarity in these latter is the comparatively long, partially flattened, hollow spur at their base, which becomes larger as it recedes from the flower, and ultimately contracts again almost to a point.

DENDRÒBIUM CHRYSÁNTHUM. This is now a somewhat old species of *Dendrobium;* but being yet scarce, and one of the finest of its tribe, we have thought the superlative excellence of a specimen in the establishment of Messrs. Loddiges worthy of record. We counted forty-four blossoms all fully expanded on one stem alone; and when we add that these are but little below those of *D. Paxtoni* (figured in our August No.) in beauty, it will be easily conceived that they present a most gorgeous picture. The stems are naturally of a half-pendent character, producing their flowers towards the summits in clusters of two, three, or more, usually four. These are of a brilliant orange tint, with two rich brownish-purple spots in the labellum. The exterior surface of the lip is covered with a delicate fringe or beard, while the sepals and petals are perfectly smooth and wax-like; these features, by their contrast, adding much to the interest of the flowers.

GASTROCHÌLUS PULCHÉRRIMUS. An Indian plant, resembling the genus *Canna* in habit, but much dwarfer and more compact. With Messrs. Loddiges, several specimens are now blossoming. It grows about eighteen inches high, has few and scattered leaves, which are sessile, ovate, acuminate, nerved, and nearly six inches long. From the tops of the stems, partly enveloped in a sheath, and disposed in two rows on opposite sides of the axis, the flowers are collected into a very close spike. They are developed with great irregularity, both in point of time and position, but there is generally two or three open at the same period. The flowers are composed of small narrow petals, and a large concave lip; the former are pure white, the latter of a white ground, with a bright streak of red down the centre, and a considerable blotch of the same colour at the orifice. Being of a transparent texture, they are very delicately beautiful, and the species deserves a place in the stove, both for this reason, and also because it continues flowering for an indefinite period, and appears to throw up a great number of suckers, whereby it may readily be multiplied.

HEMEROCÁLLIS SPECIÒSA. Messrs. Young, of the Epsom nursery, possess a plant bearing the above title, now in a flowering condition, which we believe to be new. Its leaves are radical, sword-shaped, and mucronate. The flower stem is likewise radical, not more than two inches long, bearing bright yellow flowers of full three inches in length, each elevated on pedicels of about the same extent. It is a showy species, and, from its diminutive habits, recommends itself as a desirable addition to our stock of autumnal-flowering, hardy, herbaceous plants.

ONCÍDIUM ——? A very beautiful and evidently novel species of this genus, which has not yet received a name, is blossoming in the orchidaceous house of Messrs. Loddiges. It belongs to that division which produce their leaves immediately from the roots, the foliage of this plant being, besides, of the usual thick, large, and spotted nature, though longer in proportion to its breadth, and deeply tinged with a purplish hue. But the flowers are borne on a long slender scape, have a whitish ground, and are very liberally blotched with deep pink. A yellow spot in the centre contributes much to heighten their beauty. It is superior to *O. Henchmanii*, (for which, perhaps, it might at first be mistaken,) being much larger in all its parts, and the tints of both leaves and flowers being darker.

PENTSTÈMON GENTIANOÌDES, *var*. Amongst a large quantity of seeds obtained from Mexico by Messrs. Low and Co., in 1838, a fine variety of *Pentstemon gentianoides* was introduced, which, upon being flowered in the present season, proves to be preferable to the original species. No material difference is perceptible in the foliage, but the flowers are of a reddish-pink colour externally, and much more pleasing than those of the species to which the plant is allied. We may inform those who would, with great seeming plausibility, attribute this variation to a difference of treatment, that we saw the two plants growing and blooming by the side of each other in the open ground. We were struck with the great beauty of the variety here noticed, and have no doubt that its character is inherent, and consequently lasting.

SACCOLÀBIUM GUTTÀTUM. Mr. Knight, of the King's Road, Chelsea, has lately received some extensive packages of orchidaceous and other plants from Ceylon; among which the charming plant now under remark is at present the most conspicuous object, because its flowers are just developed. Its leaves are strap-shaped, channelled down the middle, and for the most part equally terminated, while the flowers issue from the side of the stems in large clusters. They are light yellow, with a great number of pretty purplish streaks diverging from the centre, and a small white labellum. Their odour is exceedingly agreeable.

THUNBÉRGIA AURANTIACA. We have not the least scruple in declaring that this splendid species will, when its merits are properly known, speedily eclipse all the Thunbergias at present cultivated in our stoves. With the free-growing habit, and incessant propensity to flower for which *T. alata* has long been remarkable, it has blossoms of a larger size, and of a more superb light orange colour, than almost any other plant within the range of our observation. As we shall very shortly publish a beautiful drawing which has been prepared for our Magazine, we will merely now apprize our readers that its flowers are most abundantly expanded at Messrs. Young's, Epsom, and that it is a truly invaluable object.

OPERATIONS FOR OCTOBER.

In many extensive gardens which we have lately had an opportunity of visiting, cultivators are lamenting, and with reason, the little heat and extreme superabundance of moisture during the last months of the summer. Some of the more tender kinds of plants have not yet been enabled to perfect their growth; and from Camellias, Rhododendrons, and Azaleas, that were not timeously subjected to artificial heat, there is a great probability that few flowers will be obtained in the ensuing season.

It is utterly useless, at this advanced period, to endeavour to prepare any plant of this sort for flowering next year; but unless the wood is likewise properly matured, there will not be the slightest reasonable prospect of greater fertility in the one succeeding that; and plants of other genera, that flower much later, may even now derive considerable benefit from a prudent application of a trifling degree of fire-heat.

We will, however, more particularly notice those plants, including greenhouse and half-hardy species, that have been placed in the open air, or planted in the flower borders. Unless the culturist be regardless whether they are preserved or destroyed, he should immediately commence potting such as were turned out of their pots, and transferring both these, and all others that belong to warmer climes, to a greenhouse or frame. Our reasons for recommending so speedy a removal will at once be perceived by the experienced; but, for the satisfaction of those who may not so readily apprehend them, and who indulge a laudable determination not to follow blindly any precepts, by whomsoever delivered, we shall briefly insert them.

Plants that have been for some time previously kept in pots will, when transplanted into an unrestricted medium, inevitably grow with extraordinary vigour, and, in the absence of any influence to restrain their luxuriance, continue increasing till the actual occurrence of frost. This condition is, almost more than any other, to be carefully avoided; for, by allowing a plant thus to expend its energies in forming shoots that can never be ripened, we deprive the more permanent members of those agencies by which alone they can be prepared for fulfilling the design of their existence—the elicitation of flowers. In a wet and dull season, these consequences accrue with additional force, and hence the propriety of a timely attempt to avert them.

All tender exotics, whose preservation is desired, should therefore be taken from the ground as soon as possible, and introduced to a dry apartment, where a slight heat, for the purpose of hardening their shoots, will be advantageous; but care must be taken so to apportion the supply of water thereto, that no further elongation shall be induced. In potting the plants, if the soil attached to them should happen to be rich, in any measure adhesive, or more than moderately wet, it must be wholly removed, and replaced by a lighter compost: the larger roots should also be much reduced. The greatest caution is, however, necessary to maintain the small fibrous roots uninjured. Each plant should be placed in as small a pot as will contain it, because it is of importance to provide beforehand against the accumulation of stagnant water in the winter, and this is very seldom found in those pots which are full of roots.

It will be injudicious to prune, except absolute necessity exists, the branches of any of those plants which are now potted. A development of young shoots generally follows this operation, and these are unavoidably weak, immature, and unprepared for the arrival of winter.

While the weather is yet propitious, and before autumnal frosts are experienced, every potted plant should be examined, and, if needful, transferred to a smaller pot, or furnished with fresh soil. We now allude to such as have been suffered to retain too much water, and have become sickly in consequence. If these were left to stand through the winter in such a state, there would be little chance of their surviving, or, should their natural robustness of constitution bear them through it, they will scarcely ever afterwards regain their native health. The more tender, therefore, or valuable may be the specimen, the greater need is there for such a watchfulness at the present time, although every species must be more or less a sufferer by its neglect.

Shading of every kind, and under all circumstances, save the propagation of plants by cuttings, should be wholly discontinued. The temperature of the stove and orchidaceous house may be allowed to decline gradually with that of the season, resorting to artificial heat only on particular occasions, such as sudden frosts or extremely cold winds. The object of the cultivator should now be to preserve, rather than to grow, even Orchidaceæ; still there are some species which will not at once conform to his wishes, and for these he must either afford a separate house, or materially injure his other plants by maintaining an adequate temperature. It is advisable for the grower of this tribe to have a small house or pit always in reserve, where he can at any time bestow the requisite attention and treatment on such as will not succeed beneath the general system of management.

Grammatophyllum multiflorum

GRAMMATOPHÝLLUM MULTIFLÒRUM.

(MANY-FLOWERED GRAMMATOPHYLLUM.)

CLASS.
GYNANDRIA.

ORDER.
MONANDRIA.

NATURAL ORDER.
ORCHIDÀCEÆ.

GENERIC CHARACTER.—*Perianth* conspicuous, spreading. *Sepals* and *petals* nearly equal. *Labellum* attached to the column, small, three-lobed, cucullate. *Column* arched, erect, semi-cylindrical, thickened at the base. *Anthers* usually two-celled. *Pollen-masses* two, globose, furrowed at the base, with a sessile, arched gland at the extremities.

SPECIFIC CHARACTER.—*Plant* epiphytal. *Pseudo-bulbs* large, nearly round. *Racemes* partially drooping, very long, many-flowered. *Bracts* ovate-oblong, obtuse, in the form of scales, with convex backs. *Sepals* oblong, very blunt, flat; petals acute, sometimes rather narrower than the sepals. *Labellum* three-lobed, downy or hairy; middle lobe flat, roundly oblong; lateral ones erect, subfalcate, with an elevated fleshy ridge in the centre; middle lobe severed at the base before the summit fades. *Column* with a raised margin, flexuose, incurved, surrounding a deep, inversely conical cavity.

WHEN this fine species was originally introduced to Britain, considerable, expectation was excited, not only on account of the size of its pseudo-bulbs, and the apparent luxuriance of its habits, but also because it was supposed to be identical with the handsome *Letter plant* of the Malayan Archipelago, respecting which such high opinions had been entertained and circulated. A great number of plants having been sent to this country by Mr. Cuming, from Manilla, in 1837, every cultivator at once became anxious to obtain specimens, and perhaps few orchidaceæ, of such presumed value, were ever more speedily or extensively dispersed.

We are informed that to J. Bateman, Esq., of Knypersly, Cheshire, the honour is due of first flowering it, and thus eliciting its true character. About the month of May, of the present year, a plant in the excellent collection of Baron Dimsdale, Campfield Place, Herts, unfolded its blossoms, and from this we were obligingly allowed to have a drawing executed in the following month. On the flowers appearing, it was at once discovered that this species, although belonging to the same genus as the *Letter plant*, is essentially distinct, and, without question, much inferior. It is, however, very ornamental, of a remarkably free habit of growth, and a most abundant blooming plant;—three properties which, notwithstanding the detraction it has suffered by disappointing the cultivator's expectation, will ever insure it a proper degree of attention.

As it is quite impossible to give a coloured figure of *G. multiflorum*, entire, and of the natural size, we subjoin an engraving on a much less scale, in which the whole specimen is exhibited as it was seen growing.

No orchidaceous plant can be cultivated with greater facility. The most common mode is to place it in a pot, in a compost of heath soil and potsherds, with a very sufficient provision beneath for effective drainage. We have observed some plants at Messrs. Loddiges' in a remarkably vigorous state, which are merely suspended by copper wire, from the roof of the house, without the slightest protective envelope to the roots. These latter are produced in prodigious quantities, and are so densely matted together, as to afford complete security against drought. Atmospheric moisture and shade are of course indispensable to this method of treatment.

The lover of nature will find much to admire in the specimens just noticed. The roots of each year seem to form a medium for the shelter, support, and, most probably, the sustenance of those of the succeeding season; thus furnishing the plants with every assistance which the art of man has yet learned to supply.

Convolvulus Pentanthus.

CONVÓLVULUS PENTÁNTHUS.

(FIVE-FLOWERED BINDWEED.)

CLASS.	ORDER.
PENTANDRIA.	MONOGYNIA.

NATURAL ORDER.
CONVOLVULÀCEÆ.

GENERIC CHARACTER.—*Calyx* five-parted, naked, or with two small imbricated bracts, persistent. *Corolla* monopetalous, hypogynous, regular, campanulate, with five folds down the centre; limb five-lobed, deciduous. *Stamens* inserted in the bottom of the corolla, one between each of its lobes, shorter than the limb. *Germen* two-celled; cells two-seeded; surrounded at the base by an annular gland. *Style* undivided. *Stigmas* two, filiform. *Capsule* valvate; valves with an opposite, angular margin, base of the dissepiment free, seed-bearing.

SPECIFIC CHARACTER.—*Stems* twining, shrubby. *Leaves* oblong-cordate, acuminate, with a slightly sinuous margin, smooth. *Peduncles* umbellate, frequently five-flowered. *Flowers* nearly sessile, small, bright blue. *Calyx* ciliated.

CONSIDERING the abundance and extreme beauty of Convolvulaceous plants, it is possible that many will feel disposed to treat slightingly the interesting subject of our present figure.. This is a feeling which we are desirous of removing; since in no respect is *C. pentanthus* inferior to any of its allies, save in the magnitude of its flowers; while this is fully counterbalanced by their astonishing profusion, and the peculiar adaptation of the species to ornamental purposes.

Of all the plants of this tribe within the range of our information, there is not one the habit of which may be termed neat, or which can be easily rendered symmetrical by particular treatment. A striking laxness of stem, and rapidity of growth, characterize the whole of the commoner climbing species of *Ipomœa* and *Convolvulus;* and whether they are kept in the greenhouse or admitted to the stove, their tendency to occupy too large a space, without at the same time covering it pleasingly, is almost always found to be uncontrollable.

To *C. pentanthus* alone can we attach a character which is sufficiently tractable in the particular thus mentioned; and even this species requires a different mode of culture from that usually practised, to enable it to exhibit the feature which we consider so desirable. The distinction here pointed out between this and other allied plants is, therefore, not so much a natural one, (although it is such to a limited extent,) as one to which the species is susceptible of being induced by artificial treatment.

Trained to the rafters, roof, or wall, of either the greenhouse or stove, (in both of which it will thrive, though the stove appears most suitable,) this pretty plant will certainly form a showy object; as the foliage attendant on the number of its stems will effectually conceal the tenuity of the latter, as well as the distance between the former. But this is far from being the position in which it can be most advantageously displayed. A neat wire trellis, of an oblong, circular, or any other shape, less than three feet in diameter, and from three to six feet high, (about four feet is the most appropriate,) should be provided for each plant when it is first potted, and around this the stems may be directed till they have attained the summit, when their extremities must be turned downwards, and made to traverse again, but inversely, the same course. By a slight pruning, and thus continually training the young shoots between the older and original ones, a succession of healthy foliage and flowers can be maintained, and the same plant kept in an excellent blooming condition for three or four years.

Seeds, when duly ripened, may be readily germinated; and cuttings strike with tolerable freedom, if rightly attended to, and placed in bottom heat. A stock of young plants should be constantly preserved, so as to admit of the destruction of the old specimens when they become unsightly.

The flowers of this plant were primarily expanded in this country in the year 1819, when it was raised from East Indian seeds. It has subsequently been greatly neglected; but its cultivation was revived about the year 1837. We have recently seen it in most of the metropolitan nurseries, and our drawing was made in the stove of Messrs. Henderson, in the early part of last July. Treated as a stove species, it flowers during the whole of the summer and autumn; and, if several plants are possessed, there will frequently be some flowers expanded throughout the entire year.

Convolvulus is derived from *convolvo*, to entwine; most of the species being twining plants. The specific name alludes to the number of flowers in each cluster; but it is not invariably applicable.

Diplacus puniceus

DÍPLACUS PUNÍCEUS.

(SCARLET-FLOWERED DIPLACUS.)

CLASS.	ORDER.
DIDYNAMIA.	ANGIOSPERMIA.

NATURAL ORDER.
SCROPHULARIACEÆ.

GENERIC CHARACTER.—*Calyx* prism-shaped, with five segments at the summit. *Corolla* ringent, five-parted, lobes nearly equal, commonly emarginate. *Stigma* two plated. *Capsule* linear-oblong, two-celled. *Placenta* broad, then bipartite, adnate. *Seeds* awl-shaped on both sides.

SPECIFIC CHARACTER.—*Plant* shrubby, glutinous, smooth. *Leaves* linear-lanceolate, nearly connate, slightly serrulated, acute. *Calyx* with five unequal, acuminate lobes. *Corolla* scarlet-coloured; margin irregularly jagged.

BEFORE this beautiful plant had flowered in British collections, an opinion was current among cultivators, that the figures published from Mr. Nuttall's drawing were much exaggerated, and that the colour of the blossoms was scarcely a shade richer than those of the old *Mimulus glutinosus*. The appearance of the flowers in several gardens around London during the spring of the present year, at once dissipated this impression, and the species is now established as a most valuable acquisition.

To enforce more effectively the above declaration, we now furnish our readers with an accurate representation of a branch of the specimen which first developed its blossoms in the neighbourhood of London. Our figure was obtained from the nursery of Messrs. Low and Co., of Clapton, by whom the entire stock of this species was received from Mr. Buist, of Philadelphia, in the autumn of 1837, and from whose establishment it has been distributed. The particular plant above alluded to bloomed in June last.

It is somewhat singular that the original specimen from which all the thousands that are now adorning our greenhouses were raised, should have remained throughout the whole of the year 1838, without manifesting the least disposition to flower; and that immediately after the young plants procured from cuttings had obtained sufficient strength, they commenced flowering with great liberality. The well-known propensity of old plants to bloom more freely than young ones, would thus seem inverted in this instance, did it not appear probable that the quantity of cuttings taken from it must have caused this temporary barrenness. We have, however, remarked one circumstance in connexion with this subject, which may now be recorded. It is that, in proportion as this plant becomes older, its flowers diminish in size; such plants as are young and luxuriant always bearing the finest and most conspicuous blossoms. Of this fact the culturist should not be unmindful; providing timeously against the degeneracy of his stock, by maintaining a perpetual succession.

In its natural localities, our plant grows generally to the height of five or six feet; and, being exceedingly bushy, makes a splendid feature in the scenery. But in this country, a specimen of such a size is not desirable; unless it be planted in the border of the conservatory, or proves hardy enough to sustain the cold of this climate through the winter. We have repeatedly witnessed its fitness for growing in the flower-garden as a summer novelty, but have not yet ascertained whether it will remain uninjured in that situation the whole year, if moderately sheltered. It certainly demands a trial, as no shrub with which we are acquainted is more showy, or blooms so prodigally and continuously.

Managed as a greenhouse plant, the routine of its culture is of the commonest kind. For soil, a sandy loam, with an addition of heath-soil of about one-fourth, should be preferred. It may be potted as often as seems requisite, and, with merely ordinary attention, will flower from June till very late in the autumn. In the open ground, or a position in the greenhouse where light is admitted in all its natural intensity, the plant will grow much more compact, and the flowers will be more numerous, but their dimensions less.

Propagation may be effected in the easiest manner by cuttings or seeds, the latter of which are occasionally matured.

With regard to the origin of the generic appellation, Mr. Nuttall says, " the name *dis*, two, and *plakos*, placenta, alludes to the splitting of the capsule, to each valve of which is attached a large placenta, and under its edges are found the slender subulate seeds."

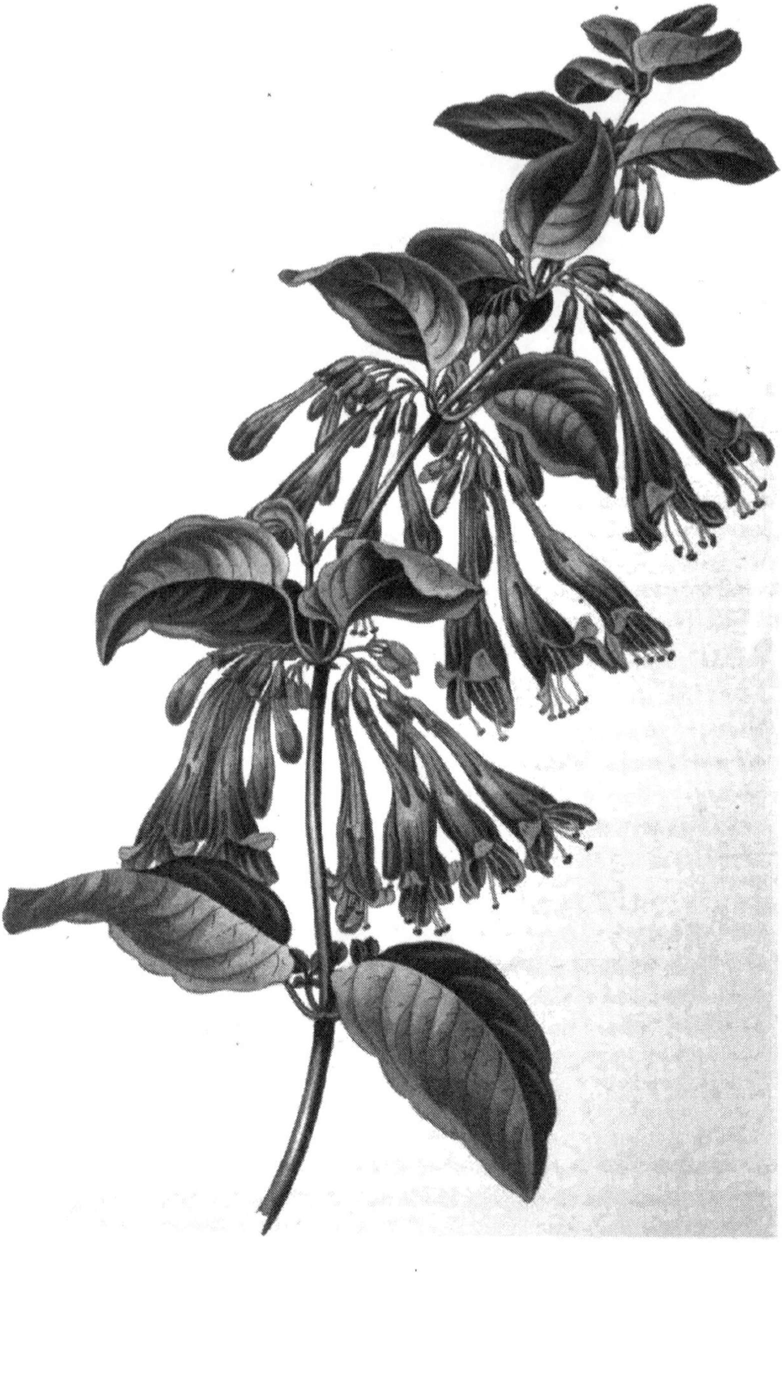

GARDOQUÌA MULTIFLÒRA.

(MANY-FLOWERED GARDOQUIA.)

CLASS.
DIDYNAMIA.

ORDER.
GYMNOSPERMIA.

NATURAL ORDER.
LABIÀTÆ.

GENERIC CHARACTER.—*Vide* vol. iii. p. 243.

SPECIFIC CHARACTER.—*Plant* shrubby, nearly glabrous, growing from eighteen inches to two feet in height. *Leaves* petiolate, ovate, obtuse, slightly crenate, a little rounded at the base, paler beneath. *Flowers* in loose whorls, usually in two large clusters, one from the axil of each leaf. *Calyx* nearly glabrous, with five acute teeth. *Corolla* three times the length of the calyx, dark purple.

THOSE of our readers who possess the third volume of this work, will find, at page 243, a drawing of an extremely elegant and graceful *Gardoquia*, bearing the name of *G. Hookerii*. We now refer to that figure because, by a comparison of the species of so small a genus, their peculiarities are much more easily discerned and remembered. It will be immediately perceived that *G. multiflora* is of a far more robust character, and develops its flowers in a very different manner.

Few plants have been so happily designated as the present species; its blossoms being produced in innumerable quantities, and throughout a very lengthened period. With regard, however, to the luxuriance of its growth, it must be observed that the small sprig exhibited in our plate formed part of a plant which was favoured with particularly appropriate treatment. We have seen many specimens which, owing to inattention, had neither leaves nor flowers more than half so large as those now delineated; but, as the mode of management is very simple, the culturist who wishes to be successful, and will take the following brief observations as his guide, can scarcely fail of rivalling the excellence to which the subject of our figure was brought.

The first point to be secured is a light and airy position in the greenhouse. Before the habitudes of both this species and *G. Hookeri* were thoroughly ascertained, they were most erroneously, and, as subsequent observation has proved, to their great detriment, confined to the stove. This naturally occasioned a weakness and smallness of all their parts, which is quite foreign to their native character. The more recent, and unquestionably the more satisfactory, because congenial practice, is to place them in a far cooler house : indeed, *G. multiflora* is occasionally transplanted to the open ground, where it displays an extraordinary degree of exuberance.

Another matter in which cultivators have too often erred, is the amount of nutritive substance which the soil should contain ; a too innutritious and sterile compost having been usually supplied. In this respect, the more immediate subject of present remark thrives best in a rather rich loamy soil, with only a small portion of sandy heath-mould incorporated. In potting, too much space should not be allowed to remain unoccupied by the roots, nor should they by any means be confined. To avoid both these extremes, the plants must be frequently shifted, employing a pot of only one size larger at each removal.

This plant may be increased with as much facility as any of the *Fuchsias*, a very trifling heat and exceedingly little trouble being required. If cuttings are struck in the early part of the autumn, they will be admirably adapted for the greenhouse or the flower-garden in the ensuing summer; and although they sometimes commence blooming in May, they are seldom destitute of flowers till the approach of winter.

We believe it has been grown in some of our leading nursery establishments for about four years; but it has only very recently been generally cultivated. Its native country is Chili, in the province of Concepcion.

The plant from which the annexed figure was prepared, flowered in great perfection in the Conservatory of his Grace the Duke of Devonshire, at Chiswick, under the skilful care of Mr. C. Edmonds.

The derivation of the generic name will be found in that of D. Diego Gardoqui, a celebrated Spaniard, to whom the genus was dedicated.

COMPARISON OF THE TWO SYSTEMS OF BOTANY.

The perusal of the Article on "Botanical Classification," July, No. 76, p. 129, has elicited the following remarks from a constant reader of "The Magazine of Botany," and which it is hoped may place—not the *merits* of the Linnæan and Jussieuan System—but the application of them, in a true point of view.

It is not at all wished to deny, or even to infuse a doubt of, any one of the positions assumed by the writer of the articles just referred to, because they are essentially sound and tenable; but while waiting for the promised "articles explanatory of its basis, (alluding to the Natural System,) principal divisions, and most extensive or interesting orders," it will be shown that there are points which have not been considered, but which ought to be known by every tyro in botanical study, in order to qualify him to form a correct judgment of what aids and sources of information he ought to have recourse to with a view to facilitate his researches.

Example is frequently better than precept; and in the present instance, one can be adduced so much to the purpose, that it would be very uncandid to withhold it.

The knowledge of structure, so much insisted upon, may exist, and be carried to a great extent, with even a total ignorance of names or nomenclature. A man therefore may be a profound scholar in Physiological botany, without being acquainted with one single plant by name; and to him the Natural System—that is, the *Science* of Physiological and Structural Botany—will be quite familiar. But to the gardener, the mere practical man, this highest knowledge is, as it were, a sealed book; yet his profession demands that he should be acquainted with names.

There are also many persons who love order and classification, and who seek to know, familiarly, the external structure and titles of the plants they cultivate or meet with. The pursuits of such persons are not only innocent, but laudable, and ought by all means to be encouraged: they have not, perhaps, time to enter deeply into scientific research, or what is more to the point, their organization does not qualify them to take rank among the learned *few*.

Imagine the case of a person having a flower sent to him which he had never seen before, its structure extremely curious, but affording no direct clue by which to discover what is its position or name among the orders of the *Natural System*. Some single prominent feature is clearly required to serve as a direction-post to the research. After patient and deliberate investigation with every kind of instrument and power that are applicable to the flower, the arrangement of the stamens is found to offer the only certain key to the hoped for discovery. Such an incident really occurred to a friend, who states the following particulars :—

The filaments were numerous, threadlike, in five distinct ranks, lying flat in close arrangement upon the five petals; they were free throughout their whole length, each parcel about twenty in number. The number and positions of these stamens directed the attention to Class 18, Order 2, *Polyadelphia Polyandria*, of Linnæus. The Corolla was pale-red, verging to orange; and referring to Loudon's *Enc. of Plants*, this circumstance *alone* threw a doubt on the plant being a *Loasa;* for, as the list contained only four species, viz. *L. Placei, nitida, volubilis,* and *grandiflora*, all of them with *yellow* flowers, it became pretty certain that the specimen must be one of recent introduction.

In the last edition of Dr. Lindley's " Natural System of Botany," p. 3, we find Order 35, Loasaceæ. "*Essential character. Calyx* superior *or inferior*, 5-parted, persistent, spreading in æstivation. *Petals* 5 or 10, arising from the recesses of the calyx, cucullate, with an inflexed, valvate æstivation; the inferior often, when present, much smaller than the outer, and truncate at the apex. *Stamens* indefinite, in several rows, arising from within the petals, either distinct or adhering in bundles before each petal, within the cavity of which they lie in æstivation; filaments subulate, unequal, the outer ones frequently destitute of anthers. *Ovary* inferior, or nearly *superior*, 1-celled, with parietal placentæ, or with 1 free central lobed one. *Style* single. *Stigma* 1-or several. *Fruit* capsular or succulent, inferior or superior, 1-celled, with parietal placentæ originating at the sutures. *Seeds* numerous, without arillus; *embryo* lying in the *axis* of fleshy albumen, with the radicle pointing to the hilum, and flat, small cotyledons. *Herbaceous* plants, hispid, with pungent hairs secreting an acrid juice. *Leaves* opposite or alternate, without stipules, usually more or less divided. *Peduncles* axillary, 1-flowered."

Viewing every part of the flower and plant now under consideration, the *texture* of calyx and corolla, their arrangement, the position of the pistillum, the succulent climbing stems, divided lax-leaves, and the prickly armature of every portion of the herbage—the pungency of which becomes evident on the slightest touch—we lean to the opinion expressed by Dr. Lindley, that herein it approaches to a plant of *Cucurbitáceæ*, (the Gourd tribe,) and that " this is the order with which, upon the whole, *Loasaceæ* must be considered to have the closest affinity."

The student in botany ought to be fully aware, that the *Orders* of the Natural System represent, or rather take the place of, the *Classes* of the Linnæan artificial classification. Loasaceæ is a *class* then, and comprises, at present, eleven genera or families. *Viz*:—

Klaprothia,	Acrolasia,	Blumenbachia,	Grammatocarpos,
Mentzelia,	Loasa (the type),	Bartonia,	and
Petalanthera,	Caiophora,	Gronovia,	Scyphanthus.

In the Linnæan arrangement some leading character can be seized, by which the labour of research may be lightened; but by what chance could a youthful enquirer be led to refer to the order Loasaceæ at all? What could suggest the idea of it? True it is that were the Essential Characters engrafted in his memory, half the work would be done; but what memory is equal to the task of grasping, and of appropriating the lengthy (and in many particulars) contradictory characters of above 291 Orders? The thing is impossible; and therefore in the commencement of his career, the student should take advantage of those more simple indications which the Linnæan classes afford, and then have recourse to the Natural Orders, by which he will be taught the physiological structure of the subject he investigates.

In the instance just alluded to, the arrangement of the stamens pointed out the Linnæan Class *Polyadelphia*: this simple, irrefragable fact, tells us in language not to be mistaken, never to discard the artificial system till we obtain some other unerring guide to conduct us to the knowledge of *Genera*.

This is all we claim. We welcome the improvements of the Natural System, and appreciate the labour and zeal of its teachers; but we will apply in every case of need to that simple instructor which puts us in the right path.

The reader will perceive that we have been endeavouring to prove the real utility of the Linnæan system, as a guide and index, not to depreciate the Natural System. The former has instructed us well, and has led us on to the present state of improvement. Like all human edifices, it will crumble under the hand of time, and be succeeded by others more refined and sublime; but it must not be discarded till a substitute be completed which can instruct, without utterly bewildering the mind in its earliest researches.

They who see all the numbers of the Magazine of Botany, will find the plant which induced these remarks figured in the Number of May, 1838, p. 77. We cannot say that the drawing does justice to the flowers; the stamens are shown erect—not as they lie reposing along the groove of *each* hooded petal—revealing clearly their Polyadelphous structure. The nectary also exhibits none of that gorgeous crimson which is so strikingly conspicuous upon the three dots of that truly wonderful piece of elastic mechanism.

We enter our protest against that part of the *Specific* Character which gives 10 *petals* to this species. "Petals 5" are one of the essential generic marks of *Loasa* as an individual genus, and though the nectary is constructed of two distinct portions, yet the lower is assuredly no petal; but, *de facto*, a member of the nectariferous organization. As we are upon the subject of the *Natural System*, it will be proper to extract from the "*Penny Cyclopædia*" the description of the Order, Loasaceæ: it is simply comprehensive.

"Loasàceæ, a small natural order of Polypetalous Exogens, consists of herbaceous, and frequently annual plants, covered over with stiff hairs or stings, which produce considerable pain by the wound they inflict. They have alternate *lobed* leaves without stipules, large yellow, *red*, or white flowers, numerous *polyadelphous* stamens, within which are stationed singular lobed *petaloid appendages*, and an inferior ovary with parietal placentæ. The fruit is a dry or fleshy capsule, with the valves sometimes *spirally twisted*. The order is nearly allied to Cucurbitaceæ."

The passages marked in italics apply strictly to *Loasa lateritia;* the *Nectary*, as a term, is discontinued, and the curious nectariferous processes are called petal-like appendages. The valves of the capsule (two thirds of which are inferior) are twisted almost as much as the seed-vessel of *Streptocarpos*.

We have no desire to render our Magazine the instrument of controversy; but we might be deemed guilty of injustice and discourtesy did we not afford a place to the preceding remarks of our respected correspondent, particularly as we believe they will meet with an unqualified response from many of our readers. Equally wanting should we be in duty to ourselves, if we allowed our previous declarations to remain undefended. Perhaps, were our own paper carefully perused in conjunction with that now inserted, further refutation of the points on which a difference of opinion is manifest would appear unnecessary. We are willing, however, to assume that the subject may yet be placed in a clearer light; and therefore trust we shall be pardoned for here reverting to it.

That a knowledge of the Linnæan arrangement is useful as a preliminary step to the acquirement of the Natural Method, or to those who can be satisfied with the vague and uncertain assistance it imparts, we have already asserted. But we profess ourselves totally at issue with our correspondent when he attempts to define the extent of its utility. Nor can we by any means admit the supposed analogy between the Linnæan *Classes* and the Natural *Orders*. The latter assuredly bring us much nearer to the *Genera* than even the *Orders* of Linnæus, and may fairly be considered as situated between these two, though decidedly less removed from the former.

It is stated that the system of Linnæus is an easier guide to genera than the Jussieuan. Could this position be maintained, our readers may be assured that no article would have ever been published by us expressive of anything but disapprobation of this much aspersed Natural System. But we undertake to show, in the papers which we shall from time to time furnish, that the direct converse of this is the case. It is barely possible that any one who has sought extensive aid from the Linnæan arrangement, can have escaped being most miserably chagrined at finding many plants comparatively as erratic in the number of stamens they produce, as in the development of flowers themselves. We may mention one instance which recently occurred beneath Dr. Lindley's observation, and is recorded in the Botanical Register, p. 47. *Bauhinia corymbosa*, a rather scarce stove plant, is found to bear flowers, some of which are distinctly referable to no fewer than eight Linnæan classes or orders. Other illustrations are omitted on account of our limited space; but we could adduce a considerable number which would equally invalidate the claims of our Linnæan apologist; and although not of so extraordinary a nature, it is not the degree in which they depart from the established rules, but the mere fact of their deviation, which lessens, indeed destroys, the value of the system.

This being an essential defect in the *arrangement itself*, we boldly ask who would entrust themselves to a guide which had frequently led them into error, or who, knowing the fallacy of such a course, would recommend others to follow it? The force of the above objection is not in the least diminished by the circumstance of *most* plants being readily assigned to their proper class. Without complete confidence in the accuracy of any method, it can never be employed advantageously; and the numerous cases in which the number of stamens is indeterminable, are calculated to beget the utmost distrust in the Linnæan classification.

But the extravagant assumptions of the admirers of this system have a tendency to bring upon it far greater disrespect than its own failings. If it were affirmed that by thus simply apportioning the vegetable kingdom into a certain number of greater or less groups, inquiries after genera are in some degree facilitated, because the number of those in each group is infinitely less than the whole, we could to this most cordially subscribe. But when we read language tantamount to an assertion that the discovery of the Linnæan class and order of any plant at once leads the inquirer to its genus, we cannot suppress our astonishment.

Without the slightest predilection towards either system, we may here declare that the Linnæan method affords very little better clue to an acquaintance with genera, than if the genera were arranged *alphabetically* in classes of similar length, with some common character affixed to each genus to determine its particular class. How, therefore, the classification of Linnæus alone could direct any person to place a plant of whose generic appearance or character he had no previous knowledge in a genus which forms a part of any of the extensive Orders of that system, we confess ourselves wholly incapable of conceiving.

It will be sufficient to remind the young gardener who may be induced, from motives which we will not endeavour to fathom, to believe that the Linnæan system is divested of all difficulties respecting nomenclature, what is his object in seeking to acquaint himself with either system. If it be (and we can imagine no other) to facilitate his acquirement of the names of plants, by an examination of their structure, a knowledge of terms is quite as indispensable in the one case as the other. That investigation of generic characters which can alone ultimately enable the student to decide upon a plant's name, is particularly requisite where only the Linnæan method is consulted; and it need not be added that such characters comprise all the phrases used in the description of the Natural Orders. The comparative apprehension with which the Jussieuan system is regarded on this account, is, therefore, wholly groundless.

We shall hereafter demonstrate that the mode of ascertaining to what Natural Order any plant belongs, is as regular, natural, and, when once the outlines of the arrangement are known, fully as easy as the way of finding its Linnæan Order. The barriers to be removed are, however, unquestionably more alarming to the beginner; but if he will consent to be inducted into the science by a regular process, we have no fear of eventually being able to verify all our present asseverations.

FAMILIAR HINTS TO YOUNG GARDENERS ON MENTAL IMPROVEMENT.

To the citation with which we closed our previous article on this subject, we may now add that observation alone can test and confirm the opinions imbibed by reading, or furnish matter for original and creditable composition and converse. Hence, it is obviously the key-stone which crowns and completes the educational structure, and secures to it the requisite strength and stability. Indeed, without observation, reason is easily deluded, and we are borne along on the wings of every airy notion which men of genius, who are lacking in practical acquirements, may conceive.

Subordinate only in importance to observation itself, is a knowledge of the readiest and most profitable manner in which it may be conducted. To afford a hurried sketch of the system we ourselves have practised, these present endeavours will be directed. What is deficient in detail, or but imperfectly connected, we leave to the adroitness of our youthful readers to elaborate and supply; only premising that, to ensure the attainment of its advantages, it must be perseveringly and indefatigably pursued, and promptly and judiciously applied.

Of all subjects of observation, that most useful to the gardener is the effect and extent of the agency of the elements, processes, and phenomena of Nature upon vegetation. The cultivation of plants—whether of an ornamental, culinary, or otherwise useful character—being the principal aim of his profession, and the treatment of these having to be regulated according to natural circumstances, will account for the importance we attach to this comprehensive particular. It being almost impossible for the memory to preserve a faithful register of daily-revealed facts and circumstances, we must commence by suggesting the use of a diary, wherein to record the occurrence, consequence, and, as far as practicable, the cause of any remarkable incident, either directly horticultural or relative thereto, with notices of such newly-presented feature of, or deviation from, the ordinary course of culture and development, as may be deemed worthy of remembrance. To the slothful, we are aware that this practice is open to insuperable objection;—but *it is* not such we address;—and the highly beneficial effects of the habit, which speedily manifest themselves, will be a sufficient stimulus to the aspiring gardener.

Diurnal changes of temperature, of humidity, and of the general state of the atmosphere, not forgetting winds and clouds, will form matter for some of the items of such memoranda; and though these are uninteresting and unsatisfactory in themselves, yet, when noted with a view of ascertaining their influence on vegetable life and functions, they will be invested with peculiar and permanent inducements to proceed. It has been the failing of those who have commenced such accounts, usually to neglect that which alone can render them either gratifying or useful; hence, they have soon become weary of the task. We would wish it to be distinctly understood, that no recorded observation of any kind can be of the slightest value unless accompanied by the influence and issue of the circumstances investigated.

Connected with atmospherical phenomena, as being the means by which many of them are modified, and which, in turn, exercise a considerable reactive agency, there are a variety of compound matters termed soils, the diversified effect of which upon plants, is too powerful and evident to be passed over by the observant gardener. Whether they are only the medium of conveyance for aqueous and gaseous fluids, or whether, as is more probable, indeed, well authenticated, they impregnate those fluids with their own particular properties, to the sustenance or injury (according as they may be inimical or congenial) of the plants growing on them, their influence must be of the highest moment. On the first assumption, a knowledge of their capability of admitting the percolation of fluids, and in the second, besides this, an acquaintance with their chemical qualities, should be sought by those who would understand correctly how to employ them. Analyses of their constituent particles, though not so easily obtained, are much more satisfactory and conclusive than a mere examination of their general appearance and consistence, and every gardener should be in some measure competent to this operation. The adaptation of the different soils to particular plants, must, however, be the ultimate object of such observations.

Ascending still higher in the scale of natural influence, there is a class of animated beings, which is included in the term insects, whose ravages upon plants it is impossible for the most negligent gardener to disregard. And yet, how little is generally known of these interesting though destructive tribes! It is our special privilege, that many departments of knowledge which the elegant and the erudite traverse as amateurs to acquire delight and wisdom from their investigation, are those with which our calling permits, nay requires us, to acquaint ourselves; and of these, Entomology will be found certainly not the least remunerative, either in imparting real pleasures or professional advantages. When it is reflected that few are familiar with the transformations, seasons, and sustenance of the more inscrutable but not less inimical species, and that many frequently confound, or fail to trace and identify, through their various metamorphoses, and in their dissimilar guises, those which are larger and more conspicuous, it will be seen how needful it is to direct attention to this important science.

Nor would inquiry into the habits of the feathered race prove superfluous. The indiscriminate slaughter and extermination of birds, is allowed by all rational and experienced men to be fatuous and impolitic. Most of them, if their numbers be discreetly regulated, are, notwithstanding temporary and apparently extensive depredation, the most efficient auxiliaries of the gardener in repressing the far more voracious hordes of vermin which would otherwise speedily defoliate all vegetation.

Apart from an examination into the influence of natural circumstances on plants, there are peculiar variations in the method and manner of treating them artificially, the applicability of which demands much and careful observation. In this instance, again, we cannot refrain from declaring the inadequacy and utter futility of a mere record of operations performed, or systems commenced, without further regard to their consequences and results. We have known young enthusiasts, who very diligently kept a journal on the above plan; but in every case have they abandoned it after its novelty has subsided, and, we are confident, from no other cause than that we have before assigned. To render these observations available, not only the particular kind of soil employed, the mode of potting, administration of water, and other similar matters, must be recorded, but the construction of plant structures, including every portion of them, and the method of heating, should be accurately noted. With such data, subsequent notice of the precise manner in which plants are affected by each and all of these different agents or media, will be invaluable.

We have now to advert to a subject which, of all others connected with our profession, is most grossly neglected; as the appearance of our modern pleasure-gardens of every description abundantly testifies. We allude to the observation of natural scenery, with a view to the impartation or improvement of an original and correct taste for landscape gardening. Far from wishing to be censorious, we state it as a remarkable fact, that not one gardener in a hundred is competent to design and execute the disposition of a garden in a manner worthy of the present or even antecedent ages. It is not our intention to direct the youthful gardener to the examination of hedge-rows and woods, for the purpose of learning the art of planting. These are as purely artificial as the plantations of gardens. Striking deeper at the root of the evil, we would point to the natural formation of hill and dale, streamlet and waterfall, rocky and mountainous districts, and say—are there not in these, ample materials and bases for more exquisite and expressive creations of art than we are accustomed to witness in most of our artificial villa gardens? The mere sciolist may, perhaps, negative this interrogatory; but, unquestionably, the man of taste and judgment will decide affirmatively.

In referring our younger professional brethren, who are desirous of attaining respectability in landscape gardening, to Nature's school, we must do so qualifiedly. A much admired piece of natural scenery is not to be examined that each particular trait may be literally or slavishly copied. It is the outlines, and not the details, the general features, and not the individual objects, that we wish to be studied; so that the student may become possessed of the spirit of beauty—the *beau idéal* of grace and congruity. It would thus be impossible for him to err greatly in design or disposition; for any deformity or constraint would be distasteful and annoying to his own eye, accustomed to the lineaments of the living landscape, to the precise extent it would be inharmonious with nature. To pursue this study successfully, the mind must be unshackled by every lovely but isolated portion of scenery which might engage its attention, that the grand distinguishing characteristics of the whole may be fully grasped, comprehended, and retained. By thus ascertaining some of the *principles* in which the striking variety and inequality of the surface of our globe is effected, and applying these *generally* in the formation of pleasure gardens, we are persuaded that a greater degree of originality, harmony, and beauty, might be attained.

Experiments may very properly be included in our remarks on observation, since it is the investigation of their results, and not their mere institution, to which we are desirous of directing the gardening student. Observation alone must be confined to natural events; but, by experiment, new and sometimes preferable systems of cultivation are elicited, and the application of horticultural art is simplified, facilitated, and improved. If it be objected that young gardeners do not possess the means for conducting inquiries of this nature, we may reply that native plants are the property of every one, and a number of most interesting experiments might be performed upon these, by which the general functions of the vegetable system could be satisfactorily ascertained. We will only add that inquiries of this, as much as of a higher order, are highly worthy of the experimenter, and personally and publicly beneficial; that they betoken true genius, increase both the resources and uses of information, and invariably tend to the discovery and establishment of truth.

FLORICULTURAL NOTICES.

NEW AND RARE PLANTS FIGURED IN THE LEADING BOTANICAL PERIODICALS FOR OCTOBER.

CLASS I.—PLANTS WITH TWO COTYLEDONS (DICOTYLEDONEÆ).

THE WATER-LILY TRIBE (*Nymphæàceæ*).

NELÚMBIUM LÙTEUM. Yellow-flowered Sacred bean. With the exception of *Magnolia macrophylla*, this handsome aquatic is said to bear larger flowers than any other plant indigenous to the North American continent. It has been known in this country many years, but Sir W. J. Hooker is not aware of any instance in which it had flowered, till its blossoms were developed in the collection of E. Sylvester, Esq., of Chorley, Lancashire, about last July. In North-America, where it is most abundant towards the Southern States, but is also found in Lake Ontario, it inhabits stagnant waters, and is called *Water Chinquepin*. Mr. Sylvester attributes his success in flowering it, to the comparatively low temperature in which it was kept during the former part of the present year; as it had for a long previous period been retained in a hot stove without producing a single blossom. Probably a cistern in a greenhouse is the most congenial situation, it being plausibly conjectured that a pool in the open air would be much too cold. *Bot. Mag.* 3753.

THE INDIAN FIG TRIBE (*Cactàceæ*).

LEPÍSMIUM MYOSÙRUS. Mouse-tail Lepismium. One of the numerous divisions into which the old genus *Cactus* has been separated. The plant under notice has a great quantity of slender, angular, branching stems, with few and scattered spines, but covered with aerial roots. The flowers appear in great profusion from all parts of the stems, but, except for their number, they do not impart much value to the plant, being small and pale yellow. Brazil is its native country, from whence it was obtained by T. Brocklehurst, Esq., of the Fence, Manchester, in whose orchidaceous-house it bloomed under rather peculiar circumstances. A branch having been accidentally detached, was placed heedlessly on the soil of another pot, where, as we presume, forming roots, it speedily flowered. Any check, short of actual mutilation of the stems of *Cactaceæ*, is well known to stimulate their flowering organs. This appears to be a species which would succeed admirably if fastened to a block of wood, and merely assisted, towards the base, with a little moss. *Bot. Mag.* 3755.

THE BIRTHWORT TRIBE (*Aristolochiàceæ*).

ARISTOLÒCHIA CILIÀTA. Fringe-flowered Birthwort. This is in all respects one of the smallest species of the genus. It is described as having a " weak, yet not climbing, slender, zigzag, glaucous, apparently simple" stem, heart-shaped, but very obtuse foliage, and green flowers ; the tip of the latter stands erect, is beautifully blotched and streaked on the upper or inner surface with deep purple, and fringed with long, succulent, glandular hairs. Seeds of it were collected by Mr. Tweedie, in Buenos Ayres, and, from some of these sent to the Glasnevin Botanic Garden, flowering plants have been liberally produced. It thrives freely in the greenhouse, and, in the more southerly parts of Britain, will perhaps be found nearly hardy. *Bot. Mag.* 3756.

THE BEAN TRIBE (*Leguminòsæ*).

LUPÌNUS BARKÈRII. Mr. Barker's Lupine. Whether, when the character of *Lupineæ* is thoroughly comprehended, the present species will be retained, is doubtful ; since it approaches pretty nearly to several previously established ones. One remarkable feature in this plant is, however, the tendency of the flower-buds to disperse themselves widely even while young ; while its "deciduous bracts, and freedom from villosity" distinguish it from *L. Hartwegii*, a native of the same district. George Barker, Esq., of Birmingham, imported seeds of it in 1338, and it bears the name of this gentleman. It is a very showy species, growing nearly three feet high, and bearing long spikes of flowers, in which there is a happy combination of blue, red, pink, and yellow. Cultivated as an annual, the seeds must be sown as early as February ; " but if managed as a biennial, the seeds should be sown in the previous year, about the beginning of August ; kept in pots protected from frost during winter, and planted out in the open borders about the middle of May." It flowers in the autumnal months. *Bot. Reg.* 56.

THE FIGWORT TRIBE (*Scrophulariàceæ*).

ANGELÒNIA GÁRDNERI. Mr. Gardner's Angelonia. A very beautiful plant, discovered by Mr. Gardner in "rather dry, open places, in the province of

Pernambuco," from whence seeds were transmitted to the Glasgow Botanic Garden, where it flowered in the stove last May. It very greatly resembles *A. salicariæfolia*, and is an erect, suffruticose, branching plant, about three feet high, and clothed with glandular hairs. The leaves are opposite, lanceolate, and much serrated; while the blossoms are deep purple, with a lighter-coloured throat, the base of which is much spotted. It is a highly ornamental plant, and, we have no doubt, would grow and flower vigorously in the greenhouse. *Bot. Mag.* 3754.

CLASS II.—PLANTS WITH ONE COTYLEDON (MONOCOTYLEDONEÆ).

THE NARCISSUS TRIBE (*Amaryllidàceæ*).

AGÀVE SAPONÀRIA. The Soap Aloe. Dr. Lindley has no hesitation in pronouncing this singular plant an *Agave*, although, unlike the other species, it is a decided perennial, and does not perish after, or, indeed, suffer any injury from, flowering. It is of Mexican origin; but Mr. Skinner is stated to have seen it used in Peru as a substitute for soap, and hence its name. "If," says Dr. Lindley, "this species should furnish a fibre capable of being used by the manufacturer, it will then, like the *Maguey*, its near ally, both produce a material from which linen may be woven, and assist in washing it afterwards." Its inflorescence is strong, and the blossoms are large, but dull yellow; the foliage is like that of the common American Aloe, and it may be treated as the *Haworthias*, and other similar genera. *Bot. Reg.* 55.

THE ORCHIS TRIBE (*Orchidàceæ*).

LÈLIA ÀLBIDA. White-flowered Lælia. Count Karwinski first discovered this charming plant in cool places near St. Pedro, Oaxaca, and, carrying it to Munich, it was from that city sent to Britain. The pseudo-bulbs are short, roundish, and with a ring round the centre; the leaves in pairs and lanceolate; while the flowers are produced in short, erect spikes from the summits of the pseudo-bulbs. Besides white, a pale flesh colour is discernible in the blossoms towards the points of the sepals, and the lip has a rich purple spot at its base, together with a yellow streak down the centre. The fragrance of its flowers is compared to " a bed of primroses, which in fact they much resemble in odour." *Bot. Reg.* 54.

THE LILY TRIBE (*Liliàceæ*).

DAUBÉNYA FÚLVA. Tawny Daubenya. There is much to interest the curious botanist in this novel plant, but little which the mere cultivator would admire. It is a bulbous species, with large, handsome leaves, from the midst of which the flowers appear in dense clusters on a short flower-stalk. Although not wholly lacking in beauty, the blossoms are of a brownish-red colour, which is necessarily somewhat dull. It was received from the Cape of Good Hope by Robert Barchard, Esq., of Wandsworth, Surrey, and is supposed to have been obtained from the East Coast of Africa, or from Madagascar. The treatment is precisely that of a Cape Bulb. *Bot. Reg.* 53.

NEW, RARE, AND INTERESTING PLANTS IN FLOWER IN THE PRINCIPAL SUBURBAN NURSERIES.

ABÙTILON STRIÀTUM. In several places which we have visited this season, the plant above named is cultivated as a supposed species of *Malvaviscus*. Indeed, its general character so resembles that of many related plants, that, unless the flowers were expanded, it might even be considered a variety of *Hibiscus rosa-sinensis*. Although of a rather straggling habit when grown in the stove, this is not so displeasingly apparent if the plant be kept in a greenhouse; while its charming orange-coloured flowers, which are beautifully striped with bright brown, depend so gracefully from the branches, that it cannot fail to excite admiration. It is now flowering abundantly in the greenhouse of Messrs. Henderson, Pine-Apple place, and also in the stove of Mrs. Lawrence, Ealing Park.

ACÀCIA KERMESÌNA. It is doubtful whether this showy plant be not assignable to *Inga* or *Anneslea* rather than *Acacia*, since its flowers are far more like those of the two former genera. It is a free-growing species, with handsomely pinnated foliage, the leaflets of which are narrow, and, in common with many others of the tribe, contract and droop in the evening of the day, resuming their natural position and office with the return of daylight. From the extremities of the branches, the flowers appear in spikes, each blossom being composed of a number of long slender filaments, of a brilliant purple hue, in which a slight dash of crimson is perceptible. In Mrs. Lawrence's splendid collection, we saw it flowering about a fortnight since.

CATTLÈYA BÍCOLOR. Of all the new species that have latterly been added to this genus, none is more distinct than the present. It has small, slender, stem-like pseudo-bulbs, and ovately-oblong, acute, alternate leaves; but the structure of the flowers constitutes its chief difference. These are principally formed in the usual manner, having pale green petals and sepals, sparingly spotted with brown; while the labellum, instead of incurving and enveloping the column, as is generally the case, is drooping, recurved, and quite detached. The sheath of the column is of a delicate white, and the lip a rich purple; the contrast in these two, between each other, and the outer members of the flower, being very striking. Specimens now blossoming at Messrs. Loddiges' were imported from Brazil. The flowers are rather sparsely produced at the summit of the younger stems.

EPIDÉNDRUM STENOPÉTALUM. With some allowance for the solitariness of its flowers, this is one of the prettiest of *Epidendra*. The stems are of a nature intermediate between the more slender kinds and *E. bicornutum*; not being longer than the latter, but far less strong, and slightly furrowed and articulated. The first leaves appear almost close to the base of the stem, but as this last advances in height, they continue decaying, so that when the stems are full grown, there are not more than eight or nine leaves remaining on each side of them. One peculiarity of the foliage is, that each leaf is a little twisted; it is, besides, long, narrow, and emarginate. Only one flower appears to expand on each stem at the same time; these being moderately large, and of a very deep pink, with a white spot at the base of the labellum, which adds greatly to their beauty. Messrs. Loddiges have a plant at present in flower. Its native country is Guiana.

FÙCHSIA GLOBÒSA; *var.* DEVÒNIA. In the greenhouse of Messrs. Henderson, Pine-Apple Place, we observed last month a very handsome *Fuchsia*, bearing the above name. It is most probably a hybrid, having been obtained from some collection near Exeter; but, notwithstanding the difficulty which both the botanist and cultivator experience in distinguishing hybrid Fuchsias on account of their great and continually increasing numbers, and the consequent injudiciousness of adding other names to the list, this plant seems to us entitled to permanent regard. It has a noble habit, fine foliage, and particularly large flowers; though these last have a much shorter and more expansive corolla, and likewise a stronger and shorter flower-stalk than the *F. globosa elegans*, of which a drawing was published in a former volume of this work.

HIBÍSCUS CAMERÒNII. We presume this is an English hybrid, named after Mr. Cameron, curator of the Birmingham Botanic Garden. It is slightly similar to *H. splendens* in the colour of the flower; these being, however, much lighter, while the leaves are smoother, and the whole plant less robust. We saw a flowering specimen at Messrs. Low and Co.'s, Clapton, in September last; and blossoms yet continue unfolding on the same plant. It appears to be a kind that, owing to its disposition to flower profusely, and at an early stage of its existence, will prove an excellent ornament to the stove, and probably to the greenhouse.

IPOMÆA LÈARII. There is undoubtedly a close affinity between this superb new species and *I. rubro-cœrulea*, and, as certainly, a decided difference. It will be sufficient at present to state that this consists chiefly in the hairiness of *I. Learii*, the deeper colour, and more conspicuous stripes of its flowers, and their production in more dense clusters on shorter lateral shoots. We shall in due time publish an excellent drawing which our artist has made from a plant that flowered in the stove of Mr. Knight, Chelsea, by whom it was imported, and named after the person who transmitted it to Britain.

JACKSÒNIA GRANDIFLÒRA. One of the elegant floral products of the Swan River Colony, plants of which have been raised in the nursery of Messrs. Low and Co., Clapton, where it is at the present time exhibiting its blossoms. The appearance of the plant is precisely that of some species of *Genista*, as it seems destitute of any other foliage than such as assimilates to the branches. This character, however, renders it graceful, and the pretty, pendent, pale yellow flowers, which are blotched in the centre with brownish purple, likewise tend to constitute it a desirable feature in a greenhouse.

NUTTÁLLIA CORDÀTA. This interesting herbaceous plant approaches nearest to

N. papaver; from which it is triflingly removed in the character of the foliage, but still more so in the hue of its blossoms. The lower leaves are, like those of *N. papaver,* divided into segments, but rather less deeply so, and more hollowed out at the base; besides which, around the entire margin, there is a broad stripe of dark brown, which appears characteristic of the present species alone. The flowers are pale pink, while, with regard to their size and the irregular and numerous fringe-like indentations along their summits, they are exactly like those of *N. papaver.* It is flowering at the Epsom nursery.

ONCÍDIUM RÒSEUM. The species of *Oncidium* which we noticed last month as flowering in Messrs. Loddiges' collection, has since received the name here given. At the present period, *O. roseum, O. Henchmanii,* and a plant which Messrs. Loddiges consider a variety of *O. sanguineum,* are all blooming in the Hackney nursery, and as they are very similar in all respects except the flowers, these having likewise several points of resemblance, it may be useful to mention their individual characteristics. The flowers of *O. Henchmanii* are the largest, the palest coloured, with the sepals and petals the least curled, and the labellum entirely brown: those of *O. roseum* are blotched with a purplish rose tint, and, with regard to the size of the lip, and the curling of the sepals, are intermediate between the other two; while the blossoms of the variety of *O. sanguineum* are much more curled, of a far darker hue, and have the smallest lip; this last member in both the latter species being stained with the same colour as the more exterior portions. All are extremely beautiful, and well-deserving of the cultivator's care.

PASSIFLÒRA ONYCHÌNA. An opportunity of witnessing the flowers of this species has at length been afforded us in the nursery of Messrs. Henderson, where a new house has just been erected for the reception of stove plants. Though greatly inferior to some other species, it is a beautiful and acceptable addition to the genus; and bears blossoms, the most prominent feature of which is the circle of deep blue rays which diverge from their centre. The leaves are small, pale green, and of the common partially tripartite form; while the plant appears to be altogether of a slender habitude.

RODRIGUÈZIA CRÍSPA. All who cultivate Orchidaceous plants, doubtless possess the interesting *Rodriguezia planifolia;* so much admired for the delightful fragrance of its simple blossoms. And to such it will be pleasing to know that a new species, with the same property, and a much more ornamental character, is now blooming at Messrs. Loddiges' nursery. *R. crispa* has pseudo-bulbs as large as, and much resembling, those of *Trichopilia tortilis,* or some species of *Oncidium.* Their base is enveloped in two small leaves, and the summits crowned with two larger and very handsome ones, of the description common to many *Oncidia.* From the axils of the lowermost pair, the floral racemes protrude. These are strong, and ultimately become drooping, bearing a considerable quantity of pale greenish yellow, successionally expansive flowers. The chief point of attraction in the blossoms is their striking disposition to curl, a bright red streak round the base of the column, their unusual size, and highly grateful odour; which last is exhaled perpetually, and not merely distinguishable at a particular period.

SACCOLÀBIUM PAPILLÒSUM. An important mistake occurred in our last Number (p. 214) respecting a species of *Saccolabium*, which we are here desirous of rectifying. *S. guttatum* was there described as a yellow species, whereas it is generally known to be of a cream colour, liberally blotched with pink; and the plant then noticed should have been called *S. papillosum*, or, as we have since discovered, a superior variety of this species.

OPERATIONS FOR NOVEMBER.

PERHAPS in no other month is the gardener required to exercise more vigilance in the superintendence of the plants committed to his charge. The almost proverbial dampness and dulness of the external atmosphere, combined with the fact that on the judicious management of exotics at this period, their maintenance in health through the winter to a very considerable degree rests, are quite sufficient to call forth a greater than usual amount of attention and care.

Every experienced cultivator is aware that it is not in the actual months of winter that the greatest difficulty respecting the healthy preservation of plants is felt. Those periods at which the most striking changes in the atmosphere and temperature occur,—the rise and fall of the seasons, or the commencement and departure of winter,—are the chief tests of skill in the treatment of tender species. In favourable years, these transitions are generally effected by slow degrees; but their influence on plants is nevertheless always somewhat sudden, and their demand upon the especial watchfulness of the culturist is never to be neglected with impunity.

The time to which these observations are especially intended to apply, is precisely one of the seasons above instanced; while the peculiarly unpropitious weather by which it has been preceded, will render its prejudicial effects doubly destructive, if these are not carefully warded off by an increased diligence in the application of preventive means; or, what is of more consequence, the cautious removal of all causes which are likely to create the evil. It is a far stronger evidence of true wisdom, to avoid the operation of any pernicious condition, than to devise means for its removal after it has created a positive injury. And if plants have been treated during the summer according to our repeated recommendations, they now need no kind of stimulation, the only point for consideration being how they may best be kept in health, without allowing the too great advancement of any exciting agent.

Concerning heat, no mistake can possibly arise, unless it be in the regulation of an artificial temperature, or the trifling and temporary admission of air. Every application of fire-heat, except in cases of forcing, or to newly imported and very young stove or orchidaceous plants, must be regarded not merely as a useless superfluity, but as decidedly detrimental. Ventilation will of course be employed only when the temperature is unusually and unduly elevated. In the greenhouse, particularly, it should be adopted whenever practicable, but always with this restriction—that the outward air be perfectly dry.

This last observation leads us at once to the most important item in the winter culture of exotics. A moderate degree of aridity, both of atmosphere and soil, is the grand desideratum throughout this trying season. To be able to preserve this at its proper standard, is a matter with which no cultivator should be unacquainted. As a first step, and one upon which the whole system mainly depends, it is of the highest moment that the plants themselves should be brought early to a fitting state of dryness. To secure this, let them be watered with the utmost care, and with the view only of keeping them alive. This timeously attended to, their exhalations will be reduced, and thus neither the roots nor the air can ever be surcharged with moisture, for it is easy to prevent its ingress from the outside.

If the course here suggested be considered an extreme one, or if it be supposed that we have carried our principle too far, let it not be forgotten that the bias is on the safe side. We never yet witnessed a plant that was killed, or even injured, by a slight drought in the winter; while, that thousands yearly perish from a contrary cause must be known to all. Anxious, therefore, to insure our readers against this loss, we have been thus particular in stating an infallible remedy. Our strictures must, however, be read in close connexion with the other portions of the system which we have for some time been attempting to establish, and by no means acted upon to the full extent, unless the summer management has been such as we have previously advocated.

In the greenhouse, stove, and every other structure in which climbing plants are trained to the pillars or roof, or in any position where they obstruct the light, and shade the more humble species, an immediate pruning should be effected, and the shoots that are left, either fastened in their proper place, or brought together in as small a compass as possible. With the hard-wooded kinds that are spread out beneath the glass, the latter of these modes is preferable, as the branches can be released, and disposed in the desired manner, before they again begin to grow. But the more succulent species, and such as are placed beneath the rafters, or where they cannot intercept light, may be at once secured in the direction in which they are wished to extend themselves when the resuscitation of their developments commences.

Miltonia candida.

MILTÒNIA CÁNDIDA.

(WHITE-LIPPED MILTONIA.)

CLASS.
GYNANDRIA.

ORDER.
MONANDRIA.

NATURAL ORDER.
ORCHIDÀCEÆ.

GENERIC CHARACTER.—*Perianth* showy. *Petals* revolute; *sepals* lateral, connate at the base, sessile, resembling each other. *Labellum* large, dilated, undivided, sessile, slightly connate with the column, lamellate at the base. *Column* dwarf, semi-cylindrical, with large lateral ears or appendages at the summit. *Pollen-masses* two, with adnate oblong caudiculæ.

SPECIFIC CHARACTER.—*Pseudo-bulbs* ovate, narrowing towards the apex, two-leaved. *Leaves* narrow, shorter than the racemes. *Bracts* ovate, membranaceous, concave, squamæform. *Sepals* and *petals* oblong, equal. *Labellum* nearly round, curled, folded about the column, five-plated at the base. *Column* pubescent, two-eared at its base.

OF this magnificent Brazilian epiphyte, Dr. Lindley truly observes, in his admirable *Sertum Orchidaceum*, that it " is one of the most noble of its race, and is scarcely rivalled by any of the beautiful species of *Dendrobium* or *Cattleya.*" Its fine and richly-mottled blossoms contain such a charming combination of lively colours, and these are rendered so pleasingly prominent by the delicate white of the labellum, that they at once arrest and fix the eye of the spectator, and occasion the most vivid emotions of delight. But what constitutes the species particularly worthy of regard, is the great prodigality with which its flowers are produced, this property being conspicuous, not merely with respect to their profusion at one and the same period, but also for the certainty of its annual occurrence.

We have found it impossible to give more than a portion of a single scape of flowers in one plate, and must apprise the reader that a strong plant will produce five or six spikes, each bearing from eight to twelve blossoms. These are disposed around the plant with such peculiar grace, inclining partially downwards by their own weight, that no moderately-sized figure could exhibit an entire specimen in its true form and proportions. To supply this defect, a small wood engraving is added on the succeeding page, by which some idea of its habit will be conveyed.

In its cultivation, it seems to require a similar treatment to the species of *Cattleya*, with, perhaps, a trifling increase of heat and moisture. Plants in the

Orchidaceous-house of Messrs. Loddiges, and subjected to the high excitation which is well known to characterize their mode of culture, thrive with great rapidity and luxuriance, and bear an astonishing number of flowers. Nevertheless, we are disposed to believe that a very high temperature is not essential, and that those who succeed best in the growth of Cattleyas will be equally fortunate in the culture of this plant.

Its flowering season appears to be the months of October and November, as we saw it blooming at Messrs. Loddiges' in November 1838, at which time our drawing was prepared, and it blossomed again last month in this and several other collections near the metropolis. On this account, and as the flowers issue from the base of the newly-perfected stems, it may very properly be allowed to rest during the winter months, by being located in a cool dry house. It should be repotted at the commencement of every spring, using the common materials (heath-soil and pot-sherds) as a compost, and sedulously providing every approved means for assisting drainage. The plants need not be elevated above the surface of the pot.

It may be increased by the usual method of separating off-sets, or detaching one of the pseudo-bulbs. No particular treatment is requisite for these, unless it be that of keeping them somewhat drier than the old plants, till they are firmly established. When the flowers are very numerous, it is sometimes necessary to support them with small stakes, but this should not be effected except when such assistance is really desirable.

Thysanotus intricatus.

THYSANOTUS INTRICATUS.

(INTRICATE-STEMMED THYSANOTUS.)

CLASS.
HEXANDRIA.

ORDER.
MONOGYNIA.

NATURAL ORDER.
LILIACEÆ.

GENERIC CHARACTER.—*Corolla* six-parted, spreading, persistent; inside segments broader; limb coloured on both sides, margin fimbriated with jointed hairs. *Stamens* six, (rarely three,) inserted in the bottom of the corolla, or hypogynous, declinate. *Filament* smooth, short. *Anthers* linear, with broad margins; three interior ones often elongated and reclinate. *Germen* celled, each cell two-seeded. *Style* filiform, declinate. *Stigma* small. *Capsule* three-celled, three-valved; valves generally seed-bearing. *Seed* in pairs, either erect or pendulous, strophiolate.

SPECIFIC CHARACTER.—*Plant* perennial, herbaceous. *Branches* very slender, filiform, intricately interwoven and entangled. *Leaves* scarce, squamæform. *Umbels* of flowers paniculate. *Flowers* hexandrous, pale blue, with a purple stripe down the middle of each petal. *Stamens* and style curved downwards.

PERSONS of the most fastidious taste will assuredly find something to gratify them in this pretty little plant, notwithstanding the tenuity of its stems, and the comparative smallness of its flowers. It is a species of a very singular habitude, as the stems and branches are so interlaced that they need no artificial support. We were favoured with an opportunity of witnessing a plant in the greenhouse of Messrs. Low and Co., about the middle of last July, which was not more than nine inches high, and on which scarcely a leaf was perceptible; but the stems formed a dense inextricable mass, from the surface of which an innumerable quantity of delicate blossoms were protruded in clusters, altogether presenting a most interesting aspect.

This natural tendency to grow compactly, is, as all must perceive, a most desirable feature in its character; for, though other species are more handsome, and have showier flowers, they are necessarily more or less straggling, owing to their flower-stems being simple and erect. Nor is the deficiency of its foliage an absolute defect; for, where the blossoms are small, as in the present case, the eye does not require a greater extent of green surface than this plant possesses in its few leaves and numerous stems; these latter being so tortuous and irregular as hardly to be distinguishable from the foliage.

Seeds of *T. intricatus* were procured from the Swan River Colony some time during the year 1838, and, amongst other collections, some were germinated in the Clapton nursery, the plants from which developed their blossoms for several months of the last summer, and furnished the subject of the present figure. Several other highly interesting new species have been introduced from the same district, some of which are named and described by Dr. Lindley in the new Appendix to the Botanical Register.

So far as we have been able to ascertain the manner in which this plant is cultivated, it appears perfectly simple. It should be potted in a very light compost, of nearly equal parts of sandy loam and heath-soil, with a small addition of sand, if necessary. While the stems are in a progressive state, and until the flowers have fallen, water must be liberally administered; always providing, however, that the drainage be perfect, and the specimen in a healthy condition; for, although a copious supply of fluid is generally necessary at this period, there are instances in which the discretion and examination of the cultivator alone can regulate its application. When in a state of torpidity, water must be almost wholly withheld, and the plants should be placed beyond the reach of all atmospheric moisture.

It is not at present known whether seeds will be perfected in our greenhouses; but, should its flowers open early in the summer, this can hardly be doubted. It may be sparingly multiplied by dividing the roots in the spring; young branches may also sometimes be detected which do not produce flowers, and which, if removed and planted in sand, in a propagation-house, will strike with tolerable freedom.

Thysanotus is derived from *thysanotos*, fringed; the three inner petals of the flowers of this genus being surrounded by a most beautiful fringe. The genus was primarily constituted by Mr. R. Brown, an eminent English botanist, and contains six or seven cultivated species, most of which are deserving of notice.

Erysimum Perofskianum.

ERÝSIMUM PEROFSKIÀNUM.

(ORANGE-FLOWERED HEDGE MUSTARD.)

CLASS.	ORDER.
TETRADYNAMIA.	SILIQUOSA.

NATURAL ORDER.
CRUCÍFERÆ.

GENERIC CHARACTER.—*Pods* four-sided. *Seeds* destitute of margins. *Cotyledons* incumbent. *Stigma* capitate, then emarginate, with spreading lobes. *Calyx* erect.

SPECIFIC CHARACTER.—*Plant* annual or biennial, with bipartite setæ, scabrous. *Stem* simple. *Leaves* lanceolate, remotely toothed. *Pedicels* half the length of the calyx. *Flowers* bright orange; claw of the petals scarcely longer than the calyx. *Seed-pods* covered with bipartite scabrous setæ, nearly round, and five times the length of the pedicels.

SEEDS of this very showy border plant were received at several places in Britain from Dr. Fischer of Petersburgh, in 1838; and, considering this is the first season in which it has flowered perfectly, we have been astonished to find it in so many collections. It is, however, one of those plants, the seeds of which ripen in such abundance, that it will very shortly be met with in every garden where new and ornamental species are grown.

In the form of its flowers, it bears so close a resemblance to the common Wallflower, that an inexperienced observer might readily mistake it for a variety of that universally-admired plant; but a marked difference in their disposition will be seen from our representation, and in this particular *E. Perofskianum* possesses a decided superiority. It is scarcely necessary to add that this consists in exhibiting a much larger surface of flowers. Like the Wallflower, also, it continues blossoming for a great length of time; specimens that commenced blooming in July, having, about a fortnight since, almost as good a display of flowers as at any previous period.

It must not be imagined from what we have just stated that old plants are as engaging as the young ones. At the present season, those that have been permitted to flower unrestrictedly during the summer months, have their flowers situated at the distance of nine inches or a foot from the leaves, the intervening space being occupied by the seed-pods. This, of course, detracts much from their beauty; and, with the exception of a few plants which may be reserved for seed, it is advisable to cut off the flower-stems soon after the seed-pods begin to appear, or when the plants become straggling. We offer this suggestion solely from analogy, as it appears likely that new flower-stems would soon be developed, and in much greater numbers; whereas, if the plants are not thus decapitated, they are apt to grow too diffuse and unsightly.

Experience has not yet determined whether this is an annual species, or whether, as the Wallflower, it will blossom for two years. If the latter term is wished to be attained, the destruction of the seed, while only in embryo, is an indispensable preliminary. Plants raised from seed in the autumn, and preserved in small pots and a cold frame, will, if planted out any time during the spring months, flower beautifully in the flower-garden from June till November. They may either be placed singly in the borders, or collected in a bed, in which latter situation their bright orange blossoms create a splendid effect.

The seeds are apparently as freely matured as those of the native species, but some care is necessary in collecting them, otherwise they will all be scattered and lost. The pods must be gathered separately, as they individually ripen; for, immediately on their becoming dry, they burst and disperse the seeds.

Of its native country, nothing certain has transpired. It is presumed to be an inhabitant of Caboul, but Sir W. J. Hooker remarks, in the Botanical Magazine, that he has been favoured with specimens from Lady Mary Cathcart, of Cathcart, who procured seeds direct from Caboul, where it is considered to be a native of Persia.

We are obliged for our drawing to Messrs. Rollison, of Tooting, in whose nursery the species has flowered during the whole of the late summer.

The generic name is from *Eryo*, to draw; some of the species containing a juice which is capable of occasioning and raising blisters.

Lobelia ignea.

LOBELIA IGNEA.

(FLAME-COLOURED LOBELIA.)

CLASS.
PENTANDRIA.

ORDER.
MONOGYNIA.

NATURAL ORDER.
LOBELIÀCEÆ.

GENERIC CHARACTER.—*Vide* vol. ii. p. 52.

SPECIFIC CHARACTER.—*Plant* an herbaceous perennial. *Stem* erect, freely branched, roundish, but slightly channelled, from three to four feet high, dark purple. *Leaves* also deep purple, sessile; lower ones lanceolate, serrated, acute, partially recurved; stem leaves longer, more attenuated, and frequently entire; floral leaves or bracts resembling the lowest ones, but much more acuminate. *Calyx* with subequal segments, sometimes triflingly serrated. *Flowers* very large, deep scarlet.

THE superb new *Lobelia*, of which the annexed figure, though accurate, is but an imperfect representation, on account of the inimitable brilliancy of the colour of its flowers, was received in England in 1838 from Mr. Makoy, of Liège. It has been doubted by many whether it be not an hybrid production; but we are credibly informed that seeds of it were originally obtained from Mexico. Indeed, the peculiar colour of the leaves and stems, and the remarkable size as well as the surpassingly rich hue of the blossoms, afford strong presumptive evidence that it is a distinct species; it being difficult to conceive how these properties could result from hybridization, when there are no other kinds at all similar.

Amongst the new half-hardy herbaceous plants which have lately been added to our collections, *L. ignea* is superior to any we have yet seen. Even the favourite *Salvia patens* is not its equal in value; the former shedding its flowers so speedily after they are unfolded, as seldom to have more than two opened at once on the same stem; whereas, on this plant, six or eight are commonly expanded together, and the branches are much more numerous.

An excellent specimen in the nursery of Messrs. Henderson, Pine-Apple Place, supplied us with the opportunity of obtaining our drawing, and also, by the merest accident, furnished a hint respecting its culture, which we shall now register, for the benefit of our readers. The plant to which we refer was kept through the last winter in a stove of a temperature rather below the usual par; and, probably from being too strongly stimulated, the main or central flowering shoot which it produced in the early spring, gradually withered, till it eventually proved a complete abortion. About the time this became manifest, a quantity of lateral shoots were observed to be issuing from all the lower and yet living parts of the stem, which soon acquired strength and vigour. The plant was then potted into a larger pot, and finally placed in the open air, where it flowered most profusely from every shoot in the months of August and September, forming a perfect and beautifully-shaped specimen, four feet high, and full three feet in diameter.

The circumstance in the above narration to which we wish now to invite attention, is the result which followed the destruction of the leading shoot. Had this continued growing, it would doubtless have attained a much greater altitude, but the lateral shoots (if put forth at all) must have been weak and stunted; while the plant would have been far less handsome with regard to form, and the size and number of its flowers, than it actually became. Cultivators should not lose sight of this fact in the management both of this and other species of *Lobelia*, as it demonstrates the importance of removing artificially the central shoot at an early period of its existence.

In other respects, *L. ignea* has hitherto been treated as more tender than the rest of its allies, and allowed a place in the stove during winter. This does not, however, appear at all requisite; and we presume it would not be injured in a frame or greenhouse, near the glass, if thoroughly protected from frost, and very cautiously supplied with water. A damp atmosphere must be especially avoided.

Propagation is performed, to almost any desired extent, by carefully detaching the young suckers, which are most liberally emitted from old roots. They will occasionally be found to have formed roots; but if otherwise, these may readily be developed by potting the suckers in a light loamy soil, plunging them in a trifling bottom heat, and shading them till they have struck. Cuttings, taken from those shoots which do not flower, or from which the blossoms are timely plucked, will root as freely as suckers, but they do not form such handsome plants. Seeds are likewise liberally produced, and may be sown in a hotbed frame as soon as they are duly dried.

For the derivation of the generic name, the reader may be referred to vol. ii. p. 52. We have adopted the specific designation as being that by which it is generally known, and also pretty accurately expressive of the colour of its blossoms.

GREENHOUSE CLIMBING PLANTS AS SUMMER ORNAMENTS TO THE FLOWER-GARDEN.

ONE of the most striking peculiarities of the system of floriculture now almost universally pursued, is what may not improperly be termed its retrogressive tendency. In this consists the chief evidence of the advancement of the science; and from it may be gathered the principal confirmation of the fact, that the cultivators of the present age have, through philosophy and experience,—those grand coadjutors in the promotion of every improvement,—attained such an exalted pre-eminence of success over their brethren of a former period.

Not to be supposed guilty of either mysticism or paradox, we will hasten to depict, in more explicit language, the character of this change. Throughout the decline of the last, and even during a considerable portion of the present century, so comparatively scarce were exotic plants, so little (speaking relatively to the present time) was known respecting their habitudes or the climates of their native countries, and such extreme caution was exercised in their management, that there were few species but were subjected to a higher temperature than they naturally required. The necessary consequences were, that a greater expense was occasioned, the plants were never healthy, but became gradually more tender, and the extension of this delightful recreation was, with regard to the less wealthy and enthusiastic, effectually checked.

To the massy, high, and dark erections in which plants were originally confined, may be traced by far the greater part of the evils above enumerated; this, indeed, being the main defect of the old system. Kept in such structures, plants could not be otherwise than strongly susceptible of injury from cold, and this susceptibility would be perpetually on the increase. Hence, the greenhouses were necessarily maintained at a much higher rate of temperature than now; while, a plant that was primarily grown as a greenhouse species, was frequently elevated, through one or two slight intermediate gradations, to a place in the stove.

With the introduction of a new method of erecting plant-houses, in which the chief objects kept in view are lowness and light, a complete alteration in the mode of culture was effected. The results, compared with those of the ancient system, have been totally reversed. Instead of a plant becoming more tender under our improved artificial treatment, it annually advances in the acquirement of a degree of hardihood; its progress being proportionately rapid to its increased exposure. This is what we have designated the *retrogressive* course of plant-culture; since, beneath its auspicious influence, plants with which we are familiar have been removed from the stove, and, by slow stages, brought to decorate the open flower-border in the summer.

How speedily, and with what particular plants, the system thus hurriedly exhibited may be carried into effect, experience and the judicious institution of every appropriate experiment and test can alone indicate. Our present object is to point out a few of those more graceful greenhouse climbing species which we have seen employed for ornamenting the pleasure-grounds. And having previously (p. 159, August No.) stated the plan of training and the form of trellis we would wish adopted, it now devolves upon us, as then promised, to make a selection of the most suitable kinds, and say a few words on their individual management.

We cannot commence better than by specifying the genus TROPÆOLUM, in which will be found several elegant species, particularly adapted for flower-garden display, or for distributing sparingly over small lawns in the immediate vicinage of the dwelling-house. *T. tricolorum, peregrinum, brachyceras, tuberosum*, and even *pentaphyllum*, may all be made to increase the charms of the pleasure-grounds, by a little attention, and the assistance of a frame in which to rear and protect them through the winter. *T. tricolorum* and *brachyceras*, being the most delicate, must be treated according to the common practice, observing to keep the bulbs or tubers perfectly dry in the winter, and not to start them by any artificial stimulus. The frame or trellis which they are intended to cover can be affixed to the outside of their pot, this last being furnished, of the precise size they are expected to require, in the early part of spring, at which time they should be repotted. When the season is sufficiently advanced to admit of their transference to the open ground without danger, they may be plunged to the rim in river sand or light soil, taking care to place a layer of ashes, two or three inches deep, at the bottom of the hole prepared for their reception, that no worms or other mining insects may find easy ingress from that quarter.

It is quite incomprehensible to us how *T. tricolorum*, notwithstanding the facility with which it may be propagated and grown, should continue so scarce, and of such an unusual pecuniary value. We can only account for these circumstances by surmising that it is treated *too unnaturally*, thereby occasioning the bulbs to rot and perish. No plant can suffer more injury from being induced to depart from the order of Nature, in regard to the time of commencing its growth, and the supply of water during its dormancy. Left to begin growing by its inherent impulses, neither over-potted nor watered immoderately in the summer, and kept entirely torpid through the winter season, it may be retained in perpetual health and vigour, and without manifesting the slightest appearance of disease or decay. To ensure the accomplishment of these ends, we cannot but believe that the adoption of the method above propounded would very materially tend; and we would add, with especial emphasis, that the plants cannot be placed too high in the pot, provided the roots are not exposed to the atmosphere, nor can the pots be plunged too deeply in the soil, so that they are not actually buried.

Respecting the multiplication of *T. tricolorum*, which may, in this point, be regarded as the type of all the other tender kinds, a few hints here may not be without their use. It is increased by cuttings ; but, to render failure otherwise than nearly certain, these must be taken from some of the strongest lateral shoots, cut off immediately below a joint, and inserted in a compost of three-fourths white sand and the remainder heath-soil, with the base of the cutting only just sufficiently below the surface of the soil to maintain firmly its erectness, and all the lower part of the pot in which the cuttings are placed (unless it be a very shallow one, which is decidedly best) filled, to within an inch and a half of its rim, with drainage materials. Each cutting should be short, taken from the strongest shoots at a period when they are half matured, and very carefully preserved from all moisture that is not essential to its progress.

We have been thus minute in our directions concerning *T. tricolorum*, because it is one of the most beautiful, and, without doubt, the most delicate of this class of plants. The rules which we have given are likewise applicable to *T. pentaphyllum* and *peregrinum*, though these are much stronger, and require far less care. *T. pentaphyllum* is scarcely suited for growing on small trellises, but where there is a high frame or arch, which will afford room enough for its full development, it will form an exceedingly interesting feature. For *T. peregrinum*, a trellis of four or five feet high is requisite, and when its shoots have been trained to the summit, they may be allowed to hang down naturally, for by this appearance of graceful negligence, their effect will be rendered doubly enchanting.

Perhaps it may be said that *T. tuberosum* is not strictly a greenhouse species, and therefore should not be mentioned among plants of that tribe. But those who are thoroughly acquainted with it will at once concede that it is as tender as any of its congeners, and that the reason of its having been more frequently exposed is its much greater abundance and cheapness. They who have never seen it flower except in a greenhouse, know comparatively nothing of its beauty ; but it unfortunately blossoms so late in the open ground, as to render its destruction almost inevitable, when at its highest perfection. To avert this, it must be started earlier; and it occurs to us that the treatment generally bestowed on some kinds of *Alstrœmeria* is exactly such as would suit this plant. The tubers may be plunged in light soil or saw-dust in the month of November, transplanted into pots as soon as they have formed shoots, and preserved till May in a greenhouse or frame, near the light. Towards the latter end of May the plants should be transferred to a prepared spot in an open lawn or border, where they would flower profusely in September and October. No plant is more ornamental, when thus treated ; but it will not thrive well if the situation chosen for it be not to some slight extent sheltered from strong or severe winds.

Many of our readers will probably be astonished when we mention *Thunbergia alata* and *T. alata alba* as fit subjects for decking the open lawn ; as these beautiful plants are not seldom imprisoned in a stove, and were, till very lately, invariably kept in that department. No sooner, however, were they introduced to the greenhouse, than they were found to grow with increased luxuriance, which suggested the idea of exposing them fully to the air, where they will succeed admirably. Young plants may be prepared annually from cuttings, about the month of August, and kept in a greenhouse, with occasional shiftings if necessary, till propitious weather for their transplantation arrives. They should then be removed from the pots, and planted in a small mound of soil, composed of nearly equal parts of loam and heath-mould, where, releasing them from the erect stakes by which, for convenience, they had previously been supported, they can be trained to any small trellis and left to bloom till destroyed by frost. Both with these and all other plants of this kind, every form of trellis that is either flat, or approximates thereto, should be discarded as improper for the purpose; since the specimen has to be viewed from all sides, and the nearer the frame approaches a circular shape, the greater symmetry of surface will it present, and the more pleasing will be its general contour.

Lophospermum erubescens and *scandens* exhibit themselves better when trained to an erect pole. The latter is, however, dwarf enough for any, even the smallest lawn; and, if allowed to do so, will emit a great number of trailing shoots from the base of its stem, which, uninterfered with, will spread around the plant, and very powerfully augment its interesting appearance. *L. erubescens* may likewise be pruned so as not to exceed four feet in height, when it will throw off an abundance of lateral shoots; and, by being attached to a feathered stake, (that is, one with a quantity of small side branches,) it will present a very imposing aspect. These species must be renewed yearly by cuttings, and managed altogether as *Thunbergia alata*, while in the greenhouse or frame.

Maurandya Barclayana is of a less vigorous habit than the preceding, and more fitted to fulfil the design pointed out in this article. If, as we have already recommended for *Tropæolum peregrinum*, the branches of this plant, after they have gained the top of the trellis, be suffered to fall loosely over the sides, a decidedly more favourable impression will be created than if it were made to conform to the stiff formality of art; while the lower portion of the plant, which often becomes bare, will be effectually concealed. Owing to the very slender nature of its stems, this species cannot be so readily increased as the Lophospermums; but with the same care as is afforded in the propagation of *Tropæolum tricolorum*, cuttings will strike with equal freedom. The plants may be taken from the ground and repotted in the autumn, if desired; but the best plan for securing a liberal show of flowers, is to obtain a fresh stock each year.

Seeds of *Loasa lateritia* may be sown in a shallow pot about the month of August, pricking out the plants into small pots, three in each pot, after the rough leaves become apparent. They should be preserved, during winter, on the shelf of a greenhouse or dry frame, near the glass; and, by being planted in the centre of a flower-plot, or on any glade of moderate extent, supporting them with the branched stakes mentioned for *Lophospermum erubescens*, they will flower throughout the entire summer, until frost occurs to kill them.

With a brief allusion to *Petunias* and *Verbenas*, we shall now dismiss this subject. Of the many lovely species and varieties comprising these genera, there are few of those which have, for the last several years, been employed in filling the beds of the flower-garden, but may also be made to assume a dwarf climbing habit by a little extra attention. We have rarely been without specimens of even *Verbena chamædrifolia*, from three to four feet in height; and the much more luxuriant species of *Verbena* that have recently been introduced, might be brought to this stature with infinitely less trouble. Plants of *Petunias*, of a similar size, are far more easily obtained; and, when planted on a lawn of somewhat limited extent, their aspect is truly fascinating.

To prepare a specimen of any suitable species of these genera for such a purpose, it is only necessary to plant it in a mound of light rich earth in the beginning of spring, and pluck off all the flower-buds immediately on their being discovered. This will induce a free, vigorous, and bushy growth. The practice may be continued till its subject has attained the requisite size, or is desired to flower; and when it is relinquished, the specimen will commence blooming, and flower in unbounded profusion till the decline of autumn. The trellises used for species of this description, should be of a particularly ornamental character; since the plants are not to be trained over, but, contrariwise, surrounded by them, as a protection against tempestuous winds. If, however, the removal of the flower-buds is duly and timeously accomplished, the lateral shoots will soon extend themselves beyond the trellis, and thus divert the eye from what, however ornate, might be considered an uninteresting object, if too conspicuous. These remarks have no further reference to the slow-growing or dwarf kinds of *Verbena*, than that, if they are wished to be managed thus, the same routine of active treatment must be followed. They will not attain a sufficient height in one season to be regarded as climbing plants, and will therefore need the shelter of a greenhouse, and the especial watchfulness of the cultivator, to preserve their first year's growth from prejudicial dampness.

It will be seen that the foregoing strictures embrace only the more showy *herbaceous* species of tender climbing plants. With regard to the shrubby sorts, there is an extremely small proportion which can with any propriety be placed in the open air, and if these should ever appear worthy of a distinct notice, we may find occasion to advert to them. All mention of several pleasing herbaceous kinds has necessarily been omitted from this sketch; but we believe there are none which do not so closely resemble some of those here treated of, that their culture may not be safely regulated by the rules thus generally inculcated.

ON THE INTRODUCTION OF FLOWERING ORCHIDACEÆ TO DRAWING-ROOMS.

There are comparatively few of those to whom the charge of exotic plants of any description is entrusted, who allow themselves to be actuated in their cultivation by all the motives to whose influence they should be alike and alone impressionable. Sometimes the health of a tribe, or even of an entire collection, is sacrificed to miscalculating economy; still oftener, to the architectural appearance of the houses in which they are grown; and, not unfrequently, from a mere want of preconsideration regarding the adaptation of an erection to its office, or a capricious, unsettled, constantly changing mode of treatment.

Rare, indeed, are the instances in which attention to the comfort and pleasure of the proprietor presents an obstacle to the attainment of the highest excellence, or where these objects are by any means sufficiently consulted. And since Orchidaceæ have become so fashionable, this point has been, at least with respect to that group, especially neglected. Not one in ten of the houses expressly devoted to their culture, can be entered by the most robust among the higher classes, much less by delicate persons or by ladies, without experiencing highly uncomfortable and overpowering sensations, and entailing unpleasant or even dangerous consequences. Every one will acknowledge that this is a state of things which urgently demands some remedial measures, if such can be applied consistently with the safety and prosperity of the plants.

We hold, as an indisputable dogma, that the method of management which furnishes facilities for affording the highest gratification to the proprietor, if, at the same time, perfectly compatible with the health of its objects, is such as every considerate and intelligent gardener must unhesitatingly adopt. That the powerfully and perpetually stimulative system of growing Orchidaceæ practised by many eminent individuals, is unnecessary to the most refined success, we have decided, after some years' patient scrutiny, perfectly to our own satisfaction. But we offer this passing hint merely as it has a strict bearing on the question now before us, and not with any intention to discuss the whole of the important inquiry it involves; for, however much this may be contested, it will be unanimously agreed that neither a rigid adherence to the colder nor the hotter ratio will suit all Orchidaceous plants; but that, where only one house is possessed, and a uniform general system of treatment is, in consequence, followed, the temperate or medium course is the most politic.

But, by a mode of transference from the Orchidaceous house to the drawing-room during the flowering season, which we have chosen the present occasion for advocating, it will be of little consequence, except to the plants themselves, whether a high or low rate of temperature, and corresponding moisture, is maintained in their permanent abode. Few would then wish to visit the whole collection, and certainly none would desire to remain long enough in a house deprived of all floral ornaments, to suffer any ill effects from its atmosphere.

Nevertheless, this plan could not be extensively acted upon without some guarantee that the plants would not be injured thereby; and, to supply this with any degree of security, the atmosphere of both departments must so far assimilate, that no violent check will be opposed to the plant's progress by such a removal. To suppose that a plant luxuriating in every species of external excitation, would derive no detriment by being suddenly transported from that position to one far cooler, drier, and darker, is assuredly incorrect and fatuous.

The safest criterion for determining the extent to which any Orchidaceous plant will bear a change of atmosphere, is the stage of growth to which it has arrived when this transition is necessary. It is notorious that the majority of Orchidaceæ flower from the pseudo-bulbs or stems of the one year's formation, just before those of the following season begin to develop themselves. Some, indeed, blossom from the summits of the new growth during its progress towards maturity, but these are comparatively scarce. How naturally, then, does this fact suggest the propriety of keeping each individual plant in a state of dormancy, so far as can be effected by withholding regular supplies of water, till the expansion of its blossoms; when it may be taken to the drawing-room and kept in the same condition till these have faded, and afterwards returned to the Orchidaceous-house to have its native energies thoroughly and seasonably elicited by more genial and active influences.

This is the simple annual circle of cultivation that is alone needful to obtain all the delights which these charming plants are capable of imparting, without any of the drawbacks inseparable from the system now in vogue. Desirous, however, of satisfying all objections that may reasonably be urged, we will anticipate those which appear strongest. It will instantly be perceived that we have based our method on the somewhat gratuitous assumption, that a general period of rest is allowed to the whole tribe during the winter, and that the principal part of them flower in the spring. We must admit that these points are at present little more than supposititious: but experience has so far invested them with plausibility, as to render them more than mere conjectures; and we are convinced that time only is requisite for the full establishment of their practicability and appropriateness.

Long ere the present period, the question above-mooted might have been decided, had it not been for the abundance of novelties continually pouring in from newly-explored countries. It is these which have virtually suppressed the cultivator's efforts to generalize and (if we may use the expression) *naturalize* his treatment. Besides concentrating his attention on them, and occupying so much of his thoughts by the ardent and worthy wish they have engendered to preserve and flower them successfully, they have generally been grown in the same house as old-established specimens, and, to administer to their feeble necessities, all others have been regarded in only a subordinate light. The slightest reflection will expose the injudiciousness of this practice; and we trust all will be induced hereafter to consign their weakly plants, as well as those of recent importation, to a pit or frame; thus overcoming one grand obstacle to the introduction of a more vigorous system of management.

Not many years since, the notion of Orchidaceæ being brought to adorn the drawing-rooms of the opulent, was considered a pure chimera. So, at the present time, our supposition that their habits may, by a discreet boldness of treatment, be assimilated to an indefinable extent, will probably be received with incredulity or even ridicule. But we have seen the former of these opinions fully corroborated, and all that is wanting to render its fulfilment universal, is the adoption and success of the latter expedient, of which we entertain the most sanguine expectations.

Although we have perhaps been rather excursive in this article, our subject demanded that we should touch lightly on the culture of Orchidaceæ in general, and we now return to give the reader a more succinct and definite idea of our design. All plants that are presumed to be capable of producing flowers, and which may possess sufficient beauty or interest to render their transference to the drawing-room desirable, should, for some time prior to their flowering, be kept as dry as their actual wants will permit, and be carried to their place of destination as soon as the first flowers expand. If watered lightly, and freely drained, the day anterior to their removal, they will seldom need any other attention till the flowers have withered, and they are restored to their original quarters.

Those species which are growing in pots, will require to be considerably elevated, in order to display their beauties; and for this purpose, a number of marble or ornamental wooden pedestals, about three or four feet high, and as many inches in diameter, with a small tablet fastened to the top, should be provided, on which the plants can be placed, according to their size. The corners of the room, and, when a fire is employed, those farthest from it, should be considered as the most suitable situations, for many reasons; the chief of which are, that they will thus be secluded from light, and bloom much longer in consequence, and that these are in all respects the most convenient positions for them.

There still remains a large proportion of species that are kept in baskets, or attached to blocks of wood, and which seem to demand suspension from the roof of the structure wherein they are kept. Some of those in baskets might easily be placed as already suggested for the species that are in pots: others, from their peculiar fitness for suspension, should be attached to brass or gilt chains affixed to the ceiling, which might be wrought in such a manner as not to be at all unsightly, and moveable when not in use. Plants thus pendent, would give an air of enchanting liveliness and elegance to a room. Drooping species should always be chosen, as well as those which are altogether most graceful and showy; while the baskets may be readily enveloped in moss, so as to render their appearance more natural.

It is needless to expatiate on the desirableness of such a system as that here delineated. All must have wished it practicable, although it has rarely been tried. We especially commend it to the enterprising culturist, as a valuable means of satisfying that peculiar *penchant* for novelty which forms so distinguished a characteristic of our era. Where the fragrance of any particular plants is found too powerful for a room that is much occupied, or the slightest inconvenience is experienced from their nocturnal exhalations, few residences are without an apartment which can be appropriated exclusively to this end; and this new appendage to a mansion would certainly not be the least interesting of its numerous departments.

FLORICULTURAL NOTICES.

NEW AND RARE PLANTS FIGURED IN THE LEADING BOTANICAL PERIODICALS FOR NOVEMBER.

CLASS I.—PLANTS WITH TWO COTYLEDONS (DICOTYLEDONEÆ).

THE INDIAN FIG TRIBE (*Cactàceæ*).

LEPÍSMIUM COMMÙNE. Common Lepismium. A very small-flowered cactaceous plant, with blossoms which would at once bring it within the genus *Rhipsalis*, but for its large triangular stems, like those of *Cereus speciosissimus*. The stems are branching, jointed, and very slender towards the base of their articulations; while the pinkish-white flowers spring from amidst the tufts of spines situated along their margins, and are usually partly buried therein. A few small roots are also produced from the furrows of the branches. It was received at the Glasgow Botanic Garden from Mr. Hitchin, and blooms in October. Brazil is presumed to be its native country. *Bot. Mag.* 3763.

CLASS II.—PLANTS WITH ONE COTYLEDON (MONOCOTYLEDONEÆ).

THE CORN-FLAG TRIBE (*Iridàceæ*).

PATERSÒNIA SAPPHIRÌNA. Sapphire Patersonia. Nothing can be more brilliant than the rich sapphire-coloured flowers of this charming plant, and it would rank as a most valuable ornament to the greenhouse were it not that these are so exceedingly fugitive. "A large plant will, however, produce numerous flower-heads, and these, by the number of their blossoms, compensate for their ephemeral existence." Seeds of it were obtained from the Swan River Colony by Mr. Mangles, with whom, we believe, it has flowered. It is to be distinguished from all its allies procured from the same district by "its long narrow leaves and scape, which are quite destitute of hairiness, except when the former are very young, at which time they are fringed with delicate down." It may be cultivated in a greenhouse, requiring no other than ordinary treatment. *Bot. Reg.* 60.

THE ORCHIS TRIBE (*Orchidàceæ*).

CYRTOCHÍLUM MYSTACÍNUM. Whiskered Curvelip. One of the least handsome species of this showy genus; the flowers being rather diminutive, and entirely of a yellow colour. Richard Harrison, Esq., of Aigburgh, imported plants of it from Peru, and it blossomed in the collection of this gentleman towards the close of the year 1837. Its pseudo-bulbs are corrugated, monophyllous at their summit, with an indefinite number of leaves enveloping their base, from the axil of the uppermost of which the flower-spike appears. This last is branched, the flowers are somewhat scattered, and have, in common with other true species of *Cyrtochilum*, " the base of the lip united to the face of the lower part of the column." *Bot. Reg.* 62.

THE LILY TRIBE (*Liliàceæ*).

SCÍLLA PRATÉNSIS. Meadow Squill. The Hon. W. F. Strangways, who has the rare merit of collecting and cultivating all the scarcer kinds of European plants, grows this highly interesting species in his garden at Abbotsbury, where it blooms in the month of June. "It is a beautiful little rock plant, quite hardy, and a welcome addition to our gardens, from flowering after the spring bulbs are gone, and before the autumnal species appear." It inhabits meadow land by the side of the river Korenicza, in Croatia. The flowers are borne in great abundance, and are of a bright purplish-blue colour. In its culture, it is indispensable that the bulbs be taken from the soil, or protected from moisture during the period of their natural torpidity. *Bot. Reg.* 63.

In an Appendix to the Botanical Register now issuing, and comprising an Index to that work from the time of its commencement, Dr. Lindley has furnished a useful account of the Flora of the Swan River Colony; and as coloured plates of the principal plants are attached, we subjoin a brief notice of those which appeared in the November Part. None of the plants figured have, we imagine, flowered in this country; but the large quantities of seeds imported, and the number of young plants at present in nurseries, render it desirable that something should be known respecting them by both grower and purchaser.

CHRYSORRHÒË NÌTENS. This species is represented as one of surpassing beauty; the dense clusters of its golden-coloured, delicately fringed, and star-like flowers, forming a most gorgeous display. It is a small shrub, with very narrow diminutive foliage, and slender, partially bare branches, the flowers being collected together at the extremities of the smaller shoots, so as to present a perfect mass of splendour. The leaves and stems resemble those of some of the weaker species of *Pimelea*.

VERTICÓRDIA INSÍGNIS. An extremely elegant little shrub, with small, opposite, divaricate, serrated, and closely-pressed leaves, and pretty pink flowers, which appear in corymbs. Like those of *Chrysorrhoë*, these last are surrounded with a beautiful fringe, or rather a great number of lobes, with hair-like protuberances round their margin; but in *Verticordia* these stand nearly erect, while, in the former genus, they spread horizontally, or are partially drooping. There are several other species equally interesting. Their leaves are described as being particularly fragrant.

HEDERÒMA LATIFÒLIUM. There appears little to admire in the flowers of this plant, unless it be the rich crimson colour of its bracts; but the leaves, which are numerous, and spotted beneath with pink, have a most refreshing odour. In reference to this property, Dr. Lindley observes, " the leaves, or rather the half-ripe fruits, of these plants (*H. latifolia* and two other species) preserve their fragrance so well that they might be worth collecting for the use of the perfumer; and if so, they would furnish a new and most agreeable article of luxury to Europe, and a small aid to the natural resources of the country."

MANGLÈSIA PURPÙREA. The principal feature in this pretty plant is its capitate inflorescence, which, according to the figure given in the work now beneath our notice, is very similar, in general outline, to our common indigenous *Jasione vulgaris*. The individual florets are, however, widely different, and exceedingly curious, while the colour is a deep purple. It is a shrubby plant, with rather a paucity of leaves, which are also minute, acuminate, and inclining towards the stem.

CÀLYTRIX AÙREA. Of ten species just added to this genus by Dr. Lindley, this is one of the most showy. It has " oval imbricated leaves and heads of the brightest yellow flowers, whose sepals end in awns, at first yellow but afterwards olive-green." *C. flavescens* and *C. sapphirina* are mentioned as the other two most remarkable.

NUYTZIA FLORIBUNDA. An affinity is at once recognizable between this plant and the genus *Acacia*; the form of the foliage, and the manner in which the flowers are produced, exhibiting, at least to our eyes, evident marks of relationship. It seems a strong-growing plant, having narrow ligulate leaves, and large terminal spikes of deep-yellow blossoms. The petals of these are by no means conspicuous, but as each footstalk bears several flowers, and from every one of them a bunch of showy stamens is protruded, their aggregate appearance is very splendid.

NEW, RARE, AND INTERESTING PLANTS IN FLOWER IN THE PRINCIPAL SUBURBAN NURSERIES.

ACÀCIA CULTRÀTA. The very extensive and handsome genus *Acacia* does not contain a more valuable species than that now under notice. It is well covered with fine, entire, knife-shaped leaves, which have a whitish appearance; and the plants grow vigorously, as well as form very symmetrical shrubs, from three to four feet in height. The flowers are borne in large spikes, frequently having twelve blossoms on each, these being large, globular, light yellow, and very showy. Specimens in the greenhouse of Messrs. Rollison, Tooting, are now blooming most exuberantly. It is well suited for placing in the rear of a group of greenhouse plants, as the lower portions of its stems are apt to remain simple, while it expands into a capacious and ornamental bush at the summit. Its flowers will continue unfolding during the greater part of the winter.

ÆRIDES ? A very remarkable new orchidaceous plant is about to flower in the collection of Messrs. Loddiges, which approaches nearest to the genus *Ærides*, but will perhaps be found distinct, when the blossoms are developed. The floral raceme has been produced more than a month; the colour, and in some degree, the shape of the flowers, are visible; and yet it will probably require another fortnight to expand and perfect them. The aspect and foliage of the plant are quite peculiar: besides having a two-edged stem, its leaves are of a very pale dull green, and sheath the stem, but are much recurved at the margin, near their base. An extensive drooping raceme of flowers issues from the stem, the individual blossoms being of a light flesh colour, with, apparently, some purple spots in the sepals and petals, and a long obtuse spur, which is of an equal thickness throughout and curved upwards. The *Ærides* described in page 187, (September No.,) has subsequently been named by Dr. Lindley *Æ. quinquevulnerum*, on account of the five purple blotches on the exterior members of the flowers.

CÁTTLEYA MÓSSIÆ, *var*. About two months since, Mr. Low, of the Clapton nursery, received a large importation of orchidaceous and other plants, among which were some very fine specimens of the genus *Cattleya*. One of these latter has just flowered, and proves to be a superior variety of *C. Mossiæ*, with immense flowers, and of a somewhat lighter hue. When flowers are obtained from a specimen in a vigorous state of health, it will undoubtedly be found a pre-eminently desirable object.

CINERÀRIA WATERHOUSIÀNA. We have seen this beautiful species flowering in several of the London nurseries during the last month, but it is clearly not equal to what it would be, if bloomed in the spring of the year. It exhibits a narrowness in the petals, and a lightness of colour, wholly attributable to the lateness of the season. To prevent this, and all other species and varieties of this favourite genus, (except that called the *King*, which may be advantageously flowered throughout the late autumnal months,) from displaying similar defects, all the flower-stems that rise before this time, should be early and regularly removed, and the plants will blossom better and more profusely at the proper period.

CONVÓLVULUS BRYONIÆFÒLIUS. The merits of this interesting species being so little known, as is evinced by its great scarcity, we shall assuredly gratify some of our readers by a short notice of it, especially since it is nearly hardy. A plant growing in an uncovered frame, at the nursery of Messrs. Henderson, Pine-Apple Place, had, about a fortnight ago, several blossoms in perfection. It is a suffruticose twining plant, with leaves resembling those of some species of Malva, and pinkish-purple flowers: both foliage and blossoms being of a very ornamental description. When planted out in the border, and supported by a bushy branch, it attains the height of three or four feet, and has a very pleasing appearance. If slightly sheltered in frosty weather, it might doubtless be retained constantly in the open ground.

CORRÆA RÙFA. The cultivation of the genus *Corræa* has, within the last two years, received a powerful stimulus by the appearance of a number of excellent hybrids in various collections; and either from this cause, or from the more extensive practice of propagation by grafting, C. rufa has now become more common. It is, so far as relates to habit, and its appearance when not in flower, without exception, the best species of the genus. The plant is well-formed, and grows luxuriantly, while its oval leaves are of the richest shining verdure on the upper side, and a deep ferruginous brown beneath. Flowering at the present dull season, it is also very serviceable in the greenhouse, and even its unhandsome whitish blossoms, so prettily pendent from the branches, have very considerable attractions, when viewed in contrast with the beautiful green and brown foliage.

CYMBÍDIUM IRIDIFÒLIUM. A newly-imported pseudo-bulb of this delightful plant, is at present producing a spike of flowers with Messrs. Rollison, Tooting; and it would appear to be a particularly choice species. It differs from the rest of the species (some of which are quite destitute of pseudo-bulbs, and bear radical leaves) in having short, thick, nearly oval pseudo-bulbs, from the base of which the flower-scape is protruded; this last depending, and disposing its blossoms in the same manner as C. aloifolium. The flowers are of a dark fuscous hue, with a deep brown, almost black spot, nearly covering the lip.

DÁPHNE ÍNDICA; var. RÙBRA. Of the few plants which are prized for enlivening the greenhouse with their blossoms in the winter months, this rare Daphne is one of the most interesting, as it possesses both a high degree of beauty, and a delicious odour. It has long evergreen foliage, which is of itself a pleasing feature, while the blossoms issue from the branches in dense clusters. They are of a dark purple externally, the interior of the petals is pale pink, and the yellow anthers which rise in the centre contribute much to heighten their charms. Plants of this variety are blossoming in a stove at Messrs. Rollison's, Tooting; but it will unquestionably succeed in the greenhouse.

HOÍTZA MEXICÀNA. There is either some peculiar way of cultivating this singular plant which British floriculturists have not yet discovered, or it is entirely worthless. The latter assumption strikes us as being the most correct; for we have attentively observed plants that were grown under every variety of circumstance, (having been led to consider it a showy species,) and the same withered, paltry appearance, with a marked deficiency of flowers, has invariably been the result of our examination. Indeed, we have never yet seen its blossoms expanded, except when it was planted in the open ground, and there is rarely more than two or three open at once on the same stem. It has usually a great number of stems, the leaves are small, much and irregularly toothed, but seldom of a lively green, and the whole plant is clothed with hairs. Its flowers are long, tubular, and reddish pink; being, however, so slender as never to be very conspicuous.

IPOMÈA PÚRGANS. While in the orchidaceous house of Messrs. Loddiges this pretty new species is flowering liberally, a plant at Messrs. Rollison's has just unfolded a few blossoms on the open wall. It is a very elegant climbing plant, with ovately-cordate, acuminate leaves, and light purple flowers, the limb of which is particularly flattened. From the two specimens above alluded to, the careful observer may readily learn the degree of temperature most congenial to this plant. That at the Hackney nursery has evidently been subjected to a too great heat, the branches, and all the other parts, being extremely weak, and preternaturally elongated. The plant at Tooting is, on the contrary, in a very vigorous condition, but it is plain that even the present mild autumn is not warm enough to occasion the full development of its flowers. A greenhouse, therefore, suggests itself, as the fittest situation, while it should either be trained to the pillars, (if there be any,) or kept in a large pot, and supported by a circular trellis; because, if fastened to the roof, it would exclude the light too much in the dark declining months of the year.

ONCÍDIUM HÌANS. This is a very neat little species, which we have yet seen in the collection of Messrs. Rollison only, with whom it blossomed last month. It assimilates slightly to *O. Harrisonianum*, having small, numerous, somewhat flattened, two-edged, and pale green pseudo-bulbs, surmounted by either one or two leaves; (generally only one;) but the foliage is most abundantly dotted with little white spots, and is likewise more coriaceous. The flowers are of the common brown and yellow colour, and are produced on short erect scapes: they are neither large nor brilliant, but interesting.

PRÍMULA SINÉNSIS; *var.* PLÈNA. Messrs. Henderson, of Pine-Apple Place, possess two charming varieties of *P. sinensis*, with fine double flowers. One, which has white or cream-coloured blossoms, is particularly valuable, combining all the beauty of the common double white primrose with the delicacy and grace of the Chinese species. The other has blossoms of a pink hue, and is only inferior with respect to the greater similarity in its colour to that of the single kinds. For decorating the windows of boudoirs, drawing-rooms, or other like situations, now that scarcely any other flowers are to be procured, nothing can be more exquisitely appropriate. They must be increased by offsets, and watered with great care.

SACCOLÀBIUM BÍFIDUM. To any other eyes than those of a botanist, or a close investigator of the forms and habits of Orchidaceæ, the plant, whose name we have here given, would appear to be a species of *Notylia*; the manner in which the flowers are produced, their structure, and exceeding minuteness, being, so far as a hasty glance can determine, in complete accordance with the members of that genus. The moment, however, that the mode of growth is examined, the delusion vanishes, and it is discovered to have terete stems (instead of pseudo-bulbs) and opposite leaves. Its small and almost imperceptible flowers are barely interesting enough to render it at all desirable, but they have a curious fork at the extremity of the peculiarly long lip, which stamps them with at least a unique character. It has lately bloomed for several months in the orchidaceous house of Messrs. Loddiges; and to those who make this tribe their study, nothing can be more useful than to search for the more palpable portions of a generic distinction among tiny plants like the present.

OPERATIONS FOR DECEMBER.

This month, like its immediate predecessor, is almost invariably fraught with danger to the more select objects of the cultivator's solicitude. In continued frosty weather, the least experienced will feel no uncertainty as to the treatment to be followed, and there is scarcely a remote probability of damage accruing, except quite fortuitously. But when the external temperature is constantly fluctuating between mildness and severity, the atmosphere being also completely saturated with moisture, the whole art and talent of the gardener are necessary to avert the impending evil.

During the entire winter season, or rather from the beginning of November to the end of the following March, the two great agents whose operation upon plants is to be dreaded, and which, when likely to be carried beyond certain limits, must be promptly checked, are cold and water. Any further allusion to the former of these might appear trite, as its effects are so speedily and distinctly palpable, that they cannot be disregarded. To a few hints on moisture, however, the same objection cannot apply; and we are particularly anxious to attract public attention to this point.

If it be philosophically true as a moral axiom, that a treacherous and insidious acquaintance is more to be suspected and feared than a candid, deliberate, avowed enemy; it is no less correct that water is more dangerous to plants in winter than frost, because its bad consequences are less evident. We wish we could perceive, amongst all cultivators, the result of a full conviction of this simple fact. Much moisture at this season, whether it be in the form of vapour or water, occasions both positive and indirect injury. Its prejudicial influence is positive, inasmuch as it causes the destruction of the leaves, stems, and roots of all plants, in which those members are in a susceptible or succulent condition; and indirect, as affording the sole means through which frost can act.

To obviate the occurrence of too much dampness in any plant structure, fire heat is very seldom necessary, if sufficient attention is given to watering, and the state of the atmosphere. No water whatever should be supplied unless the soil be quite dry, and then only in very moderate quantities; nor should air at any time be admitted, save when tolerably free from moisture: but gentle, drying winds that are not too cold, should be allowed the freest possible circulation, as these are productive of incalculable benefit.

While touching on the subject of ventilation, it may be observed that the practice of crowding the evergreen or succulent kinds of plants together in a small space, as is generally done at this period of the year, is extremely injudicious and hurtful. It tends greatly to the condensation and collection of moisture about them, and obstructs that thorough circulation of air which is so essential to preserve them from mouldiness and decomposition. With deciduous and hard-wooded species, it is not of so much importance.

In the case of the young plants that are usually struck in the autumn, and kept in frames, where either artificial heat cannot be applied, or its application would be detrimental; and likewise of those half-hardy specimens that have been taken from the open ground; a too close arrangement is particularly to be avoided. The generally immature state of their new shoots, the circumstance of their having been fresh potted, and their roots not filling the soil, (thereby affording a greater chance for the accumulation of water,) and the exhalations from the damp surface on which they are nearly always placed, all contribute to enforce a more distant disposition than is commonly effected.

We have lately seen a method of elevating frames on posts, which, though adopted for the purpose of furnishing dung-heat from beneath, is, we conceive, admirably fitted for general use in the preservation of tender plants. The four corners are raised on four posts of equal length, about two feet above the level of the ground, and two other props are also added, one at the front, and the other at the back of the frame, near the middle. A small strong ledge is made round the inner base of the frame, which rests on all the posts, and supports some slabs of slate or thin stone, long enough to extend across the whole of the bottom, and of any width at which it may be convenient to obtain them. These slabs can be pierced with any required number of small holes, so as to carry off all the water that drains from the pots, which latter are either placed flatly on the surface of the stone, or, if considered desirable, slightly raised on three small pieces of tile, placed at equal distances round their edges.

The advantages of this practice must strike persons of the dullest apprehension. Every possibility of the bottoms of the pots becoming clogged, and drainage impeded; of worms obtaining admission to the soil; of moisture stagnating below the plant; in short, of the operation of any of the ills which inevitably attend the use of soil, or even coal-ashes, for placing the pots upon, would be completely removed. The expense of slate for such an object, or of stone in those parts of the country where it abounds, would ultimately be exceedingly trifling, as it is not, like the frames, subject to any sensible decay, but would last for an indefinite period. Respecting the height to which the frame should be lifted, it is by no means necessary that it be more than one foot, and a quantity of dry litter may be placed beneath it in severe weather.

We cannot withhold the suggestion, that where brick pits are constructed for protecting half-hardy or any other ornamental kinds of plants, a small chamber should be left under the centre, throughout their whole extent, over which a similar pavement to that above noticed could be laid to support the plants intended to be grown in it. The foundation of the pit would not thus be endangered, while the same good results as are experienced in the elevated frames, would be ensured.

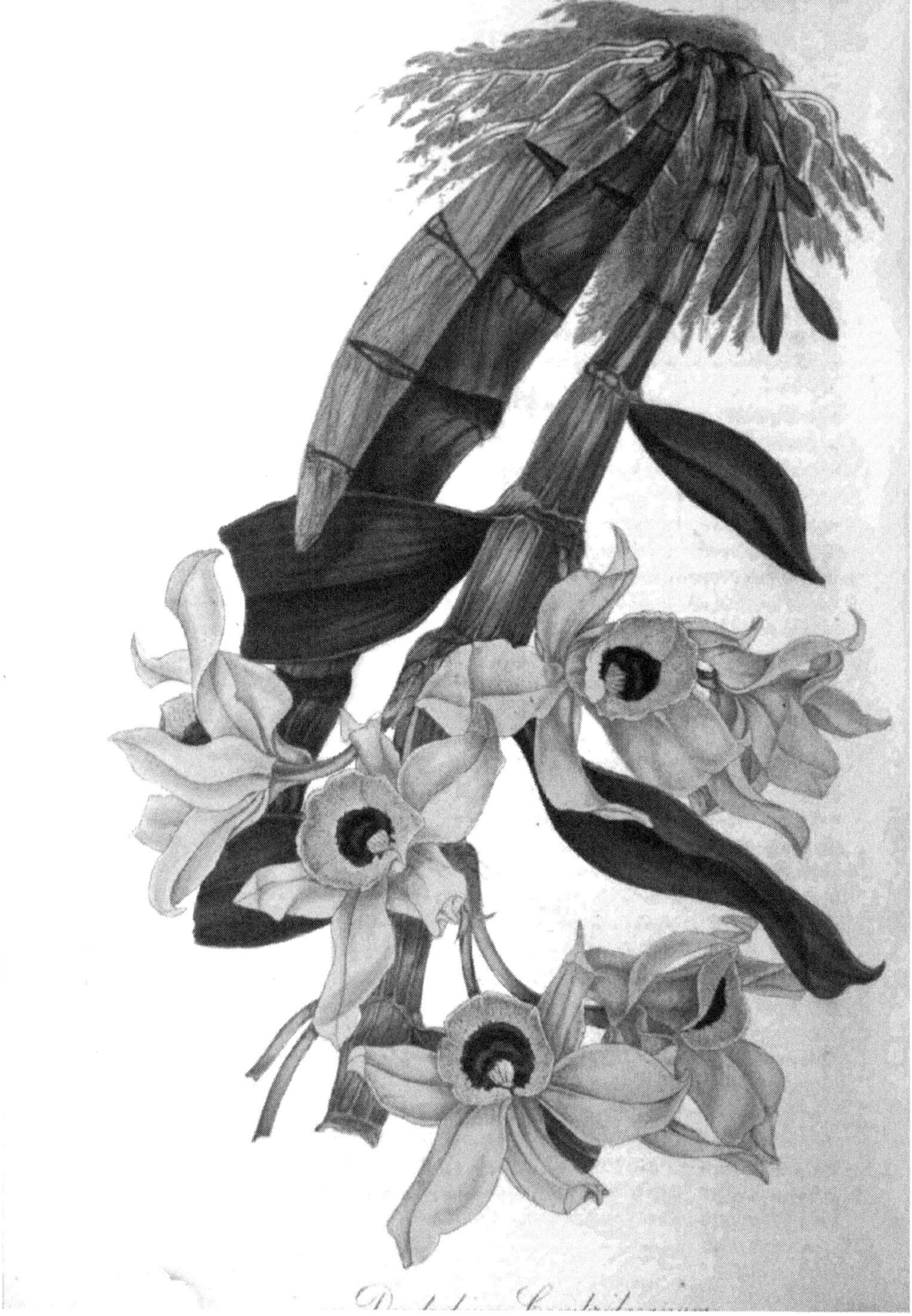

DENDRÒBIUM CAMBRIDGEÀNUM.

(DUCHESS OF CAMBRIDGE'S DENDROBIUM.)

CLASS.	ORDER.
GYNANDRIA.	MONOGYNIA.

NATURAL ORDER.
ORCHIDÀCEÆ.

GENERIC CHARACTER.—*Vide* vol. iii. p. 77.

SPECIFIC CHARACTER.—*Plant* epiphytal, caulescent. *Stems* peculiarly pendent, thick, fleshy, slightly flexuose, enlarging a little at the articulations, from nine inches to a foot long. *Leaves* lanceolate, very acute. *Flowers* solitary, or in pairs, springing from the joints opposite the leaves. *Sepals* and *petals* entire, almost equal, ovate-lanceolate, acute. *Labellum* entire, ovate, acute, concave, dark purple.

WE have great pleasure in supplying a figure of this new and highly beautiful *Dendrobium*, which, having flowered at Chatsworth during a visit of Her Royal Highness the Duchess of Cambridge to the noble occupant of that domain in the month of October last, has, by the express desire of His Grace, and with Her Royal Highness's condescending consent, received the above appellation.

The specimen from which our drawing was prepared, and which blossomed at the period already mentioned, was brought to Chatsworth by His Grace the Duke of Devonshire's botanical collector, Mr. J. Gibson, in the autumn of 1837, from the East Indies. It was found growing on the Khoseea hills, at an elevation of 4000 feet, and attaching itself to rocks or trees. Although, when depending from objects of the latter description, an impenetrable shade is afforded in the growing season, it may be useful to state that it is frequently seen clinging to the faces of rocks in situations fully exposed to the rays of the sun.

It differs from all other species either grown in the Chatsworth collection, or figured or described in any work to which we have access, in the remarkably drooping character of its stems and their striking tendency to obesity. It is also perfectly distinct in the hues of its flowers, the exterior portions of these being somewhat similar in colour to those of *D. fimbriatum*, but decidedly paler, while the lip is of a fine bright purple. The disposition of the blossoms is, moreover, quite unique among the yellow-flowering kinds, there being, in *D. Cambridgeanum*, never more than two issuing from the same point, and occasionally only one.

The extraordinary habitude of this plant will at once determine the cultivator as to the mode of treatment to be practised. Being naturally a pendent species, it will not thrive if trained in an erect position, nor even in a partially recumbent one; consequently, neither pots nor baskets of any sort are at all suitable for its reception. It must be affixed to a large block of wood, and the roots screened from light by a trifling covering of sphagnum, carefully secured with metallic wire. Living plants of the common *Lycopodium stoloniferum* are extensively employed by Messrs. Loddiges on the logs of wood and baskets which support the more luxuriant species of orchidaceæ; as they answer the threefold purpose of protecting the roots, creating a very interesting appearance, and giving certain indication of a lack of moisture whenever this occurs. The system is much to be applauded; not only on account of the neat and lively effect it produces, but likewise for the great advantages it confers on the plants, by maintaining them in a perpetually moist condition throughout their progressive stage. Whenever the moss is found to extend itself over too great a surface, or becomes too dense, it can easily be thinned or removed to any desired extent; and in the winter months, when such plants as the present should be dry and torpid, it may be allowed completely to decay, always reserving a few plants in some convenient place to renew the supply when again required.

With regard to the kind of wood best adapted for this object, it is difficult to decide what trees furnish logs of the most congenial nature. Those on which the bark is perfect, rugged, and durable, should be preferred; for the roots delight to insinuate themselves into the fissures of rough bark, and, if this is subject to a speedy decay, or separates readily upon exposure to the frequent atmospheric changes of an orchidaceous house, the plant cannot be transferred to another block without great injury to the roots.

Like all other *Dendrobiums*, this requires a period of dormancy on the cessation of its growth, of about three months' duration, during which it must be kept particularly dry. Water should, however, be very liberally administered in summer. It may be propagated after the usual manner, by merely detaching one of the younger stems, and treating it precisely as the parent plant.

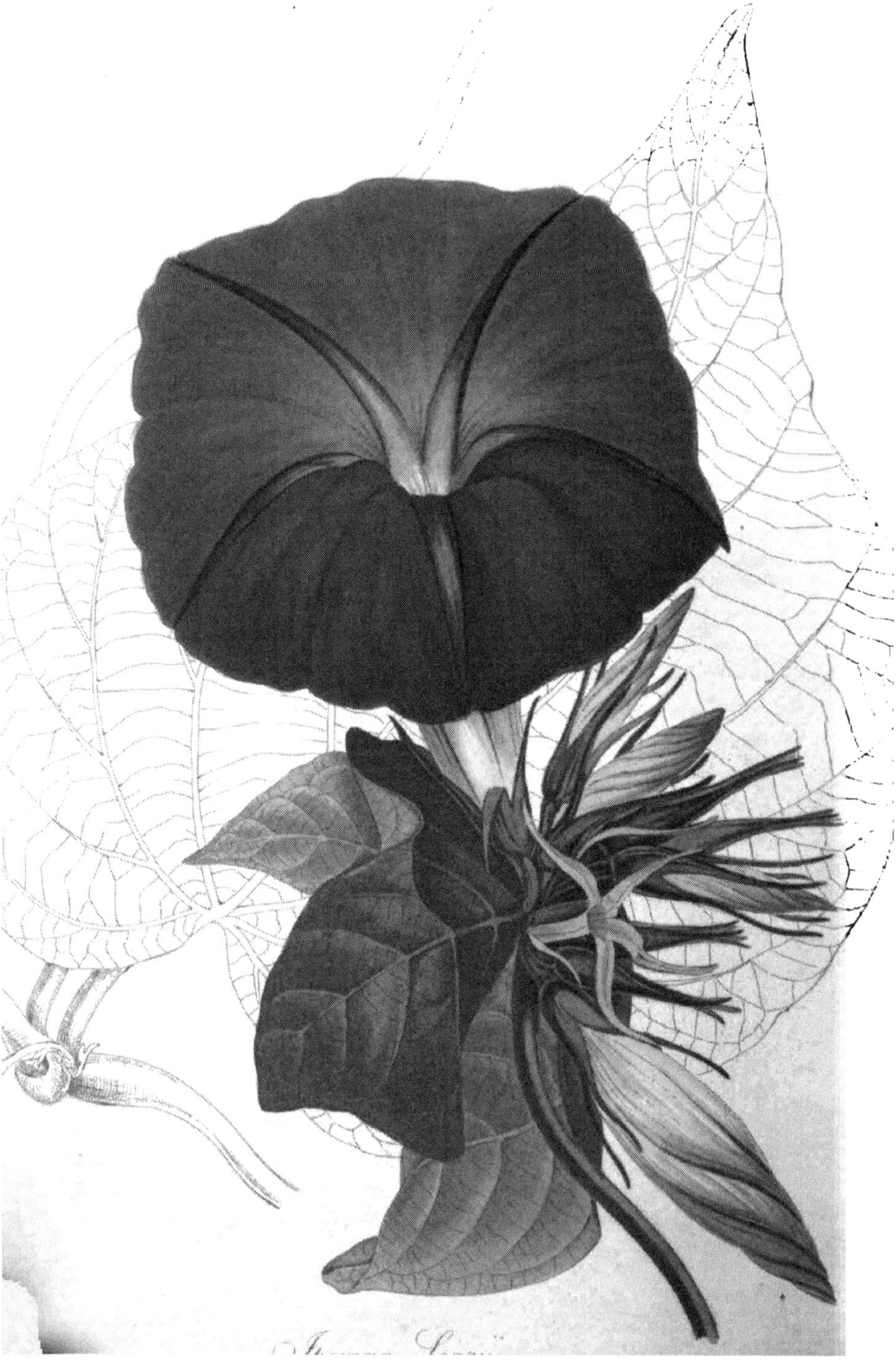

IPOMŒA LEARI.

(MR. LEAR'S IPOMŒA.)

CLASS.
PENTANDRIA.

ORDER.
MONOGYNIA.

NATURAL ORDER.
CONVOLVULACEÆ.

GENERIC CHARACTER.—*Vide* vol. iii. p. 50.

SPECIFIC CHARACTER.—*Plant* an evergreen twining shrub, hairy in all its younger parts. *Leaves* variable; most frequently cordate, but often unequally, and sometimes distinctly, three-lobed; pointletted, slightly reticulated, deep green above, thickly clothed with whitish pubescence beneath. *Calyx* composed of five unequal, long, subulate segments, with a particularly hairy tube. *Flowers* produced in clusters at the extremities of the lateral shoots; *pedicels* a nearly uniform length. *Corolla* of a deep purplish blue colour, with five conspicuous bands of a lighter hue. *Stamens* inserted in the tube of the corolla; *filaments* finely fringed at the base.

For the introduction of this splendid *Ipomœa* to British gardens, the lovers of floriculture have to thank Mr. Knight, nurseryman, of the King's Road, Chelsea, through whose persevering liberality Mr. Lear, the individual after whom it is named by the above gentleman, and by whom its seeds were sent to this country, is maintained in the beautiful and fertile island of Ceylon as a collector of botanical rarities. Our present subject is the only important novelty resulting from this mission which has yet developed its flowers; but many others have subsequently arrived, which are likely to prove real acquisitions.

To those who are not botanically familiar with *I. rubro-cœrulea*, a first glance at the annexed plate will awaken the impression that *I. Leari* is indisputably identical with that singularly lovely species. Such, however, is very far from being the case; and to establish clearly the distinction, we shall here enumerate the points in which the greatest dissimilarity exists. Every portion of *I. rubro-cœrulea* is perfectly smooth, whereas the young stems of *I. Leari* are covered with erect hairs, the upper surface of the leaves being clothed with such as are longer but appressed, and the lower surface with a dense whitish pubescence, while the hairs of the calyx are closer, more rigid, and altogether stronger. Further, the leaves of the former species are quite entire, those of the latter frequently divided irregularly. In *I. Leari*, again, the segments of the calyx are considerably longer, and the clusters of flowers are more regular, that is, their pedicels are of nearly equal length. To complete the disparity, it may be added that one is a native of the Eastern, and the other of the Western world, *I. rubro-cœrulea* being indigenous to Mexico.

We have thought it requisite to the popularity of this very deserving plant, to specify thus elaborately those particulars wherein it is so plainly distinguishable from a species to which few can be strangers; and pass immediately to a short consideration of the principal items to be observed in its management. In a newly-erected house at Mr. Knight's nursery, appropriated partly to stove plants and partly to the purposes of propagation, and in which consequently a rather high temperature is preserved, the specimen from which our figure was executed is planted in a bed formed near one of the corners, and trained to a slender wire lattice extending beneath the entire surface of the roof. It commenced flowering in this position towards the end of September, and has scarcely yet ceased; the length of the strongest shoots being fully thirty feet.

The particulars in this notice which we desire specially to dwell upon, are those of the plant being quite unrestrained at its roots, growing in a hot, moist atmosphere, and being very near the light, by the action of which it seems rather benefited than otherwise. It appears to be a shrubby species, and will probably retain its foliage through the winter in a moderate temperature. The fact of its having been raised only last year, will account for its beginning to bloom at so late a period, and in the following season it will doubtless unfold its first blossoms as early as June or July, from thence continuing to flower till the advance of winter. From the cause already assigned for the late development of its blossoms, no seeds have yet been perfected; but there is sufficient reason to expect a prodigal supply at a future time. Cuttings root with great readiness when taken from the youngest branches in their immature state, and before they have attained a flowering condition. Superfluous stems are also sometimes thrown up from the roots, which, if taken off ere they have extended themselves beyond two or three feet, form excellent cuttings.

The generic name has been explained in vol. iii. p. 50, where a delineation and description of *I. rubro-cœrulea* are given, to which the reader may be referred for a comparison between the colours peculiar to the flowers of the two species.

Thunbergia aurantiaca.

THUNBÉRGIA AURANTIÀCA.

(ORANGE-FLOWERED THUNBERGIA.)

CLASS.	ORDER.
DIDYNAMIA.	ANGIOSPERMIA.

NATURAL ORDER.
ACANTHACEÆ.

GENERIC CHARACTER.—*Vide* vol. iii. p. 28.

SPECIFIC CHARACTER.—*Plant* herbaceous, hairy. *Stems* numerous, twining. *Leaves* partially hastate, acuminate, hairy, with winged petioles, which frequently have irregularly indented margins. *Calyx* with two large, persistent, exterior envelopes, pale green. *Corolla* monopetalous; *limb* five-parted, divisions nearly equal, rounded, bright orange; throat hairy in the inside, very dark purple. *Stamens* inserted in the tube of the corolla, scarcely half so long, beautifully bearded. *Style* nearly twice the length of the stamens. *Stigma* concave, with a protuberant horn. *Capsule* almost globular, but having a conspicuous beak arising from its centre.

SELDOM have our pages been embellished with a representation of a more showy plant, or one better deserving universal and lasting dissemination. Wherever its near ally, *T. alata*, is known and esteemed,—in fact, to every collection which comprises the appurtenance of a single frame or greenhouse,—this delightful species must, immediately on being witnessed, become an indispensable desideratum.

It is no mean characteristic merit of this plant, when conjoined with its surpassing beauty, that it will flourish with almost equal vigour in a stove, a greenhouse, a house of an intermediate temperature, and, for a certain period, in the open ground. In all these situations, if proper attention is bestowed on the due maintenance of such atmospheric or other conditions as are especially requisite, the most perfect success may invariably be attained, and a truly dazzling display of its brilliant blossoms secured in little short of perpetuity. One still more interesting property, however, to those who can afford it room in a house of a temperature slightly above that of the greenhouse, is its profuse production of flowers through the most dreary winter months.

To all these encomiums, we are aware that the old *T. alata* is fully as much entitled, except that it is infinitely inferior in the richness and size of its flowers. On these last features, indeed, the chief distinction from that species depends. We

re.
ould,
led, and
ll be very
species were
Michael Clayton,
y in which it
ns are possessed,
red with these
covered with
these are lighter
accompanying

have heard it insinuated that it is a mere hybrid, between *T. alata* and some darker-flowered species; but this suggestion has not the slightest foundation, as, supposing its history were dubious, we are unacquainted with any *Thunbergias*, the colours of which, when commingled, could possibly produce the hue of *T. aurantiaca*. Besides which, if the development and thorough maturation of seeds may be relied on as a certain character of a natural and independent product, we have seen an abundance of these ripened in the Epsom nursery.

For the culture of this plant when confined to a house, a highly humid atmosphere appears necessary, at least where the structure fronts the south, or the specimen is much beneath immediate solar influence. In the arid air of a common greenhouse, or that of a stove which is at all subject to occasional drought in the summer, an attack of the red spider is nearly inevitable, the leaves of this plant, as those of *T. alata*, seeming to furnish a most agreeable resort to that detested insect. The only way of eradicating it when found to have become fully established, is by the removal of the plants infested to a very hot and close house, where the atmosphere is laden with moisture, and in which also the plant must be frequently syringed.

But the most certain mode of preventing this occurrence, and thereby saving the plant from incalculable injury, is to keep it partly secluded from the sun's beams, and constantly as moist as can be endured without damage. Notwithstanding this injunction for plants that are grown in houses, the species will succeed in the open air as freely as that above referred to, and in such an exposure needs none of the precautionary treatment which is essential in an artificial atmosphere. The soil for it should be composed of equal portions of sandy loam and heath-mould, to which, if a little of the ashes of burnt wood and some silver sand are added, and these incorporated a year before being used, the benefit to the plants will be very perceptible.

We are informed, from a respectable source, that seeds of this species were received, among many others from the Cape of Good Hope, by Michael Clayton, Esq., of Charlwood Park, Crawley, Sussex. The first nursery in which it appeared, and where in consequence the greatest number of plants are possessed, was Messrs. Young's, of Epsom. From a plant which flowered with these gentlemen about the middle of last August, and which is still covered with blossoms,—although, on account of the season and other casualties, these are lighter and smaller than those which were primarily opened,—we obtained the accompanying drawing.

Pentstemon argutus.

PENTSTÈMON ARGÙTUS.

(CUT-LEAVED PENTSTEMON.)

CLASS.
DIDYNAMIA.

ORDER.
ANGIOSPERMIA.

NATURAL ORDER.
SCROPHULARIÀCEÆ.

GENERIC CHARACTER.—*Vide* vol. iv. p. 243.

SPECIFIC CHARACTER.—*Plant* slightly suffruticose, growing from three to four feet high, covered in all its members with very short indistinct pubescence. *Stems* numerous, much branched towards the base, round. *Leaves* opposite, partly connate, upper ones lanceolate, lower spatulate, obtuse, with a great number of irregular serratures, deep green on the upper surface, and much paler below. *Calyx* equally divided into five ovate-lanceolate, acuminate, usually serrated segments, persistent. *Corolla* bilabiate; upper lip composed of two equal, rounded, slightly recurved divisions; lower lip of three somewhat larger ones; bright purple, tinged with blue towards the summits of the lobes. *Stamens* four, inserted at regular distances in the base of the corolla tube, and curving so as to lie in pairs near the mouth of the upper lip, with a barren one lying between them. *Style* rather longer than the stamens, resting on the lower lip, bearded on the upper side for about one third of its length. *Capsule* two-celled, rather compressed at the sides, with a little protuberance at the apex.

ON the numerous distinguished traits of this truly invaluable genus, we have previously had occasion to descant, in the emphatic style which we usually employ when depicting the fairer features in Flora's enchanting attire. Every constituent of her many-coloured mantle has its own individual charm, and, when viewed under auspicious circumstances, imparts a delight distinct both in kind and degree; but her brighter ornaments are dispersed with such consummate skill, that it is very rarely we meet with anything approaching to an aggregation. In the genus *Pentstemon*, however, this phenomenon most markedly occurs; as it is composed of plants which, for beauty, elegance, and everything that can render these delightful objects desirable, have few rivals.

We are induced to bestow upon them this glowing panegyric, because, as hinted in a former number of this volume, they are lamentably disregarded; and if we succeed in persuading any of our readers to investigate their claims to extensive culture, our design will have been fulfilled. Figures of several intensely interesting kinds will be found scattered through this Magazine; and we have now to furnish an account of an entirely new species, which is yet almost exclusively restricted to the higher nurseries.

P. argutus is a North American plant, inhabiting, as we have satisfactory evidence for believing, some of the southerly districts of Texas. It has perhaps been known in Britain three or four years; but, within this time, has not been very widely dispersed. We have noticed it, for two years past, in the London nurseries, although we have never seen it flower freely till the last summer; when it exhibited its beautiful blossoms at Messrs. Henderson's, Pine-Apple Place, uninterruptedly from June till November. In the month of September, our artist took the drawing which is herewith furnished.

The number and height of its stems—which last averages from three to four feet—are the prominent peculiarities of this species. From the treatment hitherto afforded, it would seem to need a place in the greenhouse. Of its equal hardihood, however, with *P. speciosus*, and likewise with *P. gentianoides*, there can be little question. To the latter plant, it assimilates most nearly in habit, being of a slightly suffruticose character. It must also be far easier to preserve through the winter than the majority of its congeners, as the leaves are neither large, numerous, nor glaucous; and to the attraction for moisture which these three properties present, all the losses of plants of this tribe may be attributed.

Planted in the open border towards the month of June, it is easy to imagine that this species would create a much more showy effect than if kept in a pot. The stems should be cut down to within a few inches of the earth in the autumn, and, with a slight mulching of old bark, it may be left through the winter; its native country, and the characteristics already named, being almost certain guarantees for its safety.

Owing to the profusion of its branches, and their half-woody character, no *Pentstemon* multiplies more readily or abundantly from cuttings. Seeds are also liberally borne, and may be sown as soon as ripe in a bed or pot supplied with a moderate heat. When the plants appear, they should be placed singly in small pots, gradually hardened, and set in a dry frame till they are required for the borders, merely repotting them when needful.

FLORICULTURAL NOTICES.

Fùchsia fúlgens. Several showy varieties of this handsome plant exist in the smaller metropolitan nurseries, and some interesting hybrids have also been obtained, although we have yet seen none that are very valuable. Probably a farther impregnation of the flowers of those already procured with the pollen of *F. fulgens* will occasion a more decided interchange of character; and we anticipate seeing many next season, in which the dwarf bushy habits and mode of flowering of the common kinds are associated with the stately flowers and foliage of our present subject. We have been attentively inquiring during the last year for every information on the culture of this plant which might assist any of our readers, but have not succeeded in eliciting anything further than has been before recorded, save the following particulars.

Kept in a stove where a liberal heat is maintained, it retains its foliage through the winter, and flowers most abundantly during the greater part of the year. In the early spring and late autumnal months, the flowers are especially profuse, and, on this account, it will, if thus managed, be of admirable service to those who possess a stove, and naturally desire flowers at that period when few others are to be seen elsewhere. It requires a considerable range for its roots, and, if the house is so constructed as to allow of its being planted out in a border, will form a magnificent shrub.

Solànum jasminoìdes. Under this name, we propose adding to our catalogues a very graceful and attractive species, which appears to us to be new, and has for some time past been blooming in the greenhouse of Messrs. Young, Epsom. Its habit and foliage are so exceedingly like those of some Jasmines, that, when not in flower, it would almost always be considered a species of that genus. It is a slender, smooth, climbing shrub, the young branches of which are deep green, as are also the leaves, these being besides either entire and ovate, imperfectly three-lobed, or equally three or five lobed. The flowers appear in extensive panicles, frequently from eight to twelve in each; they are small, flatly-campanulate, and bluish-white, with prominent yellow stamens in the centre. Altogether, this is the most elegant species of *Solanum* with which we are acquainted, and its value is much enhanced by the grateful fragrance of the blossoms. Messrs. Young received it from North America, without any knowledge of its native country; but it was probably found in some of the more southerly districts of that continent.

OPERATIONS FOR JANUARY.

January is the month in which the employment of a little fire-heat usually begins to be requisite in plant-houses, since, at this period, frosts are frequently too severe to render other means of protection completely adequate. To suggest methods for economizing this heat, should be one of the chief aims of floricultural calendars at the present season, and we therefore offer a few hints which may perhaps prove useful to cultivators.

The principal circumstance which occasions an unnecessary expenditure of heat at this time, is one to which we have before called attention, but which cannot be too often urged—the improper use of water, or the admission of air that is too much charged with moisture. All plants—at least those of a woody nature—being now torpid, seldom require watering more than once a week, and then only in small quantities. As the circulation of their sap is almost discontinued, and their exhalations scarcely perceptible, it is not surprising that they will subsist upon an exceedingly sparing supply of water, and this, both for their health and safety, should be reduced within the narrowest possible limits.

After watering the plants in any house,—which should always be done in the morning of the day,—a trifling degree of heat should be introduced during the ensuing night. This will serve to dry up the water that drains through the pots, which would otherwise create an injurious moisture in the atmosphere, and will also obviate all danger from any frost that may occur. For, let it be particularly noted that, should a slight frost immediately succeed the application of water, more real mischief will accrue than from a far greater degree of it at any other time. We saw an instance last winter in which a considerable quantity of Pelargoniums had been rather liberally watered in mild weather, which continued till three o'clock in the following morning, when a frost commenced, which destroyed all their roots that were near the edges of the pots, and the plants never properly recovered throughout the whole of the past summer.

This may be sufficient to warn those who rely on any existing state of the weather, of the necessity of a moderate supply of artificial heat after water has been administered. If the external atmosphere is warm and dry enough on these occasions, fires may sometimes be dispensed with, but great watchfulness is essential till the increased moisture has been expelled.

Another mode of moderating the expenses of a garden establishment, is the retention of heat in a plant structure by covering the glass. What we have previously advanced on this subject must, however, be duly remembered. Any thing that is placed in contact with a protected surface, if very porous, is comparatively little better than useless; because, the transference of heat being thus equally uninterrupted, it is conducted off with nearly as great rapidity as if the glass were exposed, merely having another thin substance to pass through. Mats should, consequently, always be elevated on a narrow strip of wood placed at certain distances along the house or frame, and fully an inch from its surface; but care must be taken to cover all the apertures round the edges, so as not to leave an open space between the mat and the frame, as this would admit of the partial dispersion of the heat which escapes through the glass.

GENERAL INDEX.

A.

ABUTILON striatum, 236
Acacia cultrata, 259
— kermesina, 236
Accretions of plants, character and source of the, 58, 85
Acclimatation of plants, hints on the, 61, 108, 110, 156, 184, 206
Ærides quinquevulnerum, 187, 260
— tessellatum, 139
— supposed new species of, 260
Æschynanthus ramosissimus, 195; treatment of, 196
— Roxburghii, 213
Æsculus hippocastanum, an excellent subject for botanical examination, 180
Agave saponaria, 235
Air, remarks on its admission to plant houses, 96, 143, 167, 240, 263; importance of diluting the water supplied to plants with, 12
Alburnum, derivation and meaning of the term, 57
Alstrœmeria Ligtu, 68
Alstrœmerias, brief hints on the treatment of, 68
Amphicome arguta, culture of, 80
Angelonia Gardneri, 234
Angræcum armeniacum, 213
— caudatum, 188
Anigozanthus flavidus; var. bicolor, 19
— Manglesii, 139
Annual plants, hints on rearing, 48; climates which they usually inhabit, 62
Antennaria triplinervis, 20
Arboretum et Fruticetum Britannicum, review of Loudon's, 64
Arboretums, definition and merits of, 81
Aridity, an essential feature in the winter treatment of plants, 240, 263
Aristolochia ciliata, 234
— hyperborea, cultivation of, 54
Autumn, great attention requisite for tender plants in the, 239, 263

B.

BALSAMINA Mastersiana, 75
Balsams, hints on the cultivation of, 76
Bauhinia corymbosa, 211, 228
— forficata, 186

Beauty in plants, what constitutes, 66
Begonia octapetala, 21
Bessera elegans, 138
Birds rather useful than otherwise in a garden, 231
Birthwort, northern, 53
Black glass a ready conductor of heat, but not of light, 11
Bletia Parkinsoni, 163
Books, those most profitable to a young gardener, 208
Boronia crenulata, 115
Botanical Classification, general view of, 129
Botanical Expedition to North America, particulars concerning the loss of the collectors, 135
Bouvardia angustifolia, 187
Brasavola Martiana, 20
Brassia maculata, treatment of, 5
British plants, hints on studying and collecting, 38; great advantages of acquiring a knowledge of, 39
Budding, proper season for, 192
Burlingtonia maculata, 187
— venusta, 115

C.

CACTACEOUS plants, summer exposure beneficial to, 120
Cactæ, account of an importation of, by Messrs. Low and Co., 43
Caladium petiolatum, 115
Calandrina discolor, 17
Callichroa platyglossa, 89
Calliprora lutea, 164
Calytrix aurea, 259
Camarotis purpurea, 90
Cambium, its position and consistence, 58
Camellias, method of grafting, 93, 112; general propagation of, 111
Campanula carolina, 164
— punctata, 164
Caprifolium, hybrid, 140
Caprifoliums well suited for covering the naked trunks of trees, 14
Catasetum atratum, 140
Cattleya bicolor, 236
— citrina, 187
— guttata; var. Russelliana, 19

INDEX.

Cattleya Harrisoniæ; *var.* alba, 188
— Mossiæ, *var.* 260
Ceanothus collinus, 140
Ceropegia vincæfolia, 162
Chorizema varium, 115 ; culture and propagation of, 176
Chrysorrhoë nitens, 258
Cineraria Waterhousiana, 260
Cinerarias, plants called hybrid, belong to the genus Senecio, 42
Cleisostoma rosea, 189
Clematis cærulea, culture of, 116
— Sieboldii, hardihood of, 117
Clematis, grafting the species of, recommended, 119 ; the species adapted for attaching to the stems of trees and shrubs, 14
Clerodendron squamatum, 164
Climate, its influence on plants, 33, 59, 84, 107, 132, 155, 181, 204
Climbing plants, time and mode of pruning and training exotic, 240 ; method of training some of the hardy-kinds to poles, 13 ; circular trellises most suitable for supporting, 118 ; their natural habitats, 14
Cœlogyne Gardneriana, treatment and propagation of, 73
Cœlogyne ocellata, 69, 92
— Wallichiana, general culture of, 25
Collinsia heterophylla, 18
Cold, its nature explained, 37
Comesperma gracilis, 43
Comparettia coccinea, 19
Conduction of heat, capacity of several substances for the, 36
Constitutions of plants generally similar, 85
Convolvulus bryoniæfolius, 260
— pentanthus, 219 ; culture and multiplication of, 220
Corbularia tenuifolia, 91
Corn-flag, branching, 99
Corræa cordata, 21
— Milnerii, 21
— rufa, 260
Coryanthes maculata ; *var.* Parkeri, 212
Cow Tree, account of the, 113
Cultivation of plants, the old system compared with the modern, 249
Cuticle of plants, tissue of which it is composed, 180
Cycnoches ventricosum, 189
Cymbidium iridifolium, 261
Cynoglossum cœlestinum, 163
Cyrtochilum mystacinum, 258

D.

Daphne indica ; *var.* rubra, 261
Daubenya fulva, 235
Decomposition caused by heat, 33, 34
Dendrobium, culture of the genus, 50
— divisions of the genus, 145
— aggregatum, 145
— aureum ; *var.* pallidum, 90
— Cambridgeanum, 265
— chrysanthum, 213

Dendrobium crumenatum, 90
— formosum, 49
— Jenkinsii, 163
— longicornu, 21
— macrochilum, 91
— nobile, 44
— Paxtoni, 169
— pulchellum, 91
— sulcatum, 19
— teretifolium, 70
Deutzia canescens, 70
Developments of plants not fortuitous, 58 ; induced by heat, 84
Dews, origin of, 35
Diary, its value to a young gardener, 230
Dillwynia speciosa, 116
Diplacus puniceus, 140 ; culture of, 222
Duramen, explanation of the word, 57

E.

Echites suberecta, 165
Eclipse of the sun, account of its effects on flowers, 10
Economising heat, modes of, 274
Edwardsia Macnabiana, 162
Epacris coccineus, 70, 123
— impressa ; *var.* parviflora, 89
Epidendrum diceratum, 91
— lentiginosum, 22
— macrochilum, 44
— Schomburgkii, 70
— stenopetalum, 236
Epimedium Musschianum, 185
Epiphyllum Russellianum, 88
Eria callosa, 139
— ferruginea, 139
Erica tricolor ; *var.* superba, 3
Erysimum Perowskianum, 165; culture and multiplication of, 246
Evaporation occasioned by heat, 86
Exhalations from plants, their causes, channels, and consequences, 86
Exogenous plants, general features of, 178
Exotic plants, importance of uniformity in the system of treating, 167 ; necessity for arranging them at a proper distance from each other, 119, 263
Exotic shrubs multiplied by grafting, 93
Experiments, value of, 233

F.

Fabiana imbricata, 141
Fertility of plants occasioned mainly by heat, 132
Flowering plants, rules for determining the merits of, 66
Flowers, distinct organs, 132 ; influence of heat in their production, 132 ; suggestions for promoting their formation and development, 134 ; their size, form, and colour, the chief criteria of beauty in plants, 67
Fluids, heat principally instrumental in the

production of, 35; the most rapid radiators of heat, 86
Food of plants prepared and supplied by heat, 34
Forcing flowers, hints on, 24
Forests, manner in which they affect the climate of any district, 204
Frames, advantages of growing greenhouse plants in, 201; excellent method of elevating, 264
Frost, mode in which it operates on plants, 87; means for counteracting its effects, 87; reason for its destructiveness of vegetation in spring, 86; the growth and decay of vegetable matters suspended by it, 34
Fuchsia cylindracea, well adapted for hybridization, 17
Fuchsia fulgens, suggestions for treating it as Dahlias usually are, 46; further remarks on its culture, 273
Fuchsia globosa; var. Devonia, 237
Functions of plants materially affected by heat, 84.

G.

GALACTODENDRON utile, 113
Gardeners, mental improvement of, 207, 230
Garden-mats, advantages of covering plant-houses with them in winter, 24, 274
Gardoquia multiflora, 223; cultivation of, 224
Gastrochilus pulcherrimus, 213
Gentiana gelida, 189
Geranium tuberosum; var. ramosum, 41
Gerardia delphinifolia, 165
Germination of seeds, agency of heat in the, 85
Gesneria Douglasii; var. verticillata, 29
— Marchii, 186
— oblongata, treatment of, 104
— stricta, 163
— treatment of the genus, 30
Gladioli, an open border most suitable for, 100
Gladiolus ramosus, 99
Glass, radiating and conducting power of, 37; its relative capacity for transmitting light and heat, when coloured and when transparent, 11
Gompholobium polymorphum, treatment of, 151; notice of two varieties, 116
Gompholobium versicolor, 186
Grafting Camellias, Rhododendrons, &c., 93, 111
Grafting trees, advantages of, 65
Grammatophyllum multiflorum, 217; culture of, 218
Greenhouse climbing plants, the partial acclimatation of, 159, 249
Greenhouse plants, remarks on exposing them during the summer, 119; method of inducing them to flower freely, 156
Greenhouses, substitution in them of thin canvass for glass during fine weather, 202; only calculated for display, 201
Grevillea Manglesii, 44
Griffinia hyacinthina, 44
Growth of plants, a result of the application of heat, 33, 34, 84; a distinct process from the production of flowers, 132; why, when luxuriant, it is inimical to fertility, 133
Gunnia picta, 92

H.

HABITS of plants susceptible of alteration, 84, 158
Half-hardy plants, merits of, 55; time for repotting those that are exposed, 215
Hawthorn hedges, recommendation to graft the more ornate kinds of Cratægus upon, 65
Heat, its influence on vegetable life, functions, and substances, 33, 59, 107, 132, 155, 181, 204; suppositions as to its nature, 33; its expansive power, 34; perfectly imponderous, 34; its sources, 36; its agency in the geographical distribution of plants, 59; its modification by elevated tracts or large bodies of water, 181; also by trees and forests, 204
Heath, superb three-coloured, 3
Hederoma latifolia, 259
Hemerocallis speciosa, 214
Herbaceous plants, effects of frost on such as are planted in autumn, 24
Heterotropa asaroides, 185
Hibiscus Cameronii, 237
Hills, cases in which they are suitable or unsuitable for planting tender species upon, 182
Hoitzia Mexicana, 261
Hovea fungens, 71, 101
— treatment of the genus, 102
Hoya coriacea, 89
Huntleya meleagris, 69
— violacea, 141
Hybridization of ornamental trees, its importance, 65
Hybridization of half-hardy plants, hints on the, 192

I.

ICE, a result of radiation, 35
Importation of plants, suggestions respecting the, 61
Imported seeds, directions for the germination and subsequent management of, 62
Indusium of plants, nature of the, 58
Inga Harrisii, 185
Insects, a knowledge of their forms and habits useful to gardeners, 231
Ipomœa Leari, 237; culture of, 268
— pungens, 261
— rubro-cœrulea, distinction between it and I. Leari, 267

J.

JACKSONIA grandiflora, 237

K.

KNIGHT, T. A., Esq., extracts of a letter from, on the course of sap, 9

L.

LELIA albida, 235
— anceps, 22

Lælia autumnalis, 121
— furfuracea, 114
Lælias, culture of, 122
Landscape gardening, how to obtain a knowledge of its principles, 232; instructions in, with reference to trees and shrubs, 82
Leonotis nepetæfolia, 18
Lepismium commune, 257
— myosurus, 233
Leycesteria formosa, 18
Liber, origin and application of the phrase, 57
Light, artificial, its operation on flowers similar in kind to that of the sun, 11
Lilies, general culture of the Japan species, 128, 189
Lilium aurantiacum, 127
— lancifolium roseum, 189
Linnæan system of botany, relative value of the, 129, 225, 228
Linum trigynum, 22
Lisianthus Russellianus, general cultivation of, 31
Literary composition, its importance to gardeners, 209; directions for acquiring adroitness in, 209
Loasaceæ, characteristics of the natural order, 226
Loasa lateritia, its treatment in the open border, 252
Lobelia heterophylla, management of, 198
— ignea, 165; cultivation and increase of, 248
— Milleri, 166
— ramosa, 166
Lophospermum erubescens and scandens, treatment in the open border, 251
Lupinus Barkerii, 234
— Hartwegii, 138
Lycopodium stoloniferum, useful for protecting the roots of Orchidaceæ, 266

M.

MALLOW, showy red-flowered, 16, 55
Malva Creeana, 16; culture of, 55
Manglesia purpurea, 259
Marica gracilis, 68
Marshallia cæspitosa, 17
Mats, or other covering to plant-houses, why preferable to the introduction of fire-heat, 109
Maturation of wood indispensable to fertility, 157
Maurandya Barclayana, treated as a half-hardy plant, 252
Maxillaria aureo-fulva, 22
— lentiginosa, 190
— tenuifolia, 42
— vitellina, 69
Mental improvement of gardeners, hints on the, 207, 230
Metals, imperfect radiators, but rapid conductors of heat, 36
Miltonia candida, 241; culture of, 242
Moisture, quantity supplied to plants to be regulated by the temperature, 48; relative proportion to heat in which it should exist, where flowers or seeds are desired, 133

Moon, suggestions concerning the abstraction of heat by the, 37
Morna nitida, 141
Mountains, varied temperature and vegetation of, according to their elevation, 181

N.

NAMES of plants, objections to commemorative ones, 51
Native countries of plants, a knowledge of their medium, extremes, and monthly variations of temperature, essential to the cultivator, 60
Natural system of botany, its merits considered, 129, 225, 228; its rudiments and prime divisions, 177
Nelumbium luteum, 233
Nuttallia cordata, 237
— malvæflora, 190
— papaver, 173; treatment of, 174
Nuytzia floribunda, 259

O.

OBSERVATION, importance of, 230; subjects for, 230
Odontoglossum Rossii, 212
Œnothera parviflora, 190
Oncidium Cavendishii, 45
— concolor, 212
— Forbesii, 43
— Henchmanii, 238
— hians, 262
— lunatum, 45
— luridum; var. guttatum, 69
— pulvinatum, 141
— Reidianum, 141
— roseum, 214, 238
— sanguineum, 238
— stramineum, 92
— trulliferum, 190
Operations for January, 274
— February, 23
— March, 47
— April, 71
— May, 95
— June, 119
— July, 143
— August, 167
— September, 191
— October, 215
— November, 239
— December, 263
Orchidaceæ, season of rest necessary for, 50; their nature, 157; proper time for their repose, 107; best mode of shading, 168; kind of logs most suitable for growing the epiphytal species on, 266; necessity for a pit in which to keep particular sorts, 216, 256; uniformity of treatment necessary for, 255; preparatory procedure requisite for their introduction to drawing-rooms, 254; their general period of flowering, 255
Orchidaceous-house, stained glass suggested as a fit material for glazing the, 12

P.

PÆONIA Brownii, 137
— papaveracea rubra, 116
— tenuifolia plena, 116
Passiflora onychina, 238
Patersonia sapphirina, 257
Pentstemon argutus, 142 ; culture and propagation of, 272
Pentstemon barbatum ; *var.* carneum, 89
— gentianoides ; *var.*, 214
— speciosus, 171 ; treatment of, 172
Peristeria stapelioides, 142
Petunias treated as climbing plants, 253
Phaius bicolor, 166
— Wallichii, 193 ; culture of, 194
Phalocallis plumbea, 42
Philadelphus Gordonianus, 138
Philibertia grandiflora, cultivation of, 7
Pimelea Hendersonii, 88
— incana, 22, 71
Pinus, the rarer species of, increased by grafting, 94
Pith, nature, position, and contraction of, 178
Plantations, directions for disposing shrubs in, 82 ; those formed for shelter usually inimical to plants, 204
Plant-houses, comparison of ancient with modern, 249 ; necessity for consulting the comfort of proprietors in, 254
Platycodon grandiflorus, 166
Platystemon leiocarpum, 211
Pleasure grounds, greenhouse climbing plants as summer ornaments to, 172
Poles recommended for supporting roses and other hardy climbing plants, 13
Polygonum amplexicaule, 186
Pores, nature and offices of vegetable, 85
Potentilla Hopwoodiana, 149
Potting plants, proper season for, 71
Primula sinensis ; *var.* plena, 262
Propagation of all kinds of plants by cuttings, best time for the, 72, 144 ; general directions for the, 192
Protection of plants, rules to be observed in the, 108

Q.

QUEKETTIA microscopica, 23

R.

RADIATION, its nature, causes, laws, and effects, 108 ; most copious and injurious in the spring months, 23 ; best means of checking, 24 ; capacity for, in different substances, 36
Rays of the sun, different descriptions of, 11
Reading, excellent method of, 208
Repose of plants, a periodical one necessary, 105 ; conditions to be observed during its continuance, 106 ; caused by climate, 105
Repose requisite for orchidaceæ, nature of the, 50, 157 ; proper period of, 107
Reproductive power of plants increased in proportion to the elevation of temperature, 84

Rhododendrons propagated by grafting, 93
Rodriguezia crispa, 238
Roella elegans, management of 27
Roofs of plant-houses, a covering of garden mats over them in winter economises heat, 23
Roots, advantages of reducing those of some plants, 156
Roses, suggestions for budding, 192 ; training the climbing species to poles, 13 ; soil and situation best suited to the climbing sorts, 15
Rubus, many species of, interesting when trained to poles, 16
Rudbeckia Drummondii, 51
Rudiments of plants, inquiry into their organization, 58, 153
Ruellia ciliatriflora, 90
Rustic baskets for the pleasure grounds, 161

S.

SACCHARINE matters generated by heat, 159
Saccolabium bifidum, 262
— calceolare, 97 ; culture of, 98
— papillosum, 214, 239
Sacred bean, yellow-flowered, 233
Salvia confertiflora, 114, 166
— linarioides, 191
— patens, 1 ; treatment of, 2
Sap vessels, Mr. T. A. Knight's opinion respecting, 9
Schomburgkia marginata, 139
Scilla pratensis, 258
Seeds, much more easily and safely transportable from foreign countries than plants, 61 ; heat essential to elaborate and mature them, 192 ; their production beneficial to strong plants, 34 ; but injurious to weakly ones, 157 ; those most prolific which are obtained from very fertile plants, 134 ; plants raised from seeds are always more or less hardy or tender according to the climate in which these are ripened, 158
Senecio cruentus, 42
Shelter, directions for the efficient employment of, 108 ; that of a permanent description inappropriate, 184
Shrubberies, diversity of character necessary in, 82
Shrubs, advantages of planting them solitarily, 83
Soap aloe, 235
Soils, value of a chemical analysis of, 208 ; very slightly influential in promoting fertility, except as ready vehicles of nutritive fluids, 132
Solanum jasminoides, 273
Solar heat, its agency on vegetation, 33, 59, 84, 107, 132, 155, 181, 204
Solar light, its influence on plants, 10
Sophronitis grandiflora, 42
Sphenogyne speciosa, 77
Spiral vessels in plants not conductors of fluids, 9
Spring one of the most trying seasons for exotic plants, 239
Stanhopea tigrina, 20
Staking and supporting plants, importance of timely attention to, with directions for, 120

Stephanotus floribundus, 142
Stimulation, its value to tropical plants in the summer, 48
Stylidium fasciculatum, 142
Summer ornaments of the flower-garden, period for rearing the, 72
Symmetry of parts, necessary to constitute beauty in plants, 66
Syringing plants, great utility of in the summer, 144
Systematic arrangement of living plants deprecated, 82

T.

TECOMA jasminoides, 199; best mode of flowering, 200
Temperature of plant-houses, should be increased in the summer, 47
Temperature of plants, 108
Thunbergia alata suitable for planting on lawns, 251
Thunbergia aurantiaca, 215; culture of, 216
— Hawtayneana, 147; treatment and propagation of, 148
Thysanotus intricatus, 167; culture and propagation of, 244
Thysanotus proliferus, 142
Torenia cordifolia, 68
Tourrettia lappacea, 212
Transplanting annual and hardy plants, time and mode of, 96; why it is useful, 133
Trees and shrubs, remarks on arranging and planting, 81; manner in which they modify the temperature of any district, 205
Trellises, arched, for covering small walks in the pleasure grounds, 160; form most suitable for supporting dwarf climbing plants, 161
Trichinium alopecuroideum, 114
Tropæolum tricolorum and brachyceras, remarks on exposing and propagating, 250
Tropæolum tuberosum, peregrinum, and pentaphyllum, partial hardihood and treatment of, 251
Tweedia cœrulea, 125; culture of, 126

U.

UNIFORMITY in the treatment of exotic plants, desirableness of, 167, 255

V.

VALLEYS, those traversed by streams particularly cold, 183
Vanda lamellata, 143
Vegetable fluids compared with animal, 154
Vegetable life dependent on heat, 85
Vegetable organization to a great extent uniform, 85
Vegetable physiology, articles in elucidation of, 9, 57, 153; facilities afforded by British plants for obtaining a knowledge of, 40
Ventilation, general remarks on, 96, 143, 167, 240, 263
Verbenas, method of imparting a climbing habit to, 253
Verticordia insignis, 258
Vital principle in plants, suggestions as to its position, 153

W.

WALLS, not most suitable for climbing plants, 160
Water, importance of mingling air with, before applying it to plants, 12; its tendency to lower the temperature of any atmosphere in which it exists, 183; equally dangerous to plants in winter as cold, if excessive, 263
Watering plants, general principles to be observed in, 96, 144, 168
Winds, reduction of temperature by, 205; productive of drought, and therefore, unless violent, generally beneficial to plants, 206
Wistaria consequana, its suitability for training to a pole, 16
Witsenia maura, 92
Wood, its formation and constituent parts, 179; different hypotheses respecting its enlargement, 179

Y.

YOUNG gardeners, familiar hints to, 207
Young plants, reason for their peculiar perviousness to cold, 87

Z.

ZICHYA tricolor, 211

www.ingramcontent.com/pod-product-compliance
Lightning Source LLC
LaVergne TN
LVHW011916260125
802204LV00001B/102